Financing California Real Estate

2nd Edition

ROCKWELL
PUBLISHING

Table of Contents

Preface

It is good practice for real estate agents to "qualify" their buyers and properties before writing up a sale. By doing so, the agent can be nearly certain that both are eligible for the type of financing being contemplated. To qualify a buyer and property for a loan is to select the most appropriate form of financing based on the buyer's needs as well as the value, condition and location of the property. Not only is it a waste of time and effort to write a sale that has little or no hope of success, it is difficult to re-ignite a buyer's fire once he or she has been told the disappointing news that the necessary financing is impossible.

It is a fact that the buyer looks to his or her agent for guidance with respect to financing and tends to hold the agent responsible if the loan is turned down. To the uninitiated this may seem unfair; but when you consider that the vast majority of homebuyers are both inexperienced and uninformed, this dependence on the real estate agent for direction is understandable.

Prior to the 1980's, the number of financing options was relatively small. Qualifying buyers and properties for the most appropriate type of loan was relatively easy. Then the '80's brought a myriad of financing alternatives devised to cope with the money shortages brought on by high interest rates. Many different financing programs were introduced; some were with merit, others with none. In each case, however, the objective was the same: to make financing packages available to homebuyers at affordable rates, while simultaneously offering profits to investors that were competitive with high yield investment alternatives. With the rapid decline in interest rates, many of these creative financing methods lost popularity. During times of low interest rates, buyers tend to return to the traditional methods of financing that have proven successful in the past.

Whether a particular buyer wishes to utilize a creative or traditional method of finance, whether interest rates are high or low, it is the real estate agent's function to offer expert assistance in obtaining that financing. This book is devoted to that principle. Its purpose is to acquaint agents with the array of financing programs available to them, and through examples and exercises, to enable agents to use these essential tools effectively, thereby satisfying the needs of their buyers and sellers. Finance is the key to the real estate market of the '90's. By studying the materials in this volume, you will increase your ability to turn that key and unlock the many sales opportunities that await you.

PREPARATION OF LEGAL FORMS

The purpose of this book is to familiarize real estate professionals with the theory and mechanics of today's financing arrangements. Towards this end, we have included sample documents to illustrate various plans. These sample documents are meant to draw your attention to important features of the plans; they are not intended to be used to consummate actual sales. The preparation of documents for an actual sale should always involve competent legal counsel, since binding legal rights and responsibilities are created by the documents. Don't take chances with the rights of your buyers and sellers.

Chapter 1
HISTORY OF FINANCE

Like many of our current institutions, the American finance system has its origins in the history of England. As early as the 1600's, British merchants were depositing their excess funds for safekeeping with the King's treasurer. This was better than keeping the money stashed under the bed, but the deposits earned no interest and had a habit of disappearing when the King ran short of funds. Always looking for greater security, merchants turned to private individuals in their communities who possessed vaults or safes. For a service charge, these individuals (often goldsmiths or bullion dealers) would store the merchants' money until they needed to withdraw it.

Banking history: deposits with bullion dealers, loans of deposits, checks

It wasn't long before the new class of moneyholders caught on to the fact that they could increase their profits by making use of the money in their safes. Since the merchants tended not to withdraw all of their deposits at the same time, it was possible for the moneyholders to make short-term loans from the deposits, charging interest to borrowers while still maintaining sufficient deposits to satisfy the withdrawal requirements of their depositors. Eventually this system became so profitable that it could stand on its own instead of being just a sideline for a bullion dealer. Thus was born the first true commercial bank, whose function was to provide safety for depositors while making a profit by lending the deposits to other merchants.

Once banking became an established fact of life, the number of depositors and borrowers increased greatly, to the point where it was inefficient to directly transfer cash and bullion back and forth in each transaction. The next step was the development of checks that could be written by the

Checking accounts and
use of checks:
• simplified transactions
• reduced need for cash
• increased available
  bank reserves and loan
  funds

Little regulation in early
history of American
banks:
1863—National Bank
Act established some
regulation for banks
1913, 1916—Federal
Reserve System created
and modern American
banking system
established

depositors and then cashed at any convenient time. This system gained rapid acceptance, and soon banks were confident enough in the system to honor checks from other banks as well as their own. They could then meet periodically with other bankers to settle accounts. By this time the system had grown to the point where an overall central banking system was both possible and desirable.

An important ramification of the development of checking accounts was the fact that the actual cash remained in the banks for a longer time, until the checks were presented for payment. Often there was no need for money to change hands at all, since entire transactions could be handled on paper. For example, if a depositor wrote a check against his or her account, and the person receiving the check deposited it in another account at the same bank, no money was needed to accomplish the sale. This fact enabled the banks to loan even higher percentages of their deposits while still satisfying the cash demands of their depositors. In banking terms, the reserve requirements of the banks were reduced, leading to an increase in the availability of credit.

The English banking system was imported to America with the colonists, but soon began to develop along independent lines as the new country took shape. In the years following the American revolution, banks were subject to little if any regulation, and the only real security rested in the integrity of the bank managers. Many banks kept no reserves whatsoever, or overextended by selling securities in excess of their ability to repay. Things got so out of hand that it became necessary for the federal government to step in. In 1863, Congress passed the National Bank Act to establish some rules and procedures for supervision of the banks.

When the Federal Reserve System was established by the Federal Reserve Acts of 1913 and 1916, our modern banking system was created. Limits were placed on the amount and types of loans that a bank could offer, thus insuring that the banks would not become overextended. In general, banks were precluded from investing too heavily in long-term real estate loans because their deposits had to be available for immediate withdrawal by the depositors.

During the 1800's, two new forms of financial institutions were born, the mutual savings bank and the savings and loan association. Mutual savings banks were created to fill the needs of the emerging industrial working class, who wanted a safe depository where their hard-earned money could be kept and made to grow. Savings and loans grew up to fill the need for non-commercial construction financing. Originally called building and loan associations, in the beginning they were designed to serve only members of the association, who would pool their assets and then take turns using the money to build their homes. After all the members had satisfied their financing needs, the association would be dissolved. Over the years however, S & Ls began to make some loans to non-members, and to place more emphasis on soliciting and servicing deposits, to the point where they eventually became permanent institutions.

Both S&Ls and mutual savings banks developed during 1800's

The nineteenth century was a period of rapid growth in the U.S., fueled by the opening of vast new territories for development. Money flooded into the country for investments that promised high returns and quick turnovers. Mortgage loans were considered very safe at this time because they usually had low loan-to-value ratios and matured in no longer than five years. During this period, many private investors became involved in real estate lending, in expectation of continued increases in property values. This attitude persisted into the early years of the twentieth century, up until the Great Depression.

The economic collapse of the 1930's had a major influence on the development of financial institutions in America. The large number of foreclosures that took place caused lenders to become wary of real estate investments, so much so that it once again became necessary for the government to step in. Some of the more notable programs that were developed at that time include Federal Housing Administration (FHA) mortgage insurance to help prevent defaults and foreclosures, the Federal Home Loan Bank (FHLB) to supervise and assist savings and loan associations,

In the aftermath of the economic collapse of the Great Depression came greater government involvement:
- FHA
- FHLB
- FDIC
- FSLIC

and the Federal Deposit Insurance Corporation (FDIC) and Federal Savings and Loan Insurance Corporation (FSLIC) to insure customer deposits in banks and S&Ls.

In 1989, the Financial Institutions Reform, Recovery, and Enforcement Act (FIRREA) was enacted in response to a crisis in the Savings and Loan industry. Under this Act, the Federal Home Loan Bank Board (FHLBB) was eliminated and replaced by the Office of Thrift Supervision (OTS). The Federal Savings and Loan Insurance Corporation (FSLIC) was also eliminated. The Federal Deposit Insurance program was reorganized and renamed the Deposit Insurance Fund (DIF). DIF now controls two separate insurance funds: the Bank Insurance Fund (BIF), which insures deposits in commercial banks and savings banks, and the Savings Association Insurance Fund (SAIF), which replaces the FSLIC and insures deposits in savings and loan associations.

Since the thirties, the world of modern finance has grown exceedingly complex, with ever-increasing government regulation and a proliferation of private, institutional and governmental lenders. A full discussion of this system would fill many volumes, and is beyond the scope of our discussion. The next chapters will present an overview of some of the more important real estate lenders and their characteristics.

CHAPTER SUMMARY

1. The history of finance has seen the development of financial institutions from little more than private citizens who charged for safeguarding treasure to a variety of different financial institutions. These institutions (including commercial banks, mutual savings banks, and savings and loans) began offering checking and savings accounts, and have since added a wide range of other banking and financial services.

2. The first banks in this country operated essentially without regulation and often without reserves or insurance to protect depositors. Imprudent banking practices led to the failure of many banks.

3. Frequent financial panics and bank failures led to the implementation of federal and state regulation of banking activities and the creation of government agencies to assist and regulate banking institutions and to protect the interests of depositors.

4. These regulations and agencies include the National Bank Act, the Federal Reserve Acts of 1913 and 1916, the Federal Housing Administration, the Federal Home Loan Bank Board, the Federal Deposit Insurance Corporation, the Federal Savings and Loan Insurance Corporation, and the Financial Institutions Reform, Recovery and Enforcement Act of 1989.

Office of Thrift Supervision
OTS

Don't Worry About Acronyms.

Chapter 2
CALIFORNIA REAL ESTATE CYCLES AND THE SECONDARY MARKET

Activity in the California real estate market fluctuates according to the real estate cycle. The term "real estate cycle" refers to the responses of the real estate marketplace as it reacts to the forces of supply and demand. A widely accepted rule of economics is that supply and demand will always seek to balance each other. When demand for a product (such as housing) exceeds the supply, the price for the product tends to rise, thereby stimulating more production. As production increases, more of the demand is satisfied until eventually the supply outstrips demand and a buyer's market is created. At that point, prices will fall and production will taper off until demand catches up with supply, and the cycle begins again.

In a healthy economy, supply and demand are more or less in balance. This is an idealized situation, since the forces affecting supply and demand are constantly changing, thereby shifting the balance. But as long as supply and demand are reasonably close, the economy functions well. When supply far exceeds demand, or vice versa, the economy suffers. While most borrowers are unlikely to give much thought to where the money they are borrowing comes from, the source of mortgage funds has a great deal to do with their supply. Quite simply, the source of all mortgage funds is savings. The source of the savings can vary from individual savings accounts to the profits of large corporations. Savings are invested in mortgage loans by private investors, institutional lenders (e.g., savings and loan associations) or government agencies.

As can be expected, the demand for mortgage funds comes in large part from households desiring to finance,

7

refinance or improve residential property.

FACTORS INFLUENCING REAL ESTATE CYCLES

Factors influencing the
real estate cycle:
1. economic
2. political
3. social

Disintermediation: the
loss of funds to higher
yielding investments

Imbalances in supply and demand may be either short term or long term, depending on their causes. It is not always possible to know whether a particular cycle is short or long term, because many different factors interact to create the cycles. Some of the more influential causes of real estate cycles are the state of national and local economies, the availability of credit, the cost of construction labor and materials, population shifts, and political attitudes.

Economic factors. Local economic trends are generally thought to be one of the strongest influences on real estate cycles. If an area is experiencing prosperity, there should be funds available to finance the purchase and construction of housing, and in theory the marketplace will function smoothly. The experience of the past several years has cast some doubt on this theory, however. Although local economic health is still a major factor, it has been somewhat overshadowed by the national economic picture. The availability of high return, non-real estate investments, resulting from national economic forces such as high interest rates, may diminish the supply of funds for real estate investment even in areas of relative prosperity. The forces of disintermediation (a term meaning the loss of deposits by savings institutions to higher yielding competitive investments) can greatly reduce the impact of local economics on the real estate marketplace. If local investment funds are no longer deposited on a large scale in savings institutions, where they could be made available to local homebuyers and developers, community development must be increasingly financed by funds from the national finance market.

The local economy still plays a significant role in California's housing market. For instance, the increasing population and continued economic prosperity of many California regions has led to a housing shortage. Because there is such a vigorous demand for homes, their prices have risen drastically in the last few years. Four out of the ten most expensive housing regions in the country are in California. As of June, 1988, only 25% of the state's households had the financial capacity to buy a median-priced, single-family home, which sold for $167,000. In particular regions, the median-priced home is even more expensive. For instance, in Orange County, the median-priced home was $204,000 in 1988. (The national average was $90,000.) Obviously, the local economy has played a significant role in California's housing market.

Political factors. The supply and demand for both housing and credit depend on political forces that are notoriously unpredictable. Because the government is the largest borrower in the country, its activities have a huge influence on the national economy. A decision by the Federal Reserve Board to loosen credit by increasing the supply of money could cause a rapid turnaround in the current finance market. Likewise, if Congress were to reduce the federal deficit, then the government would not have to borrow as much money, leaving more available for other borrowers such as homebuyers and developers. The likelihood of these actions taking place depends on the complex interactions between voters, lobbyists and politicians, and it is this human factor that defies attempts to predict the course of political events and their effect on the real estate market.

Political activities of a more local nature also affect the market. California's overcrowded cities are beginning to resort to "no-growth" policies. Both city governments and residents are increasingly supporting regulations limiting the number of new housing starts. Some analysts go so far as to compare the no-growth enthusiasm to the tax revolt of ten years ago, when Proposition 13 was passed (severely limiting the increase of property taxes). If no-growth policies are widely adopted, the housing shortage will become even more acute, leading to yet more price increases.

Social factors. Social behavior patterns and the distribution of population can have a major effect on supply

Government activities include:
• deficit spending
• Federal Reserve monetary policies

Deficit spending govt controls interest rates.

Social factors include:
• population distribution
• average household size

and demand. A modern example is the increase in the portion of the population that is in its prime home buying years. The children of the "baby boom" are now of age to be seeking their own housing, and this has been one factor in the overwhelming demand for housing that has pushed prices up so drastically in the past decade. High divorce rates and a trend towards later marriages also stimulate demand, because there are fewer persons per household. This trend has been significant in creating the modern phenomenon of condominiums, which are designed to accommodate smaller households. Migrations of the population are also powerful forces. Housing values benefit from an influx of population, but can be devastated by a large exodus from a region or community.

In California, the effects of migration are easily spotted. San Diego alone sees approximately 1,500 new residents a month. Demographers predict that the state's population of 28 million will increase by another 4 million in the next several years. This massive influx of migrants has helped cause the rapidly escalating housing prices previously discussed.

Over the years, the disruptive effects of real estate cycles have led the government to attempt to moderate the duration and severity of those cycles. This has been done primarily through the creation of a national secondary market which seeks to limit the effects of adverse economic factors.

THE NATIONAL (SECONDARY) MARKET

The supply of funds available for investment in real estate mortgages is channeled into mortgage finance through either the primary or the secondary market.

Primary market: lenders who make mortgage loans

The **primary market** is the most familiar market; it is made up of the various lending institutions in local communities. For example, if Brown wishes to borrow money to finance the purchase of a home, Brown will seek a loan from the primary market, which may be the local savings and loan association. The source of funds for the primary market is largely made up of the savings of individuals and businesses in the local area. For instance, Seaside Savings is a typical lender in the primary market. As a savings and loan association, it gets its funds from the savings deposits of members of the community. It will use those savings to make real estate loans to members of that same community. Seaside Savings may get additional funds for real estate lending by selling the mortgage loans it has already made. As additional funds are freed to make more loans, Seaside Savings will be able to provide more continuous service to the community by being able to provide additional real estate financing. Seaside Savings would sell its mortgages on the **secondary market**.

The national secondary market consists of private investors and government agencies that buy and sell real estate mortgages. Presently, private investors simply do not have the same influence on real estate markets that government agencies that buy and sell mortgages on the secondary level have. It is estimated that non-agency investors make up only 2% of the secondary market. For these reasons, our discussion of the secondary market will focus exclusively on government agencies.

Buying and selling loans. A real estate loan is an investment, just like stocks or bonds. The lender (be it a bank, savings and loan, or private party) commits its funds to an enterprise (in this case the purchase or construction of a home) in the expectation that the money will generate a return in the form of interest payments. Real estate loans can be bought and sold just like other investments. The present value of the lender's right to receive future payments over the life of the loan can be calculated by comparing the rate of return on the loan to the rate of return on other investments with the same degree of risk.

> **Example:** A bank makes a home loan of $135,000 at 11% interest, secured by a deed of trust. One year later, approximately $134,500 of principal remains to be paid on the loan. If market interest rates have gone up to 12.5% for similar

Secondary market: investors who buy and sell mortgage loans

FNMA Fonnie Mae

GNMA Ginnie Mae.

FHLMC Freddy Mac

11

quality investments, then the present value of the loan is less than $134,500. The present value is the amount of money it would take to generate the same amount of income at a 12.5% rate of return. An 11% return on $134,500 would be $14,795 per year. This same return could be achieved by investing $118,360 at 12.5% interest, so the present value of the loan (all other factors being equal) is $118,360 rather than its face value of $134,500.

It should be noted that many other factors can influence the value of a loan. A primary influence is the degree of risk associated with the loan. The degree of risk refers to the likelihood of default by the borrower and also to the ability of the lender to recover the loan proceeds by selling (foreclosing) the security property. The degree of risk in real estate loans is controlled mainly by qualifying the buyer and the property before the loan is made. To qualify a borrower is to insure that he or she has a large enough and stable enough income to minimize the risk of default. To qualify a property is to make sure the property is worth enough to satisfy the loan in the event of default and foreclosure.

Why buy and sell loans? The secondary market serves two vital functions: it promotes investments in real estate by making funds available for real estate loans and it provides a measure of stability in the primary (local) market by moderating the adverse effects of real estate cycles. Consider the following examples.

Example 1: Acme Savings and Loan has a long list of prospective borrowers who need funds for the purchase of homes. Acme's problem is that all of its deposits are already tied up in real estate loans. But by selling its existing mortgage loans to a secondary market investor, Acme can get the funds it needs to make the new loans and thereby satisfy its credit-hungry customers. The effects of a tight money market in Acme's local community

Secondary market functions:
- promotes investment
- provides funds
- stabilizes market

are moderated because Acme can get funds in the national market.

Example 2: If Acme Savings and Loan had a surplus of deposits instead of a shortfall, it might encounter difficulty finding enough local investments to absorb its funds. In this case, Acme could buy real estate loans on the secondary market, in essence investing in real estate located all over the country. Because of the uniform standards applied to secondary market loans, Acme can feel fairly secure in its investments, even though it may never see the actual borrowers and properties it is helping to finance.

The availability of funds in the primary market depends a good deal on the existence of the secondary market. This can be seen by taking a brief look at the flow of mortgage funds: first, mortgage funds are given to the homebuyer by a lending institution in the primary market; the mortgage is then sold to a secondary market agency, which may in turn sell it to other investors in the form of mortgage-backed securities. As mortgage-backed securities are sold by the agency, more funds become available to the secondary market for the purchase of new mortgages from the primary market. As more mortgages are purchased from the primary market, more funds become available for lenders to pass on to borrowers.

Major secondary market agencies:
• FNMA
• GNMA
• FHLMC

Pvt Sector about 2/6

How does the secondary market work? For the purposes of our discussion, the secondary market may be said to include three agencies:

- the Federal National Mortgage Association (FNMA or "Fannie Mae"),
- the Government National Mortgage Association (GNMA or "Ginnie Mae"), and
- the Federal Home Loan Mortgage Corporation (FHLMC or "Freddie Mac")

Secondary market agencies apply standardized underwriting criteria

The secondary market is able to function as it does because of the standardized underwriting criteria applied by these agencies. Underwriting criteria are used to qualify the borrower and the property and include such items as loan-to-value ratios and income-to-expense ratios. Each mortgage issued by each individual lender must conform to the secondary market's underwriting standards or it will not be purchased on the secondary market. These standards assure a uniform quality control which inspires confidence in the purchasers of the mortgage-backed securities. The purchasers know that the mortgages which back the securities must be of a minimum quality; this lessens their risk in investing in properties they cannot view or assess for themselves. Without the assurance of the underlying underwriting standards, someone in California would be unlikely to invest in site-unseen property in New Jersey.

Because the secondary market performs such an important function in providing liquidity of mortgage funds, the standards set by the secondary market have a large influence on lending activities in the primary market. For example, once secondary agencies began accepting adjustable-rate mortgages (ARMs), 15-year fixed-rate mortgages, and convertible ARMs, these types of financing became more readily available in the primary market. Lenders were more willing to make these kinds of loans when they knew the loans could be sold to the secondary market.

A relatively recent development in the activities of the secondary market is the current offerings of mortgage packages to foreign investors, thus further expanding the sources of funds available for mortgage investment purposes.

FEDERAL NATIONAL MORTGAGE ASSOCIATION

Fannie Mae
FNMA

FNMA is the nation's largest investor in residential mortgages. FNMA was created in 1938 as the first government-sponsored secondary market institution. It was originally formed as a wholly-owned government corporation. While the specific purpose of FNMA was to provide a secondary market for FHA-insured mortgages, FNMA did not start buying FHA mortgages on a large scale until 1948. At that same time, FNMA was also authorized to purchase VA-guaranteed loans. FNMA underwent several reorganizations and is now a **privately** owned and managed corporation, although it is still supervised by the Department of Housing and Urban Development. The role of FNMA was further expanded in 1970 (after it became a private corporation) with the passage of the Emergency Home Finance Act which permitted FNMA to purchase conventional mortgages as well as FHA and VA mortgages.

FNMA:
- privately owned corporation supervised by HUD
- buys FHA, VA, conventional loans
- obtains funds from sale of securities backed by mortgages it holds
- participates with lenders in joint ownership of mortgages

FNMA funds its operation by selling securities which are backed by its pool of mortgages to the public. It buys the mortgages from lenders. Lenders who wish to sell loans to FNMA are required to own a certain amount of stock in FNMA, the required amount being based on the principal balance of mortgage loans. FNMA posts the prices daily that it is willing to pay for the standard loan programs approved for purchase. The required yield and prices may also be obtained from a hotline operated by FNMA and from various financial services and publications. Loans sold to FNMA may be serviced by FNMA or by the originating lender. FNMA pays a service fee to the lender if it continues to service the loan.

In 1981, FNMA started a participation program with lenders. A master participation agreement is entered into between a lender and FNMA. The lender then assembles a pool (collection) of loans and a participation interest in that pool (50%—95%) is then sold to FNMA. In this way, both the lender and FNMA own an interest in the loans instead of the lender selling them outright. In that same year, FNMA also announced the sale of conventional mortgage-backed securities that are guaranteed by FNMA as to full and timely payments of both principal and interest. A service fee is charged by FNMA for issuing securities backed by the mortgage pool as well as a monthly fee for the guarantee provision.

15

Ginny Mae (handwritten)

Ginny Mae Does Not Buy Loans But Does Guarantee (handwritten)

GOVERNMENT NATIONAL MORTGAGE ASSOCIATION

GNMA:
- government-owned corporation under HUD
- guarantees payment of FHA and VA loans through mortgage-backed securities program
- mortgage-backed securities are issued by approved FHA and VA lenders

The Government National Mortgage Association was created with the passage of the Housing and Urban Development Act in 1968. It is a wholly-owned government corporation which, in effect, replaced FNMA when FNMA became privately owned. GNMA operates under the Department of Housing and Urban Development.

At the time of its creation, GNMA was given the responsibility for managing and eventually liquidating the remaining FNMA mortgages. Another function of GNMA is that of "special assistance:" GNMA assists the financing of urban renewal and housing projects by providing below-market rates to low-income families.

A primary function of GNMA is to promote investment by guaranteeing the payment of principal and interest on FHA and VA mortgages. GNMA carries out this function through its mortgage-backed securities program. GNMA's activities in the "special assistance" area have lessened in importance as its activities in its mortgage-backed securities program have increased. This program, supported by the federal government's borrowing power, guarantees timely interest and principal mortgage payments to the mortgage holders. The added security of the guarantee enables the mortgage holders to pledge a pool of their loans as collateral for securities. The repayment of the mortgages is the source of the funds used to pay off the securities when they become due. The mortgage-backed securities offer safety to investors, they can be easily traded, and they can be purchased in smaller denominations than many comparable investment instruments.

In order to issue GNMA mortgage-backed securities, the issuer must be an FHA- or VA-approved mortgagee, be an acceptable GNMA servicer-seller, and have a specified net worth. A fee is paid for the GNMA commitment to guarantee the mortgage pool. The issuer (lender) continues to service the mortgage.

2 Types.

Mortgage-backed securities fall into two general types: **bond-type securities** and **pass-through securities**. Bond-type securities are long-term, pay interest semi-annually, and provide for repayment at a specified redemption date. Pass-through securities pay interest and principal on a monthly basis. Pass-through securities are the more prevalent. Fully modified pass-through securities pay interest and principal monthly, regardless of whether the payments have been collected from the mortgagors. Any proceeds from foreclosure or prepayment are also passed on to the security holder as soon as received. If the issuer of the security (the lender) fails to make the payments, GNMA takes over the mortgage pool and makes the payments. Straight pass-through securities pay monthly interest and principal only when it is collected from the mortgagor.

MODIFIED & STRAIGHT
GUARANTEED   NOT GUARANTEED
LOWER   BUT HIGHER
RATE   RATE

FEDERAL HOME LOAN MORTGAGE CORPORATION

WAS FHLBS
FED HOME LOAN BANK SERVICE
FREDDY MAC

The Federal Home Loan Mortgage Corporation was created through the Emergency Home Finance Act of 1970. FHLMC is a nonprofit, federally chartered institution which is controlled by the Federal Home Loan Bank System. The primary function of FHLMC was to aid savings and loan associations who were hit particularly hard by the recession of 1969-1970. FHLMC was to help S&Ls acquire additional funds for lending in the mortgage market by purchasing the mortgages they already held. FHLMC was authorized to deal in FHA, VA and conventional mortgages. While FNMA emphasizes the purchase of mortgage loans, FHLMC also actively sells the mortgage loans from its portfolio, thus acting as a conduit for mortgage investments. The funds which are generated by the sale of the mortgages are then used to purchase more mortgages.

FHLMC has been actively involved in developing underwriting standards for conventional mortgage loans which have been of further assistance to S&Ls, who deal chiefly in conventional mortgages. All members of the Federal Home Loan

FHLMC:
- nonprofit federally chartered institution controlled by FHLB
- assists S&Ls by purchasing FHA, VA and conventional loans
- sells mortgages and mortgage-backed securities

Bank System, now under the Office of Thrift Supervision, are eligible to sell mortgages to FHLMC. Commercial banks, credit unions, and other nonmembers may be approved by FHLMC as eligible sellers. Nonmember sellers are charged an additional fee for the mortgage purchase.

FHLMC issues its own mortgage-backed securities, which are backed by the conventional mortgages it purchases. FHLMC purchases mortgages through its **immediate delivery program** or its **forward commitment purchase program**. In the immediate delivery program, sellers have up to 60 days in which to deliver the mortgages FHLMC has agreed to purchase. Failure to deliver can mean that the seller will be banned from making sales to FHLMC for two years. The immediate loan delivery program can involve either whole loan purchases or participation purchases. Under the forward commitment purchase program, commitments are made for six- and eight-month periods. Delivery of the mortgages is at the option of the seller. There is a non-refundable commitment fee payable to FHLMC.

QUALITY CONTROL

The secondary market has an enormous influence on the primary market, not only because of the increased availability of funds that it provides, but also because of the standards of quality it imposes on lenders. Because lenders wish to be able to sell their loans to the secondary agencies, they must follow the underwriting guidelines of those agencies. In the 1980's, the rate of mortgage delinquencies and foreclosures has risen sharply. In response to this higher loss rate, both FNMA and FHLMC have implemented changes in their underwriting guidelines. The secondary market is trying to improve the quality of the loans it purchases and ensure the reputation of residential mortgages as a safe investment.

In their efforts to increase the quality of the loans they purchase, the agencies necessarily force the lenders to upgrade the quality of the loans they make. Not only can the agencies refuse to purchase loans that do not follow their underwriting guidelines, they can also request lenders to repurchase loans already sold if it is later discovered the lender violated an underwriting guideline.

The secondary market encourages lenders to implement their own quality control programs. The secondary market considers it the lender's responsibility to submit investment quality loans for purchase. According to FHLMC, an investment quality loan is "a loan from a borrower whose timely repayment of the debt can be expected, that is secured by a property of sufficient value to recover the lender's investment if a mortgage default occurs." By encouraging lenders to carefully review property appraisals, legal documentation (e.g., the mortgage instrument), origination documentation (e.g., the loan application, credit report, and employment verification) and the ultimate underwriting decision, the secondary market exerts its influence to increase the overall quality of loans made and to decrease the rate of delinquency and foreclosure.

CHAPTER SUMMARY

1. Real estate cycles are the response of the real estate and mortgage markets to the forces of supply and demand. As long as supply and demand are fairly balanced, the economy functions well. But when there is too much demand and not enough supply, or vice versa, either inflation or recession result.

2. These cycles are affected by economic, political and social factors. Economic factors include population growth, unemployment rates, the cost of money (interest rates), and availability of investment funds.

Political factors include government regulations and activities (for instance the amount of government debt that must be financed), decision by the Federal Reserve to raise or lower interest rates, and local "no-growth" regulations.

Social factors include the age of the majority of the population, the size of families, and migrations of the population.

3. In recent years, the government has taken steps, especially through the regulation of secondary mortgage markets, to attempt to alleviate severe fluctuations and lengthy slumps in real estate cycles.

4. The national secondary market consists of both private investors and governmental or quasi-governmental agencies, who buy loans from the real estate lenders themselves and then sell them to other investors. The availability of funds in the primary markets depends on the activities in the secondary market, because as loans are purchased from the lenders, the lenders receive more funds to make new loans with.

5. FNMA, GNMA and FHLMC account for the great majority of the secondary market. FNMA, GNMA and FHLMC have provided greater stability and liquidity to the nation's real estate lending industry by bringing many new investors into real estate markets. The dominant factor in attracting more funds for real estate finance has been the creation of the various mortgage investment securities issued by these agencies.

6. The secondary market has also contributed to a greater standardization of qualifying standards and loan programs throughout the country. Because it will only purchase loans that comply with its standards, lenders who want the option of selling loans to the secondary market must be more careful about the loans they make. Also, the secondary market can encourage lenders to participate in new loan

programs. For example, lenders were wary of adjustable-rate mortgages until the secondary agencies agreed to buy them.

Chapter 3
TYPES OF CALIFORNIA LENDERS

Our discussion of real estate lenders will focus on the major sources of financing in California's primary market. The primary or local market consists of individuals and institutions that make loans directly to borrowers. This is in contrast to the secondary or national market, discussed in Chapter 2, where the primary lenders obtain much of the funds they supply to borrowers.

The major lenders in the primary residential market fall into three categories:

- savings and loan associations,
- commercial banks, and
- mortgage companies.

In addition to these lenders, there are numerous other lenders which make residential loans either on a smaller scale or in a different way. There are private individuals and credit unions, for example, that make many home improvement or equity loans and, in some cases, purchase money loans. Life insurance companies and pension funds, (especially life insurance companies), on the other hand, place a great deal of money in residential loans but rarely do so directly, preferring instead to use intermediaries, called loan correspondents, such as mortgage companies, banks, and savings and loan associations, to place and service their loans.

The 1980's saw many changes in the attitudes and practices of lending institutions, as well as in the regulations that govern those institutions. Lenders had to respond to constantly fluctuating economic conditions, rather than the relatively stable economic situations more common in the

Types of Lenders

Primary market lenders:
- S&Ls
- commercial banks
- mortgage companies
- mutual savings banks

INSURANCE COMPANIES
Pension funds
Private individuals
Credit unions

past. In order to understand today's lending market, we must first examine the historical roles of the more significant lenders and then look at how the modern economic climate has affected those roles.

SAVINGS AND LOAN ASSOCIATIONS

Savings and loans:
- traditionally, the leading residential lender
- recently, fewer portfolio loans and more reliance on secondary market

One of the major real estate lending institutions is the savings and loan association (S&L). State chartered savings and loans are regulated by the California Department of Savings and Loans, and can participate in the market to the full extent of the national laws regulating financial institutions. State law imposes many restrictions on S&L lending activities. By law, state chartered S&Ls may lend up to 100% of the appraised value of the property if the loan is financially sound and the property acts as security for the loan (in practice, S&Ls lend less than 100% of the appraised value). No single loan may exceed $500,000 or 1% of the association's real assets. An S&L may invest no more than 40% of its total assets in nonresidential real estate loans.

MUST INVEST 60% IN RESIDENTIAL

The History of Savings and Loans

Savings and loan associations have traditionally been the largest single source of funds for financing residential property. Over the years they have carried on their original function, investing roughly 75% of their assets in single family residential loans. They were able to dominate local mortgage markets despite the fact that commercial banks had more assets to invest, mainly because the deposits placed with savings and loans were savings deposits that were less susceptible to immediate withdrawal than the demand (checking) deposits held by commercial banks.

In the years from 1945 to the late 1970's, S&Ls expanded their mortgage operations aggressively. While other lenders feared the risks inherent in long-term conventional loans, S&Ls believed they could succeed by virtue of their knowledge of the local market and their ability to attract long-term deposits. Since they could offer higher interest on savings accounts than the commercial banks, they had no trouble attracting depositors during times of prosperity. This strategy worked very well until the surge in interest rates in the late '70s—early '80s turned the tables. Since savings and loans were limited by law with respect to how much interest they could pay their savings depositors, they found themselves in the unfamiliar position of being unable to offer attractive enough returns to depositors. The result was that they lost a large portion of their deposits to competing investments (such as money market funds and government bonds) that offered substantially higher returns. To make matters worse, the S&Ls were saddled with long-term, non-liquid mortgages at low interest rates (by 1980's standards) and were unable to liquidate their loans and reinvest their funds in higher return investments.

Disintermediation

These problems led to major changes in the characteristics of S&Ls. Instead of concentrating on lending money within their local communities, they broadened their market to avoid the potentially severe consequences of local economic slumps. They also began to rely much more heavily on the secondary market as a source of funds, to offset the continuing drain of customer withdrawals. This has made it necessary for S&Ls to adopt the uniform qualifying standards set by the major secondary market investors—the FNMA and the FHLMC.

If lenders intend to resell their loans on the secondary level, immediately or at some time in the future, the conditions of those loans must be acceptable to the secondary investors. Historically, S&Ls could set their own property and borrower standards because their loans were kept in portfolio rather than resold.

Savings and Loans in Today's Market

The early 1980's saw the deregulation of the banking industry—interest rates and investment powers were deregulated so that banks and S&Ls could compete with money-market funds. Many banks and thrifts tried new, riskier investments that regulators didn't always have the ability to evaluate. Management mistakes, economic slumps, and sometimes even fraud led many institutions toward insolvency. And when insolvency loomed, some S&L officers decided to gamble even more. Since their deposits were insured by the federal government, the officers felt there was little to lose.

The result of these risky investments was a dramatic increase in the failure rate of S&Ls. Up until the 1980's, fewer than ten S&Ls failed each year. In 1987, 48 S&Ls failed and hundreds more were insolvent. In 1988, it was estimated that there was a total of 504 insolvent S&Ls.

The problem of insolvent savings and loans became so severe that a reshaping of America's financial system was required. In August of 1989, the **Financial Institutions Reform, Recovery, and Enforcement Act (FIRREA)** was signed into law. This law completely restructured the thrift industry.

Under FIRREA, the Office of Thrift Supervision was formed. This office took over the duty of regulating the thrift industry. (A duty formerly handled by the Federal Home Loan Bank Board).

The Resolution Trust Corporation (RTC) was formed to manage the disposition of bankrupt thrifts. It manages and sells the insolvent institutions and their assets. The Resolution Funding Corporation (RFC) was created to sell the bonds needed to finance the bail-out operation.

FIRREA eliminated the Federal Savings and Loan Insurance Corporation (FSLIC). The Federal Deposit Insurance program was reorganized and renamed the Deposit Insurance Fund (DIF). DIF now controls two separate insurance funds: the **Bank Insurance Fund (BIF)**, which insures deposits in commercial banks and savings banks, and the **Savings Association Insurance Fund (SAIF)**, which replaces the FSLIC in insuring deposits in savings and loan associations.

The FIRREA changes reaffirmed the government's commitment to back all federally insured deposit accounts. As a result, depositors were reassured and many began returning their accounts to savings and loan associations. With the

[handwritten: sells bonds to raise funds]
[handwritten: RFC Resolution Funding to bailout Corp. savings or loans]
[handwritten: RTC Resolution Trust Corp. bailes out]
[handwritten: BIF Bank Insurance Fund]

numerous insolvencies and reorganizations, the number of individual savings and loan associations will undoubtedly drop. However, the financially secure organizations will survive, and the overall amount of deposits in savings and loan associations is expected to remain at or even slightly above current levels.

COMMERCIAL BANKS

Commercial banks remain the largest source of investment funds in the country today. As their name implies, they are oriented towards commercial lending activities, supplying capital for business ventures and construction activities on a comparatively short-term basis. Up until recently, residential mortgages were not a major part of their business, primarily because of government limitations on the amount of long-term investments they can make. These limitations were imposed because the vast majority of deposits held by commercial banks are demand deposits—deposits payable on demand anytime a depositor elects. They are considered less reliable for reinvestment in long-term real estate loans than the more stable savings deposits.

However, in recent years, commercial banks, especially large commercial banks, have increased their participation in home mortgage lending. Their share of the total residential mortgage market originations rose to 31% in 1989.

There are several reasons for the increase. One reason is the ability to take advantage of existing customer relationships built through checking account and other traditional services. Commercial banks want to be able to offer home mortgage loans to their customers instead of sending them off to a different lender. A second reason is the flip side of the same coin: the banks hope that mortgage loan borrowers will become new customers for checking accounts, credit cards, and home equity loans. In the last few years, commercial banks have seen a growth in consumer loans and a decline in business loans. And, because of tax changes on interest

Commercial banks:
- largest source of investment funds
- mostly short-term loans, such as construction loans
- most real estate loans are sold on the secondary market

[handwritten: Federal Reserve Bank (Fed) oversees Banks.]

27

Construction Loans "
Auto "
Business "
2nd Mortgage "
Credit Card "

deductibility, mortgage loans are expected to make up a larger portion of the banks' vital consumer loan business.

Changes in state and federal regulations have also spurred additional mortgage activity. Government regulations will require that banks hold back different percentages of funds on reserve for different types of loans, based on the perceived risk of those loans. First lien home mortgages are in the lowest risk category. This would mean a bank would have to maintain less funds on reserve for home mortgage loans than for other types of loans, which would leave more funds available for additional loans or investments. As with savings and loans, state law regulates the types of real estate loans banks can make. For example, fully amortized loans are limited to 90% of the property's appraised value. If the excess is insured or guaranteed by a government or private agency, it can make loans with higher loan-to-value ratios. State banks are regulated by the California Department of Banking.

MORTGAGE COMPANIES *Called Intermediaries*

Mortgage companies:
• intermediaries for insurance companies, pension plans, FNMA
• loans sold on the secondary market

Also got money from FNMA Fannie Mae

Mortgage companies function more in the role of intermediaries than as sources of lending capital. Their basic function is the origination and servicing of loans on behalf of large investors such as insurance companies, pension plans, or the Federal National Mortgage Association. Since these large investors often operate on a national scale, they have neither the time nor the resources to understand the particular risks of local markets or to deal with the day-to-day management of their loans. Mortgage companies fill the gap. Because they operate on a local level, they can more effectively choose which loans to make based on the risks involved. These loans are then resold to secondary market investors, with the mortgage company acting as an agent to service the loans for a fee. Because mortgage companies invest little of their own money, their activities are largely controlled by the availability of investment capital in the secondary market. Of course

MORTGAGE BANKER HAS HIS OWN SOURCE of Money

MORTGAGE BROKER - BEGS BORROWS STEALS FROM WHOEVER.

their loan qualification criteria must reflect the standards of the national market in order to facilitate resale of the loans.

MUTUAL SAVINGS BANKS

Mutual savings banks (MSBs), found mostly in eastern and northwestern states, have always been among the most conservative of lenders. Their activities are oriented towards the communities they serve, allowing close supervision of their loans. MSBs have not altered their conservative lending stance, but they have taken steps to adapt to modern economic realities. Their involvement in the secondary market has increased as local sources of deposits have dried up, and they have begun investing in outside communities, seeking the safety of diversification.

Mutual savings banks:
• conservative lenders
• recently, more reliance on secondary market

LIFE INSURANCE COMPANIES

Insurance companies control vast amounts of capital in the form of insurance policy premiums which are held for relatively long terms. Money invested in life insurance policies is generally not subject to early or sudden withdrawal (as are the deposits in banks and S&Ls) and does not earn the high returns that are now common in other investment forms. For these reasons, insurance companies are able to safely invest large sums in long-term real estate loans.

Because of their concern for long-term stability in their investments, insurance companies tend to prefer loans for large scale commercial projects as opposed to residential mortgages. Insurance companies rarely make loans directly to borrowers, preferring instead to buy loans from intermediaries, like mortgage companies, at the secondary market level. California insurance companies are regulated by the Department of Insurance.

Life insurance companies:
• long-term assets (life policies)
• long-term loans
• prefer large commercial loans
• usually operate through loan correspondents and the secondary market

REAL ESTATE INVESTMENT TRUSTS

REITs:
- investment property
- at least 100 owners
- issues shares
- 90% of gross income from investments
- 75% of gross income from real estate investments

A trust is an unincorporated association of investors managed by a trustee (or trustees). In 1960, by means of the Real Estate Investment Trust Act, Congress made it possible for investors to enjoy the flow-through tax advantages of a partnership while retaining some of the more important qualities of a corporate operation. The Act allows investors who prefer real estate as an investment to receive tax benefits similar to those granted to mutual funds and other regulated investment companies. Unlike ordinary corporations, whose earnings are subject to double taxation (first at the corporate level and again as personal income when distributed to stockholders), the real estate trust earnings are taxed only once, after they have been distributed to their investors.

There are several requirements for an REIT:

- it cannot hold property primarily for sale to customers,
- it must have at least 100 beneficial owners,
- no five or fewer persons can hold over 50% of the beneficial interest,
- it must issue shares or certificates of interest,
- each share must have a proportionate vote in trust policy decisions,
- 90% of its gross income must be from investments, and
- 75% of its gross income must come from real estate investments.

PRIVATE INDIVIDUALS

Private individuals have always been a force in the world of real estate finance. The majority of private lenders are sellers who extend credit to their purchasers. This is referred to as "taking back" or "carrying back" part of the sales price.

When interest rates are high or money is in short supply, buyers are more inclined to ask owners to sell their properties on installment terms. Accordingly, private financing becomes much more prevalent when funds from traditional sources are scarce or too expensive, or both.

The following chart illustrates the percentages of loans for one- to four-unit residences originated by savings and loan associations, mortgage bankers, commercial banks and other investors in 1988.

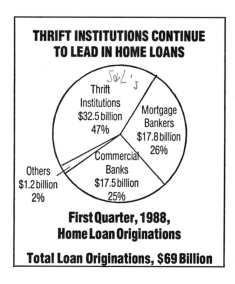

THRIFT INSTITUTIONS CONTINUE TO LEAD IN HOME LOANS

S&L's

Thrift Institutions $32.5 billion 47%

Mortgage Bankers $17.8 billion 26%

Commercial Banks $17.5 billion 25%

Others $1.2 billion 2%

First Quarter, 1988, Home Loan Originations

Total Loan Originations, $69 Billion

CHAPTER SUMMARY

1. The major real estate lenders in the primary market are savings and loans, commercial banks, mortgage companies, and mutual savings banks. Life insurance companies also make a large number of real estate loans, although usually through loan correspondents, such as mortgage companies.

2. In 1989, the Financial Institutions Reform, Recovery, and Enforcement Act (FIRREA) was passed. This law restructured the regulation of Savings and Loan Associations and reorganized the Federal Deposit Insurance Corporation.

3. Deregulation of the banking industry and changing economic conditions in the last decade have led to a number of changes in the practices of lenders on the primary market. The trend is towards conservatism in investment and greater uniformity in the lending characteristics of institutional lenders. As depositors moved their savings out of the banks and S&Ls, these institutions were forced to turn to the secondary market for funds.

4. Since secondary investors tend to know little about local economies and property values, they require a higher safety margin for their investments. In general, this means that their property and borrower qualifying standards will be more stringent. If a local lender has any plans to sell its loans on the secondary market, it must apply the investor's standards when underwriting the loans or face the consequences of keeping them in portfolio for their entire terms.

5. Additionally, since most lenders now depend heavily on the secondary market, their regional and institutional differences are disappearing. In essence, primary institutional lenders are moving towards a uniform national primary market.

Chapter 4
GOVERNMENT INFLUENCES ON REAL ESTATE FINANCE

It is a generally accepted economic theory that the cost of money (interest rates), like the cost of other things in our society, is controlled primarily by the law of supply and demand (excepting the control imposed by state usury laws). If the supply is large—that is, if there is a large amount of money in circulation—interest rates will tend to fall. Business activity will tend to increase as the cost to finance expansion decreases. Conversely, if the money supply is smaller than the demand for borrowed money, then interest rates will tend to rise. There are, of course, many factors which affect interest rates, but the forces of supply and demand have the greatest effect on them.

To a large degree, the supply of money in the United States is controlled by the federal government. The United States Treasury, the Federal Reserve System, and the Office of Thrift Supervision are the major federal influences on the cost of borrowed money. Of these, the Federal Reserve System plays the largest and the most direct role.

Supply of money controlled by government:
- U.S. Treasury
- Federal Reserve
- Office of Thrift Supervision

The federal government influences the supply of money in two ways: with **fiscal policy** and with **monetary policy**. Fiscal policy is implemented by the executive and legislative branches of the government by means of spending, taxation, and public debt management. Monetary policy, a more direct control of the supply and cost of money, is implemented by the Federal Reserve System. The ultimate goals of both fiscal and monetary policy are economic growth, full employment and a balance of international payments.

Two methods of control:
- fiscal policy
- monetary policy

Fiscal policy can be broken down into two further categories: federal spending and debt financing, and taxation. Federal spending is determined by the federal budget,

33

created by the joint efforts of Congress and the administration. The actual spending and debt financing is handled by the United States Treasury. Taxation is also determined by both Congress and the administration.

UNITED STATES TREASURY

U.S. Treasury: fiscal manager of the nation

The United States Treasury, as fiscal manager of the nation, is responsible for managing the government's finances, including the national debt. Treasury funds come from a number of sources, but the largest source is personal and business income tax.

When federal income is less than federal expenditures, a shortfall called a **federal deficit** results. A deficit has occurred in most years since the Great Depression of the 1930's. When a deficit occurs, the Treasury obtains funds to cover the shortfall by issuing interest-bearing securities to investors. Depending on their term, these securities are referred to as **Treasury Bills** (less than one year), **Treasury Notes** (one to five years) or **Treasury Certificates** (five to ten years). In issuing these securities the federal government is actually borrowing from the private sector. When the government borrows money to cover the deficit, less money is available for private borrowers.

Federal deficits:
• at historical high
• largest single demand on loan funds

While some economists believe that federal deficits have little, if any, effect on interest rates, many believe that large-scale federal borrowing can have a dramatic effect on interest rates as private borrowers compete for the limited funds remaining. Although there have been deficits in most recent years (the last surplus occurred in 1969), deficits in the last several years have been much higher than those previously. The following graph depicts federal deficits for the federal fiscal years 1979 through 1989.

In recent years, the federal deficit (government borrowing) has been the single largest drain on the supply of loan funds. In 1979, when federal borrowing amounted to $37.4 billion, mortgage financing accounted for as much as 42%

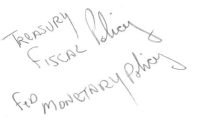

34

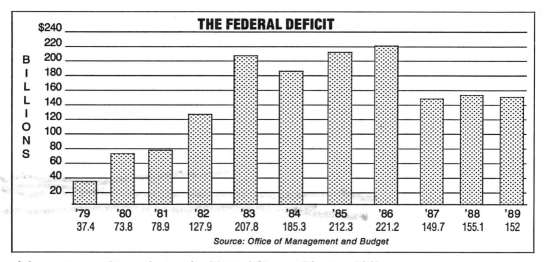

THE FEDERAL DEFICIT

BILLIONS

	'79	'80	'81	'82	'83	'84	'85	'86	'87	'88	'89
	37.4	73.8	78.9	127.9	207.8	185.3	212.3	221.2	149.7	155.1	152

Source: Office of Management and Budget

of the entire credit market in the United States. That is, 42% of the money supply available for borrowing was invested in real estate mortgages. In recent years, mortgage financing amounts to approximately 30% of the credit market, and financing the federal deficit takes up approximately another 30% of available loan funds.

One of the methods chosen by Congress to drastically cut the deficit was the passage of the Gramm-Rudman-Hollings Budget Act. The Act calls for the gradual reduction of the deficit to zero over a five-year period. If the law proves successful in bringing about a significant reduction in the federal deficit, the consequences may include increased availability of mortgage funds and lower interest rates. However, the reduction will likely be brought about at least in part through reduced federal funding for government-sponsored mortgage finance programs (e.g., FHA, VA, GNMA) and thus could mean less mortgage credit available for those with low to middle incomes.

Taxation

The second tool of fiscal policy is taxation. Lower taxes mean taxpayers have more funds for lending and investing. Higher taxes mean that taxpayers will not only have fewer

Tax policies:
• tax levels affect supply of funds for investment
• deductions/exemptions affect attraction of real estate investment

funds to lend or invest, but that they will be more likely to invest in tax-exempt securities instead of real estate mortgages or other taxable investments.

Taxation has a secondary effect on mortgage financing as well. Along with raising revenue, tax provisions are used to implement social policies. This is done through tax deductions and exemptions. For example, the deduction for mortgage interest has the effect of stimulating housing and implementing the government's policy of encouraging adequate housing and home ownership. Tax code changes in 1986 and 1987 limited to some degree the deductibility of home mortgage interest, which previously had been fully deductible. Beginning in 1988, home mortgage interest is deductible for loans of up to $1,000,000 to buy or improve a residence. Interest on other home loans, such as home equity loans for purposes other than acquisition or home improvement, is deductible on loans of up to $100,000 for a married couple filing jointly and up to $60,000 for a taxpayer filing separately.

Other provisions of the Tax Reform Act of 1986 also limited or eliminated tax benefits previously available for real property owners. The capital gains exclusion for long-term capital gains was eliminated. Accelerated cost recovery methods were eliminated, and straight-line cost recovery periods for income and investment property were increased to 27½ or 31½ years from the 15- to 19-year periods permitted for property placed in service in 1981 through 1986. The ability to offset losses from income property (termed "passive losses") against income from wages and salaries was restricted for many taxpayers.

The tax law changes probably have minimal impact for most home buyers, since most home loans are for less than $1,000,000. Also, the two other significant tax breaks for homeowners were retained: 1) the reinvestment deferral for replacing a primary residence, and 2) the $125,000 exclusion of gain on the sale of a home by an owner over 55. However, the elimination of the long-term capital gains exclusion, the longer cost recovery periods, and the restrictions on the deductibility of losses from rental property tend to make investments in income real estate less attractive.

THE FEDERAL RESERVE SYSTEM

The Federal Reserve System, usually referred to as the "Fed," is responsible for the nation's monetary policy and the regulation of commercial banks. The objectives of the Fed's monetary policy are:

The Fed:
- monetary policy
- regulation of commercial banks

1) high employment,
2) economic growth,
3) price stability,
4) interest rate stability,
5) stability in financial markets, and
6) stability in foreign exchange markets.

Although these goals are interrelated, we are most concerned with the Fed policies that affect the availability and cost of borrowed money and that, therefore, have the most direct impact on the real estate industry.

History and Organization of the Federal Reserve System

The Fed was established in 1913 as a "lender of last resort." The Fed was to provide funds to the banking system to avoid the bank panics that were common occurrences in the last half of the 1800's and early 1900's. In fact, the large losses suffered by depositors in the bank failures of 1907 finally overcame the American public's resistance to a central bank.

Do Not Have To Know.

The general hostility felt by average citizens towards banks, Wall Street interests, and centralized authority in general led to a system of checks and balances in the Federal Reserve Act of 1913. The Act established the Federal Reserve System with 12 regional Federal Reserve Banks. Its structure was designed to spread the power three different ways: geographically, between the private and government sectors, and among bankers, businesses and the public. The Federal Reserve System is made up of the:

- Federal Reserve Banks,
- Board of Governors (Federal Reserve Board),
- Federal Open Market Committee,
- Federal Advisory Council, and
- over 5,000 member banks.

Federal Reserve Board:
- sets reserve requirements
- controls discount rates
- controls open market transactions

The Federal Reserve System is controlled by a seven-member Board of Governors, called the **Federal Reserve Board**. The governors are appointed by the President and confirmed by the Senate for 14-year terms. The Board members control the Fed's monetary policy, set reserve requirements for commercial banks, and control the discount rates set by the Federal Reserve Banks. The governors also have substantial control over regulations affecting the activities of commercial banks and bank holding companies.

The **Federal Open Market Committee (FOMC)** controls the Fed's open market operations—the sale and purchase of government securities. Since these operations are the most important tool for controlling the money supply, the FOMC is the most important policy-making organization in the Fed.

12 Regional Federal Reserve Banks:
- owned by member banks
- make discount loans
- set discount rates with Fed approval

There are 12 Federal Reserve districts, each with one main **Federal Reserve Bank**. Technically, each Federal Reserve Bank is an incorporated banking institution owned by the member commercial banks in the Federal Reserve district (the member banks are required to purchase stock in their Reserve Banks). Each Reserve Bank has a nine-member board of directors.

Tools for Conducting Monetary Policy
There are three tools relied upon by the Fed for implementing monetary policy:

- reserve requirements,
- federal discount rates, and
- open market operations.

Tools of monetary policy:
- reserve requirements
- federal discount rates
- open market operations

Federal Reserve Map of the United States

O Reserve Bank Cities
• Branch Bank Cities
▬ District Boundaries
▬ Branch Territory Boundaries
★ Board of Governors of the Federal Reserve System
Note: Alaska is in the Seattle Branch Territory and Hawaii in that served by the Head Office of the Federal Reserve Bank of San Francisco. Both are in the Twelfth District.

Of these, open market transactions in government bonds are the most important.

Reserve requirements. The reserve requirement is the percentage of deposits that commercial banks are required to maintain on deposit. Prior to 1980, only member banks were required to keep reserves on deposit at the Federal Reserve Banks. However, since banking deregulation in 1980, all commercial banks must comply with the reserve requirements.

The original purpose of the reserve requirement was to help avert financial panic by giving depositors some confidence that their deposits were safe and accessible. The reserve requirement protects depositors by ensuring that enough funds are available to meet unusual customer demand. The reserve requirement also enables the Fed to exercise some control over growth of credit. By increasing the

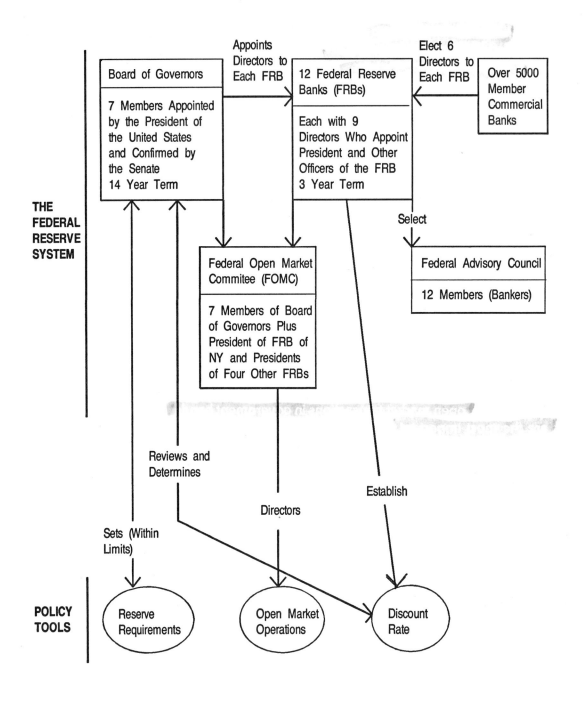

reserve requirement, the Fed can reduce the amount of money that banks have available to lend. On the other hand, a reduction in reserve requirements frees more money for investment or lending by banks. An increase in the reserve requirement, then, tends to decrease available loan funds and increase interest rates. Conversely, a decrease in the reserve requirement tends to increase funds available for lending and to decrease interest rates.

Discount rates. Federal discount rates are the interest rates charged by Federal Reserve Banks on loans to commercial banks. Increasing the discount rate usually results in the banks charging higher interest rates to their customers, since they have to charge more interest on the money they lend if they have to pay more interest on the money they borrow.

Open market operations. When the Fed buys and sells government securities, it is called an "open market transaction." Open market transactions are the main method relied upon by the Fed in its efforts to control the money supply, and with the money supply, inflation and interest rates. Only money in circulation is considered part of the money supply, so actions by the Fed which tend to increase or decrease money in circulation increase or decrease the money supply.

Purchases of government securities increase the money supply. The Fed may pay for the securities by cash, check or, if purchasing from a bank, simply by crediting the bank's reserves with the Fed. Any of these actions increases the amount of money in circulation.

Sales of government securities decrease the money supply. If the Fed sells securities, the purchaser may pay by cash, check, or, if the buyer is a bank, by reducing the bank's reserve with the Fed. Regardless of how payment is made, the money used to pay for the securities is taken out of circulation.

Other things being equal, it is believed that an increase in the money supply leads to lower interest rates. However, other things are seldom equal and several factors may apply upward pressure on interest rates at the same time that an increase in money supply is exerting downward pressure.

Reserve requirements:
- increase—decreases amount of funds available for investment and increases interest rates
- decrease—increases supply of funds and decreases interest rates

Know.

Example: Increases in money supply are often associated with increases in inflation and, if inflation is anticipated, interest rates tend to rise.

The balancing efforts of the Fed are directed to managing the growth of the money supply to adequately serve the growth of the economy at reasonable interest rates without fueling inflation or fears of inflation which could lead to higher interest rates.

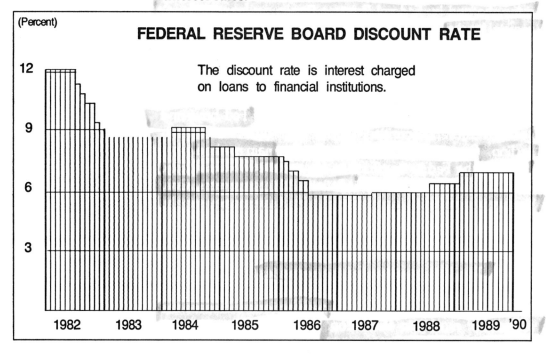

(Percent)

FEDERAL RESERVE BOARD DISCOUNT RATE

The discount rate is interest charged on loans to financial institutions.

12
9
6
3

1982   1983   1984   1985   1986   1987   1988   1989 '90

Recent Monetary Policy

Prior to 1979, the Federal Reserve System attempted to moderate interest rates by increasing the money supply when interest rates started to rise, thereby causing rates to fall. The result of this policy was relentless inflation as more and more money was pumped into the economy to satisfy the demands of borrowers.

In 1979, the Fed adopted a different approach. Because of increasing concern over inflation, the Fed discontinued efforts to control interest rates by adjusting the money supply and, instead, attempted to control inflation by restricting the growth of money. In the following months, long- and short-term interest rates fluctuated widely but remained much higher than they had been before. In 1982, the Fed again shifted course to put less emphasis on inflation, which by then seemed to be under control, and more emphasis on preventing large fluctuations in interest rates. Since then, inflation has remained at moderate levels, hovering around 4%-5%, and the discount rate and other interest rates have remained relatively stable and at lower levels than in 1980 and 1981.

OFFICE OF THRIFT SUPERVISION

The Federal Home Loan Bank System (and the Federal Home Loan Bank Board) was organized in 1932 to help stabilize the savings and loan industry. It served a parallel function to the Federal Reserve System. It was organized in a similar fashion and regulated savings and loan associations in the same manner that the Fed regulates commercial banks.

In the late 1980s, a crisis developed in the Savings and Loan industry. In response to this crisis, the Financial Institutions Reform, Recovery, and Enforcement Act (FIRREA) was enacted in 1989. This Act reorganized the Federal Home Loan Bank System. The Federal Home Loan Bank Board was eliminated and was replaced by the Office of Thrift Supervision (OTS).

The OTS now acts as the regulator of the thrift industry. A new board was created called the Federal Housing Finance Board (FHFB). This board took over the duties of the Federal Home Loan Bank board. The FHFB now acts as the overseer of mortgage lending by the Federal Home Loan Banks.

The OTS has regulatory powers similar to the Federal Reserve. However, the policies of the OTS have less impact

[Margin notes:] FHLBB replaced by FIRREA

RTC

OTS — Fed
|
S&L's   Commercial banks

OTS: regulates S&Ls in same manner that Fed regulates commercial banks on the national economy, since commercial banks control a much greater volume of deposits than do savings and loans.

WHAT ABOUT THE FUTURE?

While no one knows the future, at the time of this writing, most economists expect a relatively stable economy for the near future. The current moderate rates of inflation help keep interest rates down because investors are more assured of a safe rate of return on investments when inflation is low. The passage of legislation to compel lower federal deficits and thus less federal borrowing has also created optimism in the financial market. (Of course, continued hope depends on the concrete efforts of the President and Congress to actually reduce the deficit.) Both inflation and interest rates are expected to continue to climb slowly in the next year; however, no dramatic increases are expected.

A key factor to bear in mind with regard to the future of the real estate finance market is the vastly increased influence of the secondary market. No longer are real estate loan rates insulated from the day-to-day vagaries of national and international financial markets. It can safely be said that mortgage rates will respond with even more fidelity to the same influences which guide the markets for other long-term, fixed-income investments such as bonds.

CHAPTER SUMMARY

1. Interest rates on real estate loans, like most other things in our economy, are controlled primarily by the law of supply and demand. The federal government, through its policies of budgeting, taxation, and control of the money supply, has a great influence on the supply of money available for real estate investment.

2. For example, large government deficits may lead to a reduction in the availability of loan funds or to efforts by the government to increase the money supply to avert that shortage. Tax policies also influence real estate finance: the higher the tax rate, the less money people can put aside in savings. Also, tax changes can influence the desirability of real estate as an investment.

3. The Fed is the major force in the country influencing interest rates and the growth of the money supply. The Federal Reserve System is responsible for the nation's monetary policy and for the regulation of commercial banks. It uses three approaches to control the cost and supply of money: reserve requirements, discount rates, and most importantly, its open market transactions in government securities. Using these methods, the Fed tries to maintain the delicate balance between a healthy, growing economy and runaway inflation.

Chapter 5
CALIFORNIA FINANCE INSTRUMENTS

This chapter on real estate finance documents is an introduction to the contents and operation of these instruments. It is not intended as a substitute for competent professional advice and it should not be used as the basis for personal action, or to advise clients or customers regarding the operation of particular documents. The laws governing creditor-debtor relations are subject to change by judicial or legislative action. Therefore, it is advisable to consult an attorney for current, local advice concerning the effect of these instruments in any particular transaction.

The 'instruments' that will be discussed in this chapter are written documents. Written agreements are an integral part of most real estate financing transactions. This chapter will discuss promissory notes, mortgages, deeds of trust (or trust deeds), real estate contracts, and some of the more common and, for the real estate practitioner, more significant clauses found in those documents.

Instruments of finance:
- promissory notes
- mortgages
- deeds of trust
- real estate contracts

① Real Estate Contracts
Contract of Sale
Installment Sale
Conditional Sales Contract
Land Contract

① Owner Retains Ownership until fully paid by Borrower

PROMISSORY NOTES

Before a lender will finance the purchase of a house, the borrower must promise to repay the funds. That promise is put in writing in the form of a promissory note. Simply stated, a promissory note is a written promise to pay money. The one promising to pay the money is called the "maker" of the note. Usually, the maker is the homebuyer. The one promised payment is called the "payee." Usually, the payee is either a lender (if the purchaser has borrowed money from a bank

Promissory note:
- maker is borrower
- payee is lender
- note is evidence of debt and promise to repay

mortgage no   Deed of Trust yes.

or other lender to buy the property) or a seller (if the seller is financing the transaction in whole or in part by taking back a promissory note and mortgage or deed of trust). The promissory note, then, is the basic evidence of debt; it shows who owes how much money to whom. Promissory notes are usually rather brief and simple documents, as legal documents go. They normally are less than a page long and state:

A promissory note is the basic evidence of debt

- the names of the parties,
- the amount of the debt,
- how and when the money is to be paid,
- whether there is an acceleration clause (discussed below),
- the payee's remedies if the money is not properly repaid, and
- the signature of the maker.

Other provisions of the financing agreement between the debtor (maker) and creditor (lender or seller) are found in the mortgage or deed of trust.

NEGOTIABLE INSTRUMENTS

Negotiable means freely transferrable

Virtually all promissory notes used in real estate financing are negotiable instruments. Negotiable instruments are promissory notes that are freely transferable. "Freely transferable" means a bank or other creditor can sell the note and obtain immediate cash. The sale is usually at a discount, meaning the note is sold for a cash amount that is less than the face value of the note. The Uniform Commercial Code (which governs negotiable instruments) defines a negotiable instrument as a written, unconditional promise or order to pay a sum certain of money, either on a certain date or on demand, payable either to order or to bearer, and signed by the maker.

The promissory note (or promise to pay) is almost always accompanied by a security instrument. A security instrument

NOTE

...., 19..........   ...., ...
                                                                     [City]   [State]

....
[Property Address]

1. BORROWER'S PROMISE TO PAY

In return for a loan that I have received. I promise to pay U.S. $.................... (this amount is called "principal"), plus interest, to the order of the Lender. The Lender is ....' Savings and Loan Association I understand that the Lender may transfer this Note. The Lender or anyone who takes this Note by transfer and who is entitled to receive payments under this Note is called the "Note Holder".

2. INTEREST

Interest will be charged on unpaid principal until the full amount of principal has been paid. I will pay interest at a yearly rate of ....%.

The interest rate required by this Section 2 is the rate I will pay both before and after any default described in Section 6(B) of this Note.

3. PAYMENTS

(A) Time and Place of Payments

I will pay principal and interest by making payments every month.

I will make my monthly payments on the 1st day of each month beginning on .... 19........ I will make these payments every month until I have paid all of the principal and interest and any other charges described below that I may owe under this Note. My monthly payments will be applied to interest before principal. If, on .... I still owe amounts under this Note. I will pay those amounts in full on that date. which is called the "maturity date".

I will make my monthly payments at .... or at a different place if required by the Note Holder.

(B) Amount of Monthly Payments

My monthly payment will be in the amount of U.S. $..

4. BORROWER'S RIGHT TO PREPAY

I have the right to make payments of principal at any time before they are due. A payment of principal only is known as a "prepayment." When I make a prepayment, I will tell the Note Holder in writing that I am doing so.

I may make a full prepayment or partial prepayments without paying any prepayment charge. The Note Holder will use all of my prepayments to reduce the amount of principal that I owe under this Note. If I make a partial prepayment, there will be no changes in the due date or in the amount of my monthly payment unless the Note Holder agrees in writing to those changes.

5. LOAN CHARGES

If a law, which applies to this loan and which sets maximum loan charges, is finally interpreted so that the interest or other loan charges collected or to be collected in connection with this loan exceed the permitted limits, then: (i) any such loan charge shall be reduced by the amount necessary to reduce the charge to the permitted limit; and (ii) any sums already collected from me which exceeded permitted limits will be refunded to me. The Note Holder may choose to make this refund by reducing the principal I owe under this Note or by making a direct payment to me. If a refund reduces principal, the reduction will be treated as a partial prepayment.

6. BORROWER'S FAILURE TO PAY AS REQUIRED

(A) Late Charge for Overdue Payments

If the Note Holder has not received full amount of any monthly payment by the end of the 16th calendar day after the date it is due. I will pay a late charge to the Note Holder. The amount of the charge will be 5% of my overdue payment of principal and interest. I will pay this late charge promptly but only once on each late payment.

(B) Default

If I do not pay the full amount of each monthly payment on the date it is due, I will be in default.

(C) Notice of Default

If I am in default, the Note Holder may send me a written notice telling me that if I do not pay the overdue amount by a certain date, the Note Holder may require me to pay immediately the full amount of principal which has not been paid and all the interest that I owe on that amount. That date must be at least 30 days after the date on which the notice is delivered or mailed to me.

(D) No Waiver By Note Holder

Even if, at a time when I am in default, the Note Holder does not require me to pay immediately in full as described above, the Note Holder will still have the right to do so if I am in default at a later time.

(E) Payment of Note Holder's Costs and Expenses

If the Note Holder has required me to pay immediately in full as described above, the Note Holder will have the right to be paid back by me for all of its costs and expenses in enforcing this Note to the extent not prohibited by applicable law. Those expenses include, for example, reasonable attorneys' fees.

7. GIVING OF NOTICES

Unless applicable law requires a different method, any notice that must be given to me under this Note will be given by delivering it or by mailing it by first class mail to me at the Property Address above or at a different address if I give the Note Holder a notice of my different address.

Any notice that must be given to the Note Holder under this Note will be given by mailing it by first class mail to the Note Holder at the address stated in Section 3(A) above or at a different address if I am given a notice of that different address.

MULTISTATE FIXED RATE NOTE—Single Family—FNMA/FHLMC UNIFORM INSTRUMENT

8. OBLIGATIONS OF PERSONS UNDER THIS NOTE

If more than one person signs this Note, each person is fully and personally obligated to keep all of the promises made in this Note, including the promise to pay the full amount owed. Any person who is a guarantor, surety or endorser of this Note is also obligated to do these things. Any person who takes over these obligations, including the obligations of a guarantor, surety or endorser of this Note, is also obligated to keep all of the promises made in this Note. The Note Holder may enforce its rights under this Note against each person individually or against all of us together. This means that any one of us may be required to pay all of the amounts owed under this Note.

9. WAIVERS

I and any other person who has obligations under this Note waive the rights of presentment and notice of dishonor. "Presentment" means the right to require the Note Holder to demand payment of amounts due. "Notice of dishonor" means the right to require the Note Holder to give notice to other persons that amounts due have not been paid.

10. UNIFORM SECURED NOTE

This Note is a uniform instrument with limited variations in some jurisdictions. In addition to the protections given to the Note Holder under this Note, a Mortgage, Deed of Trust or Security Deed (the "Security Instrument"), dated the same date as this Note, protects the Note Holder from possible losses which might result if I do not keep the promises which I make in this Note. That Security Instrument describes how and under what conditions I may be required to make immediate payment in full of all amounts I owe under this Note. Some of those conditions are described as follows:

Transfer of the Property or a Beneficial Interest in Borrower. If all or any part of the Property or any interest in it is sold or transferred (or if a beneficial interest in Borrower is sold or transferred and Borrower is not a natural person) without Lender's prior written consent, Lender may, at its option, require immediate payment in full of all sums secured by this Security Instrument. However, this option shall not be exercised by Lender if exercise is prohibited by federal law as of the date of this Security Instrument.

If Lender exercises this option, Lender shall give Borrower notice of acceleration. The notice shall provide a period of not less than 30 days from the date the notice is delivered or mailed within which Borrower must pay all sums secured by this Security Instrument. If Borrower fails to pay these sums prior to the expiration of this period, Lender may invoke any remedies permitted by this Security Instrument without further notice or demand on Borrower.

WITNESS THE HAND(S) AND SEAL(S) OF THE UNDERSIGNED.

....(Seal)
-Borrower

....(Seal)
-Borrower

....(Seal)
-Borrower

[Sign Original Only]

gives the creditor the right to have the security property sold to satisfy the debt if the debtor fails to pay the debt according to the terms of the agreement. The security instrument may be either a deed of trust or a mortgage. The relative rights of the creditor and debtor under these security instruments vary according to whether it is a deed of trust or a mortgage. The next two sections of this chapter will cover deeds of trust and mortgages: the rights of the parties, the method of foreclosure, and the advantages and disadvantages of the two documents.

THE DEED OF TRUST (TRUST DEED)

The deed of trust (or trust deed) is the most commonly used security device in California. The deed of trust is a three-party device. The borrower is called the trustor; the lender is called the beneficiary; and there is an independent third party, called the trustee. The trust deed was originally designed to convey naked title (legal title with no rights to possession) to the trustee throughout the period of indebtedness. In some states, called title theory states, the trust deed still conveys title. In California, as in most states (called lien theory states), the deed of trust creates a lien against the property in favor of the beneficiary. It is this lien that gives the creditor the right to force the sale of the property if the debtor defaults on the obligations under the promissory note or the trust deed.

[handwritten margin notes: TRUSTOR; grantor is TRUSTOR; TITLE Co.]

Deed of trust:
• grantor is borrower
• beneficiary is lender
• trustee is independent third party with power of sale
• nonjudicial foreclosure

REQUIREMENTS FOR A VALID TRUST DEED

To be valid, a deed of trust must contain certain provisions. These include a statement pledging the property as collateral for a debt (a granting clause), a complete and unambiguous property description, the amount of the debt, the maturity date of the debt, a defeasance clause (the trust deed will be canceled when the debt is paid), and a power of sale clause.

Requirements for valid deed of trust:
• granting clause
• property description
• amount of the debt
• defeasance clause
• power of sale clause

[handwritten margin notes: Title Co. / Borrower / Lender / Trustee Sale / Time-minimum / 3 mos 21 Days / 3rd]

When the debt is paid in full, the beneficiary directs the trustee to reconvey the title to the trustor. The trustee releases the lien of the trust deed by signing and recording a **deed of reconveyance**. (When a beneficiary fails to release a trustor in a timely manner, the beneficiary is liable in an action for damages and subject to a statutory penalty of $300.)

The first page of a standard deed of trust is shown on the following page. Most lenders use this standard FNMA/FHLMC trust deed form so the loan will be easily salable to these agencies. If FNMA or FHLMC had to carefully inspect the provisions of each individual deed of trust they purchased, it would be an impracticably time-consuming process. When all lenders use a standard form, secondary investors can be assured of receiving a deed of trust with acceptable provisions.

FORECLOSURE

A deed of trust allows the beneficiary to foreclose the lien without the burden of bringing a legal action. This is called a **nonjudicial foreclosure**, that is, foreclosure without having to go to court.

Nonjudicial foreclosure:
- *under power of sale*
- *public notice of sale*
- *no post-sale redemption*
- *no deficiency judgment*

Power of Sale

The deed of trust contains a power of sale clause which authorizes the trustee to sell the property without court supervision if the debtor defaults. A typical power of sale clause might read as follows:

> If the default is not cured on or before the date specified in the notice, Lender at its option may require immediate payment in full of all sums secured by this Security Instrument without further demand and may invoke the power of sale . . . .If Lender invokes the power of sale, Lender shall execute or cause Trustee to execute a written notice of the occurrence of an event of default and of Lender's election to cause the Property to be sold.

———————————————————————— [Space Above This Line For Recording Data] ————————————————————————

DEED OF TRUST

THIS DEED OF TRUST ("Security Instrument") is made on ....,
19.......... The trustor is ....
.... ("Borrower"). The trustee is ....
.... ("Trustee"). The beneficiary is
...., which is organized and existing
under the laws of ...., and whose address is ....
.... ("Lender").
Borrower owes Lender the principal sum of ....
.... Dollars (U.S. $................................). This debt is evidenced by Borrower's note
dated the same date as this Security Instrument ("Note"), which provides for monthly payments, with the full debt, if not
paid earlier, due and payable on .... This Security Instrument
secures to Lender: (a) the repayment of the debt evidenced by the Note, with interest, and all renewals, extensions and
modifications; (b) the payment of all other sums, with interest, advanced under paragraph 7 to protect the security of this
Security Instrument; and (c) the performance of Borrower's covenants and agreements under this Security Instrument and
the Note. For this purpose, Borrower irrevocably grants and conveys to Trustee, in trust, with power of sale, the following
described property located in .... County, California:

which has the address of ...., ...,
                                                          [Street]   [City]
California .... ("Property Address");
                        [Zip Code]

TOGETHER WITH all the improvements now or hereafter erected on the property, and all easements, rights,
appurtenances, rents, royalties, mineral, oil and gas rights and profits, water rights and stock and all fixtures now or
hereafter a part of the property. All replacements and additions shall also be covered by this Security Instrument. All of the
foregoing is referred to in this Security Instrument as the "Property."

BORROWER COVENANTS that Borrower is lawfully seised of the estate hereby conveyed and has the right to grant
and convey the Property and that the Property is unencumbered, except for encumbrances of record. Borrower warrants
and will defend generally the title to the Property against all claims and demands, subject to any encumbrances of record.

THIS SECURITY INSTRUMENT combines uniform covenants for national use and non-uniform covenants with
limited variations by jurisdiction to constitute a uniform security instrument covering real property.

CALIFORNIA—Single Family—FNMA/FHLMC UNIFORM INSTRUMENT   Form 3005 12/83

Deed of trust may also be foreclosed judicially like a mortgage, in which case the rights and remedies are the same as those under a mortgage foreclosure.

Trustee's Sale

At the direction of the beneficiary, the trustee conducts an out-of-court sale, or auction, called a trustee's sale. The proceeds from the sale are used to pay off the trustor's debt.

However, before the trustee can sell the property, certain legal requirements must be met. First, the beneficiary (lender) prepares a document called the **Declaration of Default**, requesting the trustee to begin the foreclosure proceedings. The trustee then prepares a **Notice of Default and Election to Sell**, which is sent to the borrower. The trustee also notifies anyone who has subsequently recorded a request for notice of default and sale. The trustee is required to provide notice to all lienholders.

The borrower can prevent the sale of the property by **reinstating** the loan. A loan is reinstated by paying all past due installments, plus any late charges imposed by the lender. A borrower may reinstate the loan at any time from the notice of default until five business days before the sale date. During the five days before the sale, the borrower can stop the sale only by paying the full balance of the loan.

If the loan is not reinstated within three months of the notice of default, the trustee publishes a **Notice of Sale** of the property in a newspaper of general circulation. The notice of sale must appear weekly and the sale cannot take place until at least 20 days have elapsed from the first date of publication. Additionally, a notice of sale must be sent to the borrower, and posted on the property.

At the sale (usually a public auction), any person, including the debtor or creditor, may bid. The trustee can reject any, or all, inadequate bids and can postpone the sale if there are no acceptable bids. Otherwise, the sale is made to the highest bidder. The purchaser receives a "Trustee's Deed," which eliminates all liens junior to the trust deed being foreclosed, and any interest the debtor had in the property. The trustee applies the sale proceeds in the following order: to pay the trustee's costs and sales expense; to satisfy the beneficiary's debt; to junior lienholders in order of priority; and, finally, any surplus goes to the debtor.

The entire process, then, of selling property through the power of sale clause in a deed of trust may be accomplished in well under a year without the expenses involved in court proceedings. There are, of course, expenses connected with a trustee's sale, but these are usually substantially less than those connected with a court-ordered sheriff's sale. The relative speed and economy of the trustee's sale has caused trust deeds to all but replace mortgages in California.

Since no judge is involved in the trust deed foreclosure process, it is impossible to obtain a **deficiency judgment** at a trustee's sale. If the sale of the property fails to cover the debt, the beneficiary cannot then sue the debtor for the remainder. He or she must be satisfied with the proceeds of the trustee's sale. However, it is possible to foreclose a deed of trust like a mortgage, and then all the procedures and rights relating to mortgages are applicable.

ADVANTAGES AND DISADVANTAGES OF THE TRUST DEED

For the creditor, the primary advantage of the deed of trust is the quick and inexpensive nonjudicial sale process. Disadvantages are that deficiency judgments are usually unobtainable and that the debtor may stop the sale by making any back payments up until five days before the sale.

This right to reinstate by making up back payments (plus interest, trustee's fees and attorneys' fees) is probably the main advantage of the trust deed for borrowers. The speed of the process, the lack of judicial supervision, and the lack of redemption rights following the trustee's sale are all disadvantages for the borrower.

For creditor:
—advantages of deed of trust:
* no post-sale redemption

—disadvantages:
* no deficiency judgment
* no right of acceleration

For debtor:
—advantages of deed of trust:
* right to reinstate
* no deficiency judgment

—disadvantages:
* speedy foreclosure
* no redemption
* no judicial oversight

MORTGAGES

Mortgage:
- mortgagor is borrower
- mortgagee is lender
- creates lien against collateral property
- foreclosure by judicial process

A mortgage is a two-party instrument in which the borrower (called the mortgagor) mortgages his or her property to the lender (called the mortgagee). For the most part, California lenders prefer the deed of trust to the mortgage. A foreclosure under a mortgage requires a court-ordered sale conducted by the sheriff or other court-appointed official. This sort of foreclosure process is called **judicial foreclosure**.

FORECLOSURE

Judicial foreclosure:
1. acceleration of debt
2. foreclosure lawsuit
3. order of execution
4. equitable right of redemption
5. public notice of sale
6. sheriff's sale
7. possibility of deficiency judgment

In the event of default, the mortgagee accelerates the due date of the debt to the present and notifies the defaulting debtor to pay off the entire outstanding balance at once. If the debtor fails to do so, the mortgagee initiates a lawsuit, called a foreclosure action, in the county where the land is located. The purpose of this legal proceeding is to get a judge to order the county sheriff to seize and sell the property. The judge's order is called an order of execution. Acting under the order of execution, the sheriff notifies the public of the place and date of the sale. This requires posting notices at the property and the courthouse and running an advertisement of the sale in a newspaper circulated in the county. This process takes several weeks.

Redemption

At any time up until the sheriff's sale, the debtor may save the property by paying the mortgagee what is due. This right to save or redeem the property prior to the sale is called the **equitable right of redemption**. The debtor may also be obligated to pay delinquent interest, court costs, attorneys' fees, and sheriff's fees in order to redeem the property.

Sheriff's Sale

The sheriff's sale is a public auction, normally held at the courthouse door, and anyone can bid on the property. The property is sold to the highest bidder and the proceeds are used to pay for the costs of the sale and to pay off the mortgage. As with the trust deed, any surplus goes to the debtor.

If the property does not bring enough money at the sale to pay off the mortgage, the debtor may be able to obtain a deficiency judgment against the debtor for the remaining debt. California law prohibits deficiency judgments if the mortgage secured a loan to purchase a personal residence (a one- to four-unit property occupied by the owner). To obtain a deficiency judgment, the creditor must apply to the court within three months of the judicial sale.

Post-sale Redemption

After the sale, the debtor has another opportunity to save or redeem the property. The debtor can do this by paying the purchaser the amount paid for the property plus accrued interest from the time of the sale. This right to redeem the property following the sheriff's sale is called the **statutory right of redemption**. In California, the period lasts for one year if the proceeds from the sale are less than the indebtedness, three months if the proceeds are enough to satisfy the indebtedness. If there has been no redemption within this period, the purchaser at the sheriff's sale receives a deed to the property.

Depending on the court congestion and the availability of the sheriff for foreclosures, a judicial mortgage foreclosure may take anywhere from several months to several years from the time of default until a sheriff's deed is delivered to the purchaser, finally divesting the debtor of title.

ADVANTAGES AND DISADVANTAGES OF THE MORTGAGE

For the creditor (mortgagee), the main advantages of a mortgage are the right to accelerate the entire outstanding debt in the event of a default and the right to obtain a

For creditor:
—mortgage advantages:
 • right of acceleration
 • right to deficiency
  judgment

—mortgage disadvantages:
 • time and expense of
  foreclosure

For debtor:
—mortgage advantages:
 • long redemption
  periods
 • judicial involvement

—mortgage disadvantages:
 • acceleration
 • deficiency judgment

personal judgment against the debtor for any deficiency if the property does not bring enough at the sheriff's sale to satisfy the debt.

The main disadvantages to the creditor concern the time and expense involved in executing a judicial foreclosure. Legal fees and court costs may easily amount to several thousand dollars, which must be paid out of the creditor's pocket and may or may not be recovered at the sale. The entire process, as has already been mentioned, can take a long time to complete.

The advantages and disadvantages of a mortgage for the debtor (mortgagor), for the most part, correspond to those of the creditor, but in reverse. The creditor's right of acceleration may mean that a home purchaser who misses one or two payments will be faced with the prospect of having to pay off the debt completely in order to save the home. On the other hand, the debtor in most states is going to have a long time to get the money together, due to court proceedings and the statutory redemption period. Another advantage to the debtor is the requirement for a legal proceeding in which the debtor will have an opportunity to tell his or her story to the judge and possibly have the foreclosure stopped. This is unlikely to happen, but is possible in an unusual case.

REAL ESTATE CONTRACTS

Real estate contract:
seller retains legal title,
buyer obtains right to
possess and enjoy
property

Real estate contracts are also called contracts for deed, installment sales contracts, conditional sales contracts, and land contracts. They differ significantly from mortgages and deeds of trust. Under both mortgage and trust deed security arrangements, the debtor acquires title to the property. Under a real estate contract, the seller (vendor), retains legal title until the buyer (vendee), pays off the entire contract. During the period the purchaser is paying on the contract (which may be many years), the purchaser has the right to possess and enjoy the property, but is not the legal owner.

Real estate contracts normally provide that if the buyer defaults on the contract obligation, all the buyer's rights in the property are forfeited, any payments made may be retained by the seller as liquidated damages, and the seller has a right to retake possession of the property immediately. However, California law provides that to foreclose a land contract, the judicial procedures of foreclosure must take place.

ADVANTAGES AND DISADVANTAGES OF REAL ESTATE CONTRACTS

For the vendor, one advantage of contract sales is the personal satisfaction or security that the vendor may feel by remaining the title owner, by not giving the buyer a deed until the entire purchase price has been paid. However, since a land contract can only be forfeited by judicial foreclosure, this feeling of security may be largely illusory.

The main disadvantage to the vendor under a real estate contract is similar to the main disadvantage of the creditor under a mortgage: the expense and time required for foreclosure.

For the buyer, one advantage of real estate contracts is the fact that it takes the vendor so long to forfeit out the vendee, that the buyer may be able to look forward to several years (in counties with congested court calendars) of payment-free ownership and enjoyment of the property.

A serious disadvantage for the vendee under the contract that does not exist with mortgages or deeds of trust is that the vendor remains the legal owner. This often makes it difficult, if not impossible, for the vendee to obtain bank financing for construction or improvements. Banks are usually reluctant to lend to persons who do not have legal title. Judgments against the vendor may cloud the buyer's title, since the vendor remains the legal owner.

TYPICAL CLAUSES IN SECURITY INSTRUMENTS

Clauses commonly found in finance documents:
- acceleration
- prepayment
- alienation
- subordination
- partial release or satisfaction

We will now take a brief look at some clauses commonly used in real estate finance instruments.

ACCELERATION

Acceleration: lender may call entire debt due immediately on any default by borrower

Almost all promissory notes, mortgages and deeds of trust and many real estate contracts contain an acceleration clause. This allows the creditor or seller to accelerate the debt, that is, to declare the entire outstanding balance immediately due and payable in the event of a default. This means that a debtor who missed one payment may discover the following month that he or she does not owe just two payments, but rather the entire remaining balance. Most lenders will wait until payments are at least 90 days delinquent before enforcing an acceleration clause.

> In case the Mortgagor (or Trustor) shall fail to pay any installment of principal or interest secured hereby when due or to keep or perform any covenant or agreement aforesaid, then the whole indebtedness hereby secured shall forthwith become due and payable, at the election of the Mortgagee (or Beneficiary).

PREPAYMENT

Prepayment clause: additional charge imposed for early payment of debt to compensate lender for lost interest

Many conventional loans have prepayment provisions. (They are prohibited on FHA and VA loans.) While the time periods and the amount of payment vary considerably, the basic effect of a prepayment provision is to charge the debtor for paying off the loan too early and depriving the lender of receiving the anticipated interest. An example might be a provision which charged the debtor 3% of the original loan amount if more than 20% of the principal were repaid in any one of the first five years of the loan.

> If, within five years from the date of this note, Borrower makes any prepayments of principal in excess of twenty percent of the original principal amount in any 12-month period beginning with the date of this note or anniversary dates thereof ('loan year'), Borrower shall pay the Note Holder six months' interest on such excess principal payments.

California law prohibits imposing prepayment penalties beyond the first five years of the loan.

ALIENATION CLAUSES

Alienation refers to transfer of ownership, and alienation clauses found in loan documents are designed to limit the debtor's right to transfer the property without the permission of the creditor. Depending on the clause, it may be triggered by a transfer of title or by the transfer of any significant interest in the property (including long-term leases or any lease with an option to purchase). The alienation clause may give the lender the right to declare the entire loan balance immediately due (called a due-on-sale clause), to adjust the interest rate to current rates if they are higher than the existing loan rate or to do either at its option. Alienation clauses are not allowed in FHA and VA loans but are fairly common in conventional fixed-rate loans. ARM loans seldom have alienation clauses because the adjustable interest rate feature of ARM loans allows the lender to keep the interest rate at or close to market rates even if the ownership does not change.

> If all or any part of the Property or an interest therein is sold or transferred by Borrower without Lender's prior written consent, Lender may, at Lender's option, declare all the sums secured by this instrument to be immediately due and payable.

[Handwritten margin notes:]

SHERIFFS SALE: You have 3 mos To Go AFTER BORROWER for Deficiency.

difference between Amount owed and Amount Received from sheriffs sale!

Alienation clause: if property is sold, lender may increase interest rate, or accelerate debt

see page 148

Prior to 1982, the enforceability of such clauses varied widely from state to state. Some states regarded such provisions as enforceable according to their terms. Other states refused to enforce them unless the lender could show that its security was impaired by the transfer. Still other states distinguished between the various types of clauses, regarding some as enforceable and others as unenforceable.

In 1982, two actions on the federal level had the effect of limiting the power of the states with respect to the enforceability of due-on-sale clauses. The first action resulted from a lawsuit involving the enforceability of alienation clauses by a savings and loan association in California (*Fidelity Savings and Loan Association v. De La Cuesta, et al.*). In that case, the U.S. Supreme Court upheld a Federal Home Loan Bank Board regulation which preempted state law and permitted federally chartered savings and loans to enforce due-on-sale clauses regardless of whether such clauses were enforceable under state law.

This decision affected only the enforceability of alienation clauses by federal savings and loans; it was not directly applicable to actions by other lenders. However, passage of the Deposit Insurance Flexibility Act (the *Garn-St. Germain Act*) in the same year gave all lenders the right to enforce due-on-sale clauses in their security instruments. The act provided for a three-year transition period from October 15, 1982, to October 15, 1985, to phase in enforceability of alienation clauses in states where they had previously been unenforceable. In those states, the enforceability of due-on-sale clauses in loans which had been made during the period beginning when state law declared alienation clauses unenforceable and ending with passage of the *Garn-St. Germain Act* was delayed until October 15, 1985. The states where the window period applied were given the right to extend the window period by action of their state legislature. In California, the window period ran between August 1978 (the date of a California Supreme Court decision ruling alienation clauses unenforceable) and October 1982.

NOTE: If the seller decides to sell the property without an assumption of the mortgage taking place (e.g., the buyer takes out a new mortgage, the proceeds of which are used to pay off the seller's mortgage), any prepayment penalty provision may then apply. This "due-on-sale catch-22" is something the seller should be aware of. In California a lender may not enforce the alienation clause and also the prepayment on one- to four-unit dwellings. On other properties, the lender may enforce both clauses only if the borrower has separately agreed to pay a prepayment penalty on acceleration.

SUBORDINATION

Generally, the priority among mortgages, trust deeds and real estate contracts is determined by the date of recording, the first recorded being the first in priority. In some situations, however, the parties may desire that a later recorded instrument have priority over an earlier recorded instrument. This is particularly common in construction financing. Because of the high-risk nature of construction loans, construction lenders frequently refuse to lend any money unless they can be assured of first lien priority. Since the developer in many circumstances has purchased the land on some sort of deferred payment plan, there is often a security instrument (mortgage, trust deed or contract) which has already been recorded. In order for the later construction loan mortgage or trust deed to take priority over the earlier instrument, the earlier instrument must contain a subordination clause.

The subordination clause states that the instrument in which it is contained will be subordinate (junior) to a construction loan lien (mortgage or deed of trust) to be recorded later. The inclusion of a subordination clause must be negotiated and obtained at the time of the earlier transaction (in our example, at the time of the land purchase.)

> Subordination: creditor who is prior in time and recordation agrees to take junior lien position

> Lender agrees that this instrument shall be subordinate to a lien to be given by Borrower to secure funds for the construction of improvements on the Property, provided said lien is duly recorded and also provided that the amount secured by said lien does not exceed $85,000.

PARTIAL RELEASE, SATISFACTION, OR RECONVEYANCE

A partial release, satisfaction, or reconveyance clause obligates the creditor to release part of the property from the lien when part of the debt has been paid.

Example: A real estate contract for the purchase of five acres of land may contain a clause that states that when the vendee has paid 20% of the purchase price, the vendor will execute a deed to the vendee for one acre of the land. This would allow the vendee to acquire clear title to one acre, which may then be used to build upon.

The fact that the vendee has title will make it much easier to obtain construction financing. Such clauses are also frequently found in blanket mortgages or trust deeds covering subdivisions in the process of being developed and sold. The partial release (for real estate contracts), partial satisfaction (for mortgages) or partial reconveyance (for trust deeds) clause permits the developer to acquire, and therefore convey, clear title to one lot for which he or she has a purchaser, without having to pay off the entire lien against the development.

> Upon payment of all sums due with respect to any lot subject to this lien, Lender shall release said lot from the lien at no cost to Borrower.

CHAPTER SUMMARY

1. Instruments of real estate finance are documents that evidence debt and give the lender the right to proceed against the collateral property if the borrower defaults on the loan. The promissory note is the basic instrument of debt, signed by the borrower and showing the amount of the loan, interest rate, method and manner of repayment, and the borrower's promise to repay the debt. Mortgages, deeds of trust, and real estate contracts give the lender or seller the right to foreclose against or repossess the property if the buyer defaults. The deed of trust provides a speedier method of foreclosure than does a mortgage.

2. Some particular clauses found in many mortgages, trust deeds, and installment contracts include acceleration clauses, prepayment provisions, and alienation (due-on-sale) clauses. Subordination agreements and partial release or satisfaction clauses are less common in residential loans, but are frequently found in construction or development loans.

Chapter 6
OVERVIEW OF THE LOAN PROCESS

While the principles behind real estate finance are basically simple and straightforward, they will be even easier to understand after taking a brief look at the financing process. The procedures for financing real estate can be conveniently broken down into four steps:

1) loan application,
2) analysis of the borrower and property,
3) processing the loan application, and
4) closing the loan.

Loan process
1. application
2. underwriting
3. processing
4. closing

A fifth step could be added: servicing and sale to the secondary market. However, because this step takes place after the loan has been placed, it is primarily a matter of administration rather than analysis and judgment.

THE LOAN PROCESS

THE LOAN APPLICATION

As might be expected, the first step in obtaining a real estate loan is to fill out the loan application. The loan application is not designed for those merely inquiring about real estate loans, but for those who will follow through and actually borrow the funds (provided the loan is approved). The home buyer (or the real estate agent on behalf of the buyer) sets up an appointment with the lender. The buyer will attend

Loan application:
1. set up appointment
2. take necessary information
3. bring deposit receipt
4. choose type of mortgage
5. pay deposit

this appointment armed with a good deal of personal and financial data which will be the basis of the lender's decision whether or not to make the loan. The types of information the buyer should take to this interview will be discussed shortly. It should be noted that if the buyer does not have all the necessary data at the interview, it will be necessary to provide the missing information at a later date, which will cause a delay in the loan application process.

During the initial interview, the buyer will learn about the various types of financing programs offered by the lender. These will probably include 30-year, fixed-rate mortgages, 15-year, fixed-rate mortgages, and several different versions of adjustable-rate mortgages. Based on the information given by the lender and the buyer's own personal circumstances, the buyer will decide which program best suits his or her needs.

The lender will also require a deposit to cover the expenses that must be paid up front. These include the costs of the credit report, property appraisal, and preliminary title report. This deposit will assure the lender that these fees will be paid for, even if the loan does not close.

The deposit receipt will be examined at this interview as well. This is so the lender can be sure that the terms of the agreement are in keeping with the terms of the loan the lender can offer (e.g., interest rate and length of the term of the loan). Of particular concern is the agreed-upon closing date. Often, the deposit receipt will provide for a closing date which is far too early to be realistic. If it is impossible for the lender to meet the closing date, a more feasible one can be agreed on and later frustration avoided.

ANALYSIS OF THE BORROWER AND PROPERTY

Once the application has been properly filled out, the lender can begin gathering other pertinent information on the buyer. Verification forms will be sent out to the buyer's employer, banks or other financial institutions, and any previous mortgage lender. The lender will order a credit report and have a preliminary title report prepared. An approved appraiser will also be contacted to have an appraisal done on the property. After examining the application, the lender may also ask the buyer to submit further information, including:

Underwriting:
• verify employment
• verify funds
• order credit report
• order appraisal

- a copy of any divorce decree (to verify any child support or alimony obligations and any settlement agreement that may be the source of the downpayment);
- investment account records;
- pension plan documentation;
- tax returns (if the buyer is self-employed or retired and living on investment income); and
- any other documentation that may have an effect on the buyer's income or credit status.

The lender will be very concerned with the source of the buyer's downpayment. Savings, the previous sale of a home, or gifts are all acceptable sources of the downpayment. However, it is usually not permitted to use borrowed funds for the downpayment.

Equal Credit Opportunity Act

The federal Equal Credit Opportunity Act prohibits discrimination based on age, sex, race, marital status, color, religion, or national origin. Senior citizens, young adults and single persons must be considered on the basis of income adequacy, satisfactory net worth, job stability, and satisfactory credit rating. Lenders must apply their credit guidelines to each potential borrower in the same manner.

PROCESSING THE LOAN APPLICATION

When the credit report, verification forms, preliminary title report, and appraisal have all been received by the lender, a loan package is put together and submitted to the underwriting department. The loan underwriter thoroughly examines the loan package and then makes the decision to approve it, reject it, or approve it under certain conditions. A conditional approval usually requires the submission of additional information, such as:

- the closing statement from the sale of the buyer's previous home;
- pay stubs to verify income;
- a final inspection report; and
- a commitment for private mortgage insurance (which is always a condition for the approval of a conventional loan with a less than 20% downpayment).

CLOSING THE LOAN

Escrow agent:
- gathers necessary documents
- makes sure documents properly signed
- calculates prorations and charges
- ensures all funds deposited
- provides closing statements

After the conditions are met, all the necessary documents are prepared for closing. The closing process ordinarily takes about one week if everything goes smoothly. The mechanics of closing are normally the responsibility of the escrow agent. This escrow holder may be an "in-house" escrow department of the lender, an independent escrow company, or a title insurance company (depending on the California region). The escrow agent simultaneously follows the instructions of both the buyer and the seller, and is responsible for providing the lender with a certified copy of the escrow instructions. The escrow gathers together all the necessary documents (e.g., the promissory note and deed of trust) and makes sure that all the documents are properly signed by the parties. The escrow calculates the various prorations, adjustments, and charges to be assessed against each party, assures that all required funds and documents are deposited, and furnishes each party with a settlement (or closing) statement.

If there are no unforeseen problems during closing (e.g., the seller does not have title to the property), the loan papers are signed and sent to the funding department. This department makes one final check to be sure that everything is in order and that it has the necessary instructions for the release of the funds. The loan funds are then disbursed to the proper parties.

THE LOAN APPLICATION

As mentioned earlier, the buyer fills out a loan application at the initial interview with the lender. A copy of such a loan application is shown on the following pages. This standard loan application is used in California for a conventional (non-government insured) loan.

Lenders expect the loans they make to be repaid without collection, servicing, or foreclosure difficulties with the borrower. They are obviously careful to make loans only to those borrowers who can be expected to repay the loan in a timely manner. Therefore, employment stability, income potential, history of debt management and net worth are important considerations to the lender. These are the types of information the loan application is designed to elicit.

Information required to apply for loan:
- property information
- borrower information
  - dependents
  - income
  - housing expense
  - employment history
  - credit history
  - assets and liabilities

Property Information

The application begins with a section on the property. Questions as to the type of loan sought, the terms of the loan, location and legal description of the property, the property's value, and the manner of taking title must be completed. This information is used to determine how much security for the loan will be provided. Because lenders must live with their lending decisions for long periods of time, they are interested in the trend of the collateral's value as well as its current value.

Borrower Information

The next section of the application requests the borrower's name, address, phone number, social security number, marital status, and employer. There is a parallel section for the same information on any co-borrower (e.g., spouse). This

71

information helps the lender determine both the borrower's ability and willingness to repay the loan.

Dependents

The lender will want to know how many dependents the borrower must support. Although children help stabilize a borrower, while they are young they also add considerably to the financial obligations of the borrower.

Income

The section regarding income provides spaces for primary employment income, overtime, bonuses, commissions, dividends and interest, net rental income, and income from any other sources.

Monthly Housing Expense

The monthly housing expense is made up of such items as rent, principal and interest payments, any secondary financing payments, hazard insurance premiums, real estate taxes, mortgage insurance premiums, homeowners' association dues and utilities.

Details of Purchase

The next section asks for information on the real estate transaction itself. The buyer is to fill in the purchase price, closing costs, prepaid escrow expenses, mortgage amount, any secondary financing amounts, other equity, amount of cash deposit, closing costs to be paid by the seller, and an estimate of the cash amount that will be required for closing.

Employment History

If the borrower has been at his or her present job for less than two years, the name, address and type of business of previous employers must be included, along with the borrower's position, income, and the dates of employment.

FINANCING CALIFORNIA REAL ESTATE

Residential Loan Application

MGIC

MORTGAGE APPLIED FOR	[X] Conventional [ ] FHA [ ] VA [ ]	Amount $76,500.	Interest Rate 10½ %	No. of Months 360	Monthly Payment Principal & Interest $685.52	Escrow/Impounds (to be collected monthly) [X] Taxes [X] Hazard Ins. [X] Mtg. Ins. [ ] _____

Prepayment Option

Subject Property

Property Street Address 712 N. 1st	City Seaside	County Ocean	State CA	Zip 00012	No. Units 1

Legal Description (Attach description if necessary) SEE ATTACHMENT	Year Built 1971

Purpose of Loan: [X] Purchase [ ] Construction-Permanent [ ] Construction [ ] Refinance [ ] Other (Explain)

Complete this line if Construction-Permanent or Construction Loan ☞	Lot Value Data	Original Cost	Present Value (a)	Cost of Imps. (b)	Total (a + b)	ENTER TOTAL AS PURCHASE PRICE IN DETAILS OF ☞ PURCHASE
Year Acquired	$	$	$	$	$	

Complete this line if a Refinance Loan	Purpose of Refinance	Describe Improvements [ ] made [ ] to be made
Year Acquired	Original Cost	Amt. Existing Liens			
$	$	$		Cost: $	

Title Will Be Held In What Name(s) James Turner, Sarah Turner, husband and wife	Manner In Which Title Will Be Held community property

Source of Down Payment and Settlement Charges

savings

This application is designed to be completed by the borrower(s) with the lender's assistance. The Co-Borrower Section and all other Co-Borrower questions must be completed and the appropriate box(es) checked if [ ] another person will be jointly obligated with the Borrower on the loan, or [ ] the Borrower is relying on income from alimony, child support or separate maintenance or on the income or assets of another person as a basis for repayment of the loan, or [X] the Borrower is married and resides, or the property is located, in a community property state.

Borrower			**Co-Borrower**		
Name James Turner	Age 35	School Yrs 16	Name Sarah Turner	Age 36	School Yrs 16
Present Address No. Years 2 [ ] Own [X] Rent			Present Address No. Years 2 [ ] Own [X] Rent		
Street 7280 Cherry Avenue			Street 7280 Cherry Avenue		
City/State/Zip Seaside, California 00012			City/State/Zip Seaside, California 00012		
Former address if less than 2 years at present address			Former address if less than 2 years at present address		
Street _____			Street _____		
City/State/Zip _____			City/State/Zip _____		
Years at former address [ ] Own [ ] Rent			Years at former address [ ] Own [ ] Rent		
Marital Status [X] Married [ ] Separated [ ] Unmarried (incl. single, divorced, widowed)			Marital Status [X] Married [ ] Separated [ ] Unmarried (incl. single, divorced, widowed)		
Name and Address of Employer Qwik Copy 722 - 6th Avenue Seaside, California 00012	Years employed in this line of work or profession? 2 years Years on this job 1 [ ] Self Employed*		Name and Address of Employer Oceanview Community College Seaside, California 00012	Years employed in this line of work or profession? 5 years Years on this job 3 [ ] Self Employed*	
Position/Title Print Shop Asst. Mgr.	Type of Business Printing		Position/Title Minority Affairs Counselor/Student Counseling	Type of Business	
Social Security Number *** 333-22-111	Home Phone 423-7890	Business Phone 221-7070	Social Security Number *** 111-22-333	Home Phone 423-7890	Business Phone 435-2666

Gross Monthly Income				**Monthly Housing Expense****			**Details of Purchase**	
Item	Borrower	Co-Borrower	Total		Present	Proposed	Do Not Complete If Refinance	
Base Empl. Income	$1,558	$1,800	$3,358	Rent	$550	—	a. Purchase Price	$85,000
Overtime	—	—	—	First Mortgage (P&I)	—	$685.52	b. Total Closing Costs (Est.)	11,050
Bonuses	50	—	50	Other Financing (P&I)	—	—	c. Prepaid Escrows (Est.)	300
Commissions	—	—	—	Hazard Insurance	—	20	d. Total (a + b + c)	$96,350
Dividends/Interest	—	25	25	Real Estate Taxes	—	50	e. Amount This Mortgage	(76,500)
Net Rental Income	—	—	—	Mortgage Insurance	—	23	f. Other Financing	(0)
Other† (Before completing, see notice under Describe Other Income below.)	—	—	—	Homeowner Assn. Dues	—	—	g. Other Equity	(0)
				Other:	—	—	h. Amount of Cash Deposit	(1,000)
				Total Monthly Pmt.	$550	$751.52	i. Closing Costs Paid by Seller	(7,650)
				Utilities	55	75	j. Cash Reqd. For Closing (Est.)	$11,200
Total	$1,608	$1,825	$3,433	Total	$605	$826.52		

Describe Other Income		
▷ B-Borrower C-Co-Borrower	NOTICE:† Alimony, child support, or separate maintenance income need not be revealed if the Borrower or Co-Borrower does not choose to have it considered as a basis for repaying this loan.	Monthly Amount $

If Employed In Current Position For Less Than Two Years, Complete the Following						
B/C	Previous Employer/School	City/State	Type of Business	Position/Title	Dates From/To	Monthly Income
B	Copy King	Seaside, CA	Print Shop	Clerk		$1,350

These Questions Apply To Both Borrower and Co-Borrower	Borrower Yes or No	Co-Borrower Yes or No		Borrower Yes or No	Co-Borrower Yes or No
If a "yes" answer is given to a question in this column, please explain on an attached sheet.					
Are there any outstanding judgments against you?	no	no			
Have you been declared bankrupt within the past 7 years?	no	no			
Have you had property foreclosed upon or given title or deed in lieu thereof in the last 7 years?	no	no	Are you a U.S. citizen?	yes	yes
Are you a party to a law suit?	no	no	If "no," are you a resident alien?		
Are you obligated to pay alimony, child support, or separate maintenance?	no	no	If "no," are you a non-resident alien?		
Is any part of the down payment borrowed?	no	no	Explain Other Financing or Other Equity (if any).		
Are you a co-maker or endorser on a note?	no	no			

*FHLMC/FNMA require business credit report, signed Federal Income Tax returns for last two years, and, if available, audited Profit and Loss Statement plus balance sheet for same period.
**All Present Monthly Housing Expenses of Borrower and Co-Borrower should be listed on a combined basis.
***Optional for FHLMC
FHLMC 65 Rev. 10/86

Fannie Mae Form 1003 Rev 10/86

This Statement and any applicable supporting schedules may be completed jointly by both married and unmarried co-borrowers if their assets and liabilities are sufficiently joined so that the Statement can be meaningfully and fairly presented on a combined basis; otherwise separate Statements and Schedules are required (FHLMC 65A/FNMA 1003A). If the co-borrower section was completed about a spouse, this statement and supporting schedules must be completed about that spouse also.

☒ Completed Jointly   ☐ Not Completed Jointly

Assets		Liabilities and Pledged Assets				
Description	Cash or Market Value	Creditors' Name, Address and Account Number		Acct. Name if Not Borrower's	Mo. Pmt. and Mos. Left to Pay	Unpaid Balance
Cash Deposit Toward Purchase Held By	$	Installment Debts (Include revolving charge accounts)	Acct. No		$ Pmt./Mos.	$
Stella George, Broker	1,000	Co World Bank VISA				
Checking and Savings Accounts (Show Names of Institutions/Account Numbers)		Addr 71258 – 132nd Ave.	4567 82			
Bank, S & L or Credit Union		City Saratoga, NY	9271		$ 25/15	$ 375
Seaside Credit Union	8,023	Co Sears & Roebuck	Acct. No.			
Addr 712 Main Street		Addr 512 Main St.	4956 213			
City Seaside, CA 00012		City Seaside, CA 00012	72		$ 15/10	$ 150
Acct No. 932157		Co	Acct No			
Bank, S & L or Credit Union		Addr				
First National Bank	4,098	City				
Addr 2203 Market Street		Co	Acct. No			
City Seaside, CA 00012		Addr			/	
Acct No 2172-813		City				
Bank, S & L or Credit Union		Co	Acct. No.			
First National Bank	574	Addr				
Addr 2203 Market Street		City				
City Seaside, CA 00012		Other Debts including Stock Pledges				
Acct No 5769-813						
Stocks and Bonds (No. Description)						
		Real Estate Loans	Acct. No			
		Co				
		Addr				
		City				
Life Insurance Net Cash Value		Co	Acct. No			
Face Amount $		Addr				
Subtotal Liquid Assets	13,695	City				
Real Estate Owned (Enter Market Value from Schedule of Real Estate Owned)		Automobile Loans	Acct. No			
		Co Seaside Credit Union				
Vested Interest in Retirement Fund		Addr 712 Main Street	72160 C			
Net worth of Business Owned (ATTACH FINANCIAL STATEMENT)		City Seaside, CA 00012			$210/27	$5,670
		Co	Acct No			
Automobiles Owned (Make and Year)						
Ford 1984	8,750	City			/	
Toyota 1981	3,000					
Furniture and Personal Property	15,000	Alimony, Child Support, Separate Maintenance Payments Owed to			/	
Other Assets itemize						
		Total Monthly Payments			$ 250	
Total Assets	$40,445	Net Worth (A minus B) $ $34,250			Total Liabilities	$ 6,195

SCHEDULE OF REAL ESTATE OWNED (If Additional Properties Owned Attach Separate Schedule)

Address of Property (Indicate S if Sold, PS if Pending Sale or R if Rental being held for income)		Type of Property	Present Market Value	Amount of Mortgages & Liens	Gross Rental Income	Mortgage Payments	Taxes, Ins. Maintenance and Misc	Net Rental Income
	◇		$	$	$	$	$	$
TOTALS →			$	$	$	$	$	$

List Previous Credit References

◇ B-Borrower C-Co-Borrower	Creditor's Name and Address	Account Number	Purpose	Highest Balance	Date Paid
B/C	Atlas Savings & Loan, 352 Cherry, Seaside, CA	71116-3	Personal-furn.	$ 8,000	
C	Seaside Credit Union, 712 Main, Seaside, CA	56052 D	Auto loan	5,600	
B	First Bank Mastercard, 87632-189th N.E., Portland, ME	8926-438-92-41	1/Revolv.Credit	1,375	

List any additional names under which credit has previously been received _____

AGREEMENT   The undersigned applies for the loan indicated in this application to be secured by a first mortgage or deed of trust on the property described herein, and represents that the property will not be used for any illegal or restricted purpose, and that all statements made in this application are true and are made for the purpose of obtaining the loan. Verification may be obtained from any source named in this application. The original or a copy of this application will be retained by the lender, even if the loan is not granted. The undersigned ☐ intend or ☐ do not intend to occupy the property as their primary residence.
I/we fully understand that it is a federal crime punishable by fine or imprisonment, or both, to knowingly make any false statements concerning any of the above facts as applicable under the provisions of Title 18, United States Code, Section 1014.

Borrower's Signature _____ Date _____   Sarah Turner   Co-Borrower's Signature _____ Date _____

Information for Government Monitoring Purposes

The following information is requested by the Federal Government for certain types of loans related to a dwelling, in order to monitor the lender's compliance with equal credit opportunity and fair housing laws. You are not required to furnish this information, but are encouraged to do so. The law provides that a lender may neither discriminate on the basis of this information, nor on whether you choose to furnish it. However, if you choose not to furnish it, under Federal regulations this lender is required to note race and sex on the basis of visual observation or surname. If you do not wish to furnish the above information, please check the box below. (Lender must review the above material to assure that the disclosures satisfy all requirements to which the Lender is subject under applicable state law for the particular type of loan applied for.)

Borrower ☒ I do not wish to furnish this information
Race/National Origin
☐ American Indian Alaskan Native   ☐ Asian Pacific Islander
☐ Black   ☐ Hispanic   ☐ White
☐ Other (specify) _____
Sex ☐ Female   ☐ Male

Co-Borrower ☒ I do not wish to furnish this information
Race/National Origin
☐ American Indian Alaskan Native   ☐ Asian Pacific Islander
☐ Black   ☐ Hispanic   ☐ White
☐ Other (specify) _____
Sex ☐ Female   ☐ Male

To Be Completed by Interviewer

This application was taken by:
☐ face to face interview
☐ by mail
☐ by telephone

Interviewer _____
Interviewer's Phone Number _____

Name of Interviewer's Employer _____
Address of Interviewer's Employer _____

FHLMC Form 65 Rev 10 86
Form #71-3973 (10/86)

Fannie Mae Form 1003 Rev 10 86

Credit History

This section is for information on the buyer's credit history, e.g., any outstanding judgments, bankruptcies, foreclosures, etc.

Assets and Liabilities

In the next section of the application, the buyer is to list all assets and liabilities. Assets include cash deposits, checking and savings accounts, stocks and bonds, life insurance policies, real estate, retirement funds, automobiles, and personal property. Liabilities would include any installment debts, automobile loans, real estate loans, and alimony and/or child support payments.

Credit References

In this segment, the buyer is to list other credit references, such as personal loans or revolving credit debts which have been paid off.

Borrower's Signature

Finally, there is a space for the buyer to date and sign the application.

LOAN APPLICATION CHECKLIST

In order to properly fill out the loan application, the buyer will need to know a variety of information that may not be easily recalled from memory. To ensure that all necessary data is at the buyer's fingertips, it would be wise for him or her to take the following information to the initial interview:

1) The deposit receipt
2) A residence history:

- where the buyer has lived for the past two years,
- if the buyer is currently renting, the landlord or rental agency's name, address, and phone number; and

- if the buyer owns his or her present home, the name, address, and phone number of the lender and the type of loan (e.g., FHA or conventional).

3) Employment history:

- names, addresses, and zip codes of where the buyer has been employed for the last two years; the position held; whether the employment was full-time, part-time or temporary; and the income earned upon departure;
- if self-employed or fully commissioned, the tax returns for the past two calendar years, plus a year-to-date income and expense statement; and
- if a major stockholder in a corporation (owns 25% or more of the stock), three years of corporate tax returns.

4) Income:

- the amount and sources, including regular salary and secondary sources, such as:
  - military retirement,
  - company pensions,
  - social security benefits,
  - disability benefits, and
  - child support or alimony; and
- the lender will need a statement of benefits from the corresponding sources of income listed above; child support or alimony will require a copy of the divorce decree.

5) A list of assets:

- names, addresses, and account numbers for all bank accounts;
- the value of household goods and personal property;

- the make, model, year, and market value of automobiles;
- the cash and face value of insurance policies; and
- the address, description, and value of any other real estate owned; income properties should have a spread sheet showing relevant data (similar to the one shown below).

| | | | | | | | MORTGAGEE NAME, LOAN NUMBER, & MAILING | SUBDIVISION NAME & |
ADDRESS	MARKET VALUE	MORTGAGE BALANCE	EQUITY	GROSS RENT	MORTGAGE PAYMENT	INCOME	ADDRESS	COMMENTS

SCHEDULE OF REAL ESTATE

6) A copy of the gift letter:

- if a gift is the source of the downpayment or closing costs; and
- the letter must be signed by the donor (a close relative) and state that the funds are not to be repaid.

7) A list of liabilities:

- the name, address, and phone number for each creditor and the balance, monthly payment, and account number; and

- a copy of the divorce decree if there is any child support or alimony obligation.

8) A Certificate of Eligibility for VA loans.

9) If there is to be the sale of a present home:

- the net dollar amount from the sale after deducting the sales commission and any expenses; and
- if the buyer is being relocated by an employer who is paying all or part of the closing costs, a letter from the employer stating exactly what costs will be paid by the company.

CHAPTER SUMMARY

1. The loan process consists of four general steps:

- filling out the loan application,
- analyzing the borrower and property,
- processing the loan application, and
- closing the loan.

2. Each of these steps can be simplified if the borrower (and real estate agent) knows what is required of him or her. By supplying all the necessary data the lender needs, the borrower can ensure a much smoother loan process for all concerned. Some of the information the lender will require includes:

- the deposit receipt,
- a residence history,
- an employment history,
- income information,
- a list of assets,

- a copy of any gift letter, and
- a list of liabilities

Chapter 7
STATE AND FEDERAL REGULATION OF REAL ESTATE FINANCE

There are several laws, both state and federal, which regulate various aspects of the real estate financing process. These include laws prohibiting discrimination in real estate transactions and laws requiring certain finance disclosures to be made.

Heavy in Mid-term

DISCRIMINATION

Both the state and federal governments have enacted laws which prohibit discriminatory behavior in the real estate industry. Federal legislation includes the *Civil Rights Act of 1866* and the *Federal Fair Housing Law of 1968*. State legislation includes the *Unruh Civil Rights Act*, the *Housing Financial Discrimination Act of 1977* and the *Fair Employment and Housing Act*. The *California License Law* also prohibits real estate licensees from acting in a discriminatory manner (such acts are grounds for disciplinary action), so it is important that the real estate agent be aware of these laws and the types of actions that are prohibited. The prohibition of discrimination applies to the financing of real property as well as its sale or rental.

Laws prohibiting discrimination:
- Civil Rights Act of 1866
- Federal Fair Housing Law of 1968
- Unruh Civil Rights Act
- Housing Financial Discrimination Act of 1977
- Fair employment and Housing Act
- California License Law

FEDERAL LAWS

The Civil Rights Act of 1866

This act provides that all citizens of the United States shall have the same right, in every state and territory, as enjoyed

Civil Rights Act of 1866: all citizens have same property rights as white citizens
• upheld in *Jones v. Mayer*

by white citizens to inherit, purchase, lease, sell, and convey real and personal property. The act prohibits any discrimination based on race and was upheld in 1968 by the United States Supreme Court in the landmark case of *Jones v. Mayer*. The court ruled that the 1866 federal law "prohibits all racial discrimination, private or public, in the sale and rental of property." Its constitutionality was upheld, based on the 13th Amendment to the U.S. Constitution, which prohibits slavery.

The Federal Fair Housing Act

Federal Fair Housing Act: illegal to discriminate based on:
• race
• color
• religion
• sex
• national origin
• handicap
• children

Contained in Title VIII of the Civil Rights Act of 1968, this law took the 1866 Act one step further, making it illegal to discriminate on the basis of race, color, religion, sex, national origin, handicap, or families with children in the sale or lease of residential property or in the sale or lease of vacant land for the construction of residential buildings.

Some residential sales and leases are exempt from the provisions of the Fair Housing Law. The sale of a single-family home is exempt if three conditions are met:

1. the owner does not own more than three such homes at one time;
2. there is no real estate broker or agent involved in the transaction; and
3. there is no discriminatory advertising.

This exemption is limited to one transaction in any 24-month period, unless the owner was the most recent occupant of the home.

The rental of a unit or a room in an owner-occupied dwelling containing four units or less is exempt from the Fair Housing Law, provided rental advertisements are not discriminatory and a real estate broker is not used to locate tenants. This is called the **Mrs. Murphy exemption**.

Religious discrimination is permitted with respect to rentals in dwellings owned by religious organizations; lodgings in private clubs are also exempt from the law if the club is truly private and non-commercial.

The Fair Housing Law prohibits specific acts if they are based on race, color, religion, sex, national origin, handicap, or families with children. These prohibited acts include the following: refusing to sell, rent, or negotiate the sale or lease of residential property; changing the terms of a sale or lease for different people; discriminating in advertising; making false representations regarding the availability of certain property for sale or lease; blockbusting; steering; and limiting participation in a multiple listing service or similar service.

Blockbusting is the process by which a person induces property owners in a neighborhood to sell their property by predicting the entry of minorities into the neighborhood. The person buys the property from the owners and then resells it to minority buyers for a profit.

> Blockbusting: inducing homeowners to sell by predicting entry of minorities into neighborhood

Steering is the channeling of various applicants to specific areas in order to maintain or change the character of those neighborhoods.

> Steering: channeling prospects to specific areas to maintain or change the character of those neighborhoods

In addition to the above, Title VIII makes it unlawful to discriminate in lending practices. For example, it is illegal to refuse to grant a loan or alter the terms of a loan because of a borrower's race, color, religion, sex, national origin, handicap, or children. Also, **racial redlining** is prohibited. Racial redlining is the refusal to make loans on property located in a particular area for discriminatory reasons. The prohibition against redlining is enforced by the *Home Mortgage Disclosure Act of 1975*, which requires institutional lenders with assets in excess of $10 million to file an annual report of all loans made during that year. The loans are categorized according to the locations of the various properties so that cases of redlining can be more easily discovered.

> Racial redlining: refusing to make loans on property in specific areas for discriminatory reasons

CALIFORNIA LAWS

Unruh Civil Rights Act *also called Rumford Act*

This act states that all persons are entitled to the full use of any services provided by a business establishment. Of course, the act applies to real estate brokers, since a brokerage firm is considered to be a business establishment. Thus the act prohibits a broker from discriminating in the performance of his or her work. (The California License Law also prohibits real estate licensees from acting in a discriminatory manner.)

The Financial Discrimination Act

With this act, sometimes called the Holden Act, the legislature declared that the practice of denying mortgage loans or adversely varying the terms of a loan because of neighborhood characteristics unrelated to the creditworthiness of the applicant or the value of the real property was against public policy. In the past, in certain geographic areas, lenders had sometimes denied or decreased the amount of financial assistance available, regardless of the creditworthiness of the applicant or the condition of the property. The legislature found that this practice contributed to the decline of available housing, contributed to the abandonment of neighborhoods, undermined the value of the equity of current property owners, and perpetuated racially and economically segregated neighborhoods in those geographical areas.

In an effort to prevent continued discriminatory actions by lenders, the Holden Act was passed. Its purpose is to prevent discrimination in the financing, refinancing, construction, rehabilitation, or improvement of housing based on conditions, characteristics, or trends in the neighborhood surrounding the property. The legislature sought to encourage increased lending in neighborhoods where conventional residential mortgage financing had been unavailable, to increase the availability of housing to creditworthy persons, and to prevent the abandonment and decay of neighborhoods.

Under the act, financial institutions (any banks, savings and loan associations, or other institutions that regularly make, arrange or purchase residential real estate loans) are prohibited from the following activities:

Holden Act: prohibits discrimination in lending activities

- discriminating in the provision of financial assistance to purchase, construct, rehabilitate, improve, or refinance housing on the basis of the characteristics of the neighborhood surrounding the property, unless the lender can demonstrate that such consideration is required to avoid an unsafe and unsound business practice;
- discriminating in the provision of financial assistance to purchase, construct, rehabilitate, improve, or refinance housing on the basis of race, color, religion, sex, marital status, national origin, or ancestry; and
- considering the racial, ethnic, religious, or national origin composition of the neighborhood surrounding the property, or considering whether or not such composition is changing or is expected to change, when appraising housing or determining whether and under what conditions to provide financial assistance to purchase, construct, rehabilitate, improve or refinance housing.

Race
Color
Creed Religion
Sex
National Origin
Handicap
Children
Marital Status
Ancestry.

The act does not require a lender to provide financial assistance if it is clearly evident that occupancy of the housing would create an imminent threat to the health or safety of the occupant. It also does not preclude a financial institution from considering the fair market value of the property.

Fair Employment and Housing Act (Rumford Act)

Discrimination in the financing of housing is also prohibited by the Fair Employment and Housing Act. The act declares the practice of discrimination in housing accommodations on the basis of race, color, religion, sex, marital status, national origin, or ancestry to be against public policy. Under the Act, it is unlawful for any person, bank, mortgage company, or other financial institution to discriminate against any person or group of persons because of the race, color, religion, sex, marital status, national origin or ancestry of the person or of the prospective occupants or tenants.

Fair Employment and Housing Act: prohibits discrimination in housing accommodations

California License Law prohibits discrimination; licensees should be familiar with:
- Regulation 2780
- Regulation 2781
- Regulation 2782

California License Law and Commissioner Regulations

California License Law (*Business and Professions Code, §125.6*) prohibits discriminatory conduct by a licensee. Three Commissioner Regulations implement this provision by addressing the duties and requirements of real estate agents with respect to unlawful discrimination based on race, color, sex, religion, ancestry, physical handicap, marital status or national origin. Regulation 2780 lists a number of actions or types of conduct which are grounds for disciplinary action. Regulation 2781 concerns panic selling or blockbusting. Regulation 2782 describes the duty of a broker to supervise agents so they are familiar with the requirements of federal and state civil rights laws.

Regulation 2780 is an explanatory regulation intended to give licensees some guidance as to the types of discriminatory conduct that are prohibited and the kinds of actions that are permissible, even though they may involve discriminatory treatment. The regulation takes the form of several pages of examples of prohibited and permissible conduct. The examples are intended to be merely illustrative of some, not all prohibited actions. Some of the examples given of prohibited actions based on race, color, sex, religion, ancestry, physical handicap, marital status or national origin are listed below:

- refusing to negotiate for the sale, rental or financing of real property;
- refusing to show, rent, sell or finance real property;
- refusing or failing to provide information regarding real property;
- channeling or steering a person away from real property;
- discriminating in the terms or conditions of sale, rental, or financing of real property;
- discriminating in providing services or facilities in connection with the sale, rental, or financing of real property (this includes processing applications differently,

using codes or other means of identifying minority prospects if done with a discriminatory intent or effect, and referring prospects to other licensees or assigning agents on the basis of the prospect's race, color, sex, religion, ancestry, physical handicap, marital status or national origin);

- representing that real property is not available for inspection, sale, or rental when it is in fact available;
- processing an application more slowly or otherwise acting to delay or hinder a sale, rental, or financing of real property;
- making any effort to encourage other persons to discriminate in showing, renting, selling, or financing of real property;
- refusing or failing to cooperate with or assist another real estate licensee because of the prospect's race, color, sex, religion, ancestry, physical handicap, marital status or national origin;
- soliciting sales, rentals, or listings from one person but not from another person within the same area because of differences in race, color, sex, religion, ancestry, physical handicap, marital status or national origin;
- making any effort to discourage any person from renting, purchasing, or financing real property by representing actual or alleged community opposition based on race, color, sex, religion, ancestry, physical handicap, marital status or national origin;
- providing differing information to different persons concerning the desirability of a particular property or neighborhood because of differences in race, color, sex, religion, ancestry, physical handicap, marital status or national origin;
- refusing to accept a listing;
- entering an agreement or carrying out explicit or "understood" instructions not to show, lease, sell or finance the purchase of real property;
- making or causing to be made any advertising which indicates a preference, restriction or limitation or intent

to make a preference, restriction or limitation based on race, color, sex, religion, ancestry, physical handicap, marital status, or national origin;

- selectively using or designing any notice, statement, or advertisement in such a way as to increase discrimination by restricting or enhancing exposure of the notice or advertisement to persons of particular race, color, sex, religion, ancestry, physical handicap, marital status, or national origin;
- discriminating in the treatment of occupants or the provision of services in the course of providing property management services for housing;
- making any effort to instruct or encourage real estate licensees, either expressly or impliedly, either by words or acts, to violate any federal or state fair housing law;
- establishing or implementing any rules which have the effect of making it more difficult for a person to obtain property through a multiple listing service, because of the person's race, color, sex, religion, ancestry, physical handicap, marital status or national origin; and
- assisting or aiding any person in any way in the sale, rental, or financing of real property if there are reasonable grounds to believe that the person intends to discriminate.

It is important to remember that the regulation is only intended to provide some examples of prohibited practices, not to list all prohibited acts. Other discriminatory acts may also constitute unlawful conduct and be grounds for license suspension or revocation.

In certain situations, some discriminatory conduct is permitted:

- to fail to show, rent, sell or finance property because of a person's physical handicap if the property has characteristics or conditions which render it dangerous or inaccessible to the physically handicapped;

- charging a different price or rent or requiring different terms for properties having particular facilities for the physically handicapped;
- placing advertising directed to the physically handicapped for the purpose of calling their attention to the availability or unavailability of housing accommodations for the physically handicapped;
- treating people differently based on marital status in the sale, purchase, financing of, or negotiation for property if the acts are taken in recognition of California community property laws regarding the acquisition, financing, holding or transferring of real property; and
- designing affirmative marketing programs to attract persons of a particular race, color, sex, religion, ancestry, physical handicap, marital status or national origin who would not otherwise be attracted to the particular property or area.

Regulation 2781 is directed to panic selling (blockbusting). As does Regulation 2780, this regulation lists several types of prohibited behavior. Regulation 2781 states that it is prohibited for a licensee to solicit listings by making any written or oral statements, warnings or threats, or acting in any other manner or making any representations, express or implied, to induce owners to sell or lease property because of present or anticipated entry in the neighborhood of one or more persons of another race, color, sex, religion, ancestry, marital status, or national origin.

Regulation 2782 concerns the supervisory duties of real estate brokers in connection with civil rights laws. The regulation imposes a duty on brokers to take reasonable steps to familiarize themselves with state and federal discrimination laws and regulations, and also to take reasonable steps to familiarize their salespersons with the requirements of such laws.

FINANCE DISCLOSURES

The real estate agent should be aware of the various disclosure requirements in the field of finance. Some disclosures must be made by the agent, some must be made by the lender, and some must be made by the principal parties to the transaction. The source of the duty to disclose varies according to which disclosures are involved. Some disclosures are imposed by federal law, some are imposed by state statute, and others are imposed by the licensee's responsibilities as an agent.

FEDERAL DISCLOSURE REQUIREMENTS

Various federal regulations impose disclosure requirements on real estate financial transactions. The two most pertinent are *Regulation "Z"* of the *Truth-in-Lending Act* and the *Real Estate Settlement Procedures Act*. These acts require institutional lenders to make disclosures to borrowers at the time of loan application and prior to the close of escrow. The agent should understand these disclosures and what they mean so as to be able to explain them to the borrower.

In this segment of this chapter, we will discuss the Truth-in-Lending Act. Refer to Chapter 16, *Escrow and Closing* for a discussion of the Real Estate Settlement Procedures Act.

Truth-in-Lending Act

Truth-in-Lending Act promotes informed use of consumer credit. It is implemented by Regulation Z.

The purpose of the Truth-in-Lending Act, enacted in 1969, is to promote the informed use of consumer credit. The disclosures are required so the consumer will know exactly what he or she is paying for credit. It is hoped this knowledge enables the consumer to compare credit costs and shop around for the best credit terms. The act is implemented by **Regulation Z**. While Regulation Z does not set limits on interest rates or other finance charges, it does regulate the disclosure of these items. Disclosures are required in two general areas—when lenders offer credit/funds to borrowers, and when credit terms are advertised to potential customers.

Coverage of the Act

The provisions of the act apply to each lender who offers or extends credit to consumers (if the consumer is a natural person) in the ordinary course of business, primarily for personal, family or household purposes. The credit offered must be subject to a finance charge or payable in more than four installments. One exemption from coverage of the act is credit of over $25,000 which is NOT secured by real property.

Under the act, the definition of credit includes all real estate loans made to consumers, no matter what the amount, if the purpose is for other than business or commercial reasons.

Disclosures

Lenders who offer the above described types of credit are responsible for making certain disclosures to the consumer. These disclosures must be made before the credit transaction is consummated. Lenders engaging in a residential mortgage transaction must make a good faith estimate of the required disclosures no later than three business days after the lender receives the buyer's written application. Most lenders give the applicant the disclosure statement when he or she applies for a real estate loan. If any of the estimated figures change over the course of the transaction, new disclosures must be made before settlement.

For residential mortgage transactions, the most important disclosure required is the annual percentage rate (APR). The APR tells the borrower the cost of the loan in percentage terms. The APR is the relationship of the total finance charges to the total amount financed. Finance charges include interest, any points required by the lender, loan fees, etc. If the seller must pay points and a loan fee, the APR will be higher than the interest rate. For example, the loan may bear an interest rate of 11%, but the APR may be 11¼%. Many borrowers are confused by this apparent contradiction. They thought

TRUTH IN LENDING

Most important Regulation Z disclosure is the APR: the cost of the loan in percentage terms they were getting a loan at one interest rate, but it appears as if they are being charged another. It would be helpful at this point for the real estate agent to explain that the APR includes not just the interest rate, but the total costs of the loan, including all other finance charges spread out over the life of the loan.

The APR and other required disclosures are made to the borrower in the form of a disclosure statement. Copies of two standard disclosure statement forms are shown on the following pages. The first form is the type of form a bank or savings and loan association would use; the second form is the type a real estate broker would use if he or she were the one arranging the credit.

The disclosure statement includes the following items:

Disclosure statement:
1. creditor's identity
2. amount financed
3. notice of right to itemization
4. finance charge
5. APR
6. number, amount, and due dates of payments
7. payment provisions and penalties
8. description of security
9. assumability of loan

1. the identity of the creditor;
2. the amount financed;
3. notice of a right to receive an itemization of the amount financed;
4. the finance charge—the interest rate plus the costs of obtaining the funds, e.g., an origination or loan fee, a commitment fee, prepaid interest, an assumption fee, prepaid mortgage insurance, prepaid credit or life insurance, etc.;
5. the finance charge expressed as an annual percentage rate (the APR is labeled with a phrase such as, "The cost of your credit as a yearly rate.");
6. the number, amount and due dates of the payments;
7. new payment, late payment, and prepayment provisions;
8. a description and identification of the security (e.g., "There is a security interest in the property purchased."); and
9. whether or not the loan can be assumed by a subsequent purchaser.

FEDERAL REAL ESTATE LOAN DISCLOSURE STATEMENT
CALIFORNIA ASSOCIATION OF REALTORS® STANDARD FORM

Broker: Creditor:

_____   _____
(name)   (name)

_____   _____
(address)   (address)

YOUR LOAN IN THE AMOUNT OF $_____ IS TO BE SECURED BY A DEED OF TRUST IN FAVOR OF
CREDITOR ON REAL PROPERTY LOCATED AT _____
_____

ANNUAL PERCENTAGE RATE The cost of your credit as a yearly rate. _____%	FINANCE CHARGE The dollar amount the credit will cost you. $	AMOUNT FINANCED The amount of credit provided to you or on your behalf. $	TOTAL OF PAYMENTS The amount you will have paid after you have made all payments as scheduled. $

YOUR PAYMENT SCHEDULE WILL BE:

Number of Payments	Amount of Payments	When Payments Are Due

ITEMIZATION OF THE AMOUNT FINANCED OF $ _____

Amount given to you $_____
Amount paid on your account $_____
Amount paid to others on your behalf:
    1. Appraisal............................$_____
    2. Credit report........................$_____
    3. Notary..............................$_____
    4. Recording...........................$_____
    5. Title insurance ....$_____
    6. Document preparation ....$_____
    7. Property insurance...................$_____
    8. Other _____$_____
               (DESCRIBE)
    9. Other _____$_____
               (DESCRIBE)

Insurance:

Property insurance may be obtained by Borrower through any person of his choice. If it is to be purchased through Broker or Creditor, you will pay $_____.

Credit life and disability insurance are not required to obtain this loan.

Late Charge: If any payment is not made within _____ days after it is due, a late charge must be paid by Borrower as follows: _____.

Prepayment: If you pay off early, you ☐ MAY   ☐ WILL NOT have to pay a penalty.

Acceleration: If the property securing this loan is sold or otherwise transferred, the Creditor ☐ HAS   ☐ DOES NOT have the option to require immediate payment of the entire loan amount.

SEE YOUR CONTRACT DOCUMENTS FOR ANY ADDITIONAL INFORMATION ABOUT NONPAYMENT, DEFAULT, ANY REQUIRED REPAYMENT IN FULL BEFORE THE SCHEDULED DATE, AND PREPAYMENT REFUNDS AND PENALTIES.

I HAVE READ AND RECEIVED A COMPLETED COPY OF THIS STATEMENT.

Date_____, 19_____.

Borrower _____

Borrower _____

*IMPORTANT NOTE:

Asterisk denotes an estimate.

To order, contact—California Association of Realtors®
525 South Virgil Avenue, Los Angeles, California 900020.
Copyright©1970, 1978, by California Association of Realtors®
(Revised, 1983)

FORM LD-11

CREDIT SALE DISCLOSURE STATEMENT

 REAL ESTATE CREDIT SALE DISCLOSURE STATEMENT
(For use when Broker/Arranger or Creditor sells property on credit.)

CALIFORNIA ASSOCIATION OF REALTORS® STANDARD FORM

BROKER/ARRANGER OF CREDIT   CREDITOR:

_____   _____
(name)   (name)

_____   _____
(address)   (address)

SELLER (Same as either Broker or Creditor):

_____
(name)

I.   **SALE OF PROPERTY**

     A.   Cash Price $ _____

         Less: Cash Downpayment (Include proceeds of any separate loan) $ _____

     B.   Unpaid Balance of Cash Price $ _____

     C.   Charges not part of Finance Charge:

            1.   Appraisal .... $ _____

            2.   Credit Report .... $ _____

            3.   Notary .... $ _____

            4.   Recording .... $ _____

            5.   Title Insurance .... $ _____

            6.   Document preparation .... $ _____

            7.   Property insurance .... $ _____

            8.   Termite inspection .... $ _____

            9.   Sale escrow fee .... $ _____

            10.   Other _____ $ _____
                                (describe)

                        Total Charges $ _____

     D.   Unpaid Balance (B + C) $ _____

         Less: Prepaid Finance Charge (Item II. A. below) $ _____

     E.   AMOUNT FINANCED $ _____

II.   **FINANCE CHARGE:**

     A.   Prepaid FINANCE CHARGE

                        Loan Broker's commission .... $ _____

                        Loan escrow fee .... $ _____

                        Other _____ $ _____

                       _____ $ _____
                                (describe)

                                   (Total of A) $ _____

     B.   Interest for period of loan .... $ _____

                               FINANCE CHARGE   (A + B) $ _____

Finance Charge accrues from _____ , 19 _____ .

III. ANNUAL PERCENTAGE RATE: _____ %

IV. INSURANCE:

      Property insurance may be obtained by Buyer through any person of his choice. If it is to be purchased through the Broker or Creditor, the cost appears at Item I. C. 7. above.

      Credit life and disability insurance are not required to obtain this loan.

V. SECURITY:

      Payment of the Unpaid Balance plus interest (Finance Charge Item II. B.) is to be secured by a note and Deed of Trust in favor of the Creditor on the property purchased in this transaction, which is located at _____ ,
_____

      and is □ is not □ expected to be the location of the Buyer's principal residence. (NOTE: If it is, a Rescission Statement must be provided unless this transaction involves a first lien for the purchase or initial construction of a dwelling.)

      The Deed of Trust may secure additional advances and may cover after-acquired property. This credit may also be secured by an assignment of proceeds from any required insurance protecting the property.

VI. PAYMENT TERMS:

      Payable in _____ payments of principal and interest as follows: _____ monthly installments of $ _____ each, beginning _____ , 19 _____ , and a final/balloon payment of $ _____ due on _____ , 19 _____ .

                  TOTAL OF PAYMENTS   (Item I. D. + Item II. B.) $ _____

      There are no arrangements for refinancing balloon payments.

      If any payment is not made within _____ days after it is due, a late charge must be paid by Buyer as follows: _____ ,
_____

      In addition, Creditor has the option to accelerate the indebtedness and to declare all payments immediately due and payable.

      In the event of acceleration or other prepayment in full, unaccrued interest is cancelled and a default or prepayment charge will be computed as follows: _____

VII. DEFERRED PAYMENT PRICE (Items I. A. + I. C. + II.: cash price plus all charges and the Finance Charge) $ _____

I HAVE READ AND RECEIVED A COMPLETED COPY OF THIS STATEMENT.

Date: _____ , 19 _____ .

* IMPORTANT NOTE:
      Asterisk denotes an estimate.

BUYER: _____

BUYER: _____

Right to Rescind

Under the act, the consumer has the right to rescind any credit transaction in which a security interest (e.g., mortgage) is given in his or her principal residence. The right to rescind extends until midnight of the third business day after the close of the transaction. A major exception to this right is a residential mortgage transaction that is used to finance the purchase or construction of the residence. This exception covers the typical mortgage transaction. However, the consumer would still have the right to rescind a transaction when the security interest is given for a home improvement loan, a loan for educational purposes, etc.

The lender must always inform the consumer of the right to rescind. The notice of the right to rescind must be in a separate document from the sale or credit document and must describe the acquisition of the security interest, how the right to rescind is to be exercised, the effects of rescission, and the date the period of rescission expires.

Right to rescind
- until third business day
- does not apply to residential purchase money loans

doesn't apply to purchase of your personal home

Advertisement

The Truth-in-Lending Act also contains provisions that apply to advertising. Prior to the passage of the act, an advertiser might have disclosed only the most attractive credit terms, thus distorting the true costs of the financing. For example, the advertisement could have included the low monthly payments (e.g., $75.00 a month) without indicating the large downpayment necessary to qualify for that payment level. Advertisers did not have to disclose the APR or whether the transaction was a credit sale or lease. The act now requires the advertiser to tell "the whole story."

If an advertisement contains any one of the terms specified in the act, that advertisement must also include the required disclosures. The specified terms "trigger" the disclosures. In other words, if the advertiser uses a "trigger" in the advertisement, the disclosures must be made; if the advertisement does not use a "trigger," no disclosures must be made.

Anyone placing a consumer credit or lease advertisement must comply with the provisions of the act. This includes real estate agents who advertise private homes for sale.

The "triggering" terms for real estate advertisement include:

Advertising terms that trigger disclosure:
1. amount of downpayment
2. amount of any payment
3. number of payments
4. repayment period
5. amount of finance charge

1. The amount of the downpayment (e.g., "20% down").
2. The amount of any payment (e.g., "Pay less than $700 per month").
3. The number of payments (e.g., only "360 monthly payments").
4. The period of repayment (e.g., "30-year financing available").
5. The amount of any finance charge (e.g., "1% finance charge").

Some examples of terms which do NOT trigger the required disclosures are:

"No downpayment"
"12% Annual Percentage Rate loan available here"
"Easy monthly payments"
"Graduated payment mortgages available"
"VA and FHA financing available"
"Terms to fit your budget"
"100% VA financing available"

Terms that must be disclosed:
1. amount of downpayment
2. terms of repayment
3. the APR

If any of the listed triggering terms are used in the advertisement, ALL of the following disclosures must be made:

1. the amount or percentage of the downpayment;
2. the terms of repayment; and
3. the annual percentage rate, using that term spelled out in full. If the APR may increase (e.g., for adjustable-rate mortgages), that fact must also be disclosed.

If an advertisement discloses only the APR, the additional disclosures are not required. For example, an advertisement may simply state, "Assume an 11% annual percentage rate mortgage."

If an adjustable-rate mortgage is being advertised, it should be described as "11% annual percentage rate, subject to increase after settlement." Fixed-rate buydowns are not adjustable-rate mortgages and must not be so described. The buydown involves different interest rates in effect during the life of the loan, but all the rates are known at the time of settlement. When more than one simple interest rate is to be applied to the transaction, these rates may be advertised if all the interest rates and the terms during which the rates apply are disclosed and the annual percentage rate is stated.

Example: Assume a buydown plan where the interest rate the first year is 9%, 10% the second year, 11% the third year, and 12% for the remainder of the term. The following would be an acceptable method of disclosure:

9%	1st year
10%	2nd year
11%	3rd year
12%	remainder of loan
11¾%	annual percentage rate

Even though different interest rates may apply during the loan term, the loan only has one annual percentage rate.

On the following pages are illustrations of typical real estate advertisements. Any violations of the Truth-in-Lending Act appearing in the illustrations are pointed out, along with advice on how they should be changed to meet the Act's requirements.*

---

* Illustrations obtained from "How to Advertise Consumer Credit," published by the Federal Trade Commission. Copies of this publication can be obtained from regional Federal Trade Commission offices.

WRONG

MODELS NOW OPEN . . .

Largest Traditional Townhomes located in

... **Priced from $58,000**

V.A. Financing Available . . .

Up to 95% Conventional Financing Available . . .

Designed for contemporary living . . .

Features Include:

- **Walk-out basement**
- **Brick & frame construction**
- **Energy Package—G.E. Heat Pump & Air Conditioner**
- **Storm Windows**

- **Customising selections for your kitchen.**
- **Convenient to modern schools and Shopping areas**
- **5 floor plans**

Triggering term

Required disclosures needed

WRONG

Triggering terms

Required disclosures needed

WOULD YOU INVEST $299.
FOR THE BEST DEAL
OF YOUR LIFETIME?
VA, FHA FINANCING $500   CASH DOWN TO VETERANS

Open Noon To Dark   Closed Thursday

3 Bedrooms • 2½ Baths • Great Kitchens
$46,550 To $48,250

Chances are you haven't seen these spectacular townhomes in
Exciting
contemporary floor plans with everything you will need included
in our sales price. Walk to your own swimming pool and recrea-
tion area. Public golf course and tennis courts almost completed
nearby.

RIGHT

Triggering term →

Required disclosures →

$7,900. ON THE HOUSE.

Right now, we're selling $474 a month townhomes starting at only $356 a month. It's all part of a plan to save you $7,900 during the first ten years of your mortgage. It's called the FHA-245 Graduated Mortgage Payments Program. And _____ is one of the few places that has it. Make lower payments now—up to $118 less per month in the first year—and higher payments after the tenth year when you can better afford them. It's as easy as this:

FHA-245, Plan V

Purchase price: $54,490. Minus $3,690.00 down payment. Mortgage amount: $50,800 at 9½% interest plus ½% Mortgage Insurance Premium with the following monthly payments:

Year	Monthly Payment
1	$356.34
2	$387.03
3	$378.04
4	$389.88
5	$401.06
6	$413.09
7	$425.45
8	$438.25
9	$451.40
10	$464.94
Years 11-30	$478.89

For an Annual Percentage Rate of 10.06%. Taxes not included.

If you'd rather pay a little more at first and a little less later, you can, because altogether, we offer 5 flexible GMP plans. All structured to allow you to choose a plan that fits your needs. So that you can buy a condominium townhome at _____ now. While prices are still in the mid 50's.

Townhomes from the mid 50's. All with full basements. V.A. and conventional financing also available.

OUR VALUE IS DOUBLED IN STAFFORD COUNTY

The Bunker Hill – 3 bedroom split level with expandable lower level.

Two exceptional Virginia communities with large wooded lots.

Hickory Ridge Priced from $46,200. Large wooded lots close to major shopping, schools and commuter transportation. And you'll love the low taxes. The Bunker Hill 3 bedroom pictured above—from $49,800. Directions:

Patriot's Landing Priced from $50,600. Our new community of 3, 4 and 5 bedroom quality homes, tucked away in the woods, just off I-95. The Bunker Hill 3 bedroom pictured above.—from $54,400. Directions:

Typical financing: The Bunker Hill – (Hickory Ridge) – cash price $49,800, $2,500 down payment (5%) at 9-7/8% interest (10½ annual percentage rate). Mortgage $47,300 to be paid in 360 equal and consecutive monthly installments of $411 plus taxes and insurance.

We pay all closing costs except prepaid items and loan origination fees.

VA Financing and 5% down* Conventional Financing 9-7/8% Interest (10-1/2% Annual Percentage Rate)

...talk to in Stafford

Proper disclosure

Triggering term

Proper disclosure of the rate of finance charge

STATE DISCLOSURE REQUIREMENTS

Federal regulations are not the only sources of disclosure requirements. In addition, California statutes provide for certain disclosures by those involved in real estate transactions.

Seller Financing Disclosures

Seller financing disclosures required when:
1. for purchase of dwelling
2. seller financing present
3. credit is subject to finance charge or payable in more than four installments
4. arranger of credit present

State law requires certain disclosures to be made when all or a portion of residential financing is provided by the seller. These disclosures are required when:

1. the transaction is for the purchase of a dwelling of one to four units;
2. credit is extended by the seller;
3. the credit involved is subject to a finance charge or is payable in more than four installments (not including the downpayment); and
4. there is an arranger of credit.

An arranger of credit is either:

1. a person who is NOT a party to the transaction who is involved in negotiating the credit terms, participates in the completion of the credit documents, and directly or indirectly receives compensation for arranging the credit or the transfer of the real property facilitated by the extension of credit (this does not include an attorney or escrow officer involved in the transaction); or
2. a real estate licensee or an attorney who is a party to the transaction if neither party is represented by a real estate licensee.

If transactions fall under Truth-in-Lending Act, disclosures not required

Disclosures are not required for those transactions which fall under the provisions of the Truth-in-Lending Act or the Real Estate Settlement Procedures Act. If disclosures are required, they must be made as soon as practicable, but in any case before the execution of any promissory note or security document (i.e., mortgage or deed of trust). The disclosure statement is to be signed by the arranger of credit and delivered to both the buyer and seller. The arranger of credit is to keep a copy of the statement for three years.

A standard disclosure form is shown on the following page. Some of the required disclosures are as follows:

1) description of the terms of the note and security documents and the property that is to be the security for the transaction;

2) the terms and conditions of any senior liens on the property (e.g., a first mortgage), including the original balance, the current balance, the periodic payment, any balloon payment, the interest rate, the maturity date, and whether or not there is any current default in the payments;

3) a warning that, if refinancing is required because the note is not fully amortized, such refinancing might be difficult or impossible in the conventional mortgage marketplace;

4) if negative amortization is a possibility, a clear statement of this fact and an explanation of its potential effect;

5) if the financing is a wrap-around mortgage, information regarding the person responsible for making payments to the prior lienholders, who the person to be paid is, and information relating to balloon payments or prepayment penalties on any prior encumbrances;

6) the identity, occupation, employment, income and credit data of the buyer;

7) a statement that a request for a notice of default has been recorded; and

8) if the buyer is to receive cash from the proceeds of the transaction, a statement of that fact, plus the amount, source of the funds, and purpose of the disbursement.

Disclosures required:
1. terms of note and description of security
2. terms of any senior liens
3. refinancing warning
4. negative amortization warning
5. wrap-around warning
6. buyer data
7. notice of default
8. statement of buyer proceeds
9. balloon payment disclosures

FINANCING CALIFORNIA REAL ESTATE

SELLER FINANCING DISCLOSURE STATEMENT
(California Civil Code 2956-2967)
CALIFORNIA ASSOCIATION OF REALTORS® (CAR) STANDARD FORM

This three page disclosure statement from the Purchaser (Buyer) and Vendor (Seller) is prepared by an arranger of credit [defined in Civil Code 2957(a)] and provided to both the Purchaser (Buyer) and Vendor (Seller) in a residential real estate transaction involving four or fewer units whenever the seller has agreed to extend credit to the Buyer as part of the purchase price.

Buyer: _____

Seller: _____

Arranger of Credit: __A C E N T_____

Real Property: __ADDRESS_____

A. Credit Documents: This extension of credit by the Seller is evidenced by ☒ note and deed of trust, ☐ all-inclusive note and deed of trust, ☐ installment land sale contract, ☐ lease/option (when parties intend transfer of equitable title), ☐ other (specify) _____

B. Credit Terms:
1. ☐ See attached copy of credit documents referred to in Section A above for description of credit terms; or
2. ☒ The terms of the credit documents referred to in Section A above are: Principal amount $_____ 100K _____ interest at __10__ % per annum payable at $_1200_ per_mo__ (month/year/etc.) with the entire unpaid principal and accrued interest of approximately $_____ due_____ 19___ (maturity date).

Late Charge: If any payment is not made within _____ days after it is due, a late charge of $_____ or _____% of the installment due may be charged to the Buyer.

Prepayment: If all or part of this loan is paid early, the Buyer ☐ will, ☒ will not, have to pay a prepayment penalty as follows:_____
_____

Due on Sale: If any interest in the property securing this obligation is sold or otherwise transferred, the Seller ☐ has, ☐ does not have, the option to require immediate payment of the entire unpaid balance and accrued interest.

Other Terms: _____
_____
_____

C. Available information on loans/encumbrances* that will be senior to the seller's extension of credit:

	1st	2nd	3rd
1. Original Balance	$_____	$_____	$_____
2. Current Balance	$_____	$_____	$_____
3. Periodic Payment (e.g. $100/month)	$_____ / _____	$_____ / _____	$_____ / _____
4. Amt. of Balloon Payment	$_____	$_____	$_____
5. Date of Balloon Payment	_____	_____	_____
6. Maturity date	_____	_____	_____
7. Due On Sale ('Yes' or 'No')	_____	_____	_____
8. Interest Rate (per annum)	_____%	_____%	_____%
9. Fixed or Variable Rate: If Variable Rate:	☐ a copy of note attached ☐ variable provisions are explained on attached separate sheet	☐ a copy of note attached ☐ variable provisions are explained on attached separate sheet	☐ a copy of note attached ☐ variable provisions are explained on attached separate sheet
10. Is Payment Current?	_____	_____	_____

☐ SEPARATE SHEET WITH INFORMATION REGARDING OTHER SENIOR LOANS/ENCUMBRANCES IS ATTACHED.

IMPORTANT NOTE: Asterisk (*) denotes an estimate.

D. Caution: If any of the obligations secured by the property calls for a balloon payment, then Seller and Buyer are aware that refinancing of the balloon payment at maturity may be difficult or impossible depending on the conditions in the mortgage marketplace at that time. There are no assurances that new financing or a loan extension will be available when the balloon payment is due.

Buyer and Seller acknowledge receipt of copy of this page, which constitutes Page 1 of 3 Pages.
Buyer's Initials (_____) (_____)   Seller's Initials (_____) (_____)

_____OFFICE USE ONLY_____

Reviewed by Broker or Designee _____
Date _____

Copyright© 1989, CALIFORNIA ASSOCIATION OF REALTORS®
525 South Virgil Avenue, Los Angeles, California 90020

SELLER FINANCING DISCLOSURE STATEMENT (SFD-14 PAGE 1 of 3)
Reprinted with permission, California Association of Realtors® Endorsement not implied

E. Deferred Interest:

"Deferred interest" results when the Buyer's periodic payments are less than the amount of interest earned on the obligation, or when the obligation does not require periodic payments. This accrued interest will have to be paid by the Buyer at a later time and may result in the Buyer owing more on the obligation than at origination.

☐ The credit being extended to the Buyer by the Seller does not provide for "deferred interest," or

☐ The credit being extended to the Buyer by the Seller does provide for "deferred interest."

    The credit documents provide the following regarding deferred interest:

    ☐ All deferred interest shall be due and payable along with the principal at maturity (simple interest); or

    ☐ The deferred interest shall be added to the principal _____ (e.g., annually, monthly, etc.) and thereafter shall bear interest at the rate specified in the credit documents (compound interest); or

    ☐ Other (specify) _____

F. All-Inclusive Deed of Trust or Installment Land Sale Contract:

☐ This transaction does not involve the use of an all-inclusive (or wraparound) deed of trust or an installment land sale contract; or

☐ This transaction does involve the use of either an all-inclusive (or wraparound) deed of trust or an installment land sale contract which provides as follows:

    1) In the event of an acceleration of any senior encumbrance, the responsibility for payment or for legal defense is:

    ☐ Not specified in the credit or security documents; or

    ☐ Specified in the credit or security documents as follows:

    2) In the event of the prepayment of a senior encumbrance, the responsibilities and rights of Seller and Buyer regarding refinancing, prepayment penalties, and any prepayment discounts are:

    ☐ Not specified in the credit or security documents; or

    ☐ Specified in the credit or security documents as follows:

    3) The financing provided that the Buyer will make periodic payments to _____

    [e.g., a collection agent (such as a bank or savings and loan); Seller; etc.] and that_____

    will be responsible for disbursing payments to the payee(s) on the senior encumbrance(s) and to the Seller.

CAUTION: The parties are advised to consider designating a neutral third party as the collection agent for receiving Buyer's payments and disbursing them to the payee(s) on the senior encumbrance(s) and to the seller.

G. Buyer's Creditworthiness: Section 580(b) of the California Code of Civil Procedure generally limits a Seller's rights in the event of a default by the Buyer in the financing extended by the Seller, to a foreclosure of the property.

☐ No disclosure concerning the Buyer's creditworthiness has been made to the Seller; or

☐ The following representations concerning the Buyer's creditworthiness have been made by the buyer(s) to the Seller:

1. Occupation: _____	1. Occupation: _____
2. Employer: _____	2. Employer: _____
3. Length of Employment: _____	3. Length of Employment: _____
4. Monthly Gross Income: _____	4. Monthly Gross Income: _____
5. Buyer ☐ has, ☐ has not, provided Seller a current credit report issued by: _____	5. Buyer ☐ has, ☐ has not, provided Seller a current credit report issued by: _____
6. Buyer ☐ has, ☐ has not, provided Seller a completed loan application.	6. Buyer ☐ has, ☐ has not, provided Seller a completed loan application.
7. Other (specify): _____	7. Other (specify): _____

H. Insurance:

☐ The parties' escrow holder or insurance carrier has been or will be directed to add a loss payee clause to the property insurance protecting the Seller; or

☐ No provision has been made for adding a loss payee clause to the property insurance protecting the Seller. Seller is advised to secure such clauses or acquire a separate insurance policy.

I. Request for Notice:

☐ A Request for Notice of Default under Section 2924(b) of the California Civil Code has been or will be recorded; or

☐ No provision for recording a Request for Notice of Default has been made. Seller is advised to consider recording a Request for Notice of Default.

    Buyer and Seller acknowledge receipt of copy of this page, which constitutes Page 2 of 3 Pages.

    Buyer's Initials (_____) (_____)   Seller's Initials (_____) (_____)

_____OFFICE USE ONLY_____

Reviewed by Broker or Designee _____

Date _____

SELLER FINANCING DISCLOSURE STATEMENT (SFD-14 PAGE 2 of 3)

Reprinted with permission, California Association of Realtors® Endorsement not implied

EQUAL HOUSING
OPPORTUNITY

J. Title Insurance:
   ☐ Title insurance coverage will be provided to both Seller and Buyer insuring their respective interests in the property; or
   ☐ No provision for title insurance coverage of both Seller and Buyer has been made. Seller and Buyer are advised to consider securing such title insurance coverage.

K. Tax Service:
   ☐ A tax service has been arranged to report to Seller whether property taxes have been paid on the property. _____ (e.g., Seller, Buyer, etc.) will be responsible for the continued retention and payment of such tax service; or
   ☐ No provision has been made for a tax service. Seller should consider retaining a tax service or otherwise determine that the property taxes are paid.

L. Recording:
   ☐ The security documents (e.g., deed of trust, installment land contract, etc.) will be recorded with the county recorder where the property is located; or
   ☐ The security documents will not be recorded with the county recorder. Seller and Buyer are advised that their respective interests in the property may be jeopardized by intervening liens, judgments or subsequent transfers which are recorded.

M. Proceeds to Buyer:
   ☐ Buyer will NOT receive any cash proceeds at the close of the sale transaction; or
   ☐ Buyer will receive approximately $_____ from _____ (indicate source from the sale transaction proceeds of such funds). Buyer represents that the purpose of such disbursement is as follows: _____

N. Note of Delinquency:
   ☐ A request for Notice of Delinquency under Section 2924(e) of the California Civil Code has been or will be made to the Senior lienholder(s); or
   ☐ No provision for making a Request for Notice of Delinquency has been made. Seller should consider making a Request for Notice of Delinquency.

The above information has been provided to: (a) the Buyer, by the arranger of credit and the Seller (with respect to information within the knowledge of the Seller); (b) the seller, by the arranger of credit and the Buyer (with respect to information within the knowledge of the Buyer).

Arranger of Credit_____

Date_____, 19_____   By_____

Buyer and Seller acknowledge that the information each has provided to the arranger of credit for inclusion in this disclosure form is accurate to the best of their knowledge.

Buyer and Seller hereby acknowledge receipt of a completed copy of this dislcosure form.

Date_____, 19_____   Date_____, 19_____

Buyer _____   Seller _____

Buyer _____   Seller _____

A REAL ESTATE BROKER IS THE PERSON QUALIFIED TO ADVISE ON REAL ESTATE. IF YOU DESIRE LEGAL ADVICE, CONSULT YOUR ATTORNEY.

This form is available for use by the entire real estate industry. The use of this form is not intended to identify the user as a REALTOR® REALTOR® is a registered collective membership mark which may be used only by real estate licensees who are members of the NATIONAL ASSOCIATION OF REALTORS® and who subscribe to its Code of Ethics.

_____OFFICE USE ONLY_____

Reviewed by Broker or Designee _____

Date _____

Page 3 of _____Pages.

SELLER FINANCING DISCLOSURE STATEMENT (SFD-14 PAGE 3 of 3)
Reprinted with permission, California Association of Realtors® Endorsement not implied

EQUAL HOUSING
OPPORTUNITY

If the financing transaction includes a balloon payment, the following requirements must be met:

1) the holder of the note must give the borrower written notice, not less than 60 nor more than 150 days before the balloon payment is due, and the notice must include:
   a) the name and address of the person to whom the balloon payment is to be made;
   b) the due date of the payment;
   c) the amount of the payment; and
   d) a description of the borrower's right, if any, to refinance the debt.
2) if proper notice is not given, the due date of the balloon payment is extended to 60 days from the date the notice is given. During the interim, the borrower is obligated to make payments according to the regular payment schedule.

Mortgage Loan Transactions

Frequently real estate agents not only help the buyer apply for financing but actually negotiate the real estate loan as well. The agent may represent a mortgage lending institution or private investor who is interested in making real estate loans. The California Real Estate Law has long required that anyone acting for compensation in arranging or negotiating a real estate loan must be a real estate licensee. However, controlling loan brokerage activities solely with the license law proved inadequate, and in 1955 the Real Property Loan Brokerage Law was passed.

The passage of this law was an attempt to curb a variety of abuses, including the charging of exorbitant commissions, costs and expenses; the negotiating of short-term loans with large balloon payments; and misrepresentation or concealment of material facts by licensees negotiating the loans. This legislation is variously known as the Real Property Loan Law, the Mortgage Loan Brokers Law, and the Necessitous Borrowers Act.

When the Real Property Loan Law Applies

The provisions of the law apply when a licensee is engaged in arranging a first trust deed loan of less than $20,000 or a second trust deed loan of less than $10,000. The law does not apply to employees of institutional lenders (e.g., a bank or savings and loan association), sellers lending part or all of the purchase price to purchaser, or to any first trust deed loan of $20,000 or more, or any second trust deed loan of $10,000 or more.

The various provisions of the Mortgage Loan Broker Law:

1) prohibit the lender or broker from conditioning the making of a loan on the purchase of credit life or credit disability insurance by the borrower,
2) prohibit the use of a balloon payment in a promissory note with a term of six years or less where the security for the loan is the dwelling unit of the borrower,
3) impose monetary limits on late payment and prepayment charges to the borrower,
4) prohibit a real estate licensee from charging the borrower a fee for the servicing of a loan, and
5) authorize certain civil penalties against a licensee for violating the act's provisions.

Mortgage Loan Disclosure Statement

The Mortgage Loan Disclosure Statement, also often referred to as the Mortgage Loan Broker's Statement, is at the heart of the Real Property Loan Law. Its purpose is to provide a prospective borrower with information on all the important aspects of the loan.

A disclosure statement must be completed when a licensee negotiates a mortgage loan in any amount that is to be secured by a lien on real property. The licensee must present the disclosure statement to the prospective borrower and obtain the borrower's signature on the statement prior to the time the borrower becomes obligated to complete the loan. In addition, if the loan is within the loan amount limitations stated above (first trust deeds of less than $20,000 and

Real Property Loan Law:
- applies when arranging first loan of less than $20,000 or second loan of less than $10,000
- imposes restrictions on conditions and fees for loan

110

MORTGAGE LOAN DISCLOSURE STATEMENT (BORROWER)

CALIFORNIA ASSOCIATION OF REALTORS® (CAR) STANDARD FORM

(As required by the Business and Professions Code Section 10240 and Title 10, California Administrative Code, Section 2840)

_____
(Name of Broker/Arranger of Credit)

_____
(Business Address of Broker)

I. SUMMARY OF LOAN TERMS
   A. PRINCIPAL AMOUNT OF LOAN . . . .$_____
   B. ESTIMATED DEDUCTIONS FROM PRINCIPAL AMOUNT
      1. Cost and Expenses (See Paragraph III-A) . . . .$_____
      *2. Commission/Loan Origination Fee (See Paragraph III-B) . . . .$_____
      3. Liens and Other Amounts to be Paid on Authorization of Borrower
        (See Paragraph III-C) . . . .$_____
   C. ESTIMATED CASH PAYABLE TO BORROWER (A less B). . . . .$_____

II. GENERAL INFORMATION ABOUT LOAN
   A. If this loan is made, you will be required to pay the principal and interest at _____ % per year, payable as
   follows:_____ _____ payments of $_____
              (number of payments)   (monthly/quarterly/annually)
   and a FINAL/BALLOON payment of $_____ to pay off the loan in full

        " NOTICE TO BORROWER: If you do not have the funds to pay the balloon payment when it comes due, you may have to obtain a new loan against your property to make the balloon payment. In that case, you may again have to pay commissions, fees, and expenses for the arranging of the new loan.

        In addition, if you are unable to make the monthly payments or the balloon payment, you may lose the property and all of your equity through foreclosure. Keep this in mind in deciding upon the amount and terms of this loan."

   B. This loan will be evidenced by a promissory note and secured by a deed of trust in favor of lender/creditor on property located at (street address or legal description):

   _____
   _____

   C. 1. Liens presently against this property (do not include loan being applied for):

Nature of Lien	Priority	Lienholder's Name	Amount Owing
_____	_____	_____	_____
_____	_____	_____	_____

      2. Liens that will remain against this property after the loan being applied for is made or arranged (include loan being applied for):

Nature of Lien	Priority	Lienholder's Name	Amount Owing
_____	_____	_____	_____
_____	_____	_____	_____

        NOTICE TO BORROWER: Be sure that the amount of all liens is stated as accurately as possible. If you contract with the broker for this loan, but it cannot be made or arranged because you did not state these lien amounts correctly, you may be liable to pay commissions, fees, and expenses even though you did not obtain the loan.

   D. If you wish to pay more than the scheduled payment at any time before it is due, you may have to pay a PREPAYMENT PENALTY computed as follows:

   _____
   _____

   E. The purchase of credit life or credit disability insurance is not required of the borrower as a condition of making this loan.

   F. The real property which will secure the requested loan is an "owner-occupied dwelling."   YES _____   NO _____
                                                                             (Borrower initial opposite YES or NO)

        "For purposes of restrictions on scheduled balloon payments and unequal payments, an "owner-occupied dwelling" means a single dwelling unit in a condominium or cooperative or a residential building of less than three separate dwelling units, one of which will be owned and occupied by a signatory to the mortgage or deed of trust for this loan within 90 days of the signing of the mortgage or deed of trust. For certain other purposes relating to this loan, "dwelling" means a single dwelling unit in a condominium or cooperative, or any parcel containing only residential buildings if the total number of units on the parcel is four or less, which is owned by a signatory to the mortgage or deed of trust."

        Borrower hereby acknowledges the receipt of a copy of this page, which constitutes page 1 of 2 pages.
              Borrower's Initials (_____) (_____)

THIS FORM HAS BEEN APPROVED BY THE CALIFORNIA DEPARTMENT OF
REAL ESTATE (D.R.E.), DECEMBER, 1989.

Copyright© 1989, CALIFORNIA ASSOCIATION OF REALTORS®
525 South Virgil Avenue, Los Angeles, California 90020
(Revised 12/7/89)

____OFFICE USE ONLY____

Reviewed by Broker or Designee _____
Date _____

MORTGAGE LOAN DISCLOSURE STATEMENT (BORROWER) (MS-14 PAGE 1 of 2)
Reprinted with permission, California Association of Realtors® Endorsement not implied

III. DEDUCTIONS FROM LOAN PROCEEDS
  A. ESTIMATED MAXIMUM COSTS AND EXPENSES to be paid by borrower out of the principal amount of the loan are:

	PAYABLE TO	
	Broker	Others
1. Appraisal		
2. Credit investigation		
3. Delivery		
4. Drawing/Document preparation		
5. Escrow:		
6. Notary:		
7. Notice of delinquency:		
8. Processing:		
9. Recording:		
10. Tax service.		
11. Title insurance:		
12. Other costs and expenses		
TOTAL COSTS AND EXPENSES.................................	$	

*B. LOAN BROKERAGE COMMISSION/LOAN ORIGINATION FEE .... $_____

  C. LIENS AND OTHER AMOUNTS to be paid out of the principal amount of the loan on authorization of the borrower are estimated to be as follows:

	PAYABLE TO	
	Broker	Others
1. Fire or other hazard insurance premiums		
2. Credit life or disability insurance premium (see Paragraph II-B)		
3. Beneficiary statement fees		
4. Reconveyance and similar fees		
5. Discharge of existing liens against property:		
6. Other:		
TOTAL TO BE PAID ON AUTHORIZATION OF BORROWER	$	

If the loan which this disclosure statement applies is a loan secured by a first deed of trust in a principal amount of less than $20,000 or a loan secured by a junior lien in a principal amount of less than $10,000, the undersigned licensee certifies that the loan will be made in compliance with Article 7 of Chapter 3 of the Real Estate Law.

*This loan ☐ may/ ☐ will/ ☐ will NOT (check one) be made wholly or in part from broker-controlled funds as defined in Section 10241(j) of the Business and Professions Code.

NOTICE: This disclosure statement may be used if the broker is acting as an agent in arranging the loan by a third person or if the loan will be made with funds owned or controlled by the broker. If the broker indicates in the above statement that the loan "may" be made out of broker-controlled funds, the broker must notify the borrower prior to the close of escrow if the funds to be received by the borrower are in fact broker-controlled funds.

_____		_____
(Name of Broker)		(Name of Designated Representative)
_____		_____
(License Number)		(License Number)
_____	OR	_____
(Signature of Broker)		(Signature)

NOTICE TO BORROWER

DO NOT SIGN THIS STATEMENT UNTIL YOU HAVE READ AND UNDERSTOOD ALL OF THE INFORMATION IN IT. ALL PARTS OF THE FORM MUST BE COMPLETED BEFORE YOU SIGN.

Borrower hereby acknowledges the receipt of a copy of this page which constitutes page 2 of 2 pages.

DATE: _____   _____
                                                   (Borrower)

                                             _____
                                                   (Borrower)

D.R.E. Ref.: MLDS-423 12-7-89

MORTGAGE LOAN DISCLOSURE STATEMENT (BORROWER) (MS-14 PAGE 2 OF 2)
Reprinted with permission, California Association of Realtors® Endorsement not implied

junior trust deeds of less than $10,000), the licensee must certify in the disclosure statement that the loan is in compliance with the provisions of Law.

If a licensee is negotiating a loan to be made by specified institutional lenders and the licensee will receive a commission from the borrower of 2% or less, a Mortgage Loan Disclosure Statement is not required.

The following information must be included in the disclosure statement:

- The estimated maximum costs of making the loan which are to be paid by the borrower, including the:
  - appraisal fees
  - escrow fees
  - title charges
  - notary fees
  - recording fees
  - credit investigation fees.

> The costs of making the loan cannot exceed 5% of the loan amount, or $195, whichever is greater. In no event may the costs exceed either $350 or the actual costs. Regulations preclude the broker from charging costs or fees which exceed those customarily charged for the same or comparable services in the community where the services are rendered.

- The amount of the commission to be received by the licensee. The statutory maximum commission amounts are:

  First Trust Deeds
  - 5% of the principal of a loan of less than three years
  - 10% of the principal of a loan of three years or more

Disclosure statement must include:
1. estimated costs
2. amount of commission
3. amount of liens
4. amounts to be paid from loan
5. balance of loan funds to borrower
6. principal amount of loan
7. interest rate
8. terms of loan repayment
9. name of broker
10. statement re broker-controlled funds
11. prepayment terms
12. insurance statement

113

Second or Other Junior Trust Deeds
- 5% of the principal of a loan of less than two years
- 10% of the principal of a loan of between two and three years
- 15% of the principal of a loan of three years or more

- Any liens against the real property and their approximate amount.
- The estimated amounts to be paid from the loan proceeds on the order of the borrower, such as:
  - fire insurance premiums
  - amounts due on prior liens
  - amounts due other creditors
  - assumption fees
- The estimated balance of the loan funds to be paid to the borrower (after deducting the previous items).
- The principal amount of the loan.
- The interest rate.
- The term of the loan, the number of installments, the amount of each installment, and the approximate balance due at maturity.
- The name of the real estate broker negotiating the loan and his or her license number and business address.
- If the broker anticipates that the loan may be made from broker-controlled funds, a statement to that effect. Broker-controlled funds are funds owned by the broker or close relation of the broker or by any entity (e.g., corporation) of which the broker owns an interest of more than 25%.
- The prepayment terms.
- A statement that the purchase of credit or credit disability insurance is not required as a condition for making the loan.

Other Disclosure Duties

The Mortgage Loan Disclosure Statement is a requirement of state law. A separate disclosure statement by a person extending consumer credit is required by the Federal Truth-in-Lending Act (as previously discussed).

A real estate licensee's duty of disclosure in a mortgage loan transaction does not begin and end with the preparation of a Mortgage Loan Disclosure Statement. The California court has held that a licensee has the obligation to inform prospective borrowers of the differences between the commission amounts brokers could charge for loans subject to the Real Property Loan Law as opposed to loans not covered by the Law. In other words, if a borrower tells the broker the loan amount required and that amount falls within the provisions of the Mortgage Loan Broker Law, and the broker then suggests, without any other economic justification, the possibility of a larger loan amount (putting it outside the Law's provisions), the broker is obligated to inform the borrower that if the latter borrows above the statutory limit, the broker's commission, escrow fees and charges may be more than the ceilings imposed by the Mortgage Loan Broker Law. (*In Realty Project, Inc. v. Smith*).

Other Restrictions

Loans subject to the provisions of the Mortgage Loan Broker Law may not provide for a balloon payment if the term of the loan is less than three years. A balloon payment is defined as an installment payment that is greater than twice the amount of the smallest installment payment called for in the promissory note.

If the property securing the loan is an owner-occupied dwelling, a balloon payment is not permissible if the term of the loan is six years or less. Neither of these restrictions apply to seller financing.

Other restrictions on loans subject to the mortgage Loan Broker Law include the following:

115

1. Charges for late payment of an installment are limited to 10% of the installment payment. If a payment is made within ten days of its due date, no late charge may be imposed.

2. Any prepayment penalty is limited by statute if the security for the loan is a single-family, borrower-occupied dwelling. No charge may be assessed for prepayment made more than six years from the date of the loan. During the first six years of the loan, 20% of the principal balance of the loan may be paid off during any 12-month period without penalty. Six months' interest on the amount prepaid over 20% of the unpaid principal balance is the maximum prepayment penalty allowed. This provision applies to loans of any dollar amount if negotiated by a real estate licensee for compensation.

Disclosures Imposed by Status as an Agent

The real estate licensee's status as an agent imposes additional disclosure requirements on the licensee. The real estate agent is a fiduciary of the principal. This means that the agent owes certain duties to the principal, such as acting in the principal's best interest, obeying the principal's instructions, and refraining from taking unfair advantage of the principal. One of these is the duty of full disclosure. In addition to these principles of agency, the California License Law also imposes on the real estate agent the duty to refrain from engaging in fraudulent or dishonest dealings and making misrepresentations.

Agency principles combined with statutory duties require the real estate agent to make full disclosure regarding any transaction and to act in the utmost good faith. The real estate agent may well ask, "Just what must be disclosed?" Courts have interpreted the disclosure requirement to mean that the real estate agent must make a full disclosure to the principal of all material facts that might affect the principal's decision. A full disclosure includes all material facts that have or are likely to have a bearing on the desirability of the transaction from the point of view of the principal. A material fact is one that the agent should realize would be likely to affect the judgment of the principal in giving his or her consent to the transaction.

Obviously, this standard is rather vague. Just what is a material fact in any given situation? How is the agent to know what will or will not affect a principal's decision? Practically speaking, what constitutes full disclosure will vary from situation to situation. In fact, courts have stated that the question of whether an agent has made full disclosure is one that is to be determined on a case by case basis. What is material to one person may not be material to another.

To help get a feel for what may or may not be material in a particular set of circumstances, some true factual situations are presented below. It is hoped these will give the agent a general idea of what types of information must be disclosed. When deciding what should be disclosed, the agent should bear in mind that the courts feel that real estate licensees, by virtue of their semi-professional status and generous compensation, hold themselves out as experts on real estate financing and are justifiably relied upon as such by lenders and borrowers alike. Therefore, courts believe agents have an affirmative duty to give expert advice to their clients as to the economic sense of a transaction.

Examples of Full Disclosure

Three factual situations are presented below that, it is hoped, will give the real estate agent a better understanding of the meaning of "full disclosure" and "fiduciary duty."

1. **Security and assets of purchaser.** A property owner, named Alhino, owned property improved with an apartment and commercial units. A real estate agent, Senjo, learned that the property was for sale and discussed the price and other terms of the sale with Alhino. Shortly thereafter, Senjo showed the property to a previous customer, Ranker. Ranker told

Senjo that he would buy the property only if the owner agreed to carry back the loan on an unsecured promissory note. Ranker told Senjo that he, Ranker, wanted to finance the property this way so that he could be late in making the payments without risking losing the property.

Senjo presented Ranker's offer to the owner, stating that Ranker was a very wealthy man with extensive property holdings, some of which Senjo was personally familiar with. He also told Alhino that he was better off taking an unsecured promissory note than a mortgage because if there was a default, he could get a money judgment against Ranker instead of the property, which might be in a state of disrepair by then. The owner accepted the offer.

Before the transaction closed, Ranker asked Senjo if he could pay his commission in the form of a promissory note and that he needed to borrow the downpayment. Senjo did not inform Alhino of Ranker's need to borrow these funds nor of Ranker's desire to be able to make late payments safely.

Ranker soon defaulted on the note and, two years after the close of escrow, committed suicide. Alhino sued Ranker's estate, which was insolvent. Alhino then sued Senjo and his broker for fraud and misrepresentation. The court ruled in favor of Alhino. The court listed the following misrepresentations or failures to disclose as supporting the claim of breach of fiduciary duties: the representation that Ranker was a wealthy man and claims of personal knowledge as to some of his holdings (which Senjo did not have); failure to disclose Ranker's need to borrow the downpayment and amount of the commission; and failure to disclose the fact that Ranker wanted to finance the property without a mortgage or trust deed so that he could default with impunity. (*Alhino v. Starr*)

2. **Escrow instruction.** A real estate agent, Kateen, negotiated the sale of a parcel of property. The purchase price was to be $165,000. The buyer was to assume an existing loan of $140,000 (secured by a first deed of trust) and execute a note for $25,000 (secured by a second deed of trust). There was to be no downpayment.

Kateen, without the knowledge of the buyer or seller, had escrow instructions prepared that reflected a sales price of $206,250 and a cash downpayment of $41,250. This was done to encourage the mortgage company to purchase the note secured by the second deed of trust. In fact, relying on the escrow instruction, the mortgage company did approve the loan package and sold the note to two investors. The company would not have done so if it had known there was to be no downpayment.

Shortly after the close of escrow, the purchaser defaulted on both loans. Accusations were filed against Kateen with the Department of Real Estate, charging substantial misrepresentations and fraudulent and dishonest dealings. The Department revoked Kateen's license. Her actions in causing false escrow instructions to be prepared constituted sufficient grounds for revocation of her license. (*Kateen v. Department of Real Estate*)

3. **Inquiry as to ability to repay.** Peirce was a 77-year-old widow who owned four parcels of property. Her rental income was barely enough to subsist on, so she contacted Hom, a real estate agent, to arrange a loan on her properties. Hom's real estate office was around the corner from where Peirce lived and they had known each other for many years on a non-business basis.

Hom arranged for two different loans on Peirce's properties, charging commissions of over 13% for each loan. Each loan also called for substantial balloon payments at the end of the loan terms. Both loans violated the California Real Estate Law (the commission cannot exceed 10% and no installment, including the last, can be more than twice the amount of the smallest payment). Hom prepared and presented to Peirce a "Broker's Loan Statement" which stated that the loans were in compliance with the Real Estate Law. Peirce later testified that the loan terms were never fully explained to her but that she trusted Hom and believed the terms were legal.

Hom did not inquire as to Peirce's ability to repay the loans. He assumed she would use the proceeds to pay for living expenses, but in fact she had other debts to pay, including other mortgage loans. Eventually, Peirce was unable to keep up with all of her loan payments and all of her lenders foreclosed. Peirce sued Hom, partly on the basis of breach of fiduciary duty.

The court stated that there was no doubt that Hom stood in a fiduciary relationship to Peirce (he was her agent) and that Hom breached his fiduciary duty when he failed to inquire into Peirce's ability to repay the loans. As she came to him because of his expertise in real estate financial matters, he should at least have determined whether there was a reasonable likelihood of her repaying the loans. He also should have advised her as to a more prudent means of raising money on her property. He should have discussed the possibility of default and loss of her property, and suggested the alternative of selling one of her properties instead of further borrowing. (*Peirce v. Hom*)

These examples are, for the most part, rather blatant instances of breaches of fiduciary duties. Other situations may not seem so obvious. The wisest thing for the real estate agent to do is to err on the side of caution, always acting with the utmost good faith and disclosing to the fullest extent possible.

CHAPTER SUMMARY

1. Both state and federal law regulate some aspects of real estate financing. They prohibit discrimination in lending and require certain disclosures to be made to the borrower in residential transactions.

2. The federal Civil Rights Act of 1866 and Fair Housing Act of 1968, and California's Unruh Civil Rights Act, Financial Discrimination Act, and Fair Employment and Housing Act all prohibit discrimination in real estate transactions and/or real property financing. In addition, the California License Law has extensive regulations relating to permitted and prohibited activities by real estate licensees.

3. The federal Truth-in-Lending Act requires disclosure of the total financing costs and the annual percentage rate (APR). Certain advertising restrictions must also be followed.

4. California requires the arranger of credit to make detailed disclosure of the financing terms to the buyer in seller-financed residential transactions. The Mortgage Loan Brokers' Law requires loan brokers to make a full disclosure to the borrower regarding the terms of the loan and the costs involved in loans they arrange. The law also limits fees and the commissions that may be paid loan brokers for some loans.

Chapter 8
CONVENTIONAL FINANCING

For the sake of simplicity and organization, we have divided the entire complex of financing programs used in California into three general categories:

1. conventional loan programs,
2. creative financing methods, and
3. government-insured loan programs.

General categories of financing programs:
- conventional
- creative
- government insured/ guaranteed

Conventional loans, government-insured loans, and certain forms of creative financing have provided the solutions to virtually all real estate financing problems since the Federal Housing Administration was formed in 1934. Until the late 1970's, most real estate loans (conventional, government insured or creative) involved long-term, fixed-rate repayment plans. A long-term, fixed-rate real estate loan is one that is repaid over 15 to 30 years at an unchanging rate of interest.

The fixed-rate mortgage* has been the cornerstone financing instrument since the Great Depression. However, in times of high or volatile interest rates it is not favored by real estate lenders, due primarily to its slow payback of principal and its inability to keep pace with inflation and rising interest rates. A fixed-rate mortgage bearing 9% interest will provide a 9% return throughout its term (up to 30 years), regardless of what happens to the cost of money during that time.

If investment money is to be attracted to real estate, it will be on the promise of yields that are competitive with other investment alternatives. This means homebuyers today and

---

* Throughout the rest of our discussion, we will use the term "mortgage" instead of the more cumbersome "mortgage or deed of trust." For the purposes of this section of the book, the two instruments are interchangeable.

in the future will have to pay higher interest rates than did borrowers of 20 years ago; furthermore, since interest levels are subject to significant change over relatively short periods, it is reasonable to expect lenders to protect themselves by committing their funds for shorter terms (15 years and less), or by offering variable-rate loans, like adjustable-rate mortgages.

THE CONVENTIONAL LOAN

A conventional loan is any loan not insured or guaranteed by a government agency. The best way to explain contemporary non-government financing is to start with a look at conventional loans as they have been structured in the past, and then follow with a recital of changes that have occurred to complete the primary elements of today's conventional financing programs.

Historical Perspective

Not only have most conventional loans made over the past several decades been for long terms at fixed interest rates, they have also been **fully amortized**.

Amortization: repayment through equal installment payments of principal and interest

Amortization. An amortized loan is one that provides for repayment within an agreed period (term) by means of regular payments (usually monthly) which include a portion for principal and a portion for interest. As each payment is received, the appropriate amount of principal is deducted from the debt and the remainder of the payment, which represents the interest, is retained by the lender as earnings or profit. With each payment, the amount of the debt is reduced and the interest due with the next payment is recalculated based on the lower balance. The total payment remains the same throughout the term of the loan, but every month the interest portion of the payment is reduced and the principal portion is increased.

Example: $90,000 loan @ 10¼%, 30-year term
(figures approximate)

PYMT. NO.	PRINCIPAL BALANCE	TOTAL PYMT.	INTEREST PORTION	PRNCPL. PORTION	ENDING BALANCE
1	$90,000.00	$806.49	$768.75	$37.74	$89,962.26
2	89,962.26	806.49	768.43	38.06	89,924.20
3	89,924.20	806.49	768.10	38.39	89,885.81
4	89,885.81	806.49	767.77	38.72	89,847.09
5	89,847.09	806.49	767.44	39.05	89,808.04

The long-term amortized or level payment loan has obvious advantages for the borrower. Its repayment is spread out over 25-30 years, which keeps the monthly payment at a manageable level; it is self-liquidating as the loan balance steadily declines to zero (the borrower is not faced with balloon payments of any kind); and the principal and interest payment remains constant for the entire term of the debt.

The long-term, fully amortized, fixed-rate real estate loan is the one borrowers are most familiar with and, in most cases, the type they would like to obtain when financing a home.

THE 15-YEAR, FIXED-RATE MORTGAGE

The 15-year, fixed-rate mortgage has gained increasing popularity over the last few years. Before the advent of the Federal Housing Administration some 50 years ago, a home loan normally was made for a period of five, seven or 15 years. However, most of those loans involved partial or no amortization with balloon payments at the conclusion of their terms.

Since 1979, there has been increased usage of fixed-rate mortgages that are amortized over a 15-year period. Homebuyers were more than twice as likely to use 15-year mortgages in 1986 than in 1983. In early 1987, some lenders

15-year, fully amortized, fixed-rate mortgage:
advantages:
1. often lower interest rate
2. clear ownership in half the time of a traditional 30-year loan
3. great savings in interest over life of loan

disadvantages:
1. larger monthly payments
2. smaller tax deduction

reported that up to 30% of their mortgages were 15-year, fixed-rate. The secondary agencies also reported ever increasing volumes of 15-year mortgages. A 15-year mortgage saves money. There are several advantages to the 15-year mortgage. One is that lenders will often offer lower fixed interest rates on a 15-year mortgage than a 30-year mortgage because the shorter term means less risk for the lender. A 15-year mortgage also offers free and clear home ownership in half the time. The major benefit is the thousands of dollars that borrowers can save because of lower total payments over the life of the loan. A borrower who can do simple arithmetic will understand that for the relatively small additional monthly payment, the 15-year mortgage offers significant savings over its 30-year counterpart. In the graph below, a comparison is made between $70,000, $100,000, and $125,000 mortgages at 10% for 15-year terms and 10½% for 30-year terms.

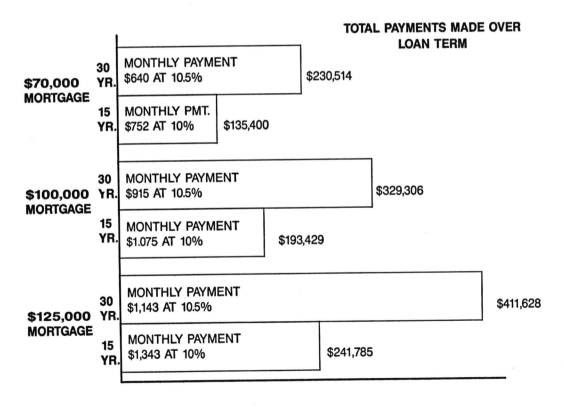

TOTAL PAYMENTS MADE OVER LOAN TERM

$70,000 MORTGAGE

30 YR. | MONTHLY PAYMENT $640 AT 10.5% | $230,514
15 YR. | MONTHLY PMT. $752 AT 10% | $135,400

$100,000 MORTGAGE

30 YR. | MONTHLY PAYMENT $915 AT 10.5% | $329,306
15 YR. | MONTHLY PAYMENT $1.075 AT 10% | $193,429

$125,000 MORTGAGE

30 YR. | MONTHLY PAYMENT $1,143 AT 10.5% | $411,628
15 YR. | MONTHLY PAYMENT $1,343 AT 10% | $241,785

Disadvantages. A 15-year mortgage requires higher monthly payments. Larger downpayments are often also required to reduce the monthly payments and the homeowner loses the tax exemption on the interest payments sooner (because homeownership is attained sooner).

CONFORMING vs. NONCONFORMING LOANS

The particulars of the conventional loan programs detailed in this chapter reflect the criteria established by the national secondary market investors, primarily the FNMA and FHLMC.

Every conventional lender who has the option of keeping its loans in portfolio (primarily banks and savings and loans) can, within the limits of the law, deviate from the standards set by the secondary investors. But when a loan does not meet secondary market criteria it is considered nonconforming and is not salable on the secondary market. For example, so-called "Jumbo" loans are loans that exceed the maximum loan amount that FNMA or FHLMC will purchase (currently $~~187,450~~ for a single-family residence). A loan larger than the FNMA/FHLMC maximum would not conform to their standards and could not be sold to FNMA or FHLMC.

Today the trend is almost exclusively towards conforming loans, that is, loans that meet secondary market standards. So while lenders in your community may occasionally set policies that differ from those explained below, because of the importance of being able to liquidate real estate investments (loans) in the event of a financial predicament, the vast majority of lenders will consistently tailor their policies and standards to conform to those set by major secondary market investors.

Conforming and nonconforming loans:
- conforming loans meet FNMA/FHLMC standards
- today's trend is toward conforming loans to keep option of selling on the secondary market

Now 191,250.

THE 80% CONVENTIONAL LOAN

For many years now, the standard conventional loan-to-value ratio (LTV) has been 80% of the appraised value or sales price, whichever is less. With this type of loan the buyer makes a 20% downpayment and obtains a 30-year, fixed-rate conventional loan for the balance of the purchase price.

If a buyer does not have enough money for a 20% downpayment but still wants a conventional loan, he or she has a number of options:

1. a 90% conventional loan with a 10% downpayment;
2. a 95% conventional loan with a 5% downpayment;
3. a downpayment of 10% with a conventional loan for up to 75% and the seller carrying a second mortgage for the remaining portion of the purchase price.

Example: $120,000 sales price

$90,000	75% first mortgage
18,000	15% 2nd mortgage (seller's)
12,000	10% downpayment
$120,000	

Asking the seller to carry a portion of the purchase price on installment has been a popular way to finance conventional transactions ever since the long-term, fully amortized loan came into existence in the 1930's. Its popularity increases when interest rates are high and money from institutional sources (banks and savings and loans) is scarce.

LOAN ORIGINATION FEE

To cover the administrative costs of making a real estate loan, the local lender will always charge a loan origination fee, also called a loan fee or loan service fee. The loan fee is a percentage of the loan amount, not the sales price, and on conventional loans it will range from 1½% to 3% or more.

Example:

$$
\begin{array}{rl}
\$120,000 & \text{sales price} \\
\times\ .80 & \text{80\% loan-to-value ratio} \\
\hline
\$96,000 & \text{loan amount} \\
\times\ .02 & \text{2\% loan fee} \\
\hline
\$\ 1,920 & \text{loan fee}
\end{array}
$$

The charge is customarily paid by the buyer. The lender generally charges lower loan fees on loans with 80% or lower ratios, and higher fees on the riskier 90% and 95% loans.

SECONDARY FINANCING

When a purchaser borrows money from any source to pay a portion of the required downpayment or settlement costs, it is called secondary financing. In the preceding example, a 25% downpayment would have been $30,000 ($120,000 purchase price less $90,000 loan equals $30,000 downpayment). However, the borrower arranged for the seller to "carry" a portion of the purchase price over a period of time. In effect, the borrower has been extended credit by the seller and it is viewed as secondary financing, just as if the money had been borrowed from a local finance company. Conventional lenders allow secondary financing provided the following requirements are met.

Secondary financing: a loan to pay part of the downpayment, usually short-term, approximately five years
1. at least 10% cash downpayment by borrower
2. term 5-30 years
3. no prepayment penalty
4. regular scheduled payments
5. no negative amortization

1. **The borrower must make a 10% downpayment.** For owner-occupied property, the total of the first and second mortgage must not exceed 90% of the

appraised value or sales price, whichever is less. The borrower must pay the remaining 10% of the purchase price out of his or her own funds. The first mortgage may not exceed 75% loan to value.

2. **Term not to exceed 30 years or be less than five years.** The "term" of a loan, in this context, refers to the repayment period, and a repayment period for secondary financing cannot extend beyond 30 years. The rationale for the 30-year limit is that it should not take longer to pay off a second mortgage than it will take to pay off a first mortgage, and traditionally the repayment period for a long-term, fully amortized first mortgage has been 30 years.

3. **No prepayment penalty permitted.** The second mortgage must be payable in part or in full at any time without a prepayment penalty.

4. **Scheduled payments must be due on a regular basis.** Payments on the second can be monthly, quarterly, semi-annual, or on any other regular basis. The scheduled payments can be designed to fully amortize the debt during its term, to partially amortize the debt during its term (with a balloon payment at the end of the term), or to pay interest only with a balloon payment at the conclusion of the term.

5. **No negative amortization.** The payment on the second mortgage must at least equal the interest on the loan. No negative amortization is allowed.

Fully Amortized Second

A five-year, $9,000 fully amortized second bearing 9¾% interest will cost the borrower approximately $190.12/month. When underwriting the loan, the lender will include this amount in the borrower's monthly housing expense.

Example:

$632.00   payment on 10%, 30-year, $60,000 first mortgage (includes principal, interest, real estate taxes and insurance)

190.12   payment on 9¾%, five-year, $9,000 second mortgage (fully amortized)

—————

$822.12   total housing expense

Second mortgage may be:
1. fully amortized
2. partially amortized with balloon
3. interest only with balloon

Partially Amortized with Balloon Payment

If a second mortgage is scheduled to fully amortize within its term, the monthly payments will be larger than if it is scheduled to partially amortize (partially pay off) during the same period. The thinking behind the partially amortized mortgage is that the smaller monthly payments make the total housing expense less burdensome for the borrower and, thus, it is easier to qualify for a loan.

Example:

$632.00   payment on 10%, 30-year, $60,000 first mortgage (includes taxes and insurance)

77.32   payment on 9¾%, five-year, $9,000 second (partially amortized, based on 30-year repayment schedule)

—————

$709.32   total housing expense

When compared to the example for the fully amortized second mortgage, it is clear the partially amortized second mortgage eases the qualifying burden somewhat and may be a preferred financing arrangement when a borrower's income is borderline.

Setting Up A Partial Amortization Schedule

The above example states that the payments for the partially amortized mortgage are based on a 30-year repayment (amortization) plan. This means the payments were scheduled as though the debt would be paid in full over a 30-year period, even though the entire balance would be due and payable after five years. When the repayment term is 30 years, as opposed to five years, the payments are lower and the debt is retired very gradually. In fact, after five years, payments based on 30-year amortization will have reduced the original loan balance by a relatively small amount, and if the second mortgage is to be paid at that time, there will be a substantial balloon payment. The following chart illustrates how the $9,000 second mortgage would steadily decline over 30 years if allowed to do so. A 30-year, $9,000 loan at 9¾% will have an $8,677 (approximate) balance at the end of five years. This would be the amount of the balloon payment.

AMORTIZATION CHART
9¾% INTEREST

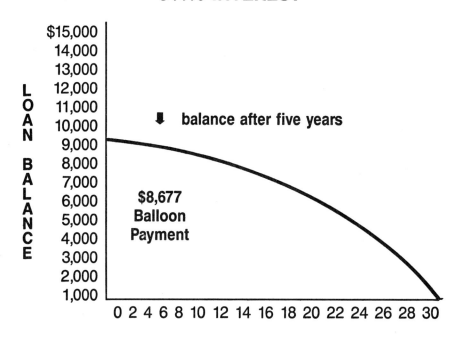

Interest-Only Second

The second mortgage can call for "interest only," which will reduce the amount of the monthly payments still more. Of course, if no principal is paid during the term of the loan, the balloon payment will be the original amount (in the case of our prior example, $9,000). Monthly interest-only payments are computed by multiplying the mortgage debt by the stipulated interest and dividing that figure by 12 (months).

Example:

$$\begin{array}{r} \$9,000 \\ \times\ .0975 \\ \hline \$877.50 \end{array}$$

$$12\ \overline{)\ 877.50}\quad \dfrac{73.13}{}\quad \text{monthly interest payment}$$

[handwritten margin notes: Fanny Mae will Not go along on a second unless: A balloon payment is out at least 5 yrs. B No Negative Amortization. C. Must be periodic payments (monthly). D. at least 10% down. E. No Prepayment Penalty]

Lender First and Lender Second

The seller does not necessarily have to carry the second mortgage when secondary financing is included. The lender, for example, can make a normal 80% loan and a 10% second loan. The buyer makes a 10% downpayment. A typical lender second under these circumstances might have payments based on 30-year amortization with a five-year **call provision** (balloon payment in five years), or it might be a fully amortized ten-year loan. The repayment plan is a matter of agreement between borrower and lender. Keep in mind, the lender will normally charge a loan fee for both the first and second loans.

Secondary financing is often from the seller, but may be a long-term first and short-term second from the institutional lender

PRIVATE MORTGAGE INSURANCE *[handwritten: PMI]*

Eighty percent conventional loans have traditionally been considered "safe" by the mortgage industry because the

PMI: FNMA/FHLMC requirement for loans over 80% LTV

substantial equity the borrower has in the property (20% of the purchase price) is incentive to keep mortgage payments current. Even if there is a default, a foreclosure sale of the property is more than likely to produce enough funds to cover 80% of the original sales price (or appraised value). However, once borrowers begin making downpayments of less than 20% of the sales price, lenders regard the loan as more risky. Under these circumstances, as assurance against loss, the lender will require the borrower to pay for private mortgage insurance. The presence of mortgage insurance compensates the lender for the reduced borrower equity.

Both FNMA and FHLMC require third-party insurance on home loans with less than 20% downpayments. Needless to say, the smaller downpayment requirement of the 90% loan made it very popular with buyers, sellers, and real estate agents. Mortgage insurance is sometimes available for loans with up to 95% LTV.

PMI:
1. protects lender
2. insures position of loan, usually about 20%
3. premium paid by borrower

How Mortgage Insurance Works

When insuring a loan, the mortgage insurance company shares the lender's risk but actually assumes only the primary element of risk. This is to say the insurer does not insure the entire loan amount but rather the upper portion of the loan. The amount of coverage can vary but typically it is 20% to 25% of the loan amount.

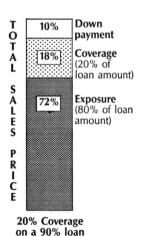

20% Coverage
on a 90% loan

Example: 20% coverage

$200,000	sales price
× .90	LTV
$180,000	90% loan
× .20	amount of coverage
$36,000	amount of policy

In the event of default and foreclosure, the lender, at the insurer's option, will either sell the property and make a claim for reimbursement of actual losses (if any) up to the face amount of the policy or relinquish the property to the insurer and make a claim for actual losses up to the policy amount. Losses incurred by the lender take the form of unpaid interest, property taxes and hazard insurance, attorney's fees, and costs of preserving the property during the period of foreclosure and resale, as well as the expense of selling the property itself.

1.
	$10,950	unpaid interest
	2,061	unpaid taxes and insurance
	1,750	attorney's fees
	6,075	resale costs
	+ 310	miscellaneous expenses
	$21,146	total cost of foreclosure and resale

2.
	$195,000	resale price
	−187,000	loan balance
	$ 8,000	gross profit on resale

3.
	$ 8,000	
	− 21,146	foreclosure and resale costs
	($13,146)	net loss — amount of claim

Private mortgage insurance premium (PMI). In return for insuring the loan, the mortgage insurance company charges a one-time fee at the time the loan is made and a recurring fee, called a **renewal premium**, that is added to the borrower's mortgage payment. Real estate agents and lenders refer to the charges as the **PMI** (private mortgage insurance) or **MIP** (mortgage insurance premium).

Fee at closing. The one-time fee charged at loan closing for a 90% fixed-rate mortgage is generally less than 1% of the loan amount, depending upon the amount of coverage requested. Typical coverage would call for a one-time fee of .5% of the loan amount for 20% coverage.

PMI premium:
1. one-time fee at closing
2. annual renewal premium
3. financing of one-time premium, now available from some users

Example:

$155,000	sales price
139,500	90% loan

$139,500	loan amount
× .0050	one-time fee
$698	PMI at closing

Renewal premium. The renewal premium for a standard fixed-rate, 90% loan averages about .34% of the loan amount annually. The annual fee is divided by 12 and added to the buyer's monthly payment.

Example:

$139,500	loan amount
× .0034	(.34%)
$474	annual premium

$39.50 monthly premium

12 ⟌ 474.00

Below is a mortgage insurance rate chart for primary residences published by a national mortgage insurance company. Although the focus of this discussion has been on insuring fixed-rate mortgages, private mortgage insurance companies also insure adjustable-rate mortgages (ARMs). The rates for ARMs are also set forth below. Today, rates vary somewhat between companies for different types and amounts of coverage. The chart is intended to serve only as a general price guide.

FIXED-PAYMENT MORTGAGES [1] [7]

MGIC Coverage	LTV	SINGLE Term to 80% [8] No Refund	Refund [9]	ANNUAL 1st-Year Premiums	RENEWAL PREMIUMS Declining[3]	Constant [4] Yrs. 2-10	Yrs. 11-Term
25%	90.01 - 95%	3.60%	4.40%	1.10%	.50%	.49%	.25%
	85.01 - 90%	2.50	3.10	.65	.35	.34	.25
	85% & under	2.15	2.45	.50	.35	.34	.25
22%	90.01 - 95%	3.25	4.30	1.00	.50	.49	.25
	85.01 - 90%	2.35	3.00	.55	.35	.34	.25
	85% & under	2.05	2.40	.45	.35	.34	.25
20%	90.01 - 95%	3.05	4.15	.90	.50	.49	.25
	85.01 - 90%	2.20	2.95	.50	.35	.34	.25
	85% & under	1.95	2.35	.40	.35	.34	.25
17%	85.01 - 90%	2.00	2.85	.40	.35	.34	.25
	85% & under	1.75	2.30	.35	.35	.34	.25
12%	85.01 - 90%	1.70	2.80	.35	.35	.34	.25
	85% & under [5]	1.50	2.00	.30	.30	.29	.25

NONFIXED-PAYMENT MORTGAGES [2] [7]

MGIC Coverage	LTV	SINGLE Term to 80% [8] No Refund	Refund [9]	ANNUAL 1st-Year Premiums	RENEWAL PREMIUMS Declining[3]	Constant [4] [6] Yrs. 2-10	Yrs. 11-Term
25%	90.01 - 95%	4.20%	5.20%	1.35%	.55%	.54%	.25%
	85.01 - 90%	3.15	3.90	.75	.45	.44	.25
	85% & under	2.50	3.15	.60	.45	.44	.25
22%	90.01 - 95%	3.85	5.05	1.20	.55	.54	.25
	85.01 - 90%	2.90	3.80	.65	.45	.44	.25
	85% & under	2.35	3.10	.55	.45	.44	.25
20%	90.01 - 95%	3.60	4.90	1.10	.55	.54	.25
	85.01 - 90%	2.75	3.75	.60	.45	.44	.25
	85% & under	2.20	3.05	.50	.45	.44	.25
17%	85.01 - 90% [5]	2.50	3.65	.50	.45	.44	.25
	85% & under	2.00	2.65	.40	.40	.39	.25
12%	85.01 - 90%	2.05	3.20	.40	.40	.39	.25
	85% & under [5]	1.65	2.30	.35	.35	.34	.25

*An ARM will only be insured by many mortgage insurance companies if the only negative amortization that occurs does so as a result of payment caps; scheduled negative amortization is not allowed.

One-time PMI premium. In 1987, some private mortgage companies introduced one-time mortgage insurance premiums, an alternative to the traditional initial premium and renewal premium program. Under the new program, the initial premium and renewal premium are combined into a single, one-time premium which may be financed by the borrower. The amount of the one-time premium is simply added to the mortgage amount. The new program has two advantages for borrowers: there is no cash requirement at closing, and the monthly payments are usually smaller (for most loans the original mortgage payment needed to amortize the mortgage amount plus premium is less than the monthly charge formerly imposed for the renewal premium alone).

Cancellation

Cancellation:
1. when loan is less than 80% of home value
2. borrower may have to pay for appraisal
3. loan payments reduced to reflect canceled premium

Lenders require mortgage insurance on high loan-to-value, low downpayment loans as protection against borrower default. Once the increased risk of borrower default is eliminated, usually when the loan balance has been reduced to 80% or less of the home's present value, the mortgage insurance has fulfilled its purpose. Traditionally, even when the risk was reduced, many lenders did not cancel the insurance policy. Because the policy is between the insurer and the lender, only the lender can cancel the policy, not the borrower.

Until a few years ago, lenders were not required to cancel the policy, and thus the lenders either did not cancel the policy or canceled the policy but neglected to pass on the savings to the borrower.

Example: Sometimes insurance premiums are written into the interest rate charged on the loan. If the lender's interest rate is 12% and the cost of the mortgage insurance is .5%, the total interest rate on the mortgage will be 12.5%. Often, in the past when the lender canceled the insurance policy, it kept the interest rate at 12.5% instead of lowering it back to 12%.

This practice is called **"loaded couponing."** FHLMC revised its mortgage insurance cancellation rule in 1985 to prevent this and other practices. Under FHLMC's rule, when the insurance is canceled the lender must modify the mortgage interest rate to reflect the cancellation. However, cancellation is not automatic; the borrower must request the cancellation and often must pay the costs of a new appraisal.

FHLMC requires lenders to drop coverage at the request of borrowers under certain conditions. The insurance must be canceled if the loan is at least seven years old and has been paid down to 80% or less of the home's current value. If the mortgage is less than seven years old, lenders must cancel the policy only if the loan has been paid down to 80% of the home's value and the borrower meets established payment history criteria. If the borrower has a fixed-payment mortgage, payments must not have been more than 30 days past due in the immediately preceding 12 months. If the loan is an adjustable-rate mortgage, there must have been no payment over 30 days past due for the preceding 24 months.

FHLMC deals directly with less than 20% of the lenders who originate home loans, so these rules are not universal. However, because FHLMC is a major provider of mortgage funds, it does exert a significant influence over the entire mortgage market.

Canceling mortgage insurance but failing to pass on the savings to the borrower is also a violation of the Real Estate Settlement Procedures Act (RESPA), according to the Department of Housing and Urban Development. The practice of collecting premiums on canceled insurance (referred to as **"self-insurance"**), is thought to be common, although no accurate figures are available. The RESPA ruling is similar to the HUD policy on FHA loans, which considers self-insurance a fraudulent practice.

FNMA also requires lenders to cancel PMI under certain conditions. In 1987, FNMA implemented a rule which required all lenders who sell their mortgages to FNMA to cancel PMI if a new appraisal shows that the loan has been paid down to 80% of the property's current value (no

---

FHLMC MORTGAGE INSURANCE CANCELLATION RULES

IF:	REQUIREMENT
1. Insurance is cancelled	Lender must reduce interest to reflect cancellation
2. Loan is at least seven years old and has been paid down to 80%	Insurance must be cancelled and rate reduced
3. **Fixed-rate** loan is less than seven years old but paid down to 80% of home's current value*	Insurance must be cancelled and rate reduced provided no mortgage payments have been more than 30 days past due during the preceding **12 months**
4. **Adjustable-rate** loan is less than seven years old but paid down to 80% of home's current value*	Same as above except no mortgage payments have been more than 30 days past due during the preceding **24 months**

*Buyer must obtain appraisal at own expense

---

matter how old the loan is).

The borrower must pay for a lender-approved appraisal and if the appraisal shows the loan balance to be 80% or less of current value, the borrower then makes a formal request to terminate the PMI. The lender must cancel the policy and reduce the monthly mortgage payment by the amount of the PMI premium.

It is estimated that FNMA deals with approximately 3,000 lenders.

Rising Mortgage Delinquency

In the early 1980's, the amount of past-due mortgages and foreclosures began to rise dramatically. In 1985, the delinquency rate was up to 6.19% (the highest since the 1930's). These increases in loan delinquencies and foreclosures prompted the mortgage insurance industry to raise its premiums and institute new underwriting guidelines. Although the rate of delinquencies has dropped off somewhat, private mortgage insurance companies continue to apply strict standards to the mortgages they insure.

Why increased delinquencies? Most loan defaults occur between the third and fifth year of the life of the loan. Therefore, the losses experienced in 1984 and 1985 were largely due to loans originated in 1980-1982. The defaults occurred at a time of high unemployment and high interest rates which depressed home values and the housing market. Those who lost their jobs lost their homes as well because they could not sell at a price equal to the mortgage balance. In the current economy, homebuyers can no longer expect inflation alone to bail them out of problem loans, as was the case during the 1970's. Previous high inflation rates almost always ensured that the selling price of the home would exceed the original mortgage balance, so that a hard-pressed homeowner could sell the home for a profit, or at least enough to pay off the mortgage. When inflation levels lowered, the value of the home no longer rose quickly enough to allow the homeowner to recoup enough from the sale of the home to pay off the mortgage.

Higher delinquency rates in recent years led to:
1. higher PMI premiums
2. greater involvement of insurers in effort to increase quality of underwriting

Efforts at quality control. In 1985-1986, mortgage insurance companies began to exert considerable effort to increase the quality of the loans they insure in an attempt to avoid future losses. These efforts resulted in both new policies and new products.

A major change in the private mortgage insurance process is the active role that mortgage insurance companies are taking with their own underwriting procedures. No longer are these companies simply reviewing loans made by lenders and then accepting them with few questions. Mortgage insurance companies now have their own comprehensive set of underwriting guidelines. For example, one national insurance company has its own list of documentation requirements, including: lender loan application, credit report, verification of employment and income, verification of deposit, sales agreement, appraisal, and borrower payment history. The mortgage insurance company also requires a comprehensive borrower analysis, involving his or her personal history, employment history, an income ratio analysis (see chart below for ratios), a review of assets, credit ratings and credit reports. There are certain acceptable sources of equity (cash, gift letters, lot equity, sweat equity, etc.) and a set policy for property appraisals.

	ACCEPTABLE INCOME RATIOS	
Type of Loan	Total Monthly Housing Expense To Income	Total Monthly Expense To Income
Over 90% LTV, nonfixed payment	25%	33%
Other	28%	36%

In another effort to improve quality control in underwriting, one national mortgage insurance company provides in its master policy that the insurance will not cover losses suffered from misrepresentation, negligence, or fraud; representations made by the lender, borrower or any other party are considered to be the lender's own representation. These provisions will hopefully encourage more care in the underwriting process as lenders will bear the burden of any misrepresentation or fraud that escapes their attention. The effect of these types of provisions in policies may be somewhat modified by state law. For instance, in California in 1985, a law was passed that provides that fraudulent statements in applications and attached documents for mortgage insurance will block a claim to recover. If the application contains incorrect information that is not fraudulent, the legislation provides that the misrepresentation shall not prevent a recovery unless it was material to the acceptance of the risk, or the insurer in good faith would not have issued the policy if the true facts had been known. There are now over 30 states with similar legislation.

Additional steps taken by mortgage insurers in an effort to control losses include employing spot-check appraisers to reevaluate the value of the loan properties. Both lenders and insurers are becoming increasingly careful of those with whom they do business. Lenders are examining the financial health of the mortgage insurance company to ensure that they are able to pay all claims. Mortgage insurance companies are rechecking the underwriting standards of the lender to make sure that the loans being made are sound and less likely to default. Many insurance companies have refused to do business with those lenders who have made a large number of defaulted loans. Usually, a very small number of lenders are responsible for most of the loans that default. One mortgage insurance company concluded that 90% of its defaults had come from only 10% of its lenders.

Over the next few years, lenders who make relatively few claims with insurers may qualify for lower insurance rates, thus gaining a competitive edge against those with high losses. However, insurance companies would need prior approval from state regulatory bodies before they could vary rates between lenders.

THE 90% CONVENTIONAL LOAN

Ninety percent loans became increasingly popular with the advent of private mortgage insurance. However, the qualifying standards for such loans tend to be more stringent and lenders adhere to those standards more strictly (even though the loan is insured). Marginal buyers and properties are more likely to be rejected if the loan amount requested exceeds 80% of the value or purchase price, whichever is less.

Minimum 10% downpayment. When seeking a 90% loan, the buyer must make at least a 5% downpayment out of his or her own cash reserves. The rest of the downpayment may be a gift from a family member, equity in other property traded to the seller, or credit for rent already paid under a lease/purchase.

90% conventional loan:
• stricter adherence to underwriting standards
• minimum 5% down by borrower
• may have higher loan fee and interest rate

Loan fee and interest higher. Ninety percent loans usually call for larger loan origination fees and higher interest rates than do 80% loans. This is a generalization and there are certainly exceptions, but when thinking in terms of 90% financing, it is a good idea to expect a more expensive loan.

THE 95% CONVENTIONAL LOAN

The success of the 90% loan in the 1960's and early 1970's encouraged lenders and private mortgage insurers to experiment with an even higher loan-to-value ratio—the 95% conventional loan. Made primarily by savings and loans and mortgage companies, the 95% loan makes it possible to obtain conventional financing with as little as 5% cash down.

95% conventional loan:
• higher underwriting standards and ratios
• strict adherence to standards
• may have higher loan fee, interest rate, PMI premium

More expensive than 80% and 90% loans. If you apply the generalization "the smaller the downpayment the greater the risk of default" (this represents the view of most lenders), it is easy to understand why in most cases the 95% conventional loan is more costly than 80% and 90% loans. Both interest rates and loan fees are generally increased for 95% loans. In fact, private mortgage insurance companies may charge up to a 1.10% one-time premium at closing for 95% loans, as opposed to the .65% for 90% loans (at 25% coverage). Also, the borrower's renewal premium on 95% loans is usually higher than on 90% loans. Depending on the type of coverage requested, the renewal premium will be around .49%. The following chart shows a comparison of the mortgage insurance rates for the various LTV loans:

PMI COMPARISON CHART (for $95,000 loan at 20% coverage)		
LTV	**1st Year**	**Annual Renewal Premium**
80%	N/A	N/A
90%	$475.00 (.50%)	$323.00 (.34%)
95%	$855.00 (.90%)	$465.50 (.49%)

No secondary financing. The buyer must make the downpayment on his or her own, without resorting to secondary financing or gifts.

More stringent underwriting requirements. Ninety-five percent loans are becoming more and more difficult to obtain. Underwriting guidelines are extremely strict for a 95% loan and those guidelines are followed very closely. Lenders are much more careful today when making 95% loans than they have been in the past, due to the high foreclosure rate of high loan-to-value loans. A marginal buyer will rarely qualify for a 95% loan. Underwriters "ride the credit line" when evaluating risk with just 5% down. If your borrower's application is weak in certain areas, it is probably advisable that some alternate form of financing be considered, such as government-insured or seller financing. Owner occupancy is required.

FNMA guidelines for 95% loans. As an example of stricter underwriting requirements for 95% loans, FNMA guidelines state that the borrower should fall into **one** of the following three sets of circumstances:

1. The borrower has a good mortgage payment history, good credit, sufficient financial assets and a credit history indicating the borrower is willing and able to devote a substantial portion of his or her income to a mortgage payment.

2. The borrower has no mortgage payment history, good credit and sufficient financial assets, and the borrower's total monthly debt service-to-income ratio is **30%** or less.

3. The borrower has no mortgage payment history (first-time buyer), but has good credit, sufficient financial assets and financial reserves to carry the mortgage payment. For this category, the borrower must normally have on deposit sufficient cash or other very liquid assets to cover **three months' mortgage payments** (principal, interest, taxes, insurance, mortgage insurance) after the downpayment and closing costs.

Exercise No. 1

A borrower is seeking a 95% conventional fixed-rate loan to buy a home. The sales price is $136,000. The appraisal came in at $139,000. The buyer plans to make a 5% cash downpayment.

1. Will the interest rate and loan fee be more or less than for an 80% loan?

More

2. Can the buyer use secondary financing or a gift to make the downpayment?

No

3. Under FNMA Guidelines, can the borrower be a first-time buyer?

Yes,

70% "EASY QUALIFIER" LOANS

In accordance with the general rule that lower downpayment loans are more expensive and subject to stricter underwriting scrutiny, higher downpayment loans are generally less expensive for the borrower and underwriting standards are less stringently applied. For example, many lenders are willing to waive verification of employment or documentation of income if the borrower is willing to make a larger than normal downpayment, usually at least 25%-30%, and has good credit. These loans are often referred to as "easy qualifier," "time saver," or "no documentation" loans. They are particularly attractive for high-income borrowers whose income is from self-employment or from a variety of sources, and for whom documentation may be more burdensome than for borrowers whose income is solely from wages or salary.

In addition to the simplified, faster qualifying procedure, these low loan-to-value ratio loans are often less expensive since the lender may impose lower loan fees or slightly lower interest rates. Also, since the downpayment is well over 20%, mortgage insurance is not required.

ASSUMING CONVENTIONAL LOANS

Do not take chances when writing sales that call for assumptions of existing conventional loans. Do not give buyers and sellers advice on the assumability of a loan unless it is a certainty. When there is some question about what will happen if an assumption is attempted, consult the lender, an attorney or other individual who is particularly qualified to advise you.

When attempting to assume a loan, one of three things will happen:

1. The lender will accept the assumption and the loan terms will be left intact.

Assumption of conventional loans:
- check for alienation clause
- check with lender

If there is an alienation clause, lender may:
1. approve assumption and not change loan terms
2. increase interest rate
3. call loan

2. The lender will accept the assumption but will insist on an assumption fee and/or will increase the loan's interest rate, possibly to present market levels. This frequently defeats the purpose of the assumption, which was to take advantage of the loan's lower-than-market interest rate.

Assumption fees vary from lender to lender; some are inconsequential, others are prohibitive, up to 3% of the loan balance or more. The charges are usually spelled out in the mortgage instrument.

3. The lender will refuse to allow the assumption and will call the note, which means demanding full payment of the loan at once. The right to do this must be spelled out in the promissory note or mortgage.

Do not discover after the sale has been made what the lender plans or is entitled to do. Find out before you write the sale, even if it means not making the sale at all.

Conventional Prepayment Penalties

Historically, most conventional lenders have penalized borrowers who paid off their loans sooner than agreed; some still do.

Prepayment penalties:
- additional charge for early payment of loan
- usually apply during first 3-5 years of loan
- less common in today's loans

But because of the volatility of interest rates today, lenders are inclined to make shorter term loans. They like the idea of being able to invest their money in real estate at today's rates, to recover it after a relatively short period (three to 15 years for real estate loans) and to reinvest the funds at whatever rates prevail at the time.

Prepayment penalties discourage early payment of a loan, and this runs counter to most lenders' objectives in today's real estate market. FNMA and FHLMC do not have prepayment penalties in their standard promissory notes and mortgages or trust deeds. In California, lenders are prohibited from charging prepayment penalties beyond the first five years of the life of the loan for loans on owner-occupied, one- to four-unit dwellings.

Exercise No. 2

A borrower is seeking conventional, fixed-rate financing in order to purchase a home. The sales price is $85,000 and the property has been appraised at $88,000. The buyer will make a 10% downpayment and finance the balance with a 75% conventional first loan at 9½% interest for 30 years and a 15% second loan. The second bears interest at 11% and calls for a balloon payment after five years; it is amortized on the basis of a 30-year schedule. There will be a 1.5% loan fee on the first loan.

1. **What will be the loan amounts for the first and second loans?**

2. **How much will the buyer pay at closing for downpayment and loan fee?**

3. **What is the amount of the balloon payment on the second loan?**

CHAPTER SUMMARY

1. Traditional conventional loans are fixed-rate, fully amortized 30-year loans. However, recently 15-year loans have been gaining in popularity because of the significant savings in interest payments. Also, loans may be fully amortized, partially amortized, or interest only with a balloon payment. Today, virtually all conventional loans are conforming loans, meaning they conform to FNMA/FHLMC standards.

2. Different standards apply to loans of differing loan-to-value ratios: loans of not more than 80% LTV, loans of more than 80% LTV and loans of more than 90% LTV. Generally speaking, the smaller the downpayment, the stricter the underwriting standards applied. The loan fees also tend to be higher for loans with higher LTVs.

3. Secondary financing is allowed on many conventional loans, but there are specific restrictions that must be followed. For example, a borrower may borrow part of the downpayment from another source but must pay at least 10% out of his/her own resources. Also, no prepayment penalties are allowed on the second loan.

4. For loans over 80% LTV, private mortgage insurance is required to insure the lender for part of the loan amount. The borrower pays an initial fee and then an annual renewal premium for the mortgage insurance. Requirements of private mortgage insurers impose another set of standards in addition to the FNMA/FHLMC guidelines for underwriting loans.

5. Before you try to assume a conventional loan, study the original loan papers carefully. Lenders often have the

option of charging an assumption fee, raising the interest rate, or refusing the assumption altogether. Conventional loans may or may not include prepayment charges and/or alienation clauses (California law prohibits prepayment penalties after the first five years of the loan).

Chapter 9
ALTERNATE FINANCING

The 1980's presented California's real estate industry and its allied fields with a unique assortment of problems. In the early years of the decade, the paramount problem was to reconcile the investor's need for a high rate of return with the borrower's need for an affordable loan. The search for a solution to this problem spawned many innovative plans, such as buydowns, adjustable-rate mortgages (ARMs), graduated payment mortgages (GPMs), growth equity mortgages (GEMs), and shared appreciation mortgages (SAMs).

As interest rates declined in the latter part of the decade, interest in most alternate financing plans quickly evaporated. The return of affordable fixed-rate conventional financing relegated many of the alternate financing plans to the dust bin (with the sole exception of ARMs). However, today's lower interest rates are not guaranteed to continue, and rising rates can easily rekindle interest in alternate financing programs.

In this chapter, we will examine some of the most popular and successful of the alternate financing methods: buydowns, ARMs, and GEMs.

Alternate financing plans:
- buydowns
- ARMs
- convertible ARMs
- GPMs
- reduction option mortgages
- GEMs
- SAMs

DISCOUNTS AND POINTS

Before discussing specific alternate financing programs, it is important to address the subject of discounts. Discounts or discount points (often referred to as just "points") have traditionally been associated with FHA and VA financing in residential loans. However, payment of points has become

Discounts:
1 point = 1% of loan amount

commonplace for conventional loans as well. The term "point" is a contraction of the larger term "percentage point." A point is one percentage point or one percent of a loan amount. On a $90,000 loan, one point would be $900; six points would be $5,400.

Example:

$$\begin{array}{r} \$90,000 \\ \times\ .06 \\ \hline \$\ 5,400 \end{array}$$

Two types of points:
1. loan fee to cover lender's administrative costs
2. discounts to increase lender's yield

Discounts have the effect of adding to the lender's yield. If a lender can "discount" a loan, the interest rate charged the borrower does not have to be as high to meet minimum yield requirements.

There are two sorts of points charged by lenders in real estate loan transactions. One type is designed to pay the lender's administrative costs in processing a loan. It is called a loan origination fee, loan fee, service fee or administrative charge. The fee is normally somewhere between one point (for FHA and VA loans) and two to four points (for conventional loans). The loan fee is usually paid by the buyer.

The other type of point, which may be called a discount, discount points or just points, is designed to increase the lender's yield to something above the interest rate stated in the promissory note, which is called the coupon rate or the nominal rate. Depending on the circumstances, this sort of charge may be paid by either the buyer or the seller, but it is most often paid by the seller. Keep in mind, the discount is computed on the loan amount, not the sales price.

Example:

$122,000	sales price
$97,600	loan amount
6%	discount

$97,600 loan
× .06
$5,856 discount

Points are paid at closing by deducting the amount of the points from the amount of the loan to be advanced. For instance, if the loan were for $145,000 and the lender required four points, 4% of the loan ($5,800) would be deducted from the amount actually advanced to the borrower (the loan would be discounted 4%) and the remainder, $139,200, would be delivered to the borrower to finance the purchase. The borrower would sign a promissory note and mortgage agreeing to repay the entire $145,000 at the stipulated rate of interest. The lender would advance only $139,200 but would be repaid $145,000. The buyer would transfer the loan proceeds ($139,200) to the seller without making up the difference. In effect, the seller paid the lender $5,800 to induce the lender to make the loan with a lower than market interest rate. The $5,800 compensated the lender for the lower yielding loan.

Discount points are subtracted (discounted) from the face value of the loan and the lender advances the remainder

Who pays the points?
• seller in VA transactions
• in FHA and conventional transactions, may be either seller or buyer, but is usually seller

POINTS IN VA TRANSACTIONS

Payment of discount points has long been a part of most VA loans. The maximum interest rates allowed on VA loans are usually a little lower than prevailing market rates. This means that a lender making a VA loan could not charge the borrower as much interest as the same lender could have charged the same borrower for a conventional loan to buy the same house. Lenders, then, have traditionally required the seller to pay enough points to increase the lender's yield on VA loans to a rate that is competitive with conventional loans. Under VA regulations, the buyer is prohibited from paying any discount points. Any points required by the lender must be paid by the seller or a third party (e.g., builder).

Exercise No. 1

A borrower is seeking a $137,000 conventional loan and doesn't want to pay more than 10½% interest. The lender is willing to make a 10½% loan, provided the loan is discounted by eight points.

1. What is the amount of the discount?

$137K
.08
10,960
10,

† 10,960.

DISCOUNT POINTS IN CONVENTIONAL LOANS

Discount points:
1. increase lender's yield
2. decrease buyer's interest rate
3. make property more marketable

The purpose of points in conventional loan transactions is usually to increase the lender's yield from the rate the borrower is willing or able to pay to the rate the lender requires as a yield on its loans. While the buyer is not prohibited from paying discount points on conventional or FHA loans, in most instances the seller is the one who pays the points as a way of reducing the interest rate to be paid by the buyer and thus making the property more marketable. When the seller pays points to reduce the buyer's interest rate, it is called a "buydown." It is far easier to sell property if the interest rate to be paid by the buyer is relatively low and affordable.

HOW MANY POINTS?

Rule of thumb for estimating number of points:
6 points = 1% increase in lender's yield

The question of how many points must be paid can only be answered with up-to-the-minute information concerning yields required by lenders, which are often affected to a large degree by existing market conditions. The number of points required to increase the lender's yield by 1% is affected by many factors, including prevailing interest rates, the average time that loans are outstanding before being paid off, and, to some degree, the terms of the loan documents themselves. Currently the number of points to be paid is normally computed on the assumption that it takes six points to increase the lender's yield on a 30-year loan by 1%. This is a "rule of thumb" approach to computing yields and should be confirmed with the lender before a final quote is made.

Example:

$ 90,000   proposed 30-year loan
11%   required yield
10%   interest rate preferred by borrower

$ 90,000
× .06
$ 5,400   discount (usually paid by seller)

$ 90,000
5,400
$84,600   advanced by lender after discount

$ 90,000   note
× .10   nominal rate paid by borrower
$ 9,000   interest paid by borrower

.11   yield to lender
$84,600 ⟌ $9,000

BUYDOWN PLANS

One of the easiest and most agreeable ways to make expensive loans less expensive is the "buydown." A buydown is a way to lower a purchaser's initial monthly mortgage payments as an aid to qualifying for a loan. The seller, builder or any other person, including the buyer, makes a lump sum payment to the lender at the time the loan is made. The

Buydown: lump sum paid to lender to reduce interest rate charged to buyer money that has been paid to the lender is used to reduce the borrower's payments either early in or throughout the life of the loan.

Example:

Buydown advantages:
- lower payments for borrower
- easier for buyer to qualify

| $65,000 | 30-year, 15% loan |
| $ 3,900 | buydown (6 points) |

$822	quoted 15% loan payment
− 770	buyer's payment at 14%
$52	savings resulting from buydown

In the above example, the quoted rate is 15%, but the borrower's interest rate has been bought down by 1%, reducing the interest rate to 14% for a $52/month savings.

Buydowns may be:
- permanent
- temporary level payment
- temporary graduated payment

Two Advantages to a Buydown

There are two fairly obvious advantages to a buydown plan.

1. The buyer's monthly payment is lower than normal.
2. The lender evaluates the buyer on the basis of the reduced payment, thereby making it easier to qualify for the loan.

PERMANENT BUYDOWNS

Estimating permanent buydown amount:
1. yield/discount tables, or
2. rule of thumb, 6 points = 1% interest rate

A buydown can be permanent or temporary. If a portion of a buyer's interest rate is permanently bought down (e.g., for 30 years), the lender's nominal rate (the rate stated in the promissory note) will be reduced by that amount.

Example: Lender quotes 15% for a 30-year loan of $65,000. Builder agrees to buydown the note rate to 14%. Lender agrees to make the loan at this rate if Builder makes a lump sum payment to Lender of $3,900. Builder pays $3,900 to buydown the interest rate by 1%.

How to Compute Permanent Buydowns

There are two ways to be completely accurate when determining permanent interest rate buydowns. One way is to obtain a discount/yield table booklet from a lender or title company and learn to use it; the other way is to call your lender for a quote. If you just want a rough estimate of the buydown amount, the six points per 1% interest formula referred to earlier is reasonably accurate.

TEMPORARY BUYDOWNS

When interest rates are high, temporary buydowns are very popular as a means of reducing a buyer's payments—sometimes substantially—in the early months or years of the loan. Many buyers feel they can grow into a larger payment but need time to get established. Temporary buydown plans take two forms: level payment and graduated payment.

Estimating temporary buydown:
1. yield/discount tables, or
2. calculate difference between unsubsidized and subsidized payments for the buydown period

Level Payment

This plan calls for an interest reduction that is constant throughout the buydown period.

> **Example:** Lender makes a 30-year loan for $65,000 at 15% interest.* Seller agrees to buydown the purchaser's interest rate to 13% for three years.

---

* A seemingly high interest rate was used in this example because it is when market interest rates are high that temporary buydowns are most frequently used.

Year	Note Interest Rate	Buydown %	Effective Interest Rate	Monthly Payment at 15%	Actual Monthly Payment	Monthly Subsidy	Annual Subsidy
1.	15%	2%	13%	$822	$719	$103	$1,236
2.	15%	2%	13%	$822	$719	$103	$1,236
3.	15%	2%	13%	$822	$719	$103	$1,236
4.	15%	-0-	15%	$822	$822	-0-	-0-
						TOTAL BUYDOWN	**$3,708**

Graduated Payment

A graduated buydown plan calls for the largest subsidies in the first year or two of the loan, with progressively smaller subsidies in each of the remaining years of the buydown period.

Example: Lender makes a 30-year loan for $70,000 at 14¾% interest. Builder agrees to buy-down purchaser's interest rate by 3% the first year, 2% the second year, and 1% the third year.

Year	Note Interest Rate	Buydown %	Effective Interest Rate	Monthly Payment at 15%	Actual Monthly Payment	Monthly Subsidy	Annual Subsidy
1.	14¾%	3%	11¾%	$871	$707	$164	$1,968
2.	14¾%	2%	12¾%	$871	$761	$110	$1,320
3.	14¾%	1%	13¾%	$871	$816	$55	$660
4.	14¾%	-0-	14¾%	$871	$871	-0-	-0-
						TOTAL BUYDOWN	**$3,948**

How to Compute Temporary Buydowns

To be 100% accurate, use the yield/discount tables previously mentioned or obtain a quote from your lender. As an alternative, temporary buydowns can be computed with considerable accuracy with the use of the interest rate factors in the back of this book or a hand calculator programmed to calculate amortized loan payments. The subsidy computation by this method is simple:

1. Compute the buyer's monthly principal and interest payment without the subsidy.
2. Determine the buyer's monthly payment with the subsidy.
3. Subtract the subsidized payment from the actual payment and multiply by twelve for the annual subsidy.

Example: Level Payment Buydown

$76,000   loan amount
16¼%   coupon (note) rate
14¼%   subsidized rate (five years)

1. Determine monthly principal and interest without subsidy.

$76,000	
× .0136494	16¼%, 30-year interest factor
$1,037.35	monthly payment without subsidy

2. Determine payment with subsidy.

$76,000	
× .0120469	14¼%, 30-year interest factor
$915.56	monthly payment with subsidy

161

3. Subtract subsidy payment from actual payment and multiply by 12 (months).

$1,037.35 actual payment
− 915.56 subsidized payment
$121.79 monthly subsidy
×12
$1,461.48 annual subsidy

4. With a level payment plan, the annual subsidy is constant for the entire buydown period, in the case of this example, five years. So, the final step is to multiply the annual subsidy by the number of years in the buydown plan.

$1,461.48 annual subsidy
×5 years in buydown plan
$7,307.40 total buydown (subsidy)

FNMA/FHLMC LIMITS ON BUYDOWNS

FNMA and FHLMC guidelines impose limits on discounts, buydowns, and other forms of contributions by sellers or other interested parties for the purpose of paying for financing costs, including prepaid interest and impounds for property taxes, hazard insurance and mortgage insurance. Contributions are limited to a percentage of the sales price or appraised value, whichever is less.

If the contributions exceed FNMA and FHLMC guidelines, the contribution amount must be deducted from the value or sales price before determining the maximum loan amount. (Exception: contributions by an employer or immediate family member are not subject to these limits.)

LTV Ratio	Maximum Contribution
2%	Investment property
3%	Principal residence and greater than 90% LTV
6%	Principal residence and 76% - 90% LTV
9%	Principal residence or second home and 75% or less

Example:

$100,000 sales price
105,000 appraised value
90,000 90% loan
6,000 maximum contribution

Any contribution in excess of $6,000 would be deducted from the sales price (or appraised value, if it were less), with a corresponding reduction in the loan amount.

Exercise No. 2

Buyer Johnson agrees to purchase Callahan's home for $110,000, subject to obtaining a 90%, 30-year conventional loan at 13¾%. A lender is located who is willing to make the loan but insists on 14¾%. The seller is willing to make a permanent buydown for the buyer.

1. Approximately how much would the buydown cost the seller?

2. What would Johnson's monthly payment be?

163

ADJUSTABLE-RATE MORTGAGE

ARM:
• interest on loan adjusted periodically based on changes in cost of money
• margin is added to index to ensure profit for lender

Perhaps the most popular and widely accepted form of alternate financing has been the adjustable-rate mortgage, universally referred to as an ARM. Because the ARM shifts the risk of interest rate fluctuations to the borrower, lenders normally charge a lower rate for an ARM than for a fixed-rate loan. Although the majority of borrowers prefer the security of a fixed rate (provided the rate is not too high), ARMs have maintained a place in the market despite comparatively low mortgage rates. While in mid-1985 half of the new single-family mortgages were ARMs, only 30% of all borrowers used ARMs in 1987. However, as interest rates began to edge up in mid-1988, interest in ARMs began to grow. Generally, as interest rates rise, so does ARM popularity.

WHAT IS AN ARM?

An ARM is a mortgage that permits the lender to periodically adjust the interest rate so it will accurately reflect fluctuations in the cost of money. ARMs are made primarily by banks and mortgage companies. Savings and loans make a similar type of loan called an Adjustable Mortgage Loan (AML). While there are some differences between ARMs and AMLs, on the whole they are alike and will be treated as such. From this point forward, reference to an ARM is meant to include the AML.

The ARM passes the risk of fluctuating interest levels on to borrowers, and this is where many lenders feel it belongs. With an ARM, it is the borrower who is affected by interest movements. If rates climb, the borrower's payments go up; if they decline, the payments go down.

HOW DOES AN ARM WORK?

The borrower's interest rate is determined initially by the cost of money at the time the loan is made. Once the rate has been set, it is tied to one of several widely recognized and published indexes, and future interest adjustments are based on the upward and downward movements of the index. An index is a statistical report that is a generally reliable indicator of the approximate change in the cost of money. There are several acceptable indexes that are published periodically and are easily available to lenders and borrowers alike. Examples include the indexes for the monthly average yield on three-year Treasury securities, the monthly average of the weekly auction rate on Treasury Bills, the national average mortgage contract rate for major lenders on purchases of previously occupied homes, and the cost-of-funds (based on the lenders' cost of funds).

At the time a loan is made, the index preferred by the lender is selected, and thereafter the loan interest rate will rise and fall with the rates reported by the index.

In the illustration below, you will notice the loan interest rate runs roughly parallel to the Treasury securities rate but always a few percentage points above it. Since the index is a reflection of the lender's cost of money, it is necessary to add a **margin** to the index to ensure sufficient income for administrative expenses and profit. In fact, between lenders who use the same index, it is the size of the margin that makes the difference in interest charges. Margins will usually vary from 2% to 3%. The index plus the margin equals the adjustable interest rate.

$$\begin{array}{r} \text{Index} \\ +\ \text{Margin} \\ \hline \text{Interest Rate} \end{array}$$

Example: Lender selects one-year Treasury securities index.

It is the index rate that fluctuates during the term of the loan and causes the borrower's interest rate to increase and decrease; the lender's margin remains constant. It should be noted that the lender has the option of increasing or leaving unchanged the borrower's interest rate when the selected index rises, but if the index falls, a reduction in the borrower's rate is mandatory.

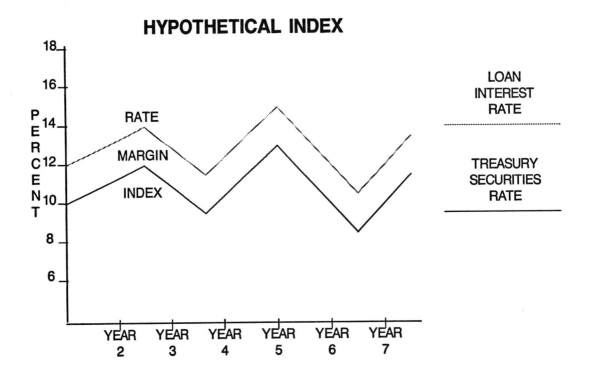

Terms, rate changes, and many other aspects of ARMs are regulated by several agencies, depending on the type of lender. National banks are regulated by the Comptroller of the Currency; the Office of Thrift Supervision regulates federally chartered savings and loan associations. Most other lenders are subject to the control of the Federal Reserve Board. Any applicable guidelines or requirements of FNMA, FHLMC, FHA and/or private mortgage insurers must be followed as well.

ELEMENTS OF AN ARM LOAN

There are several elements that give form to an adjustable-rate mortgage; they include:

1. the index
2. the margin
3. the rate adjustment period
4. the interest rate cap (if any)
5. the mortgage payment adjustment period
6. the mortgage payment cap (if any)
7. the negative amortization cap (if any)
8. a conversion option (if any)

Elements of ARMs:
- index
- margin
- rate adjustment period
- rate cap
- payment adjustment period
- payment cap
- negative amortization cap
- conversion option

Index

Most lenders try to use an index that is very responsive to economic fluctuations. Thus, most ARMs have either a Treasury security (usually the one-year) or the cost-of-funds as an index. (The cost-of-funds index is an average of the interest rates savings and loan associations pay for deposits and other borrowings with a certain range of maturities.) The cost-of-funds is a more stable index than the Treasury index. In other words, the cost-of-funds index doesn't rise as much as the Treasury index over the long term, but neither does it lower as much. In late 1987, FNMA began purchasing ARMs using the cost-of-funds index of the 11th District Federal Home Loan Bank, which is expected to make the cost-of-funds a more widely used index for ARMs. The Treasury index is more volatile, going both lower and higher than the cost-of-funds.

Margin

The margin is the difference between the index value and the interest charged to the borrower.

167

Example:

9.25%	current index value
2.00%	margin
11.25%	mortgage interest rate (note rate)

Rate Adjustment Period

This refers to the intervals at which a borrower's interest rate is adjusted, e.g., six months, one year, three years, etc. After referring to the rate movement in the selected index, the lender will notify the borrower in writing of any rate increase or decrease. Annual rate adjustments are most common.

Interest Rate Cap

Lenders use two different mechanisms to limit the magnitude of payment changes that occur with interest rate adjustments: interest rate caps and payment caps. If a limit is placed on the number of percentage points an interest rate can be increased during the term of a loan, it is said to be "capped." Today, most ARMs have caps of some kind.

Lenders, consumers, and congressional leaders alike are concerned with a phenomenon called payment shock. Payment shock results from increases in a borrower's monthly payments which, depending upon the amount and frequency of payment increases, as well as the borrower's income, may eliminate the borrower's ability to continue mortgage payments.

Teaser rates. When lenders discovered the residential adjustable-rate mortgage instrument in late 1979, they recognized an opportunity to increase earnings and to insulate themselves from the staggering losses caused by too many fixed-rate mortgages that were yielding less than the prevailing cost of money. As public acceptance of ARMs grew, so did the prevailing cost of money. As public acceptance of ARMs grew, so did the competition for mortgage loans— adjustable-rate mortgage loans.

Teaser rates:
- discounted first-year rates on ARMs
- danger of payment shock

To compete, lenders lowered the first-year interest rates on the loans they offered and introduced borrowers to discounts and buydowns. The low initial rates have subsequently been dubbed "**teaser rates**." Many lenders offered attractive teaser rates merely to enlarge their portfolio of ARMs. But since most ARMs were without interest rate caps prior to 1984, there were many instances where initial interest rates were increased by five to six percent. Clearly a crisis was developing. Consumers were losing confidence in the ARM and lenders were afraid they might experience unprecedented defaults, a phenomenon appropriately referred to as portfolio shock.

Industry leaders (especially the secondary market investors) began demanding more uniform ARM lending practices and a period of self-regulation began. To protect borrowers from payment shock and themselves from portfolio shock, lenders began imposing caps on their ARMs.

FNMA and FHLMC Caps

Both FNMA and FHLMC have guidelines relating to ARM interest rate caps. There are many different ARM plans, but as a general guideline, most ARMs purchased by FNMA are limited to rate increases of no more than 2% per year and no more than 6% over the life of the loan. FHLMC rate adjustment guidelines limit rate increases to 2% per year and 5% over the life of the loan. While these guidelines do not take the form of government regulations, most lenders include these or stricter caps in their loans.

The Federal Home Loan Mortgage Corporation (FHLMC) has developed a set of ARM guidelines that, in its opinion, sets parameters acceptable for "investment quality" ARM loans. Guidelines for periodic interest rate caps are illustrated below. In the column titled, "Illustrative Maximum Payment Increase," it is shown how a monthly payment would increase on a 30-year, $50,000 loan at a 12% interest rate with initial payments of $514.31.

Freddy Mac

Lifetime
Freddy Fanny
mac mae
5% 6%

FEDERAL HOME LOAN MORTGAGE CORPORATION
Guidelines for Periodic Interest Rate Caps

	Per Rate Adjustment Period	
Rate Adjustment Period	Maximum Rate Adjustment	Illustrative Maximum Payment Increase*
Less than six months	0.167%	$ 6.43
Six months or more, but less than one year	1.0%	$ 38.79
One year or more, but less than two years	2.0%	$ 78.13
Two years or more, but less than three years	3.0%	$117.91
Three years or more	5.0%	$198.53

* $50,000 loan, 30 years at 12% interest

Mortgage Payment Adjustment Period

This defines the intervals at which a borrower's actual principal and interest payments are changed; it is possible they will not coincide with the interest rate adjustments. There are two ways the rate and payment adjustments can be handled:

1. The lender can adjust the rate periodically as called for in the loan agreement and then adjust the mortgage payment to reflect the rate change.
2. The lender can adjust the rate more frequently than the mortgage payment is adjusted. For example, the loan agreement may call for interest rate adjustments every six months but changes in mortgage payments every three years.

If a borrower's principal and interest payment remains constant over a three-year period but the loan's interest rate has steadily increased or decreased during that time, then too little or too much interest will have been paid in the interim. When this happens, the difference is subtracted from or added to the loan balance. When unpaid interest is added to a loan balance, it is called **negative amortization**.

In an earlier illustration it was shown how a borrower's ARM payments would parallel a chosen index; but this is not always the case. If the loan agreement calls for regular rate changes but only occasional payment adjustments, the payments will not parallel the index at all, as indicated by the graph below.

Negative amortization:
• when interest rate is adjusted but payment is not
• interest shortfall is added to principal balance
• periodic reamortization and negative amortization caps to avoid excessive and dangerous negative amortization

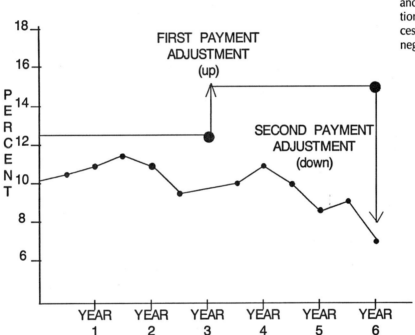

● Interest rate adjustments

Example: Borrower's interest payment is set at 12.5%, which includes a 2.5% margin and a beginning index value of 10%. The lender will use the six-month Treasury Bill index for biannual rate

171

adjustments, and the borrower's mortgage payment will be adjusted every three years.

You will notice that throughout the loan's first level payment period (years 1-3), rates were increased four times and decreased twice. Though it is impossible to say by looking at the graph, it would appear that the rate increases during this period were more sustained and, in at least one instance, sharper than the rate declines. There is a good likelihood that during this period there was more interest due than paid, resulting in negative amortization. In the second three years, with only two moderate and relatively brief exceptions, the index value declined. Any negative amortization that occurred during the first three years was probably more than offset by the surplus interest paid by the borrower during the second three years.

Mortgage Payment Cap

When there are no limits on the amount mortgage payments can be increased, borrowers are vulnerable to extreme changes in the cost of money. Inevitably, unrestricted increases would create hardships for many borrowers. Some lenders incorporate payment caps into their ARMs, usually in the area of 7½% annually. Other lenders only impose annual interest rate caps that work to limit payment increases. Still other lenders impose both rate and payment caps. Regardless of which policy a lender embraces, the objective is the same: to keep payment adjustments within a manageable range for the borrower.

Avoid Negative Amortization

There has been a dramatic movement away from negative amortization. This is probably because mortgage plans that provide for, or at least have a possibility of, negative amortization are not as attractive to borrowers as plans that do not permit negative amortization. In general, today's borrowers are better informed with respect to adjustable rate loans.

Many lenders see annual interest and payment hikes, with acceptable limitations, as a means of avoiding interest short-falls and the need for negative amortization. Still, interest fluctuations between 1983 and 1989 were minor compared to the fluctuations between 1981 and 1982. By establishing rate and payments caps (during 1984), lenders began sharing more of the risk of increased interest rates than they did in the preceding three years. But if interest rates reach the high pre-1983 levels, the rate and payment caps in use today might prove too expensive for lenders, and that might signal the return of negative amortization as a means of keeping bor-rowers' payments at manageable levels.

Exercise No. 3

Borrower Jones secures a 30-year ARM loan of $92,000. The initial interest rate is 10%. The loan agreement calls for annual interest rate and payment adjustments, with a 7½% annual payment cap. After the first year, the overall interest rate is adjusted to 12%. Use the interest rate factors and loan progress charts in the appendices.

1. **What is the adjusted principal and interest payment after the first year?**

2. **Will there be an interest shortfall in year 2? If so, how much each month?**

Negative Amortization Cap

Negative amortization has to be watched carefully or it could develop into an unmanageable problem for both the homeowner and the lender. The various lenders handle the problem in different ways.

Negative amortization becomes more important at higher initial loan-to-value ratios. The current industry practice is to set a limit of between 110%-125% of the initial loan balance. Another approach is to set the limit at 100% of the initial appraised value. This allows households that make larger downpayments to have lower payments for a longer period of time. If negative amortization reaches the ceiling, the loan must be recast and further negative amortization is prohibited.

Bear in mind that negative amortization ceilings could be reached only if the interest rate increased several percentage points a year, for a number of years, without relief. The payment caps previously mentioned allow payment increases that are substantial enough to prevent negative amortization in most cases. Negative amortization is most likely to occur where there are frequent rate changes (e.g., every six months) and infrequent payment adjustments (e.g., every three years).

Periodic reamortization. As mentioned just above, many ARM loans with a possibility of negative amortization have a maximum cap for the amount of negative amortization. If the cap is reached, the loan payments are reamortized to a level sufficient to pay off the loan over the remaining term, without regard to any payment cap that might otherwise apply. Some ARMs provide for periodic reamortization of the loan, instead of or in addition to setting maximum caps for negative amortization. For example, the loan agreement might provide that every fifth year the monthly payment will be adjusted, with no payment cap, so that the new payments fully amortize the loan balance over its remaining term. These reamortizations are in addition to the normal reamortization and new payment levels made in connection with the regularly scheduled rate and/or payment adjustments.

Example: Original loan of $65,000 at 12¾% (10% index value + 2¾% margin). During the first five years overall rate increases have exceeded payment adjustments, resulting in negative amortization of $2,250. The loan balance is $67,250. Index value at the fifth year is 12¼%; the margin remains constant at 2¾% for an adjusted rate of 15%.

$67,250	adjusted loan balance
15%	adjusted interest rate
25 years	remaining term on original 30-year loan

To determine the reamortized payment, refer to the principal and interest factors in the appendix.

$67,250	adjusted loan balance
×.0128084	factor for 15%, 25-year loan
$861.36	reamortized payment

This periodic reamortization reduces the possibility of a large buildup in the homeowner's debt, which would otherwise have to be paid in the form of a balloon payment when the house is sold or the loan becomes due.

New ARM Products

One of the most popular recent innovations in ARM loans is the introduction of a conversion option. A "convertible ARM" is one in which the borrower has the right to convert from an adjustable-rate loan to a fixed-rate loan. ARMs with a conversion option normally include the following:

- a higher interest rate (often both the initial rate and the converted rate are higher);

Convertible ARMs:
- option to convert to fixed-rate loan
- conversion at specified times
- fee for conversion
- both ARM rate and fixed rate may be higher

- a limited time to convert (e.g., between the first and fifth year); and
- a conversion fee (typically about 1%).

For example, a FNMA convertible ARM program may be converted between the 13th and 60th month for a $250 processing fee paid to the lender. The initial rate on the ARM loan is the same as for other FNMA ARMs, but if converted, the fixed rate is ⅛% higher than the standard fixed rate at the time of conversion.

ARM LOAN-TO-VALUES

ARM LTVs:
- owner occupancy
- 90% LTV

ARMs with loan to value ratios of 80%, 90%, and 95% are available. However, higher LTV loans are often subject to some restrictions. For example, many lenders refuse to make 90% or 95% ARM loans if there is a possibility of negative amortization. In most cases, borrowers seeking 90% or 95% ARMs will be required to occupy the property being purchased. FNMA and FHLMC require owner occupancy for all ARMs. Owner-occupants are considered better risks than nonoccupant borrowers.

FHLMC and FNMA LTV Guidelines for ARMs

FNMA and FHLMC have established stricter LTV guidelines for ARMs than for fixed-rate loans. Loan-to-value ratios may not exceed 90% for ARMs purchased by FNMA and FHLMC. The lower loan-to-value requirements are due to the potential risk from increasing payments when the interest rate is adjusted.

DISCOUNTS AND SUBSIDY BUYDOWNS ON ARMS

Some ARMs have initial interest rate discounts or subsidy buydowns. A discounted rate, in this context, means the borrower pays less than the note rate (index rate plus margin) prior to the first interest rate adjustment. The discounted rate is frequently referred to as a teaser rate. Loans with a subsidy buydown reduce the borrower's initial rate by payment of funds in advance. The subsidy buydown is usually paid by the seller. The probability that payment shock will occur is increased, because a payment increase after the first adjustment period is almost inevitable, even if there has been no increase in the value of the index in the interim.

Of course, an increase in the index during this same period would make the payment shock even greater.

Moreover, initial rate discounts and subsidy buydowns have been used to increase the attractiveness of ARMs for some borrowers who have trouble qualifying for financing at higher rates. Thus, these loans are inherently more risky than most other types of loans, and lenders are beginning to underwrite them more conservatively.

For ARMs with a 2% annual interest rate adjustment cap and an LTV over 80%, FHLMC requires the borrower to be qualified on the basis of payments made on the mortgage at the initial rate plus 2% (the maximum second-year mortgage rate). For example, a borrower seeking an ARM loan with an initial interest rate of 9% would have to qualify at an 11% interest rate (initial rate plus 2%).

Discounts and buydowns on ARMs:
- FHLMC requires qualifying at teaser rate + 2% if LTV over 80%

FNMA:
- no buydowns on ARMs
- other contributions limited to 2% if LTV over 90%, 6% if LTV over 75%

HOUSING EXPENSE-TO-INCOME RATIOS ON ARMS

Certain ARMs contain features that increase the likelihood that housing expense-to-income ratios will increase to dangerous levels after the first rate adjustment (expense-to-

Lower housing expense-to-income ratios may be required if:
1. no rate or payment caps
2. buydown over 2%

income ratios are covered in *Qualifying The Buyer,* Chapter 13.). ARMs with no rate or payment caps have the potential for large increases in the ratios. Likewise, loans with rate discounts or subsidy buydowns that exceed 2% add to the chances of significant payment shock. When ARMs are made with these features, secondary market investors and many private mortgage insurance companies are insisting that the traditional housing expense-to-gross income and total monthly debt payment-to-income ratios of 28% and 36% be disregarded in favor of lower, more conservative ratios.

The FHLMC recommends a 25% housing expense-to-income ratio, and a 33% total monthly debt service-to-income ratio, for ARM loans with any of the following features:

FHLMC: 25%/33% if:
1. no caps or caps outside guidelines
2. discount or buydown over 2%
3. rate cap over 1% or payment cap over 7½% per year

1) rate or payment cap outside FHLMC guidelines, or no caps;
2) discount or subsidy buydown exceeds 2%;
3) rate cap over 1% or payment cap over 7½%; or
4) difference between rate and payment adjustment periods exceeds three years, and the payment cap does not meet FHLMC guidelines.

APPRAISALS ON PROPERTIES SECURED BY ARMS

Appraisals for ARM loans are reviewed more carefully by lenders. Attempt to identify and net out effect of discounts, buydowns, or other favorable financing

Because ARMs introduce additional elements of risk to mortgage lending, a greater number of lenders are adhering more strictly to underwriting guidelines. This applies in particular to the lender's concern for the validity of the appraisal.

Today lenders insist that the appraisal report accurately reflect an estimate of the true value of the property, uninfluenced by discount rates, subsidy buydowns or other financing concessions. Such concessions must be clearly identified, preferably in the appraisal report, and their effect on the value of the property must be fully explained. When underwriting ARMs, the underwriter will carefully review the appraisal report to determine if the appraiser has performed this analysis satisfactorily. If not, the appraisal shall be considered deficient. As much as possible, underwriters attempt to net the value of the favorable financing out of the appraised value in determining the maximum loan for a given loan-to-value ratio.

ARM STANDARDIZATION AND DISCLOSURE

Standardization

The widespread acceptance of ARMs represents a major evolutionary phase in the housing industry. Initially, the estimated 200-plus adjustable-rate plans fueled sharp criticism. Customers were understandably confused by the proliferation of ARM programs. The threat of government regulation, increased dangers of foreclosure, and the refusal of the secondary market to buy ARMs caused lenders to standardize many of their ARM programs.

Uniform ARM underwriting standards have since been adopted and the secondary market agencies are now purchasing ARMs on a large-scale basis. While even a few years ago lenders were underwriting loans on the basis of their own standards and were largely keeping them in portfolio, lenders are currently following secondary market guidelines and reselling ARMs just as they do fixed-rate loans.

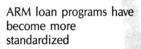

ARM loan programs have become more standardized

Disclosure

Lenders offering adjustable-rate mortgages must comply with the Federal Reserve's guidelines under Regulation Z of the Truth-in-Lending Act requiring certain disclosures to be made to ARM borrowers. These rules require a **general brochure** to be given borrowers, **certain specific disclosures** to be made if relevant to the particular ARM program and establish guidelines for calculating and disclosing the **annual percentage rate (APR)**. Disclosures must be provided to the borrower when the loan application is made or before payment of any nonrefundable fee, whichever occurs first.

A lender may comply with the requirement to provide a general informational brochure on adjustable-rate loans by giving the loan applicant the *Consumer Handbook on Adjustable Rate Mortgages*, which has been prepared by the Federal Reserve and the Federal Home Loan Bank Board. The following disclosures must be made, if appropriate to the individual loan program applied for:

ARM disclosures:
1. index
2. where to find index
3. how rate and payment determined
4. advice to ask about margin and rate
5. if initial rate is discounted
6. rate and payment adjustment caps
7. if caps may cause negative amortization
8. any call provision
9. information regarding adjustment notices
10. availability of disclosures for other ARM plans
11. maximum rate and payment
12. initial rate and payment

1) the index used to determine the interest rate;
2) where the borrower may find the index;
3) an explanation of how the interest rate and payment will be determined;
4) a suggestion that the borrower ask the lender about the current margin and interest rate;
5) if the initial rate is discounted, a disclosure of that fact and a suggestion that the borrower inquire as to the amount of the discount;
6) the interest and payment adjustment periods and any rate and payment caps;
7) a statement that rate and payment caps may result in negative amortization;
8) a statement that the loan has a demand or "call" provision;
9) a description of the information that will be contained in the adjustment notice and when such notices will be provided;
10) a statement that disclosure forms are available for the lender's other ARM loan programs;
11) the maximum interest rate and payment; and,
12) the initial interest rate and payment.

The lender must give the borrower advance notice of any change in payment, interest rate, index or loan balance. These disclosures must be provided at least 25, but not more than 120, days before the new payment level takes effect. The lender must also give the borrower an example, based on a $10,000 loan, showing how the payments and loan balance would have been affected by changes in the index to be used.

Regulation Z disclosures regarding the annual percentage rate cannot be made based solely on an ARM's initial rate; they must be based on the initial rate plus the lender's margin.

Regulation Z APR disclosures must be based on initial rate + margin

Example:

> 30-year mortgage
> 9% initial rate
> 10% six-month Treasury Bill index rate
> 2% margin

> The disclosure of the APR should reflect a composite annual percentage rate based on 9% for one year and 12% for 29 years. The payment schedule should reflect 12 payments at 9% and 348 payments at 12%.

The guidelines are an effort to ensure that when mortgage rates are adjusted, borrowers are not faced with unexpectedly large increases in their payments because their disclosure forms were based only on a discounted initial rate and not also on the interest rate index used to set future payments.

WHAT YOU NEED TO KNOW ABOUT ARMS

As an agent, you must always be prepared to answer buyers' and sellers' questions. You are expected to be knowledgeable. When it comes to ARM financing, it would be reasonable to expect the following questions:

1. What will my interest rate be?
It is usually not necessary to break the rate down into index and margin. The buyer is concerned only with the total. Monitor local rates; they change regularly.

Agent needs to know:
1. interest rate
2. when rate changes
3. when payment
   changes
4. rate caps?
5. payment caps?
6. possibility of negative
   amortization?
7. conversion option?

2. How often will my interest rate change?

The rate adjustments will be spelled out in the loan agreement. Depending on lender preference (index used), they will occur every six months, annually, every three years, or every five years. The six-month and one-year intervals are most common. In order to be specific, you have to know your lenders and their policies.

3. How often will my payment change?

Again, in order to give an accurate answer, you have to be familiar with the policies of the local lenders. The majority of lenders have shown a preference for simultaneous rate and payment changes, but there are many exceptions.

4. Is there any limit to how much my interest rate can be increased?

Most ARMs have interest rate caps. The most common life-of-the-loan caps are the 5% and 6% caps imposed by FHLMC and FNMA. Annual interest rate caps are usually between 1% and 2%.

5. Is there any limit to how much my payment can be increased at any one time?

Some ARMs have payment caps, while others keep payment hikes under control with interest rate caps. Where payment caps exist, they are usually limited to 7½%-15% of the payment amount or the equivalent of 1%-2% interest rate change.

6. What is the probability of runaway negative amortization?

The answer is: remote to nonexistent. Interest rate caps, negative amortization caps, and reamortization requirements protect borrower and lender in this regard. But the best protection is undoubtedly the changing nature of the money market itself. Interest rates rise and fall; they always have. A borrower's rate will be increased at one interval and reduced at another. If at one point there is negative amortization because the interest due exceeded interest paid, there is an excellent chance that not long afterwards index declines will result in the opposite: accelerated amortization. This up and down pattern, though always unpredictable, continues throughout the life of the loan.

7. *Can it be converted to a fixed-rate loan?*

Many ARM's now contain a conversion option which permits the borrower to convert to a fixed-rate loan, for a fee at certain periods or points in the loan term. ARMs with a conversion option often have higher interest rates than those without.

THE GROWTH EQUITY MORTGAGE (GEM)

Sometimes called a building equity mortgage (BEM) or rapidly amortizing mortgage (RAM), the GEM solves many of the problems that have limited the appeal of ARMs. Still, today it enjoys only limited public acceptance.

Though there are numerous variations of the growth equity mortgage, all of them share the following characteristics:

GEM:
- fixed interest rate
- initial payment based on 30-year amortization
- annual increases in payment (3% - 5%)
- quick reduction of principal
- pay off in 11-17 years

- the interest rate is fixed over the life of the loan;
- first year payments of principal and interest are based on a 30-year term;
- the borrower's payments are increased at specified intervals (usually annually) for all or a portion of the life of the loan;
- since the interest rate is fixed, 100% of the annual payment increases are used to reduce the principal balance.

DETERMINING ANNUAL PAYMENT ADJUSTMENTS

There are any number of annual payment adjustment plans, but by far the most popular method is to increase the payments by a fixed percentage—typically 3% or 5%.

> **Example:** $86,000 loan at 10.5% (fixed rate) based on a 30-year term. Payments to be increased 3% annually.

$$\begin{array}{r} \$86,000 \\ \times .0089610 \\ \hline \$770.65 \end{array}$$ 10¼%, 30-year factor

initial monthly payment

$842.11 × 1.03
year 4 payment

$817.58 × 1.03
year 3 payment

$793.77 × 1.03
year 2 payment

$770.65 × 1.03
year 1 payment

In the example above, the borrower's payments are increased by 3% each year, and the entire increase is always applied to the loan balance.

EQUITY BUILDS UP QUICKLY

Because payment increases are used to reduce the mortgage debt, a borrower will pay off a GEM much sooner than a 30-year fixed-rate mortgage. If payments are increased 3% per year on a 15% loan, the entire debt will be retired in 13 years and 7 months; with 5% annual increases, the same loan will pay off in just 11 years and 4 months. A GEM's repayment term is dependent on the interest rate and the magnitude of the annual payment increases. Most GEMs pay off in 11 to 17 years. The following graph demonstrates the difference between the repayment patterns of a GEM and a 30-year fixed-rate mortgage.

It is clearly illustrated by the graph below that GEM payments become substantially higher than the level fixed-

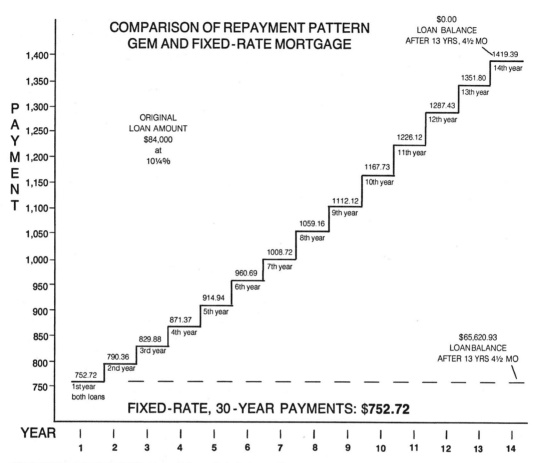

COMPARISON OF REPAYMENT PATTERN
GEM AND FIXED-RATE MORTGAGE

$0.00
LOAN BALANCE
AFTER 13 YRS, 4½ MO

ORIGINAL
LOAN AMOUNT
$84,000
at
10¼%

$65,620.93
LOAN BALANCE
AFTER 13 YRS 4½ MO

FIXED-RATE, 30-YEAR PAYMENTS: **$752.72**

* Fixed-rate loan payments based on 30-year amortization, not including taxes and insurance.
  GEM payments based on 30-year amortization with 5% annual increases.

rate payments. In the past, this annual rate of increase was well below the inflationary trends and GEM payment increases did not rise as fast as borrowers' incomes. Borrowers had few difficulties adjusting to payment hikes, and furthermore, to many borrowers the payment increase drawback was insignificant when weighed against the remarkable advantage of accelerated equity accumulation. A 30-year, fixed-rate mortgage shows a balance of $65,620.93 after thirteen years and

185

four and a half months; at the end of the same period, the GEM loan is paid in full. At current low rates of inflation, the GEM payment increases do not look so attractive. The primary advantages of GEMs, fast amortization and predictable payments, are also available with the more popular level payment 15-year, fixed-rate loans (discussed in Chapter 7).

Payments Are Predictable

The borrower's payments will increase annually, but unlike adjustable-rate mortgages that are tied to an index, the amount of the annual increase is known at the outset of the loan.

No Negative Amortization

To the contrary, there is accelerated positive amortization.

Reduced Interest Costs

A GEM borrower will pay less than half the interest he or she would pay with a traditional 30-year, fixed-rate mortgage. By referring to the "Comparison of Repayment Pattern" chart, you can see that after 13 years and 4½ months the borrower will have paid only $18,379.07 in principal on the 30-year, fixed-rate mortgage. The balance of the $120,811.56 in payments will have been applied to interest, with much more interest to be paid before the loan's 30-year term is over. On the other hand, interest on a GEM loan is much less and the interest portion of each succeeding payment declines as rapidly as the loan balance itself.

Simplicity of Loan

In contrast to ARMs, the GEM is easy to understand and explain. There is little doubt buyers are reluctant to commit to a major debt, like a home loan, if they do not understand it.

Lower Than Market Interest Rate

Very often lenders are willing to make GEM loans at lower than market rates because they will recapture the principal so quickly. Recaptured principal can be reinvested at competitive market rates. The lower than market rate makes it easier to qualify for the loan.

REDUCTION OPTION MORTGAGE

A reduction option loan is a fixed-rate loan that gives the borrower a limited opportunity to reduce the interest rate without paying refinancing costs. The FHLMC-approved program is a 30-year, fixed-rate loan with the option to reduce the interest rate once between the 13th and 59th month of the life of the loan. Market interest rates must decline at least 2% before the borrower may exercise the option to reduce the interest rate on the loan.

The cost to reduce the interest rate would be $100, plus .25% of the original loan amount. This cost is substantially lower than the one to two points that would normally be charged to refinance. On a $100,000 loan, it would cost $350 to reduce the interest rate of a reduction option loan, as opposed to $1,000 to $2,000 for a loan without the reduction option. Other costs of refinancing, such as appraisal and credit check, are also avoided.

Interest rates for reduction option loans are somewhat higher, approximately 0.125% higher than for fixed-rate loans without the reduction option.

Exercise No. 4

A borrower seeks an $82,000 GEM loan. He locates a lender who is willing to make the loan at 10%, with payments based on a 30-year term. The borrower's payments will increase 3% annually.

1. What is the buyer's initial mortgage payment?

719.61

chart

page 404

2. What is his payment at the beginning of the second year? The third year? The fourth year?

X 103   X 103   X 103

BI-WEEKLY LOANS

A bi-weekly loan is a fixed-rate mortgage set up in a fashion similar to a standard 30-year conventional loan. Both interest rate and payments are fixed. However, payments are made every two weeks instead of every month. Each payment is equal to half of what the monthly payment would be for a fully amortized 30-year, fixed-rate loan of the same amount at the same interest rate.

Bi-weekly loans offer significant savings in interest over the life of the loan. For example, if a $70,000 loan at an interest rate of 10.5% is paid on a bi-weekly schedule, instead of a monthly payment plan, the borrower would save approximately $60,000 in interest. The main reason for the interest savings is that since payments are made every two weeks (not twice a month), 26 payments are made each year, so that the equivalent of an extra monthly payment is made each year. Bi-weekly loans are usually fully paid off in approximately 20 to 21 years, instead of 30 years.

Example:

$70,000 loan, 10.5% fixed rate, 30-year amortization

Schedule	Payment	# of Payments	Total Amount Paid
Monthly	$640.32	360	$230,515.20
Bi-weekly	$320.21	532	$170,325.39

The bi-weekly loan would pay off in about 20½ years, with total interest payments of approximately $60,189.81 less than the monthly payment schedule.

NOTE: In this example, bi-weekly payments are slightly more than one-half the monthly payment in order to avoid a partial final payment.

Although bi-weekly loans have been available for some time, especially in the Northeast and Midwest, they have not been widely promoted by lenders because of the increased servicing costs associated with handling 26 payments instead of 12 payments per year. However, FNMA began purchasing bi-weekly loans in February 1988. With FNMA available as purchaser for the loans, lenders will be relieved of the burden of packaging bi-weekly mortgages for private investors and that may lead to some growth in their popularity. Loans with a payment schedule that coincides with the way many people are paid would seem to have some natural appeal.

REVERSE MORTGAGES
(or Home Equity Conversion Mortgages)

Reverse equity mortgages are designed to help elderly homeowners achieve financial security by converting their home equity into cash. A reverse mortgage borrower must be over age 62 and own a home with little or no outstanding mortgage.

Typically the homeowner mortgages his or her home to a bank or savings and loan association, and in return receives a monthly check from the lender. The amount of the monthly payment depends on the appraised value of the home, the age of the homeowner, the length of the loan, when the loan must be repaid, and the amount of interest charged.

The most basic RM is the **term loan**, which provides monthly advances for a fixed period of time (generally three to 12 years). At the end of the period, all principal advances plus interest are due. Term loans have had limited success because borrowers fear having to sell their home at the end of the term.

The **split term** loan is similar to the basic term, except that it does not have to be repaid until the borrower moves, dies, or sells the house. This type of RM provides more peace of mind for the borrower.

Under a **tenure** loan, the lender makes monthly payments only as long as the borrower occupies the house as a principal residence. Tenure payments are generally lower than other types of RMs because of the uncertainty as to when the mortgage will be repaid.

The **line of credit** loan is slightly different from the other RMs in that payments are not made on a regular basis. The borrower withdraws funds whenever necessary up to a maximum number of times. Repayment is deferred until the borrower dies, sells or moves.

CHAPTER SUMMARY

Alternate financing programs were developed in the early 1980's to meet the twin challenges of higher home prices and higher interest rates, which made it more difficult for buyers to qualify for home loans. To make it easier for the buyer to qualify, many alternate financing plans involve the payment of discount points or temporary or permanent buydowns to reduce the buyer's interest rate and payments, either for the entire term or for the initial period of the loan term. Out of the many programs introduced, only a few (primarily various ARM loan programs) have achieved continued acceptance and popularity with consumers. Buyers contemplating applying for ARM loans should be aware of and consider the following important elements: the lender's index for adjusting the interest rate, the lender's margin above the index, rate and payment adjustment periods, whether there are any periodic or lifetime caps on interest rate and payments, the possibility of negative amortization, and whether there is an option to convert to a fixed-rate loan.

Chapter 10
GOVERNMENT FINANCING – FHA-INSURED LOANS

The Federal Housing Administration, or the FHA, was created by Congress in 1934 as part of the National Housing Act. The purpose of the Act, and of the FHA, was to generate new jobs through increased construction activity, to exert a stabilizing influence on the mortgage market, and to promote the financing, repair, improvement and sale of real estate nationwide.

FHA INSURES LOANS

Today, the FHA is part of the Department of Housing and Urban Development (HUD); its primary function is to insure loans. Approved lenders are insured against losses caused by borrower defaults on FHA-insured loans. The FHA does not build homes or make loans.

FHA:
- insures loans through Mutual Mortgage Insurance Plan
- does not make loans or build homes

The FHA is a giant federal insurance agency. Its insurance program is called the Mutual Mortgage Insurance Plan. Under the plan, lenders who have been approved by the FHA to make insured loans either submit applications from prospective borrowers to the local FHA office for approval or, if authorized by the FHA to do so, perform the underwriting functions themselves (review of appraisal, mortgage credit examination, etc.). Lenders who are authorized by the FHA to fully underwrite their own FHA loan applications are called "direct endorsers." Direct endorsers are responsible for the entire mortgage process, from application through closing. When a direct endorser has approved and closed a loan, the application for mortgage insurance is submitted to FHA. Over

Direct endorsers: lenders approved by FHA to handle entire underwriting process for FHA loans half of all FHA loans are closed under the direct endorsement program.

FHA ASSUMES LIABILITY

FHA:
• insures lenders for full amount of (default) loss
• regulates conditions and terms of loan

As the insurer, FHA incurs full liability for losses resulting from default and property foreclosure. In turn, FHA regulates many of the conditions of the loan. FHA regulations have the force and effect of law; these regulations and FHA procedures and practices have done much to shape the face of the real estate lending industry today.

FHA LOANS DISTINGUISHED FROM CONVENTIONAL LOANS

FHA vs. conventional:
1. no second mortgage for any part of minimum downpayment
2. buyer must pay own reserves
3. mortgage insurance required on all loans
4. assumable
5. no prepayment charges

FHA loans have a number of features which distinguish them from conventional loans. The most significant differences are listed below.

1. **No secondary financing for the downpayment.** The FHA minimum downpayment for a particular loan must be paid by the borrower in cash. The buyer may not resort to secondary financing from the seller or another lender to borrow any portion of the minimum downpayment or other closing costs. Secondary financing is permitted for part of the purchase price (other than the downpayment) if certain conditions are met. However, the total amount financed, including the FHA-insured loan and the second loan, may not exceed the maximum allowable FHA loan.

   Example: If the maximum allowable loan were $75,000, the buyer could finance that through a $75,000 FHA-insured loan or partially through an FHA-insured loan and partially through a second mortgage to another lender (e.g., a $60,000 FHA loan and a $15,000 second mortgage to the seller).

However, the buyer would still have to make the minimum required downpayment in cash.

FHA requirements governing secondary financing in conjunction with FHA-insured loans are discussed in more detail later in this chapter.

2. **Buyer must pay own impounds (reserves).** The prepayable reserves on FHA loans for property taxes and homeowners' insurance must be paid by the borrower. With VA loans and many conventional loans, the seller is permitted to pay all of the buyer's settlement costs, including the prepaid reserves, if the seller is willing to do so. Tax and insurance reserves are referred to by several different terms, including impounds, prepaid items and prepayable expenses.

3. **Mortgage insurance (MIP) is required on all loans.** Regardless of the size of the downpayment, mortgage insurance is required on all FHA loans. Conventional loans do not usually call for mortgage insurance (PMI) unless the loan-to-value ratio exceeds 80%.

4. **FHA loans are assumable.** Most conventional security instruments (mortgages and deeds of trust) contain an alienation clause, which grants the lender certain rights if the property is sold before the loan is paid off. Most alienation clauses give the lender the election of demanding the loan be paid in full when the property is sold or of approving the transfer and assumption of the loan by the new buyer. The lender's consent to the transfer and assumption may be contingent upon a new loan agreement at a higher interest rate and payment of an assumption fee. Alienation clauses which call for full payment of the loan at the time of sale are commonly known as "due-on-sale" clauses. FHA and VA loans do not contain due-on-sale clauses. Therefore, FHA loans, with the exception of government subsidized Section 235 loans, are

assumable. (Section 235 loans may only be assumed by buyers who are also eligible for the 235 program.)

NOTE: While FHA loans are assumable, a credit check of the new borrower is required in some cases when assuming FHA loans endorsed after December 1, 1986:

FHA assumption requires credit check:
1. first 12 months of owner-occupant loan
2. first 24 months of nonowner-occupant loan

1) if the original borrower was an owner-occupant, a credit check is required for any assumption within the first 12 months after the loan is closed; and

2) if the original borrower was an investor, a credit check is required for any assumption within the first 24 months after closing.

5. **No prepayment charges.** Many conventional loans contain prepayment provisions imposing charges if the borrower pays off the loan within the first few years of origination. These charges can be quite substantial. For example, a prepayment clause may provide that if the borrower pays off the loan within five years of origination, a charge equal to six months' interest on the original amount will be imposed. FHA and VA loans do not contain prepayment clauses; they may be paid off at any time without additional charges.

INTEREST RATES AND DISCOUNT POINTS ON FHA LOANS

• FHA interst rates are freely negotiable
• buyer may pay discount

Up until 1983, the FHA set maximum allowable interest rates (usually below the prevailing conventional mortgage rates) as well as prohibiting the borrower from paying any discount points (other than the 1% loan fee). Any discount points charged by the lender had to be paid by the seller. Currently, there is no mandatory maximum interest rate—the rate on an FHA loan can be any rate agreed upon by the borrower and lender. Furthermore, if points are charged by the lender in connection with the loan, the points may be paid by the seller, the buyer, or both, depending on the agreement of the parties. FHA rates may still be lower than conventional rates due to the perceived lower risks of a government-insured loan, and points are often paid by the seller.

The legislation removing limits on interest rates and points to be paid by FHA borrowers does not apply to VA loans. The Veterans Administration still sets maximum interest rates and prohibits the borrower from paying any points other than a one-percent loan fee and a small funding fee.

CALCULATING THE FHA PAYMENT

The FHA principal and interest payments are calculated like any other real estate loan: determine the loan amount and multiply it by the appropriate interest rate factor in the back of this book. The feature which distinguishes FHA mortgage payments from conventional and VA mortgage payments is inclusion of the Mutual Mortgage Insurance premium, more popularly referred to as the MIP or the mortgage insurance premium.

The MIP

For most FHA programs, the FHA Mutual Mortgage Insurance premium is a one-time premium. It may be paid in cash at closing or financed over the term of the loan. The amount of the premium varies depending upon both the term of the loan and whether the premium is to be paid in cash at closing or financed. Premiums are smaller for shorter term loans and for premiums paid in cash.

MIP one-time premium may be:
- fully financed, or
- fully paid in cash at closing

To reduce the number of possible factors involved and to simplify calculating the MIP, the premium must be completely paid in cash or completely financed. Paying part in cash at closing and financing the rest is not permitted. The factors, then, are based upon the term of the loan with either 100% financing or 0% financing.

	FHA MIP FACTORS BASED ON TERM OF LOAN			
Portion of MIP Financed	Less Than 18 Years	18 to 22 Years	23 to 25 Years	More Than 25 Years
100%	.02400	.03000	.03600	.03800
0%	.02344	.02913	.03475	.03661

In Chapter 8 it was noted that the 15-year mortgage was gaining popularity. An added incentive for obtaining a 15-year mortgage is provided by the lower MIP factor. The financed MIP for a $70,000, 15-year mortgage is $1,680, compared to $2,660 for its 30-year counterpart.

Paying the MIP in Cash. If the MIP is paid in cash at closing, the premium for a 30-year loan is equal to 3.661% of the loan amount; if financed, the premium would be 3.8% for a 30-year loan.

Example:

$80,000   30-year loan
× .03661   factor for MIP paid at closing
$2,928.80   one-time MIP (not financed)

If the premium is paid in cash at closing, it may be paid by the borrower or the seller.

Financing the MIP. If the MIP is financed, the premium charge is 3.8% of the loan amount for a 30-year loan. The amount of the premium is added to the loan to find the total amount financed. Monthly payments are then calculated to pay off the loan, including the MIP, according to the particular loan program. If the MIP is financed, it must be paid by the borrower.

Example:

$80,000	30-year loan
× .038	MIP factor if premium is financed
$3,040	one-time MIP

$80,000	loan amount without MIP
+ 3,040	MIP premium
$83,040	total amount financed

Financed MIP is added to loan amount. Total financing may exceed FHA maximum loan amount by the amount of the MIP.

When the MIP is financed, the total amount financed may then exceed what would otherwise be the FHA maximum loan by the amount of the MIP. If, as shown in the preceding example, the maximum FHA loan permitted in the transaction is $80,000, the total amount financed may exceed the $80,000 maximum by the amount of the $3,040 MIP. The total amount financed would then be $83,040.

The loan fee paid by the borrower is based only on the maximum loan amount, not including the MIP. In the example above, the loan fee would be $800 (.01 × $80,000 = $800). The discount points, though, are based on the total amount financed, including the MIP. If the transaction included three points to be paid by the seller, the seller would pay $2,491.20 (.03 × $83,040 = $2,491.20).

If the MIP is financed it may affect how the total financing is rounded off. There is no universal practice regarding rounding off FHA loan amounts, but the rounding off procedure is often based in part on whether the MIP is financed. Many lenders round FHA loans down to the next lowest fifty dollars.

Example:

$76,452.50	maximum loan amount from LTV calculations based on acquisition cost without MIP

$76,450.00   loan amount, rounded down to next lowest $50 increment

If the MIP is financed, many lenders round down to the nearest dollar, rather than the next lowest $50 increment. It is, however, a common practice to first calculate the loan amount without the MIP, rounded down to the next lowest $50 increment, and then add on the financed MIP, rounded down to the nearest dollar.

Example:

$76,450.00   loan amount, rounded down to nearest $50 increment

× .038   financed MIP factor

$2,905.10   MIP

$76,450.00   loan amount without MIP

+ 2,905.10   MIP premium

$79,355.10   total amount financed

$79,355.00   total amount financed, rounded down to nearest dollar

MIP Assumption. There is often confusion surrounding the MIP when an FHA loan with a financed MIP is assumed by a buyer. The seller often expects to receive a refund of the unearned MIP. However, if the MIP is financed (as is the usual case), there is no refund when the loan is assumed. The buyer, in effect, assumes the obligation of paying off the financed MIP as well as the seller's loan. (If the loan is paid off or refinanced, there is a refund of the unearned MIP, based upon a 12-year schedule and the FHA loss experience).

This means that the seller sometimes receives less money at closing than he or she expects.

Example:

$85,000   sales price
$80,000   loan without MIP
$83,040   loan with MIP
  $1,040   of MIP has been earned at
           time of sale

If the loan is assumed by the buyer, the buyer assumes the MIP as well as the loan and the seller does not receive a refund of the unearned MIP.

$85,000   sales price
− 82,000   loan with MIP assumed by buyer
  $3,000   to seller

If the loan is paid off, the seller would receive a refund of the $2,000 unearned MIP.

$85,000   sales price
− 82,000   loan with MIP
   3,000
+ 2,000   refund of unearned MIP
$ 5,000   to seller

Exercise No.1

The proposed FHA loan is for $73,700 at an interest rate of 13½% and a term of 30 years.

1. What would the borrower's monthly payments be if the entire MIP were paid in cash at closing?

2. What would the borrower's monthly payments be if the MIP were financed?

ADVANTAGES OF FHA FINANCING

FHA advantages:
  1. low downpayment
  2. no prepayment charge
  3. assumable
  4. long-term loans
  5. easier qualifying standards

It is fair to say that the FHA is consumer-oriented; when administering its various programs, the FHA makes reasonable efforts to protect the interests of the borrower and to make home financing available on the most favorable terms. Attractive features incidental to FHA-insured loans include:

1. **Low downpayments.** FHA downpayment requirements are usually much less than those set for conventional loans.

2. **No prepayment penalty.** FHA loans may be prepaid at any time without penalty. Many conventional loans impose substantial penalties for paying off the loan in its early years.

   On loans made before 1985, lenders were allowed to require 30 days' written notice of an intent to prepay and to require that prepayment be made on an installment due date. As a result of this practice, most borrowers who prepaid loans were charged an additional month or month and a half of interest. Under new rules, prepayment is permitted without having to pay as much additional interest. For loans made after 1985, the lender may not require 30 days' written notice before prepayment, even if the mortgage or other debt instrument gives the lender that right. The FHA rule supersedes the agreement in the private documents. The lender may require that the prepayment be made on an installment due date (usually the first of the month) or that interest be paid until the next installment due date. Thus the borrower may prepay without giving the lender advance notice, but if prepayment is offered at any time other than on an installment due date (the first of the month), the lender may either refuse to accept payment until the next installment due date or charge interest until that date. The lender must give borrowers a written disclosure of the prepayment policy.

3. **FHA loans may be assumed.** FHA loans (with the exception of Section 235 loans) may be assumed for a nominal handling fee ($50-$75). Even when a conventional loan can be assumed, a hefty assumption fee is often charged. Remember, if an FHA loan is assumed within the first 12-24 months, the lender may require a full credit check and can charge up to $500 to process the assumption application.

4. **Long-term loans.** Most FHA loans are written for 30 years. The long term helps to minimize monthly payments.

5. **Less stringent qualifying standards.** It is generally easier for a borrower to qualify for an FHA loan than a conventional loan.

FHA loans are considered very economical by industry standards and the features cited above explain why. Historically, FHA financing has been directed toward and has had its widest appeal among the low- to middle-income segment of the home-buying market.

FHA LOAN PROGRAMS

The FHA has several programs which are of interest to homebuyers, the most popular of which is the Section 203(b). The 203(b) is the FHA's standard home loan insurance program. Over the years, approximately 70% of all FHA insurance has been written for this type of loan. Included in this section is the **FHA Veterans' Benefit Act of 1965 (203b2).**

The FHA has also adopted a mortgage insurance plan for adjustable-rate mortgages (ARMs). The adjustable-rate mortgage program has proved moderately popular and the specifics of that program will be covered later in this chapter.

Section 203(b): most popular FHA program

SECTION 203(b) — THE STANDARD FHA PROGRAM

An ordinary borrower is the one most suitable for the 203(b) insured loan. The particulars of the 203(b) program are described below.

Maximum Loan Amount

The Department of Housing and Urban Development limits the maximum loan amount for 203(b) loans. The maximum loan amount depends upon the medium range prototype housing costs for the community. This results in **varying maximum mortgage amounts** from one community to another.

Allowable loan amounts are higher in areas of higher-cost housing. The basic maximum loan amount for single-family residences is $67,500. In high-cost areas where the median price of homes significantly exceeds this amount, HUD may increase the maximum allowable loan amount up to 95% of the median home price in the area. An area is determined to be "high cost" following an application by area lenders or other interested parties showing that the median sales price of homes in the area in the preceding three months

Maximum loan amount depends on:
1. type of dwelling
2. geographic area

Maximum single-family loan limited by:
1. $67,500 basic single-family max
2. up to 95% of median home price in area
3. not to exceed $124,875

significantly exceeded the FHA maximum allowable loan amount. Regardless of area prices, HUD may not raise the maximum loan amount for single-family homes in any area higher than $124,875.

Limiting the maximum loan amount to 95% of the median-priced home means that FHA programs, as was mentioned earlier, tend to be directed at and serve persons who are in the low- to median-priced housing market. In California, where median housing prices are far higher than the FHA maximum loan amount, these loans are not as useful to low- and middle-income homebuyers. However, California lenders still report a significant amount of FHA activity. While certain metropolitan areas, such as Los Angeles and San Francisco, are too-high priced, there is a substantial number of rural areas that still take advantage of FHA financing. Also, lenders use FHA loans to finance construction in outlying regions of metropolitan areas.

There are different loan ceilings for single-family dwellings, duplexes, triplexes and fourplexes. Check with a local lender for the current maximum mortgage amounts in your community. After confirming the maximum amounts, pencil them into the space provided below. Keep in mind, maximum loan figures change periodically to reflect the rising cost of housing.

MAXIMUM LOAN AMOUNTS — 203(b)

Single family $ _124,875.00_
Duplex $ _140,600.00_
Triplex $ _170,200.00_
Fourplex $ _197,950.00_

203(b) Loan-to-Value Formula (Owner Occupied)

The loan-to-value formula for homes costing more than $50,000 involves two steps, with two percentages:

203(b) owner-occupant LTV for homes over $50,000 acquisition cost:
- 97% of first $25,000
- 95% of remainder

Step 1. Compute 97% of the first $25,000 of the acquisition cost.

Step 2. Add 95% of that portion of the acquisition cost which exceeds $25,000.

Example: sales price of $66,000

Step 1 $25,000
              × .97
              ─────────
               $24,250

Step 2 $41,000   ($66,000—$25,000)
              × .95
              ─────────
               $38,950

Step 3 $24,250
             + 38,950
              ─────────
               $63,200   loan amount

FHA LTVs based on acquisition cost: sales price (or appraised value if less) plus FHA allowable closing costs equals acquisition cost

An unusual feature of FHA loan computations is that estimated closing costs are added to the sales price and the maximum allowable loan is calculated based on the total. So, the buyer is able to finance part of the closing costs rather than being required to pay all of the closing costs in cash at the time of closing, as would be true with most other types of loans. This further reduces the buyer's cash requirements for FHA financing in comparison to conventional financing.

Example:

         $66,000   sales price
       + 1,450   estimated closing costs
        ─────────
         $67,550   TOTAL

Step 1 $25,000
                × .97
                $24,250

Step 2 $42,450   ($67,450—$25,000)
                × .95
                $40,327.50

                $24,250.00
             + 40,327.50
                $64,577.50   or $64,580.00 maximum
                              loan amount

By adding the estimated closing costs to the sales price and then working the loan-to-value formula, the buyer is able to obtain a higher loan amount. Compare the two preceding examples. The buyer is able to borrow $1,380 of the $1,450 estimated closing costs ($64,580—$63,200 = $1,380).

Estimating closing costs. FHA offices maintain a table for use by lenders in the area, which specifies the amount of closing costs which can be added to a purchase when calculating a loan amount. The table below is used for illustrative purposes only; you may find that costs in your area differ.

Allowable closing costs depend on:
• loan amount
• geographic area

Lenders in most communities provide literature in the form of booklets or pocket-size pamphlets that detail FHA loan amounts for the more popular programs. Many agents find it easier and more practical to keep an FHA loan-to-value schedule with them at all times, rather than to try to compute the loan amounts themselves.

FHA ALLOWABLE CLOSING COSTS*			
SALES PRICE/ VALUE	**ESTIMATED CLOSING COSTS**	**SALES PRICE/ VALUE**	**ESTIMATED CLOSING COSTS**
$20,000 to $24,999	$950	$110,000 to $114,999	$1950
$25,000 to $29,999	$1000	$115,000 to $119,999	$2000
$30,000 to $34,999	$1050	$120,000 to $124,999	$2050
$35,000 to $39,999	$1100	$125,000 to $129,999	$2100
$40,000 to $44,999	$1150	$130,000 to $134,999	$2150
$45,000 to $49,999	$1200	$135,000 to $139,999	$2200
$50,000 to $54,999	$1250	$140,000 to $144,999	$2250
$55,000 to $59,999	$1300	$145,000 to $149,999	$2300
$60,000 to $64,999	$1350	$150,000 to $154,999	$2350
$65,000 to $69,999	$1450	$155,000 to $159,999	$2400
$70,000 to $74,999	$1500	$160,000 to $164,999	$2450
$75,000 to $79,999	$1550	$165,000 to $169,999	$2500
$80,000 to $84,999	$1600	$170,000 to $174,999	$2550
$85,000 to $89,000	$1650	$175,000 to $179,999	$2600
$90,000 to $94,999	$1700	$180,000 to $184,999	$2650
$95,000 to $99,999	$1800	$185,000 to $189,999	$2700
$100,000 to $104,999	$1850	$190,000 to $194,999	$2750
$105,000 to $109,999	$1900		

*The maximum closing costs cannot exceed the statutory mortgage limits for the particular area.

Exercise No. 2

Sales price is $122,000. The buyer seeks a standard FHA 203(b) loan. The home is in a high-cost area.

1. **Using the 203(b) loan-to-value formula, without adding any additional costs, what would the loan amount be?**

2. **Using the chart in the book, what would be the FHA allowable closing costs?**

3. **After adding the estimated closing costs to the sales price and then using the loan-to-value formula, what would the loan amount be?**

Loan-to-Value Ratio for Homes $50,000 or Less

For homes with an FHA-appraised value (or sales price, whichever is lower) of not more than $50,000, including allowable closing costs, the loan-to-value ratio is 97% of the total value (or cost), including allowable closing costs.

203(b) owner-occupant LTV for homes with $50,000 or less acquisition cost:
- 97% of total acquisition cost

Example:

$45,000	sales price
+ 1,200	allowable closing costs
$46,200	TOTAL

$46,200	
× .97	loan-to-value ratio
$44,814	or $44,800 maximum loan amount

FHA math rhythm hot.
Can finance part of closing costs
all of MIP
Cannot add discount points to loan

Loan-to-Value Ratio for Homes Less than One Year Old

When the property being purchased with an FHA loan is less than one year old and is not warranted by an approved construction insurance program or is not an FHA-approved construction, the loan-to-value ratio cannot exceed 90% of the appraised value or acquisition cost, whichever is less.

LTV 90% if home less than one year old and not:
1. FHA/VA approved construction, or,
2. warranted by construction insurance

Exercise No. 3

Sales price is $70,250. The buyer seeks a standard 203(b) loan at 13¾% for 30 years.

1. **What is the maximum loan amount, including the MIP? Assume a minimum downpayment with buyer financing the MIP. Use the allowable closing cost table above.**

2. **What is the mortgage payment (principal and interest, including the financed MIP)?**

NONOWNER OCCUPANCY LOANS

A nonowner occupancy loan refers to a loan on investment property. An investment loan generally requires a much larger downpayment than an owner-occupant loan. This policy is consistent with the belief that in times of financial stress, a property owner will place a greater priority on protecting his or her home than will be placed on saving investment property. There used to be an FHA loan program for nonowner occupancy loans. In 1989 this program was abolished. As of December 15, 1989, the FHA no longer makes any investor loans. However, an investor loan which was made prior to this date is still assumable, if the new buyer meets the FHA qualifying standards.

203(b)2—VETERANS BENEFIT ACT

This is an FHA insurance program for veterans of all branches of the U.S. military, including the National Guard and Coast Guard. The program is often referred to as an FHA/VA loan, but this is technically incorrect. It is an FHA program and the Veterans Administration is not involved, other than to assist in establishing the borrower's veteran status. It would be more accurate to refer to this type of loan as an FHA/GI or FHA Veteran's loan.

203(b)(2) FHA/GI:
1. vets
2. single-family dwellings
3. owner-occupant

Single-Family Dwellings

Only single-family dwellings may be financed with an FHA/GI loan, and the veteran must intend to occupy the property. Investment property loans are not available under this program.

Maximum Loan Amount

The FHA/GI maximum loan amount is the same as the maximum for a standard 203(b) single-family dwelling.

203(b)(2) Loan-to-Value Formula

The primary advantage of the FHA Veteran's loan is that the downpayment requirement is smaller than under the standard 203(b) program. As with the standard 203(b) loan, the 203(b)(2) loan-to-value formula involves two steps and two percentages:

203(b)(2) FHA/GI LTV:
• 100% of first $25,000
• 95% of remainder

1. Take 100% of the first $25,000 of the acquisition cost.

2. Add 95% of the amount of the acquisition cost (sales price plus estimated closing costs) in excess of $25,000.

Example: Sales price of $60,000; estimated closing costs of $1300.

1. $25,000
     × 1.00
     $25,000

2. $36,300   ($61,300—$25,000)
     × .95
     $34,485

     $25,000
    + 34,485
     $59,485

     $59,450   loan amount (rounded down)

FHA/GI Eligibility Requirements

FHA/GI eligibility:
• 90 days in any branch of service
• other than dishonorable discharge

To be eligible for this loan program, the borrower must have served in any branch of the U.S. military for a minimum of **90 days** of continuous active duty and have been discharged under other than dishonorable conditions (**honorable** or **general discharge**).

If the veteran received an honorable discharge, the Veterans Administration will issue a **Certificate of Veteran Status** after receiving a copy of the veteran's DD-214 (a form issued to veterans upon discharge from active duty which summarizes the active duty career). The Certificate of Veteran Status certifies that the veteran has met the minimum military service requirements. If the veteran received a general discharge (better than a bad conduct or dishonorable discharge, but not as good as an honorable discharge), the VA will inquire into the circumstances of the discharge and will decide whether or not to issue the Certificate of Veteran Status. Some veterans with general discharges are approved; others are not.

203(b)(2) Program May Be Used More Than Once

A veteran may obtain 203(b)(2) loans as many times as he or she desires, as long as each time the program is utilized, it is used for a loan to buy a home which the veteran intends to occupy. However, as with the standard 203(b) program, there may be restrictions as to how many low-downpayment loans a borrower may have outstanding at one time.

THE FHA ARM

The increasing popularity of adjustable-rate mortgages (ARMs) in the early 1980's led the Department of Housing and Urban Development to initiate federal mortgage insurance for adjustable-rate loans.

FHA ARM:
- one- to four-unit dwellings
- owner-occupant
- 1% annual rate cap
- 5% lifetime rate cap
- no negative amortization
- written disclosure of terms and "worst case" scenario

The FHA ARM plan is limited to one- to four-family dwellings, including condominium units. The inclusion of an adjustable-rate feature in any FHA mortgage plan does not affect the maximum mortgage limits, loan-to-value ratios, mortgage insurance premiums or borrower qualifications. The plan is restricted to owner-occupants.

There is only one FHA ARM plan. The features include:

1. adjustments to the contract interest rate are limited to 1% annually;
2. the interest rate may not be increased or decreased more than 5% over the life of the loan;
3. no negative amortization is permitted;
4. the mortgagee is required to explain fully and in writing the terms of the ARM, including the worst case scenario (i.e., a 1% increase each year for five years for the maximum 5% increase, and then no decline thereafter for the life of the loan).

Below is an example of an ARM "Worst Case" disclosure, as required by the Department of Housing and Urban Development (HUD).

FHA ARM "WORST CASE" SCENARIO"
Monthly Installment of Principal and Interest for a 30-Year Term, $50,000 at 11% Adjustable-Rate Mortgage with a Margin of 1.0 Percent

Policy Year	Monthly Payment	End-of-Year Balance	Interest Rate	Index
1	476.16	49774.95	.11000	.10000
2	513.86	49570.67	.12000	.11000
3	551.79	49382.46	.13000	.12000
4	589.89	49206.34	.14000	.13000
5	628.10	49038.82	.15000	.14000
6	666.38	48876.90	.16000	.15000
7	666.38	48687.07	.16000	.16000
8	666.38	48464.56	.16000	.16000
9	666.38	48203.70	.16000	.16000
10	666.38	47897.92	.16000	.16000
11	666.38	47539.47	.16000	.16000
12	666.38	47119.27	.16000	.16000
13	666.38	46626.66	.16000	.16000
14	666.38	46049.21	.16000	.16000
15	666.38	45372.28	.16000	.16000
16	666.38	44578.72	.16000	.16000
17	666.38	43648.45	.16000	.16000
18	666.38	42557.94	.16000	.16000
19	666.38	41279.56	.16000	.16000
20	666.38	39780.95	.16000	.16000
21	666.38	38024.17	.16000	.16000
22	666.38	35964.75	.16000	.16000
23	666.38	33550.54	.16000	.16000
24	666.38	30720.46	.16000	.16000
25	666.38	27402.81	.16000	.16000
26	666.38	23513.65	.16000	.16000
27	666.38	18954.49	.16000	.16000
28	666.38	13609.91	.16000	.16000
29	666.38	7344.62	.16000	.16000
30	666.38	.00	.16000	.16000

Limit on Number of Insurable ARMs

There is a limit on the number of ARMs that may be insured by FHA in any one year. The limit is currently set at 30% of the number of all single-family mortgages insured under Title II of the National Housing Act during the previous fiscal year. At the time of this writing, the actual amount of ARMs insured by FHA is less than 10%. The popularity of FHA ARMs depends in large part on the interest rate level of fixed-rate loans. As with conventional loans, when fixed rates are low, interest in ARMs is significantly lower than when fixed rates begin to rise.

Availability of FHA ARMs is subject to an annual limit

SECONDARY FINANCING WITH FHA LOANS

Prior to July, 1985, no secondary financing was permitted in connection with an FHA-insured loan. The only mortgage allowed in the transaction was the FHA mortgage. It is now permissible for the buyer to have a second mortgage along with the FHA-insured mortgage. However, the buyer must still pay the FHA minimum downpayment in cash; no portion of the downpayment may be financed. The second loan may be from an institutional lender, the seller, or a third party.

Conditions for Secondary Financing

Use of a second mortgage as part of the purchase price, in conjunction with an FHA-insured mortgage, is permitted only if the following conditions are met:

1. The first and second mortgages together may not exceed the maximum allowable loan amount for the particular program.
2. The combined total of the payments under the FHA-insured first mortgage and the non-FHA second mortgage may not exceed the borrower's ability to pay (the borrower is qualified based on the total of both payments).

Secondary financing with FHA:
1. *1st and 2nd mortgages combined cannot exceed maximum loan amount*
2. *borrower qualifies for combined payments*
3. *installment payments on 2nd collected monthly and same amount*
4. *no balloon on 2nd*
5. *no prepayment penalty on 2nd*

3. If the second mortgage has periodic installment payments, those payments must be collected monthly and must be substantially the same in amount.
4. The second mortgage may not have a balloon payment due sooner than ten years (or such other term as the FHA commissioner may approve).
5. The second mortgage must permit prepayment without penalty after giving the lender 30 days' notice.

These restrictions do not apply if the mortgage is held by the federal, state or local government.

What is the Advantage of Secondary Financing with an FHA-Insured Mortgage?

If the total amount financed by both mortgages may not exceed the amount which could be financed with one FHA loan, a borrower may well ask what advantage there is to having a second mortgage. The buyer must still make the same downpayment (proceeds of a second mortgage may not be used for any portion of the downpayment or to reimburse the seller for seller contributions or buydown). When the program was first authorized in 1985, interest rates were substantially higher than they are today. It was thought that in some situations, the seller might be willing to take back a second mortgage at a lower interest rate than the rate on the FHA first mortgage. It was thought that in some situations, the seller might be willing to take back a second mortgage at a lower interest rate than the rate on the FHA first mortgage.

> **Example:** The interest rate on the FHA mortgage is 14%. The seller is willing to finance part of the purchase price at only 10%. Thus, the total payments on the first and second mortgages would be less than if the entire amount were financed by an FHA insured institutional loan.

In marginal cases, this arrangement might permit a buyer to qualify for an FHA loan who did not have sufficient income to qualify otherwise. With current relatively low interest rates, it is less likely that this type of transaction would be attractive.

BUYDOWNS AND MAXIMUM FHA LOANS

The FHA limits the amount of seller buydown (discount points) which may be paid in connection with FHA-insured loans to 6%. If a transaction involves a seller-paid buydown of more than 6%, the excess is applied, dollar for dollar, to reduce the sales price for the purpose of calculating the maximum loan amount.

> **Example:** Buyer is purchasing a house with the agreed upon sales price of $100,000. Seller agrees to a seller-paid buydown of 8% (or $8,000). However, the FHA limits the amount of seller buydown (discount points) to 6%. A buydown of only 6% would be $6,000. The extra $2,000 is applied to reduce the sales price in calculating the maximum loan amount. The maximum loan amount would be calculated based on a sales price of $98,000 ($100,000 − $2,000 = $98,000).

For this rule, a seller-paid buydown includes discount points, prepaid interest and closing costs normally paid by the buyer (such as the 1% loan origination fee) which are paid by the seller.

For FHA fixed-rate loans with temporary buydowns, the borrower may be qualified at an interest rate up to 2% below the note rate. For example, if a 10% FHA loan called for a temporary buydown of three percentage points, the borrower would have to qualify for the loan at an 8% interest rate.

CHAPTER SUMMARY

1. The FHA was created in 1934 as part of the National Housing Act to create construction jobs by making residential financing more available and more affordable. For the most part, the FHA has succeeded in these goals, making housing significantly more affordable for low- and middle-income buyers.

2. The FHA insures, but does not make, loans. The insurance premium, called the MIP, can be paid by any party if it is paid in cash. The MIP may also be financed, in which case it must be paid by the borrower. The MIP is more commonly financed along with the loan amount. The MIP premium varies in amount depending on the loan term and whether it is paid in cash or financed.

3. FHA loans have several advantages over conventional loans, including:

   - low downpayments (usually between 5% and 7%)
   - less stringent qualifying standards
   - no prepayment penalties
   - freely assumable (sometimes a credit check is required), and
   - long-term loans

4. All FHA loans are for owner-occupant borrowers. The FHA used to insure loans for investor borrowers, but this program was abolished in 1989. FHA investor loans that are already in existence are assumable if the new buyer meets the FHA qualifying standards.

5. One unusual aspect of FHA loans is that, in addition to the low minimum downpayment and being able to finance the mortgage insurance premium, the borrower may finance part of the closing costs. Each region has its own limits on the amount of closing costs that may be financed with the loan amount.

6. The FHA sets varying maximum loan amounts for types of residences (one- to four-unit and co-ops/condos) and for different geographical areas of the country based upon median home prices. The basic maximum loan amount is $67,500, or 95% of the median-priced home, up to a maximum of $124,875.

7. The FHA also offers adjustable-rate mortgages. The plan is restricted to owner-occupants and is limited to one- to four-family dwellings. There is a limit on the number of ARMs that may be insured by the FHA in any one year.

Chapter 11
GOVERNMENT FINANCING – VA-GUARANTEED LOANS

The Veterans Administration guarantees repayment of certain residential loans made to eligible veterans. VA loans are available to purchase single-family homes or multiple-family residences containing **up to four units**. **No investor loans** are guaranteed by the VA. If the property is a single-family dwelling, the veteran must intend to occupy it as his or her residence; if the property is a multiple-family dwelling, the veteran must occupy one of the units.

VA LOAN CHARACTERISTICS

Several characteristics of VA-guaranteed loans are highly attractive to borrowers:

- Unlike most loans, a VA loan may be obtained with no downpayment.
- VA loans contain no prepayment penalties and no due-on-sale clauses. Although VA loans are assumable, a complete credit check of the assumptor is required prior to the assumption of any VA loan made after March 1, 1988.
- The interest rate on VA loans may not exceed the maximum allowable rate determined by the Veterans Administration. The maximum VA rate is normally below the prevailing market rate for conventional loans.
- VA loans have no mortgage insurance (either private mortgage insurance or FHA-style mutual mortgage insurance).
- Discount points are paid by the seller.

VA-guaranteed loans:
- eligible vets only
- one- to four-unit dwellings
- owner-occupant only

Advantages:
1. no downpayment required
2. no prepayment charges
3. assumable
4. maximum interest rate set by VA
5. no mortgage insurance premium
6. points paid by seller
7. secondary financing allowed

- Finally, secondary financing is permitted in conjunction with most VA loans.

NOTE: No mortgage insurance is required for VA loans, but a **1.25% funding fee** is charged. Depending on the amount of downpayment, there may be a reduced funding fee for purchase or construction loans. When a downpayment of 5% to 10% is paid, the funding fee is only .75%. When a downpayment of 10% or more is paid, the funding fee is only .50%.

There is also a **loan origination fee** of 1%. The funding fee may be financed, but the 1% loan fee must be paid in cash at closing. If the funding fee is financed, the amount financed may not exceed the maximum VA loan amount.

Sale by assumption. Veterans who obtained loans guaranteed by the Veterans Administration are legally obligated to indemnify the United States Government for any claim paid by the Veterans Administration under the guaranty. The indemnity liability continues for the life of the loan even though the property is transferred to another owner and the foreclosure occurs because of the default of a subsequent owner.

It is therefore important that veterans who sell or transfer their homes in transactions where the VA loan will not be paid off at closing be made aware that they can be released from liability on that loan only if the following three conditions are met:

Assumption of VA loan:
1. without release
2. with release
3. with reinstatement of entitlement

Assumption with release:
1. loan current
2. purchaser has acceptable credit
3. written agreement by purchaser to assume obligation

1. The loan must be current.
2. The purchaser must be an acceptable credit risk.
3. The purchaser must assume the obligations and liabilities of the veteran on the loan, including the indemnity obligation. The assumption of obligations must be evidenced by a written agreement as specified by the Veterans Administration.

Vet can restore entitlement. In addition to being released from liability on the loan, the veteran seller may, under the proper circumstances, have his or her loan entitlement restored. In order to accomplish this, the buyer must be a veteran who has an unused entitlement which is at least equal to the veteran seller's initial entitlement and the buyer must consent to substitute his or her entitlement for the seller's. The veteran buyer must also satisfy the conditions set out just above.

Assumption with reinstatement:
1. buyer is eligible vet
2. buyer agrees to substitute entitlement
3. buyer has remaining entitlement at least equal to seller's original entitlement

Explain transfer of liability in sales contract. To facilitate a veteran's release from liability on a loan the buyer intends to assume, it is best to include in the sales contract a provision to that effect. The sales agreement should provide that the buyer will assume all the seller's loan obligations (including the potential liability for indemnity on the VA loan) and that the sale will not be closed unless and until the VA approves the income and credit of the purchaser. If the buyer is a veteran and the seller wants a substitution of VA entitlement, a stipulation to that effect should also be included in the agreement.

Unfortunately, these steps are often neglected and sales are often consummated without submitting applications to the VA for release of liability and, in many cases, without the buyer even formally agreeing to assume payment of the loan. If the sale closes without first obtaining a release from liability from the VA and/or a substitution of entitlement, it may be difficult or impossible for the veteran to obtain a release from the VA at a later date.

ELIGIBILITY

Eligibility for VA loans is based on the length of continuous active service in the U.S. armed forces. The minimum requirement varies depending upon when the veteran served.

Eligibility for VA
guarantee:
1. other than dishonor-
   able discharge
2. minimum active duty
   service requirement
3. service-connected
   disability
4. certain unremarried
   surviving spouses

90 days continuous active duty, any part of which occurred:
1. September 16, 1940, through July 25, 1947 (WWII)
2. June 27, 1950, through January 31, 1955 (Korea)
3. August 5, 1964, through May 7, 1975 (Vietnam)

181 days continuous active duty, any part of which occurred:
1. July 26, 1947, through June 26, 1950
2. February 1, 1955, through August 4, 1964
3. May 8, 1975, through September 7, 1980

24 months continuous active duty for veterans who enlisted after September 7, 1980, **except:**
1. individuals discharged for disability;
2. individuals discharged for hardship; or
3. any case in which it is established that the veteran is suffering from a service-connected disability not the result of willful misconduct and not incurred during a period of unauthorized absence.

For persons who fall into one of the exceptions to the 24-month service requirement, the 181-day service requirement applies. Veterans who are discharged for hardship or for a non-service connected disability are eligible only if they have served a minimum of 181 days. Persons who have served six months' active duty for training purposes only are not eligible. There is no minimum active duty service requirement for veterans discharged for a service-connected disability.

There is no eligibility for persons who received a dishonorable discharge.

Eligibility of a spouse. A veteran's spouse may be eligible for a VA loan if:

1. the vet was killed in action or is a possible prisoner of war because of service during the Vietnam era; or
2. the vet died of service-related injuries and the spouse has not remarried.

VA Guarantee

AMOUNT OF GUARANTY

VA loan amounts are determined by the Certificate of Reasonable Value (CRV), the appraised value for a VA loan. Only a portion of the loan will be guaranteed by the VA. The maximum guaranty has been increased over the years as follows:

Guaranty amount: based on loan amount up to maximum guaranty of $46,000 for loans over $144,000

WWII guaranty was $4,000;
increased on September 1, 1951, to $7,500;
increased on May 7, 1968, to $12,500;
increased on December 31, 1974, to $17,500;
increased on October 1, 1978, to $25,000;
increased on October 1, 1980, to $27,500;—
increased on February 1, 1988, to $36,000;
increased on January 1, 1990, as follows:

Loan Amount	Guaranty Amount
up to $45,000	50% of loan amount
$45,000—$56,250	$22,500
$56,251—$90,000	40% of loan amount
$90,001—$144,000	$36,000
Over $144,000	$36,000 plus 25% of amount over $144,000, up to a maximum of $46,000.

most will loan up to 18 Yours.
X .25 guarantee
46,000.

Example:

1. $75,000 loan amount
    × .40 guaranty of 40% of loan amount
    ─────
    $30,000 guaranty amount

2. $125,000   loan amount
      $36,000   guaranty amount (maximum guaranty for loans between $90,000 and $144,000)

3. $160,000   loan amount
     −144,000
       16,000   amount above $144,000
       × .25
      $4,000   additional guaranty amount

     $36,000   guaranty amount up to $144,000
    + 4,000   additional guaranty (25% of amount over $144,000)
    $40,000   guaranty amount

Partial Eligibility

In cases where a vet has unused entitlement, the remaining eligibility may be used for a new loan. The maximum guaranty amount used to determine unused entitlement is $36,000, unless the loan is over $144,000.

Partial eligibility: if less than current maximum entitlement was used on an earlier loan, remaining entitlement may be used for new loan

Example: A veteran obtained a VA loan in 1984 and used the maximum guaranty then available, $27,500. The veteran now wants to use any remaining entitlement for a VA loan to buy a new $130,000 home.

    $36,000   maximum guaranty for determining unused entitlement for all loans up to $144,000
  − 27,500   guaranty on existing loan
    $8,500   remaining entitlement to be used for new loan

Suppose the same veteran wanted to use any remaining entitlement for a new $150,000 VA loan.

$150,000 loan amount
− 144,000
_____
6,000 amount above $144,000
× .25
_____
1,500 25% of amount above $144,000
+ 36,000
_____
37,500 guaranty for determining unused entitlement
− 27,500 guaranty on existing loan
_____
$10,000 remaining to be used for new loan

Partial eligibility is normally used only when the vet has sold the property for which the original loan was obtained, since VA loans require owner occupancy. It is not necessary, however, that the original loan have been completely repaid. Veterans who have had a previous VA loan and are uncertain as to the amount, if any, of remaining entitlement may usually have their questions answered by their local VA office. The veteran will need the VA identifying numbers for the original loan. The VA office can then check to see what outstanding balance, if any, remains on that loan.

Reinstatement

If the original VA loan is paid in full and the vet has sold the house for which the original loan was made, then full entitlement is restored. However, the vet must demonstrate a need for new housing in order to obtain a new VA loan.

Full entitlement may be restored even if the original loan has not been fully repaid. This is possible only if the buyer who assumes the original loan is an eligible veteran and agrees to substitute his or her entitlement for the seller's and if a full release from liability is obtained from the VA. (See the earlier section in this chapter covering entitlement and transfer of

Reinstatement of entitlement:
1. original loan paid in full, or
2. original loan assumed by eligible vet who agrees to substitute entitlement

227

liability.) If these conditions are not met, then the veteran seller has only whatever partial entitlement is still available in excess of the guaranty on the original loan.

Entitlement may be used for refinancing VA or other loan

Refinancing

Unused entitlement may be applied to refinancing the vet's current home, regardless of whether a VA loan was originally used to purchase the home. The new VA loan may be applied to pay off all existing loans plus the costs of refinancing, and the veteran may even receive cash from the proceeds of the new loan in some cases. If the existing loan is not a VA loan, the veteran may refinance with a VA loan up to the value of the home and may receive some cash as shown in the example below; if the existing loan is a VA loan, the veteran may only refinance to the extent of the existing mortgage for the purpose of lowering payments.

> **Example:** A vet owns a house encumbered by a $50,000 conventional mortgage. The vet applies for a VA loan to refinance the property, and obtains a CRV indicating the property is worth $100,000. The vet obtains a $100,000 VA loan. The proceeds of the loan are applied as follows:

$100,000   loan
$- \ 50,000$ pay off existing loan
$\underline{- \ \ 3,500}$ refinancing costs
$\ \ \$46,500$ cash to vet

Exercise No. 1

John Beckler was inducted into the U.S. Navy on May 1, 1980, and was honorably discharged in March of 1982. He is now seeking a $70,000 loan to buy a home.

1. Is John eligible for a VA-guaranteed loan? If so, what is the maximum possible amount of his entitlement?

2. If John gets a $70,000 VA loan, how much of the loan will the VA guarantee?

VA LOAN AMOUNTS

There is no maximum VA loan amount, except for the requirement that the loan may not exceed the appraised value of the property as determined by the CRV or the sales price, whichever is less.

When the VA maximum guaranty amount was $36,000, most lenders would not make a VA loan of over $144,000. Now that the maximum guaranty has been raised to $46,000, most lenders will probably make larger VA loans, but not over $184,000.

Furthermore, most lenders require that the guaranty equal at least 25% of the loan amount for a zero down loan. If the veteran's remaining entitlement is insufficient, a downpayment may be made so that the combination of entitlement and downpayment equals 25% of the loan.

VA loan amount:
1. no maximum set by VA
2. loan over $184,000 unlikely
3. combination of guaranty and downpayment must equal 25% of loan

> **Example:** A veteran with $2,500 remaining entitlement wants to buy a home for $75,000 and obtain the maximum possible VA-guaranteed loan.
>
> $75,000   purchase price/desired loan amount
>
> $18,750   25% of loan amount
> – 2,500   remaining entitlement
> $16,250   required downpayment

229

As with FHA financing, VA loans have limited appeal in California's expensive metropolitan areas because of the low loan limit (which is lower than California's median home price). However, VA lenders still do a brisk business in rural areas and on the fringes of metropolitan areas.

Secondary Financing

If a downpayment is used in connection with a VA loan, VA regulations permit the buyer to finance part or all of the downpayment (secondary financing) if the following conditions are met:

Secondary financing:
1. total financing cannot exceed CRV
2. buyer qualifies based on combined payments
3. interest on second not above current VA maximum rate
4. except for due-on-sale, second cannot contain more stringent conditions than VA first mortgage

1. the total of all financing does not exceed the reasonable value of the property;
2. the buyer's income is sufficient to qualify based on the payments required for both loans;
3. the interest rate on the second does not exceed the current VA rate of interest; and,
4. there are no more stringent conditions connected with the second mortgage than apply to the VA first mortgage (such as a late payment penalty). Exception: The second mortgage may contain a due-on-sale clause.

Some instances where a veteran may use secondary financing include the following:

- when a veteran does not have enough entitlement to qualify for a large enough loan and does not have enough cash to make up the difference; and
- when the veteran can get secondary financing (e.g., seller financing) at a lower interest rate than the institutional VA loan, making the proposed loan payment smaller, and thus making it easier for the veteran to qualify for the loan.

FHA — VA COMPARISON CHART

	FHA	VA
Buyer Characteristics		
Eligibility	Any Qualified Borrower	Qualified Veterans Only
Owner-Occupant Loans Only	Yes	Yes
Property		
Units	1 - 4	1 - 4
Loan Characteristics		
Maximum Loan	$67,500 - $124,875 depending on region	No Maximum

Note: Neither FHA nor VA loans may exceed appraised value.

Maximum Interest Rate	Negotiated by Borrower and Lender	Set by VA
Downpayment Required	Yes	No
Buyer Permitted to Pay Points	Yes	No (max. 1% loan fee)
FHA or VA Fee	3.8% MIP (financed, 30-year loan)	1.25% Funding Fee
Secondary Financing Permitted	Yes	Yes
Secondary Financing for Downpayment	No	Yes
Assumable Loans (No Due-on-Sale)	Yes	Yes
Prepayment Charges	No	No
Lender Protection	Insured to Full Extent of Losses from Default	Maximum $46,000 Guaranty

Exercise No. 2

Jeffrey Bates just sold his home, allowing the buyer to assume his VA loan. The VA guaranty on the existing loan is $17,500. Bates now wants to buy another home. Assume that the lender follows the 25% rule outlined above.

1. What is the largest no downpayment VA loan Jeffrey can obtain?

2. If Jeffrey wanted an $80,000 VA loan, what would his downpayment be?

CHAPTER SUMMARY

1. The Veterans Administration guarantees loans for home purchases by eligible veterans. Loans are available for one- to four-unit dwellings, but only if the veteran occupies the property. VA loans differ from other loans in that there is no downpayment requirement and the VA sets the maximum interest rate which may be paid by the borrower.

2. Although the VA sets no maximum loan amount, it does set a maximum available guaranty, which is used by lenders for limiting the loan amounts. Currently the maximum guaranty is $46,000 and the maximum available loan may go as high as $184,000.

3. VA loans do not contain either prepayment charges or alienation clauses.

Chapter 12
GOVERNMENT FINANCING –
CAL-VET LOANS

An additional type of government-sponsored financing is available to California residents. In 1921, the California legislature enacted the California Veteran Farm and Home Purchase Program, which enabled the California Department of Veterans Affairs to provide eligible veterans with affordable financing to purchase home or farm property. The Department originates, processes, funds and services the loan until it is fully repaid.

SOURCE OF FUNDS
The funds for the loan program are raised through the issuance and sale of General Obligation Bonds and Revenue Bonds. These bonds are repaid by the veterans who are participating in the loan program so there is no direct cost to California taxpayers. By federal regulation, the majority of the Revenue Bond funds are awarded to first-time homebuyers (those who have not owned a principal residence within the past three years). If a veteran does qualify as a first-time homebuyer, he or she should so inform the Cal-Vet representative when applying for the loan.

Cal-Vet loan funds raised through sale of General Obligation and Revenue Bonds. Bonds are repaid by participating veterans

When funds for Cal-Vet loans are in short supply, there is a statutory order of preference for granting the loan funds. The loans are given in the order of the following categories:

1) Veterans who were wounded or disabled from war services. Disability must be rated at 10% by the United States Veterans Administration.
2) Former prisoners of war, unremarried spouses of veterans killed in the line of duty and unremarried

When there is a shortage of funds, order of preference is:
1. wounded or disabled veterans
2. former prisoners of war
3. Vietnam and Indian vets
4. all others

spouses of veterans designated as missing in action.
3) Veterans who served during the Vietnam period (August 5, 1964—May 7, 1975) and Indian veterans applying for loans on reservation or trust land.
4) All other qualified veterans.

APPLICATION

Application:
1. pay $25 fee
2. fill out application
3. submit military papers
4. submit title report with plat map
5. submit deposit receipt and escrow instructions
6. fill out verification forms
7. sign and return discrimination notice and authorization forms

Under state law, the application for the loan must be made within 25 years from the date of release from active duty. One exception is that veterans who were wounded or disabled as a result of their war service or who were prisoners of war have 30 years after their release in which to apply. The applicant must follow certain steps in applying for a Cal-Vet loan:

1. Pay a fee of $25 at the time of filing the application.
2. Answer all questions on the loan application form completely.
3. Submit a certified copy of his or her military separation documents showing date of entry and release.
4. Submit two legible copies of a current preliminary title report with a plat map covering the property.
5. Submit a copy of the deposit receipt for the proposed transaction and a copy of current escrow instructions.
6. Complete the applicant's portion of the Verification of Employment forms and have his or her employer complete them and return them to the Cal-Vet office.
7. If the applicant is self-employed, he or she must include a current profit and loss statement.
8. Sign and return a notice on federal laws prohibiting discrimination and credit information authorization forms.

The submission of all the required documentation at the same time will facilitate the processing of the application.

The completed Cal-Vet application must be received by the Department of Veterans Affairs **before the purchase**

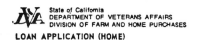

State of California
DEPARTMENT OF VETERANS AFFAIRS
DIVISION OF FARM AND HOME PURCHASES

LOAN APPLICATION (HOME)

GOVERNMENT FINANCING—CAL-VET LOANS

Office use only (Date received)

SUBJECT TO AVAILABILITY OF FUNDS AND PREFERENCE CATEGORIES

APPLICANT

1. Veteran's Name (Last) (First) (MI)	2. Date of Birth (Mo.) (Day) (Yr.)	3. Social Security Number — —
4. Spouse's Name (Last) (First) (MI)	5. Date of Birth (Mo.) (Day) (Yr.)	6. Date Married (Mo.) (Day) (Yr.)

7. Home Address (Number & Street)　City　State　Zip Code　7a. Place of Birth

8. Telephone Number	9. Years at Present Address	10. Ethnic Background (Optional)	11. No. & Age of Dependents living at Home

YOU MUST NOTIFY THE CAL-VET OFFICE OF ANY CHANGE IN YOUR ADDRESS

ELIGIBILITY

Date of Enlistment	State of Residence at Time of Enlistment	Date of Release	12. Were you wounded or disabled as a result of military service? If yes, check box and submit verification. ☐ Wounded ☐ Disabled

13. Were you ever a prisoner of war? ☐ Yes ☐ No

13a. Have you and/or your spouse owned an interest in the last 3 years in a home used as your principal residence? ☐ Yes ☐ No

14. Are you an unmarried spouse of a veteran missing in action or killed in the line of duty while on active duty. ☐ Yes ☐ No

15. Have you ever had a Cal-Vet Loan ☐ Yes ☐ No　　15a. Date Paid in full (Mo.) (Day) (Yr.)　　15b. Location

16. Have you ever requested or received a bonus or benefit from any other state for any military service? ☐ Yes ☐ No　　16a. If yes, what state　　16b. Period of service (Mo.) (Day) (Yr.)

17. Have you ever acquired an interest of record in the property being submitted? ☐ Yes ☐ No　　17a. If yes, when? (Mo.) (Day) (Yr.)　　17b. Guaranteed or insured by the Federal Government ☐ Yes ☐ No

SUBJECT PROPERTY

18. I REQUEST A CAL-VET LOAN OF $ _____ TO PURCHASE SUBJECT PROPERTY AT PRICE $ _____

19. Street Address　City　County　Zip

20. ☐ Existing Home ☐ Unimproved Home Site ☐ Under Construction　20a. ☐ Single Family Home ☐ Condominium/PUD　Mobilehome ☐ New ☐ Used ☐ Land ☐ Mobilehome Park

21. Under Construction　　Cost of Unimproved Lot $ _____　21a. Estimated Completion Date (Mo.) (Day) (Yr.)　21b. Balance Owed $ _____　21c. Proposed Construction Cost $ _____

21d. Date Lot Acquired (Mo.) (Day) (Yr.)　　22. Current F.H.A. case number (if any)　　23. Solar Heating Device ☐ Yes ☐ No

24. Property is: ☐ Vacant ☐ Occupied by:　Name of occupant　Phone Number

25. Access to property may be obtained by calling:　Name:　Address:　Phone:

PLEASE NOTIFY THE CAL-VET OFFICE OF ANY CHANGE IN PROPERTY ACCESS INFORMATION

EMPLOYMENT AND INCOME

26. Veteran's Present Employer	26a. Address of Employment		Gross Monthly Salary	Office Use Only
27. Occupation	27a. How long	27b. Telephone	$	
28. Spouse's present employer	28a. Address of Employment		Gross Monthly Salary	
29. Occupation	29a. How long	29b. Telephone	$	
30. Retirement Income: ☐ Military $ _____ ☐ Other $ _____			$	
31. V.A. Compensation			$	
32. Social Security ☐ Veteran $ _____ ☐ Spouse $ _____			$	
33. Child Support Received			$	
34. Interest/Dividends ☐ Savings ☐ Stocks/Bonds ☐ Notes/Trust Deeds ☐ Others			$	
35. Income from Real Estate: List each property. Attach additional sheet if necessary.			$	

Address of Property Indicate S if sold PS if pending sale	Status	Type of Property	Value	Gross Income	Loan Payment	Taxes & Expense	Net Monthly Income	
1		Personal Residence	$		$	$		
2			$	$	$	$	$	
3			$	$	$	$	$	

36. TOTAL MONTHLY INCOME FROM ALL SOURCES　$

37. If not on current job for more than 1 year, list previous employment. Attach additional sheet if necessary.
V — Veterans　　S — Spouse

V/S	Previous Employment/School	City	Occupation	Gross Monthly Salary	From Date To
				$	

A-1 (9/84)　LOAN APPLICATION (HOME)

FINANCING CALIFORNIA REAL ESTATE

ASSETS:		SUB-TOTALS	OFFICE USE ONLY
38. Cash on hand (Funds under personal possession and not bank accounts)		$	
39. Checking Account(s) @ _____ Branch			
40. Savings Account @ _____ Branch			
Account @ _____ Branch			
41. Stocks and Bonds (Describe) _____			
42. Total Equity in Real Estate: Market Value $ _____ Less Loan Balance _____			
43. Trust Deed(s) owned (Current Value) _____			
44. Earnest Money or Deposit on this Property (Not included in other listed assets) _____ _____			
45. Other Liquid Assets _____			
46. Additional Funds to complete this purchase ☐ Gift ☐ Personal Loan ☐ Secondary Financing			
SUB-TOTAL		$	
47. Automobiles: Year _____ Make _____			
Year _____ Make _____			
48. Household Furnishing and Personal Properties _____			
49. Other Assets: _____			
TOTAL		$	

LIABILITIES: PLEASE FURNISH NAMES, ADDRESS, AND ACCOUNT NUMBERS ON ALL LOANS AND ACCOUNTS.

	ACCOUNT NUMBER	MONTHLY PAYMENT	BALANCE OWED	OFFICE USE ONLY
50. Loans on Real Estate				
1. _____		$	$	
2. _____				
3. _____				
51. Automobile _____				
52. Furniture _____				
53. Money Owed to Relatives _____				
54. Notes Payable (Unsecured) _____				
55. Personal Loans _____				
56. Alimony—Child Support _____				
57. Other (Including credit cards) _____				
TOTAL				

58. Present Monthly Housing Expense for Residence:
Rent/Payment $ _____ Utilities $ _____ Taxes & Insurance $ _____ Total $ _____

59. Are there suits or judgments against you? (If yes, attach explanation) ☐ Yes ☐ No

60. Have you ever filed for bankruptcy? (If yes, submit schedule of debts or discharge of bankruptcy and attach explanation) ☐ Yes ☐ No

61. Names and Addresses of credit references (List accounts other than above) Account Number Open/Closed
1. _____ _____ _____
2. _____ _____ _____
3. _____ _____ _____

PLEASE READ CAREFULLY AND SIGN

I hereby certify under penalty of perjury that all information contained in this application is given for the purpose of obtaining a Cal-Vet loan and is true, correct, and complete. I authorize the Department of Veterans Affairs and its agents, employees, and officers to conduct credit investigations and to obtain information from and provide information to credit agencies and others pertaining to my credit and financial condition, except that information contained in this application may not be provided to credit agencies and others more than 120 days after the date this application is filed. I also understand and acknowledge that the Cal-Vet loan contract will provide for a flexible interest rate, which may result in periodic decreases or increases in the monthly installment.

_____ Date

_____ Signature of Veteran Applicant

_____ Signature of Spouse

is completed or an interest in the property is acquired. An exception to this rule is if the veteran has an interest in a building site, the structure has not been completed, and a certificate of occupancy has not yet been issued.

Cal-Vet loans may only be used to refinance **construction loans** or interim loans with a term of 24 months or less. The Department does not make construction loans itself and will only refinance a construction loan when the property is completed and ready for occupancy. If a veteran is building a home, he or she should apply for approval of the building site and a determination of eligibility before construction begins. Once the veteran is found qualified and the building site has been approved, the Department will issue a loan commitment, allowing 12 months for the construction to be completed.

Secondary financing may be used, but only with the Department's consent. If secondary financing is used, the total amount of financing, both secondary and the Cal-Vet loan, cannot exceed 90% of the Department's appraised value of the property and a subordination agreement must be obtained from the secondary lender.

OCCUPATION OF THE PREMISES

The veteran or a member of the Veteran's immediate family must occupy the property within **60 days** of signing the Cal-Vet loan papers and must continue to use the property as the principal place of residence for the life of the loan. An exception is made for farm properties as long as the veteran personally cultivates the property (harvesting crops and/or tending livestock).

The property may be rented out if the Department determines there is good cause. In no case may the property be rented for more than a total of four years during the life of the loan. Transfer, assignment, encumbrance or rental of the property requires the consent of the Department.

Premises must be occupied by vet or family member within 60 days of signing loan papers

If a veteran must move out of the property, he or she may qualify to have the loan transferred to another property. There are established criteria which must be met and the veteran should contact a Cal-Vet representative to be sure of proper procedures.

ELIGIBILITY

Eligibility:
1. California born or resident at time of entry
2. honorable release
3. fulfill service requirements
4. vet must not have accepted benefits from another state

Both state and federal laws determine eligibility for Cal-Vet loans. The following are the requirements for eligibility:

1) the veteran must have been born in California or be able to prove bona fide residency at the time of entry into active duty;

2) the veteran must have been released from active duty under honorable conditions;

3) the veteran must have served at least 90 days on active duty (unless discharged because of a service-connected disability). At least one day of active duty must have been during one of the following wartime periods:

   —Vietnam period: August 5, 1964—May 7, 1975
   —Korean hostilities: June 27, 1950—January 31, 1955
   —World War II: December 7, 1941—December 31, 1946
   —World War I: April 6, 1917—November 11, 1918

   A veteran who was awarded a qualifying Campaign Medal or Armed Forces Expeditionary Medal for services during a peacetime period may also be eligible. Military service solely for the purpose of processing, physical examination or training does not qualify; and

4) the veteran must not have accepted a bonus or benefit from another state for the qualifying period of military service.

LOAN FEES

There is a loan origination fee charged on all Cal-Vet loans. At the time of this writing, the fee is $425, $25 to be paid at the time of application and the remainder to be collected at the close of escrow. Property taxes and insurance are also collected at closing.

Current loan fees:
- $425
- $25 paid at time of application

LOAN TERMS

Qualifying properties, the **maximum loan amounts**, and **loan-to-value ratios** are as follows:

Qualifying Properties	Maximum Loan Amount
Single-family home, including condos and townhouses	$125,000
Mobilehomes on land owned by the borrower	90,000
Mobilehomes in approved parks	70,000
Working farms	200,000

Homes equipped with solar energy heating devices may be approved for up to an additional $5,000 loan amount. When the purchase price is $35,000 or less, the loan may be **97%** of the appraised value or purchase price, whichever is less. Where the purchase price is greater than $35,000, the loan may be **95%** of the appraised value or purchase price, whichever is less. For farm properties, the loan amount cannot be more than **95%** of the Department's appraised value which is based on net income from agricultural production.

Loan-to-value ratios range from 95%-97%

239

The **interest rate** on Cal-Vet loans used to vary over the life of the loan. This is no longer true. The interest rate is now a straight 8% on all types of Cal-Vet loans.

CHAPTER SUMMARY

1. The Cal-Vet program is designed to provide affordable financing for California veterans for homes and farms. Loans are available for homes, mobile homes, and working farms.

2. Except for short-term rentals, homes and mobile homes must be occupied by the borrower for the life of the loan and farms must be occupied or worked by the borrower. The loan origination fee is $425. The loan-to-value ratios range from 95% to 97%. There are prepayment penalties for the first five years of the loan's life.

3. To apply for a Cal-Vet loan, the veteran must pay a $25 application fee, fill out the application completely, submit the proper military documentation, submit a title report with a plat map, submit the deposit receipt and escrow instructions, and sign and return proper authorization forms.

4. To be eligible for the loan, the veteran must have: 1) been born in California or be able to prove residency at the time of entry into active duty; 2) been released under honorable conditions; 3) served the statutory amount of

time; and 4) not have accepted a bonus or benefit from another state for the qualifying period of military service.

5. Both federal and state regulations set requirements as to type of eligible property, eligibility of borrowers, maximum loan amount, and other financing terms.

Hrly Wages
X 173.33333 =

Monthly earnings .

Hrly X 173.3333 = 866.67

Chapter 13
QUALIFYING THE BUYER

Before agreeing to make a real estate loan, a lender will evaluate both borrower and property to determine that they meet minimum qualifying standards. The evaluation process is called **loan underwriting**; the individual who conducts the evaluation is an underwriter or credit underwriter.

The primary concern throughout the evaluation process is degree of risk, and the determination of acceptable risk hinges on the answers to two fundamental questions:

Loan underwriter evaluates:
1. borrower's overall financial condition
2. value of property

1) Does the borrower's overall financial situation, which is comprised of income, assets and credit history, indicate he or she can be reasonably expected to make the proposed monthly loan payments in a timely manner?
2) Is there sufficient value in the property pledged as collateral to assure recovery of the loan amount in the event of default?

The Federal Home Loan Mortgage Corporation (FHLMC) refers to loans which answer these questions affirmatively as "investment quality loans." The FHLMC publication, *Underwriting Guidelines for Home Mortgages,* defines an investment quality loan as ". . . a loan to a borrower from whom timely repayment of the debt can be expected and secured by real property which provides sufficient value to recover the lender's investment if a loan default occurs."

It was mentioned in a previous chapter that until recently, savings and loans, savings banks, and even commercial banks made most of their real estate loans from the funds of their depositors. As such, they were free to apply their own

Most lenders employ FNMA/FHLMC underwriting standards for conventional loans; FHA and VA standards apply for FHA/VA loans.

underwriting standards, sometimes without concern for whether or not a loan could be sold to FHLMC or FNMA. If a particular savings institution made a loan that did not measure up to FHLMC or FNMA standards, the loan would simply be held in portfolio.

In recent years, this country's savings institutions have experienced unprecedented **disintermediation**, which is the loss of deposits to higher yielding market investments. As a result, they have far fewer customer deposits with which to make loans, and if they are to continue in the real estate lending business, they must be in a position to sell their loans on the secondary market.

Qualifying standards can vary from lender to lender, and in some instances they do, but with increased lender dependence on the national secondary market a high degree of standardization in loan underwriting has developed. This is to say that the majority of lenders throughout the country have incorporated into their own conventional loan underwriting procedures the standards set by the major secondary market investors, specifically FNMA and FHLMC.

Since most lenders use FNMA and FHLMC conventional underwriting standards, it is important for the real estate agent to know what those standards are; otherwise, it would be impossible to expertly pre-qualify buyers and properties. Of course, if the loan being contemplated is to be insured by the Federal Housing Administration (FHA) or guaranteed by the Veterans Administration (VA), FNMA and FHLMC underwriting standards are not applicable, as FHA insurance or a VA guaranty eliminates risk for the lender or secondary market investor. The FHA and VA have their own underwriting standards which will be discussed subsequently.

As noted earlier, the real estate underwriting procedure involves an evaluation of both borrower and property. This chapter will cover qualifying the buyer. Qualifying the property is covered in Chapter 14.

When qualifying a buyer for a conventional loan, the real estate agent must use FHLMC and FNMA underwriting criteria, which are for all practical purposes the same. Of course, when qualifying a buyer for an FHA or VA loan, the FHA or VA underwriting guidelines must be followed. There are some minor differences between the FHA and VA guidelines, and they will be explained later in this chapter.

FHLMC/FNMA UNDERWRITING STANDARDS

According to the FHLMC, "underwriting mortgage loans is an art, not a science. It cannot be reduced to mathematical formulas, but requires sensitive weighing of the many aspects of the loan." There are many factors related to a borrower's application for a loan that must be considered by the underwriter; they include income, net worth, and credit history.

Factors in evaluating borrower's financial condition:
1. income
2. net worth
3. credit history

INCOME

Conventional lenders consider a borrower's income adequate for a loan if the proposed payment of principal, interest, taxes and insurance does not exceed **28%** of his or her **stable monthly income**. Stable monthly income is the borrower's gross monthly income from primary base employment and any secondary income that is considered reliable and likely to endure. We will take a closer look at acceptable income sources shortly.

Income-to-debt ratios:
—for LTV up to 90%:
  housing expense - 28%
  total debt service - 36%

—For LTV over 90%:
  housing expense - 28%
  total debt service - 33%

Example:

$2,900   stable monthly income
   700   proposed mortgage payment*

$$2{,}900\overline{\smash{)}700} \quad .24$$

---

*Includes principal, interest, taxes, insurance (PITI), and private mortgage insurance (PMI) premium, if applicable.

A second but equally important concern is that the total of the borrower's housing expenses (as explained above), plus any installment debts with more than ten (10) remaining payments, and alimony, child support or maintenance payments, if any, not exceed 36% of his or her stable monthly income.

Example:

$2,900   stable monthly income

$700   proposed mortgage payment*
225   auto payment (18 installments remain)
+ 100   child support
$1,025

$$\underset{2,900\,\overline{\big)\,1,025}}{.35}$$ total expense-to-income ratio

The total expense-to-income ratio, called a **total debt service ratio**, frequently is a more realistic measure of the borrower's ability to support the loan payments because it takes into account the borrower's other recurring financial obligations.

Using these ratios, it is a simple matter to determine the maximum mortgage payment a borrower will qualify for. First, take the borrower's stable monthly income and multiply that by the maximum housing expense-to-income ratio (0.28). The answer is the maximum mortgage payment allowable under the first ratio. Then take the stable monthly income and multiply that by the maximum total debt service ratio

---

*Includes principal, interest, taxes, insurance and PMI premium, if applicable.

(0.36). The answer is the amount of total monthly long-term debts the borrower is permitted to have. Take this total amount and subtract the monthly long-term obligations (not including mortgage payments) and the resulting figure is the largest mortgage payment allowed under the total debt service ratio. The mortgage payment determined through calculating the total debt service ratio is more than likely to be smaller than the housing expense-to-income figure. This is because other monthly debts are taken into consideration. Since the borrower must qualify under both ratios, the smaller of the two is the maximum allowable mortgage payment.

> **Example:** Mary Smith has a stable monthly income of $3,200. She has three, long-term monthly debt obligations: a $220 car payment, a $75 personal loan payment, and a $50 revolving charge card payment. What is the maximum monthly mortgage payment she can qualify for?

Housing expense-to-income ratio: 28%

$3,200.00	monthly income
× .28	income ratio
$896.00	maximum mortgage payment under housing expense-to-income ratio

Total debt service ratio:

$3,200.00	monthly income
× .36	income ratio
$1,152.00	maximum total debt service

$1,152.00	maximum total debt service
220.00	car payment
75.00	personal loan payment
− 50.00	revolving charge card payment
$807.00	maximum mortgage payment under total debt service ratio

The maximum monthly mortgage payment Mary would qualify for would be $807. Remember, Mary must qualify under both ratios, so the lower figure is the most Mary can get. Of course, if she could pay off some of her debts and reduce her total long-term monthly obligations, she would be able to qualify for a larger mortgage payment.

FNMA ratios for 95% loans. For loans which exceed 90% loan-to-value ratios (95% loans), the total expense-to-monthly income ratio is **33%** (the housing expense ratio remains 28%). These ratios may be exceeded (up to the standard ratio of 36%) only if there is sound justification which is documented by the lender.

FNMA / FHLMC RATIOS		
Loan-to-Value	**Housing Expense**	**Total Debt Service / Fixed Payments**
90% or less (downpayment 10% or more)	28%	36%
FNMA more than 90% (downpayment 5%)	28%	33%

Stable Monthly Income

Stable monthly income: base income (wage, salary, commissions, profits from primary occupation) + allowable secondary income

This is the base income of the borrower (both husband and wife), plus earnings from acceptable secondary sources. Secondary earnings take the form of, but are not limited to, bonuses, commissions (over and above base salary), part-time employment, social security payments, military disability and retirement payments, interest on savings or other investments and the like.

Analyzing a borrower's income is a three-dimensional procedure. Before concluding there is a sufficient quantity of income, the underwriter must decide what portion of the borrower's total verified earnings are acceptable as a part of his or her stable monthly income. This is accomplished by studying the quality (dependability) of the income source(s) and the durability (probability of continuance) of the income.

Quality. A quality secondary source is one that is reasonably reliable, such as an established employer, government agency, interest-yielding investment account, etc.

Durability. Durable income is that income which can be expected to continue for a sustained period. Permanent disability, retirement earnings and interest on established investments clearly are enduring types of income.

Bonuses, commissions and part-time earnings. These sources are considered durable if they can be shown to have been a consistent part of the borrower's overall earnings pattern for at least one but preferably two years. Proof of such consistency can be obtained by submitting copies of the borrower's W-2 forms or federal income tax statements from the previous year or a verification of employment and earnings from the employer.

Overtime. Overtime earnings are technically eligible for inclusion in a borrower's stable monthly income, but underwriters are most reluctant to rely on such earnings because their durability is so uncertain. It is recommended that you not count on overtime earnings when qualifying your buyers unless they are clearly a consistent part of his or her earnings pattern.

Unemployment and welfare. These earnings are almost never treated as stable monthly income because they are viewed as temporary.

Alimony, child support or maintenance. These sources of income can be considered part of the borrower's stable monthly income if it is determined they are likely to

Income is evaluated based on:
• quantity
• quality
• durability

Allowable secondary sources can include:
• bonuses
• commissions
• part-time wages
• overtime
• alimony, child support, maintenance

be consistently made. Such a determination is dependent on whether the payments are required by written agreement or court decree, the length of time the payments have been received, the age of the child (child support payments generally stop at age 18), the overall financial and credit status of the payer, and the ability of the borrower to compel payment if necessary.

A copy of the divorce decree is generally sufficient to establish the amount and the enforceability of the required payments. In some instances, where the underwriter is not satisfied that the full payments are received regularly, the borrower may be asked to submit proof of receipt.

The closer a child gets to age 18, the less durable child support income paid for him or her appears. There is no official cut-off date used by underwriters, but it is safe to say that once the child is between 16 and 17 years of age, most underwriters will see the support payments as terminal and will not include them in the stable monthly income.

Income from other family members. Generally, only the earnings of the head(s) of household will be considered when calculating the stable monthly income. Support income from teenage children or other family members could stop without notice; income of this sort lacks both quality and durability.

Self-employment income. Self-employed borrowers should be prepared to provide, if possible, audited profit and loss statements and balance sheets for the two years prior to the loan application; additionally, the underwriter will require copies of the borrower's federal income tax statements for the same two years.

Self-employed borrowers need financial records and federal income tax returns for two years.

If a borrower has been self-employed for less than two years it will be difficult to qualify him or her for a loan; if the borrower has been in business for less than one year it will be more difficult still. Underwriters are wary of new businesses and are generally unswerving in their insistence that the self-employed borrower has operated the business profitably for at least two years.

The requirement for documentation of income may be waived in some cases. Many lenders offer "easy qualifier" or "no documentation" loans for borrowers meeting certain requirements. A borrower who has sufficient assets, good credit and who is able to make a large downpayment (usually at least 25% to 30%) may be able to obtain a loan without providing documentation of income and income tax returns for the preceding two years. Under FHLMC guidelines, the loan-to-value ratio for these reduced documentation loans may not exceed 70% and the borrower must meet all income-to-debt ratios and other qualifying standards.

Co-mortgagor. Frequently a co-mortgagor is used to aid a primary borrower in qualifying for a loan. Today parents often lend their established earnings pattern and financial status to their children who otherwise would be unable to purchase a home. A co-mortgagor is simply a co-borrower, an individual who, along with the primary borrower, accepts responsibility for repayment of the loan by signing the promissory note and mortgage. Like the primary borrower, the co-mortgagor must have earnings, assets and a credit history that are acceptable to the underwriter.

Co-mortgagor provides income to assist borrower, signs note and mortgage along with purchaser

Keep in mind, if a co-mortgagor is used, he or she must be able to support both his or her own housing expense and a proportionate share, if not all, of the proposed housing expense. Marginal co-mortgagors should not be relied on very heavily; they may do more harm than good to a loan application.

Rental income. Income from rental properties can be counted as stable monthly income if a stable pattern of rental income can be verified. Authenticated copies of the owner's books showing gross earnings and operating expenses for the previous two years should be submitted along with the borrower's application for loan approval.

Rental income—usually need record of rents and expenses for two years

Verifying Income

Until early 1987, lenders were required to verify income by sending an income verification form directly to the applicant's employer. The employer filled out the form and then

Income verification:
1. form filled out by employer, or
2. W-2 forms for two years and payroll stubs for 30 days

sent it directly back to the lender. The borrower was not allowed to have any contact with the verification forms. However, FNMA and FHLMC have changed income verification procedures and now income may be verified by the borrower. The borrower can substantiate his or her own employment and income by providing W-2 forms for the previous two years and payroll stubs or vouchers for the previous 30-day period. The pay stubs must identify the borrower, employer, and the borrower's gross earnings for both the current pay period and year to date. Lenders then confirm the employment and earnings by a phone call to the employer.

Computing Monthly Earnings. When converting hourly wages to monthly earnings, multiply the hourly wage by 40 (hours in a work week), then multiply by 52 (weeks in a year) and divide by 12 (months in a year).

Example:

Hourly Wage: $9.50
Weekly Income: $9.50 × 40 = $380
Annual Income: $380 × 52 = $19,760
Monthly Income: $19,760 ÷ 12 = $1,647
(Or simply multiply the hourly wage by 173.33)

Positive employment history
1. consistency, usually two years in same job or field
2. changes for advancement
3. special education or training

Employment History. When evaluating the elements of a borrower's income (quantity, quality and durability), the underwriter will analyze the individual's employment stability. A borrower with a history of steady, full employment will be given more favorable consideration than one who has changed employers frequently, unless the changes are properly explained.

As a general rule, a borrower should have continuous employment for at least two years in the same field. However, every borrower is unique and if there is not an established two-year work history, there may be explainable circumstances which would warrant loan approval, such as having recently finished college or been discharged from the service.

Advancement. If the borrower has changed employers for the sake of advancement within the same line of work, the underwriter will likely view the change favorably. On the other hand, persistent job hopping without advancement usually signifies a problem of some kind and an underwriter will tend to regard the individual's earnings as unstable.

Education, training. Special education or training that prepares an individual for a specific kind of work can strengthen a loan application. Such education or training can offset minor weaknesses with respect to earnings or job tenure if the underwriter is convinced there is a continuing demand for individuals in this line of work that promotes job stability and opportunities for advancement.

Exercise No. 1

Roy Karnes has recently been honorably discharged from the U.S. Air Force, where he spent most of the past four years being trained as an airplane mechanic. After discharge, Karnes and his wife Judy moved to Sacramento. Roy accepted a full-time job two months ago with a major airline company, with a starting position of apprentice mechanic; two weeks after that, Judy found a job with a local hospital as a vocational nurse. Roy's hourly wage is $13.00; Judy earns $385.00 a week.

1. **What is the maximum housing expense an underwriter would approve for the Karnes?**

2. **What is the maximum total debt service an underwriter would allow?**

3. Are there any special circumstances that might result in loan approval even though the Karnes have only been with their employers for a short time?

NET WORTH

Net worth: difference between assets and liabilities; substantial net worth can offset marginal deficiency in income-debt ratios

According to the Federal National Mortgage Association, "accumulation of net worth is a strong indication of credit worthiness." A borrower who has built up a significant net worth from earnings, savings and other investment activities clearly has the ability to manage financial affairs and accumulate wealth. An individual's net worth is determined by subtracting personal liabilities from total assets.

If a borrower has a marginal debt service-to-income ratio, an above normal net worth can offset the deficiency. Underwriters know that net worth in liquid form can be used to pay unexpected bills or to support a borrower when there has been a temporary interruption in income.

Required Reserves After Closing

Reserves after closing: two months' mortgage payments on deposit after downpayment and closing costs.

As a safeguard against unexpected bills or temporary loss of income, and as a general indicator of financial ability, FNMA requires the borrower to have sufficient cash on deposit, or in the form of highly liquid assets, to cover two months' payments (principal, interest, taxes, insurance, and, if applicable, mortgage insurance) after making the downpayment and paying all closing costs. FHLMC guidelines require a minimum of two months' payments for all owner-occupant loans, without regard to loan-to-value ratio, and three to six months for nonowner-occupant loans.

Verification of Assets

Included in every loan application is a section devoted to assets. The underwriter will take whatever steps are necessary to verify the nature and value of assets held by the borrower. The purpose of the asset verification process is twofold:

Verification of assets:
1. form from borrower's bank(s) verifying deposit(s), or
2. bank statements for three months

1) It must be determined that the borrower has sufficient liquid assets to make the cash downpayment and pay the closing costs and other expenses incidental to the purchase of the property. Liquid assets include cash and any other assets that can be quickly converted to cash.
2) The underwriter wants to know that the borrower has sufficient reserves to handle typical household emergencies, whatever they might be and whenever they might arise.

Verification of deposit.

The underwriter will use the form "Request for Verification of Deposit" (see example below) to prove the borrower has the necessary funds in his or her bank account(s). This form is sent directly to the bank and returned to the underwriter without passing through the borrower's hands. When the underwriter receives the completed verification of deposit, there are four things he or she will look for:

1) Does the verified information conform to the statements in the loan application?
2) Does the borrower have enough money in the bank to meet the expenses of purchase?
3) Has the bank account been opened only recently (within the last couple of months)?
4) Is the present balance notably higher than the average balance?

Recently opened accounts or higher than normal balances must be explained, as these are strong indications that the buyer has resorted to borrowed funds to pay the downpayment and closing costs.

FINANCING CALIFORNIA REAL ESTATE

REQUEST FOR VERIFICATION OF DEPOSIT

INSTRUCTIONS: LENDER - Complete Items 1 thru 8 Have applicant(s) complete Item 9 Forward directly to
depository named in Item 1.
DEPOSITORY - Please complete Items 10 thru 15 and return DIRECTLY to lender named in Item 2.

PART I - REQUEST

1. TO (Name and address of depository)	2. FROM (Name and address of lender)
You Betcha Bank 1919 2nd St. Anytown, USA	

3. SIGNATURE OF LENDER	4. TITLE	5 DATE	6. LENDER'S NUMBER (Optional)
	loan officer	7/20/9x	

7. INFORMATION TO BE VERIFIED

TYPE OF ACCOUNT	ACCOUNT IN NAME OF	ACCOUNT NUMBER	BALANCE
checking	Carl B. Able	11616-6	$ 482
savings	Carl B. Able	61161-1	$ 3,100
			$
			$

TO DEPOSITORY: I have applied for a mortgage loan and stated in my financial statement that the balance on deposit with you is as shown above. You are authorized to verify this information and to supply the lender identified above with the information requested in Items 10 thru 12. Your response is solely a matter of courtesy for which no responsibility is attached to your institution or any of your officers.

8. NAME AND ADDRESS OF APPLICANT(s)	9 SIGNATURE OF APPLICANT(s)
Carl B. Able 1800 3rd Avenue Anytown, USA	

PART II - VERIFICATION OF DEPOSITORY

10. DEPOSIT ACCOUNTS OF APPLICANT(s)

TYPE OF ACCOUNT	ACCOUNT NUMBER	CURRENT BALANCE	AVERAGE BALANCE FOR PREVIOUS TWO MONTHS	DATE OPENED
checking	11616-6	$ 200	$ 200	1/3/9x
savings	61161-1	$ 3,600	$ 1,000	3/22/9x
		$	$	
		$	$	

11 LOANS OUTSTANDING TO APPLICANT(s)

LOAN NUMBER	DATE OF LOAN	ORIGINAL AMOUNT	CURRENT BALANCE	INSTALLMENTS (Monthly/Quarterly)	SECURED BY	NUMBER OF LATE PAYMENTS
	none	$	$	$ per		
		$	$	$ per		
		$	$	$ per		

12. ADDITIONAL INFORMATION WHICH MAY BE OF ASSISTANCE IN DETERMINATION OF CREDIT WORTHINESS
(Please include information on loans paid-in-full as in Item 11 above)

None

13. SIGNATURE OF DEPOSITORY	14. TITLE	15. DATE
	assistant vice president	7/23/9x

The confidentiality of the information you have furnished will be preserved except where disclosure of this information is required by applicable law. The form is to be transmitted directly to the lender and is not to be transmitted through the applicant or any other party.

RE 016 (Rev 3-80)

FNMA Form 1006
Rev. June 78

Alternative Verification Method

When FNMA changed its rules regarding verification of income (early 1987) it also changed its rules on verification of deposits. Lenders may now use an alternative method of verifying deposits: the borrower may submit the original bank statements for the previous three months to verify sufficient cash for closing.

Financial statement. If a borrower's assets are substantial and diverse, an audited financial statement may be the best way to explain the borrower's creditworthiness to the underwriter. A financial statement is a summary of facts showing the individual's financial condition; it contains an itemized list of assets and liabilities which serves to disclose net worth. See the example below.

Real estate for sale. If a borrower is selling a property to raise cash to buy the subject property, the equity may be counted as a legitimate asset. Equity is the difference between the market value of the property and the sum of the selling expenses, mortgages and other liens against the property. Equity is what the buyer should receive from the sale of the property. In cases where the equity is the primary or exclusive source of money for the purchase of the subject property, the underwriter might require, before making the new loan, evidence that the former property has been sold and the proceeds from that sale have been received by the borrower.

If the purpose of the loan is to finance the construction of a home on a lot owned by the borrower, the underwriter will treat the borrower's equity in that lot as cash or its equivalent.

Personal financial statement may be needed for borrower with substantial and diversified assets

Example:

```
 $75,000   estimated construction costs
+ 10,000   lot value
 $85,000   total property value
```

INDIVIDUAL FINANCIAL STATEMENT

Office As of _____ 19 ____

LAST NAME	FIRST	MIDDLE		AGE	SOCIAL SECURITY NUMBER
Parks,	Dorothy	M.		54	111-00-1111

ADDRESS	NUMBER AND STREET	CITY, STATE, ZIP CODE			
1000 East 10th St.		Metro City, Kansas			

HOME PHONE	BUS. PHONE	AGES OF DEPENDENT CHILDREN	EMPLOYER OR SELF-EMPLOYED	NUMBER OF YEARS	POSITION OR OCCUPATION
777-8010	777-9000	NONE	SELF-EMPLOYED	10	

Do not complete this marital status section or information below concerning your PRESENT spouse if you reside in Alaska, Oregon or another non-community property state and are applying for individual unsecured credit. ☐ Married ☒ Unmarried (Single, widowed, divorced) ☐ Separated

ASSETS	(Omit Cents)	LIABILITIES	(Omit Cents)
Cash on hand and in banks	$ 50,000	Open accounts payable — Schedule G	$ 2,500
Accounts receivable — Schedule A			
		Notes payable — Schedule H	
Notes receivable — Schedule B		Accrued expenses	
		Federal income tax payable	
Listed stocks and bonds — Schedule D	50,000	Due relatives and related concerns; describe:	
		Installment obligations — Schedule I	
TOTAL CURRENT ASSETS	$ 100,000	**TOTAL CURRENT LIABILITIES**	$ 2,500
Real Estate — Schedule F	5,210,000	Real Estate Mortgage and Contracts – Schedules C & F	3,440,000
Automobiles and trucks	25,000		
Machinery and tools		Other liabilities; describe	
Contracts and Mortgages Receivable — Schedule C	80,000		
Unlisted stocks and bonds — Schedule E	25,000		
Due from relatives and related concerns; describe:		Amount borrowed on life insurance	
		TOTAL LIABILITIES	$ 3,465,000
Household goods	15,000		
Other assets; describe Art & Jewelry	30,000	**NET WORTH**	$ 2,040,000
Cash Surrender value of life insurance	20,000		
TOTAL ASSETS	$ 5,505,000	**TOTAL LIABILITIES AND NET WORTH**	$ 5,505,000
INCOME FOR YEAR:		CONTINGENT LIABILITY:	$
Salary or wages		Guaranteed or cosigned loans or paper	
Proprietorship/partnership draws	45,000	Surety bonds	
Commissions and bonus		Other	
Dividends and interest	20,000	INSURANCE	
Rentals	140,000	Buildings	4,800,000
Other (See Item 2 below)		Liability (auto, etc.)	2,000,000
TOTAL NET INCOME	$ 205,000	Life insurance — face value	500,000

Payable to: Loretta Parks

Are any of the above assets pledged to secure indebtedness other than liabilities listed? Describe _____

Last filing IRS return? 19 _84_   Have you made your will? ☒ YES NO ☐   Have you ever taken bankruptcy? ☐ YES NO ☒

Income taxes paid $ _30,000_   Has your spouse made a will? ☐ YES NO ☐   Judgments, suits or litigation? ☐ YES NO ☒

COMPLETE EACH SCHEDULE BY WRITING "NONE" IN THOSE THAT DO NOT APPLY

Schedule A. ACCOUNTS RECEIVABLE

Name	Amount	Due Date
None		
TOTAL	$	

Schedule B. NOTES RECEIVABLE

Name	Amount	Due Date
None		
TOTAL	$	

Schedule C. CONTRACTS AND MORTGAGES RECEIVABLE

Name of Debtor	Security and To Whom	Receivable Balance	Receivable Mo.Payment	Owing on This Property Balance	Owing on This Property Mo.Payment
M. D. Nelson	3 Bdrm. Residence	80,000	903	--	--
	1920 South River Drive				
	Metro City				
	TOTAL	$ 80,000	$ 903	$	$

Schedule D. LISTED STOCKS AND BONDS

Name of Company	Registered Name	Number of Shares	Market Per Share	Total Mkt. Value
Blue Chip	Blue Corp.	1,000	$ 50	$ 50,000
	TOTAL			$ 50,000

Schedule E. UNLISTED STOCKS AND BONDS

Metro City Bonds Due 1995		25	1,000	$ 25,000
	TOTAL			$ 25,000

Schedule F. REAL ESTATE

Unless otherwise noted, title stands in name of: Dorothy M. Parks

Location, Size, Description	Year Acquired	Current Value Land	Current Value Buildings	Total	Payable To	Mortgages or Contracts Balance	Mortgages or Contracts Mo.Payment
50 Unit Apartment		$ 300,000	$2,000,000	2,300,000	1st Bank	$1,500,000	$ 14,475
Complex							
1500 N. 50th , Metro City							
2 Story Office Bldg.		200,000	2,500,000	2,700,000	N. B. Sailors	1,500,000	19,850
506 Main, Metro City							
Residence		60,000	150,000	210,000	1st Federal St. L.	140,000	1,540
1000 East 10th,							
Metro City	**TOTAL**	$ 5,210,000			**TOTAL**	$ 3,440,000	$ 35,865

Schedule G. OPEN ACCOUNTS PAYABLE

Payable To	Amount	Due Date
VISA	1,000	
Sara Interiors	1,500	
TOTAL	$ 2,500	

Schedule H. NOTES PAYABLE TO OTHERS

Payable To	Amount	Due Date
NONE		
TOTAL	$	

Schedule I. INSTALLMENT OBLIGATIONS

Payable To	Collateral	Balance	Final Due Date	Monthly Pmt.
NONE				
	TOTAL	$		$

Assets include:
1. cash and other liquid assets
2. equity in real estate for sale
3. equity in other real estate
4. stocks, bonds, cash value in insurance policies
5. autos, boats, furniture and other personal property

$85,000	total property value
× .80	loan-to-value ratio (80%)
$68,000	maximum loan amount
$85,000	total property value
− 68,000	maximum loan amount
$17,000	required downpayment
$10,000	lot value
− 4,000	liens against lot (mortgage)
$6,000	borrower's equity

The borrower shows $6,000 equity in the lot, which is included in the list of assets necessary to satisfy the downpayment and settlement cost requirements.

Other real estate. Regardless of whether a real estate holding is income or non-income producing (e.g., rental property versus vacant land), it is an asset and should be considered when qualifying a borrower for a loan. You should bear in mind, though, it is the equity, not the value of property, that contributes to net worth. It is the equity that can be converted into cash in the event of need.

Real estate with little or no equity or with income that is equal to or below expenses is more of a liability to a loan application than an asset.

Other assets. Any assets held by the borrower will help the loan application. Assets, other than cash and real estate, typically listed in a loan application include automobiles, furniture, jewelry, stocks, bonds and cash value in a life insurance policy. You should keep in mind that the assets which will most favorably influence the underwriter's decision are the liquid assets, those that can be quickly converted to cash.

Gift letter:
• gift of cash from immediate family member
• letter stating that money is intended as gift and need not be repaid

Gift letter. If an applicant lacks the necessary funds to close a transaction, a gift of the required amount from relatives is usually acceptable to the underwriter. The gift should be confirmed by means of a (gift) letter signed by the donor. The letter should clearly state that the money represents a gift and does not have to be repaid.

The gift usually must be from an immediate family member. Even if the gift letter requirements are satisfied, the borrower will normally have to make some cash payment out of his or her own cash resources. FNMA requires that the borrower make at least a 5% downpayment in addition to the gift, unless the gift is 20% or more of the purchase price. If the gift equals 20% or more, then the borrower is not required to make a 5% downpayment in addition to the gift.

Exercise No. 2

Mr. Able wants to buy a home, and it is estimated that his 80% conventional loan will have a $878.00 mortgage payment. He has an automobile payment of $212.00 a month with 14 installments remaining. He earns $700.00 a week. His downpayment and closing costs are estimated at $18,400. Able is selling a home with an equity of $14,000. He has a checking and savings account with a local bank and plans to draw on that account to close the transaction (refer to the Verification of Deposit below).

1. What is Able's housing expense-to-income ratio?

2. What is the total debt service-to-income ratio?

3. Is Able going to have any problems closing the transaction? Explain.

REQUEST FOR VERIFICATION OF DEPOSIT

INSTRUCTIONS: LENDER - Complete Items 1 thru 8. Have applicant(s) complete Item 9. Forward directly to depository named in Item 1.
DEPOSITORY - Please complete Items 10 thru 15 and return DIRECTLY to lender named in Item 2.

PART I - REQUEST

1. TO (Name and address of depository)	2. FROM (Name and address of lender)
You Betcha Bank 1919 2nd St. Anytown, USA	

3. SIGNATURE OF LENDER	4. TITLE	5. DATE	6. LENDER'S NUMBER (Optional)
[signature]	loan officer		

7. INFORMATION TO BE VERIFIED

TYPE OF ACCOUNT	ACCOUNT IN NAME OF	ACCOUNT NUMBER	BALANCE
checking	Carl B. Able	11616-6	$ 482
savings	Carl B. Able	61161-1	$ 3,100
			$
			$

TO DEPOSITORY: I have applied for a mortgage loan and stated in my financial statement that the balance on deposit with you is as shown above. You are authorized to verify this information and to supply the lender identified above with the information requested in Items 10 thru 12. Your response is solely a matter of courtesy for which no responsibility is attached to your institution or any of your officers.

8. NAME AND ADDRESS OF APPLICANT(s)	9. SIGNATURE OF APPLICANT(s)
Carl B. Able 1800 3rd Avenue Anytown, USA	*[signature]*

PART II - VERIFICATION OF DEPOSITORY

10. DEPOSIT ACCOUNTS OF APPLICANT(s)

TYPE OF ACCOUNT	ACCOUNT NUMBER	CURRENT BALANCE	AVERAGE BALANCE FOR PREVIOUS TWO MONTHS	DATE OPENED
checking	11616-6	$ 200	$ 200	2-7-84
savings	61161-1	$ 3,600	$ 1,000	3-1-87
		$	$	
		$	$	

11. LOANS OUTSTANDING TO APPLICANT(s)

LOAN NUMBER	DATE OF LOAN	ORIGINAL AMOUNT	CURRENT BALANCE	INSTALLMENTS (Monthly/Quarterly)	SECURED BY	NUMBER OF LATE PAYMENTS
	none	$	$	$ per		
		$	$	$ per		
		$	$	$ per		

12. ADDITIONAL INFORMATION WHICH MAY BE OF ASSISTANCE IN DETERMINATION OF CREDIT WORTHINESS:
(Please include information on loans paid-in-full as in Item 11 above)

None

13. SIGNATURE OF DEPOSITORY	14. TITLE	15. DATE
[signature]	assistant vice president	

The confidentiality of the information you have furnished will be preserved except where disclosure of this information is required by applicable law. The form is to be transmitted directly to the lender and is not to be transmitted through the applicant or any other party.

RE 016 (Rev 3-80)

FNMA Form 1006
Rev. June 78

4. Do you see any problems with his verification of deposit? Explain.

CREDIT HISTORY

As a part of the loan evaluation, the underwriter will analyze the credit history of the borrower; this is accomplished by obtaining a credit report from a responsible credit rating bureau.

Credit history indicates borrower's willingness to repay past debts

If the borrower's credit history reflects a slow payment record or other derogatory credit information, the loan application could be declined. Derogatory credit information, over and above a slow payment record, includes suits, judgments, repossessions, collections, foreclosures and bankruptcies.

Derogatory credit information includes history of:
1. slow payment
2. judgment(s)
3. repossession(s)
4. foreclosure(s)
5. bankruptcy
6. bill consolidation and refinancing

In some instances, derogatory ratings do not prevent a borrower from obtaining a loan. If the credit problems can be satisfactorily explained so the underwriter is satisfied they do not represent the borrower's overall attitude towards credit obligations and that the circumstances leading to the problems were temporary and no longer exist, the loan application might be approved.

Explaining Derogatory Credit

Most people try to meet their credit obligations on time; when they do not, there is usually a reason. A loss of job, hospitalization, prolonged illness, death in the family or even divorce can create extraordinary financial pressures and adversely affect credit paying habits. If two or three derogatory items show up on a credit report, it may be possible to successfully explain the ratings if the borrower can show that the problems occurred during a specific period of time for an understandable reason, and that prior and subsequent credit ratings have been good.

Letter of explanation for derogatory credit information:
- reason for problem during specific period
- problem no longer exists
- ratings before and since are good

When explaining credit difficulties to a lender, it is a mistake to blame the problems on misunderstandings or on the creditors themselves. Too frequently, underwriters listen to explanations from borrowers who refuse to accept responsibility for their own acts, insisting instead that the blame lies elsewhere. The reaction to such explanations is very predictable: skepticism, disbelief, and rejection. Underwriters reason that a borrower's reluctance to take responsibility for prior credit problems is an indication of what can be expected from him or her in the future.

If a borrower's credit report is laced with derogatory ratings over a period of years, there is probably little hope for loan approval. Perpetual credit problems more likely reflect an attitude instead of a circumstance, and it would be reasonable to presume that the pattern would continue in the future.

All credit problems are resolved with time, and if a buyer indicates he or she has had some credit problems in the past, it would be a mistake to automatically presume the buyer cannot qualify for a loan. Refer him or her to a competent lender and get an expert's opinion.

Bill Consolidation, Refinancing

Even in the absence of derogatory ratings, there are matters that can be revealed by a credit report which might indicate the borrower is a marginal credit risk. If an individual's credit pattern is one of continually increasing liabilities and periodically "bailing out" through refinancing and debt consolidation, he or she may be classified as a marginal risk—the pattern suggests a tendency to live beyond a prudent level. This is a subjective consideration likely to influence the underwriter's decision if the borrower is weak in other critical areas such as income or assets.

ACCOUNT NO. _____ 8572F _____
ACCOUNT NAME _____
REPORT ORDERED BY _____
DATE ORDERED _____ March 3, 199x _____
DATE COMPLETED _____ March 17, 199x _____
INDIVIDUAL OR JOINT REPORT __ JOINT _____
TYPE REPORT (CASE OR FILE NO.) _____
REPORT PREPARED BY _____
PRICE _____

BASE	NON-LOCAL	ADDITIONAL	TAX	TOTAL

STANDARD FACTUAL DATA REPORT

REPOSITORY INFORMATION OBTAINED FROM: JOHN J. JONES (BORROWER)   JOAN J. JONES (CO-BORROWER)

ALL INQUIRIES WITHIN THE LAST 6 MONTHS HAVE BEEN CHECKED AND ANY OPENED ACCOUNTS ARE REFLECTED BELOW.

This standard factual data report meets all underwriting requirements set by FHA, VA, FNMA and FHLMC.

GENERAL INFORMATION	
1. BORROWER'S NAME AND AGE / CO-BORROWER'S NAME AND AGE	JOHN J. JONES, 37; JOAN J. JONES, 35
2. CURRENT ADDRESS	101 1ST AVE., ANYTOWN, USA 00000
3. LENGTH OF TIME AT PRESENT ADDRESS / OWN?	6 MONTHS/NO
4. PREVIOUS ADDRESS	275 14TH STREET, ANYTOWN, USA 00000
5. BORROWER SS # / CO-BORROWER SS #	001-01-1111; 100-10-2222
6. MARITAL STATUS / YEARS / DEPENDENTS	MARRIED/4/3
BORROWER'S EMPLOYMENT	
7. NAME OF EMPLOYER / ADDRESS	LUCKY LARRY'S USED AUTO; 121 MAIN STREET, ANYTOWN
8. POSITION HELD / LENGTH OF EMPLOYMENT	SALESPERSON/ 8 MONTHS
9. EMPLOYMENT VERIFIED BY	LARRY JONES
10. PREVIOUS EMPLOYMENT / LENGTH OF EMPLOYMENT	TOTEM CAR SALES/18 MONTHS
CO-BORROWER'S EMPLOYMENT	
11. NAME OF EMPLOYER / ADDRESS	ABC DEPARTMENT STORE; 421 MAIN STREET, ANYTOWN
12. POSITION HELD / LENGTH OF EMPLOYMENT	DEPARTMENT MANAGER/ 8 YEARS
13. EMPLOYMENT VERIFIED BY	C. BELLOWS
14. PREVIOUS EMPLOYMENT / LENGTH OF EMPLOYMENT	——

THE REPORTING BUREAU CERTIFIES THAT: Public records have been checked for judgments, garnishments, foreclosures, bankruptcies and other legal action involving the BORROWER ☒ CO-BORROWER ☒ (or equivalent results have been obtained through the use of qualified public records reporting services) with the following results: PUBLIC RECORD ITEMS FOUND BORROWER DIVORCE 8/9x   PUBLIC RECORD ITEMS FOUND CO-BORROWER N/A

THE REPORTING BUREAU CERTIFIES THAT: The credit record of the borrower (and co-borrower if any) has been checked as to payment of obligations: a. ☐ through the credit accounts extended by designated credit grantors, if any; and, b. ☒ through accumulated credit records of such credit grantors of the community in which the subject(s) resides, with the results indicated below.

CREDIT HISTORY

BUSINESS	DATE ACCOUNT OPENED	HIGHEST CREDIT	BALANCE OWING	MONTHLY PAYMENT	PAYMENT PATTERN	PAST DUE AMOUNT	TIMES PAST DUE 30	60	90+	DATE LAST PAST DUE
BOLES INC.	7/9x	$200	–0–	$17	AS AGREED	–0–				——
ACME DRUGS	9/9x	$150	$90	REVOLV.	SLOW	$26	12	2		CURRENT
PENNEY'S	8/9x	$950	$900	$45	SLOW	$45	2	1		CURRENT
MASTERCARD	9/9x	$500	$429	REVOLV.	AS AGREED	–0–				——
ABC FINANCE	2/9x	$1,500	$1,500	$92	TOO SOON TO RATE	–0–				——
HFC FINANCE	6/9x	$4,800	$1,900	$185	SLOW	$185	4			CURRENT

POSITIVE INFORMATION

NEGATIVE INFORMATION

POSITIVE: wife with same employer for last eight years; wife shows advancement with firm
NEGATIVE: possible alimony and/or child support from recent divorce; husband changed employers within last two years; three slow ratings on credit report—all of them open accounts; recent loan from ABC Finance may represent funds borrowed to pay closing costs or downpayment

Exercise No. 3

There is information contained in the sample credit report above which could favorably or unfavorably affect the underwriter's decision. In the space allocated, list the items you feel contribute to or detract from the loan application.

POSITIVE
INFORMATION

NEGATIVE
INFORMATION

Illegal Discrimination

Credit may not be denied
for discriminatory reasons

A borrower must be of legal age (usually age 18 or older) before he or she can qualify for a loan; after that, an applicant's age is not a valid reason for rejecting a loan.

In addition to age, a lender cannot use as a basis for denying a loan the race, color, creed, national origin, religion, handicap, familial status (children), marital status or sex of the borrower. (See Chapter 7, *State and Federal Regulation of Real Estate Finance.*)

U.S. Department of Housing and Urban Development

EQUAL HOUSING OPPORTUNITY

We Do Business in Accordance With the Federal Fair Housing Law

(The Fair Housing Amendments Act of 1988)

It Is Illegal To Discriminate Against Any Person Because of Race, Color, Religion, Sex, Handicap, Familial Status, or National Origin

- In the sale or rental of housing or residential lots

- In advertising the sale or rental of housing

- In the financing of housing

- In the provision of real estate brokerage services

- In the appraisal of housing

- Blockbusting is also illegal

Anyone who feels he or she has been discriminated against may file a complaint of housing discrimination with the:

**U.S. Department of Housing and Urban Development
Assistant Secretary for Fair Housing and Equal Opportunity
Washington, D.C. 20410**

Previous editions are obsolete

form HUD-928.1 (3-89)

SUMMARY OF QUALIFYING THE BUYER

A buyer's ability to qualify for a real estate loan depends on many factors, all of which relate to income, net worth and credit history. While there are established guidelines for determining adequacy of income in relation to proposed housing expense, it would be wrong to apply them too rigidly. All aspects of the buyer's financial situation must be considered before deciding on his or her qualification for a loan. Consider the quality, quantity and durability of a buyer's income and relate it to net worth and credit history. For instance, a buyer with a very marginal income situation may still qualify for a loan if the net worth is substantial enough to indicate an unusual ability to manage financial affairs. Conversely, strong earnings and substantial assets may not be enough to offset the damage caused by poor credit paying habits. A borrower must be both able (income/assets) and willing (credit) to pay the housing expense.

Finally, keep in mind that a good property with a considerable cash equity can offset marginal credit or income because borrowers who make large investments (downpayments) in their properties are far less likely to default than borrowers with little or no equity.

FHA UNDERWRITING STANDARDS

FHA ratios are based on gross income:
- housing expense - 29%
- total debt service - 41%

FHA's qualifying ratios are based on the borrower's gross income. Once the borrower's gross income has been identified, it must be compared against the proposed housing expense. Included in FHA's estimated housing expense are principal and interest payments, the monthly property taxes, the monthly homeowner's insurance premium, an estimated monthly maintenance expense, an estimated monthly utilities expense, monthly homeowners' association dues (if any), and monthly property assessments (if any).

Sample Housing Expense:

$538.42	principal and interest
40.00	property taxes
15.00	homeowner's insurance
33.00	maintenance expense
80.00	utilities expense
- 0 -	homeowners' association dues
- 0 -	assessments
$706.42	total housing expense

The FHA will allow a maximum ratio of housing expense to gross income of **29%**.

$2,435.93   minimum gross income necessary
.29⌐ 706.42   housing expense

In addition to its concern for the borrower's ratio of housing expense to income, FHA will want to know the borrower can support the family's fixed monthly payments as well. Fixed payments include automobile and personal loans, revolving credit card obligations, and child support or alimony payments. The maximum ratio for housing expense plus fixed payments-to-gross income is **41%**.

Example:

$706.42	housing expense
	fixed monthly payments:
92.65	auto payment
20.00	revolving account
$819.07	TOTAL

$1,997.73   minimum gross income necessary
.41⌐ 819.07   housing expense & fixed payments

Exercise No. 4

Bob Johnson works for the Acme Boat Company as a bookkeeper, earning $1,800 a month; his wife, Lucy, has a part-time secretarial job which pays $785 a month. They want to buy a house with an FHA loan. They have two personal loans with a local bank. The first loan has a payment of $114 and a balance of $1,254; the second loan calls for installments of $85, with $1,755 owing. They also have a department store revolving account with $47 payments and an $888 balance.

2. What is the Johnson's monthly gross income?

2. What is the maximum housing expense the FHA will allow?

3. What is the maximum total of housing expense and fixed payments the FHA will allow?

RESIDUAL INCOME

Prior to 1989, the Department of Housing & Urban Developmen (HUD) also used a residual income method of qualifying purchasers as an alternative to the total payments to income method just described. If a borrower did not qualify under the first formula, the FHA, at its option, could use the alternative qualifying method. The FHA no longer uses the residual income method. All applicants for FHA loans must now qualify based on the total payments-to-net income method.

VA QUALIFYING STANDARDS

Prior to 1986, the Veterans Administration used a cash flow qualifying method. However, in 1986, the VA began using both the cash flow method and an income ratio method. This means that those underwriting VA guaranteed loans will have to determine two separate figures in their analysis, the residual income of the borrower and the income ratio of the borrower.

VA uses both cash flow method and income-debt ratio

CASH FLOW ANALYSIS

The borrower's cash flow is the veteran's remaining income after subtracting income taxes, housing expense, and all recurring monthly obligations from his or her gross monthly income. The veteran's residual income must meet the VA's minimum requirements, which are set out below. The minimum requirements are determined based on the geographic region, family size, and size of the loan.

Cash flow requirements differ based on geographic region, size of family, and size of loan

The amount of the veteran's residual income must meet the VA's minimum requirements. A new set of residual income requirements has been published and the figures are set out below. These figures are now determined on both a regional basis and a selling-price basis.

Exercise No. 5

Steven Gulickson works for the Peters-Davis Corporation as an accountant, earning $2,500 a month; his wife, Allison, works two days a week in an interior design shop, where she makes $13 per hour. They pay approximately $510 per month in income tax. Steve and Allison have four children and they live in what the VA considers the West Region. They want to buy a house with a VA loan.

The Gulicksons have two personal loans with a local bank. The first has a monthly payment of $136 and a balance of $3,264. The second loan calls for installments of $210, with $5,460 owning. They also have two department store accounts. One account has a balance of $750 and requires payments of $52 per month. The other account has a balance of $1,500 and requires payments of $45 per month.

1. What is the Gulickson's gross monthly income?

2. Assuming that the Gulicksons want a loan amount above $70,000, what is the residual income amount that the VA will require?

3. What are the Gulickson's total monthly expenses?

4. Using the residual income method, how much money will the Gulicksons have available for use as their monthly housing expense?

RESIDUAL INCOMES BY REGION FOR LOAN AMOUNTS OF $69,999 AND BELOW					RESIDUAL INCOMES BY REGION FOR LOAN AMOUNTS OF $70,000 AND ABOVE				
	NORTH-EAST	MID-WEST	SOUTH	WEST		NORTH-EAST	MID-WEST	SOUTH	WEST
Family Size*					Family Size*				
1	$348	$340	$340	$379	1	$401	$393	$393	$437
2	583	570	570	635	2	673	658	658	733
3	702	687	687	765	3	810	792	792	882
4	791	773	773	861	4	913	893	893	995
5	821	803	803	894	5	946	925	925	1031

*For families with more than five members, add $70 for each additional member up to a family of seven.   *For families with more than five members, add $75 each additional member up to a family of seven.

Minimum Residual Standards are Guidelines

The balance available for family support is an important factor in evaluating a loan application, but is not the only consideration. The VA standards are intended to be guidelines in judging the borrower's relative strength or weakness with regards to residual income, which is only one of the many factors to be considered in underwriting VA loan applications.

Other Factors to be Considered.

In addition to the residual income standards, other important factors considered in underwriting a loan application include:

1. the borrower's demonstrated ability to accumulate cash or other liquid assets (such as stocks or bonds);
2. the borrower's demonstrated ability to use credit wisely and to avoid incurring an excessive amount of debt;
3. the relationship between the shelter expense for the property being acquired and the expense that the borrower is accustomed to paying;
4. the number and ages of the borrower's dependents;
5. the locality and general economic level of the neighborhood where the property is located;

Minimum residual amounts are guidelines only. Lender should also consider other relevant factors:
1. liquid assets
2. ability to avoid excessive debt in past
3. current and proposed housing expense
4. age and number of dependents
5. neighborhood
6. likelihood of increase or decrease in borrower's income
7. employment history
8. credit history
9. size of downpayment
10. cash available after paying downpayment and closing costs

273

6. the likelihood that the borrower's income may increase or decrease;
7. the borrower's employment history and work experience;
8. the borrower's demonstrated ability and willingness to make payments on time;
9. amount of any downpayment made; and,
10. the borrower's available cash after paying closing costs and other prepaid items.

INCOME RATIO ANALYSIS

In addition to residual income, a ratio based on total monthly debt payments (housing expense, installment debts, child support, etc.) to gross monthly income will be considered by a VA underwriter. The ratio is determined by taking the sum of the housing expense (principal, interest, tax and insurance payments) and monthly obligations and dividing that by gross income. If the obligations-to-income ratio is 41% or less, the underwriter may approve the loan. If the ratio is above 41%, the underwriter must present other factors (e.g., sufficient residual income, significant liquid assets, a substantial downpayment) before approving the loan. A VA underwriter may generally approve the loan if the residual income is at least 20% over the required minimum.

Example: (family of two in West)

VA uses gross income for ratio:
• total debt service to gross income—41%

$733 required residual income
2000 gross monthly income
1200 total monthly expenses

$$\begin{array}{r} .6 \\ \$2,000\overline{)1,200} \end{array}$$

274

Obligations-to-income ratio: 60% (higher than 41%—will need additional factors for approval)

$$\begin{array}{r} \$2,000 \\ -\ 1,200 \\ \hline \$\ 800 \end{array}$$ residual income

$$\begin{array}{r} \$733 \\ \times\ .20 \\ \hline \$146.60 \end{array}$$ additional 20% of required residual income

$$\begin{array}{r} \$733.00 \\ +\ 146.60 \\ \hline \$879.60 \end{array}$$ required residual income plus additional 20%

The veteran's residual income is $800, less than 20% above the residual income requirements. It's possible a VA underwriter would not approve the loan.

The VA has emphasized that these underwriting standards are guidelines for approval only and should not be automatic reasons for approving or rejecting a loan.

As you have probably noticed, the FHA and VA obligations-to-income ratio formulas are more liberal than the FNMA and FHLMC conventional loan qualifying ratios, and the cash flow or residual income analysis systems are the most liberal of all. A borrower who would be considered marginal by FNMA and FHLMC might qualify more easily for an FHA or VA loan.

INCOME AND EXPENSE STANDARDS
FOR CONVENTIONAL, FHA, AND VA LOANS.

	HOUSING EXPENSE	TOTAL DEBT SERVICE/ FIXED PAYMENTS	CASH FLOW ANALYSIS
FNMA/FHLMC (conventional) Loan-to-Value 90% or Less	- principal, interest, taxes, insurance, and PMIP - not to exceed 28% of stable monthly income	-housing expense plus debts with more than ten payments remaining -not to exceed 36% of stable monthly income	
FNMA Loan-to-Value More Than 90%	- not to exceed 28% of stable monthly income	-not to exceed 33% of stable monthly income	
FHA	- principal, interest, taxes, insurance, maintenance and utilities - not to exceed 29% of income	- housing expense plus recurring debts - not to exceed 41% of income	
VA		- housing expenses plus recurring debts - should not exceed 41% of gross income	- cash flow should equal or exceed specified region figures for appropriate family size + loan amount

QUALIFYING THE BUYER — CASE STUDY

When first faced with the many rules used by lenders to qualify borrowers, you may feel overwhelmed or confused. However, these rules are really fairly simple to apply and once you have gone through the qualifying process a few times, they will begin to fall into place. This case study is designed to see you through the qualifying process step by step. You will be given all the necessary information about a potential buyer and will be asked to determine the maximum loan amount he or she would qualify for under the various programs available: conventional, FHA-insured and VA-guaranteed. Various forms are provided to help you work through the necessary calculations. Knowing the maximum price range of affordable housing prevents a potential buyer from the disappointment of choosing a house he or she can't afford.

John and Mary Smith are thinking of buying their first home. They come to your office because you advertised a house that sounded attractive and affordable. Before taking them to see the home, or any other property they might be interested in, you wisely decide to "pre-qualify" them— determine the maximum loan amount and monthly payments they could qualify for. After questioning them about their financial position, you end up with the following information:

Employment:
John served in the Army for two years during the Vietnam War.

John has been employed as a salesperson by National Tire, Inc. for three years.

Mary has been employed as a paralegal by Badley & Badley (a law firm) for two years.

Income:

John makes the following income:

monthly salary: $1,775

commission: $250 average per month (regularly received for previous two years)

bonus: $2,000 bonus last year (for the first time)

Mary makes the following income:

monthly salary: $1,750

Dependents:

John and Mary have two children, ages fourteen and seventeen.

Assets:

Savings account: $12,000

Retirement fund (IRA): $5,300

Vacation property (unimproved lot): $3,700 equity

Miscellaneous (furniture, etc.): $11,500

Liabilities (monthly):

Car payment: $215 (30 payments remaining)

Car payment: $165 (11 payments remaining)

Installment contract (on vacation property): $142 (125 payments remaining)

Revolving credit card payments: $30 (15 payments remaining)

College loan: $50 (23 payments remaining)

Federal Income Tax: $462

Other Facts:

John and Mary live in what the VA considers to be the West region.

The maximum FHA loan amount in the city where John and Mary live is $90,000. (NOTE: This FHA amount may be more or less in your area.)

Through your contacts in the mortgage market, you know that current interest rates for 30-year loans are as follows:

VA (fixed-rate): 10%
FHA (fixed-rate): 10¾%
Conventional, fixed-rate, 90% LTV: 10¾%
Conventional, fixed-rate, 95% LTV: 11¼%
Conventional, adjustable-rate: 8½%

You now have all the basic information on the Smith's finances and the current interest rates. Using the following forms to help you with your calculations, determine the maximum loan amount and payments they will qualify for. Since John was in the Army, you know that he is eligible for a VA-guaranteed loan, so you should complete the process for each program.

Note that there is a form for an FHA-insured loan, a form for a VA-guaranteed loan, and three forms for conventional loans: one for a 90% or less LTV fixed-rate loan, one for a 90% or less LTV adjustable-rate loan, and one for a 95% LTV fixed-rate loan.

You can determine the maximum loan amount from the monthly payment and interest rate by using two different methods. If you have access to one, a financial calculator will figure the loan amount for you quickly (see Appendix ? in the text for basic instructions on finding loan amounts). If a financial calculator is not available to you, you may use the Interest Rate Factors Table in Appendix ?. Simply find the appropriate interest rate factor for the interest rate and term of the loan, and add a decimal point and zero to the front of the number. Then, take the maximum monthly mortgage payment and divide it by this number. The result will be the maximum mortgage amount.

When the borrower actually applies for a loan with a lender, he or she will have already entered into a purchase and sale agreement for a particular home at a particular purchase price and will be asking for a certain loan amount. Since the lender knows the requested loan amount and purchase price, he or she can calculate (with fair accuracy) what insurance, taxes, mortgage insurance and maintenance costs will be. When you are prequalifying a buyer, however, you will usually not have a particular purchase price in mind. But you will still need to know an approximate figure for these costs. In the qualifying forms, we assume that 10% of the total mortgage payment will go towards taxes, insurance and mortgage insurance. This is only an approximation, but it should be close enough for prequalifying purposes. Average figures for these costs will vary from place to place, depending on property tax rates, etc. In practice, choose a percentage that reflects the costs in your area. If you are prequalifying a borrower with a specific loan amount in mind, you should be able to determine approximate figures for these amounts by asking a local lender.

As you figure out the loan payments and maximum loan amounts, answer the following questions:

1. What are the maximum monthly mortgage payments under each program?

2. What are the maximum loan amounts for each program?

3. Which program would the Smiths be most likely to choose?

INCOME QUALIFYING — CONVENTIONAL LOANS
FIXED-RATE, 90% OR LESS LTV

Monthly Gross Income:

Base salary	_____
Overtime	_____
Bonuses	_____
Commissions	_____
Other	_____
Total	_____

Long-Term Monthly Debt:

Car payment	_____
Child support	_____
Credit cards	_____
Other loans	_____
Other debts	_____
Total	_____

(Consider 5% payments on all revolving charges)

Housing Expense-to-Income Ratio:

_____	Stable Monthly Income
_____ x .28 _____	Income Ratio
_____	Maximum Mortgage Payment (PITI)

Total Debt Service Ratio:

_____	Stable Monthly Income
_____ x .36 _____	Income Ratio
_____	Maximum Monthly Obligations

_____	Maximum Monthly Obligations
_____ − _____	Monthly Obligations
_____	Maximum Mortgage Payment (PITI)

MAXIMUM MORTGAGE PAYMENT (PITI)_____

_____	Maximum PITI
	(less 10% of mortgage payment)
_____ − _____	(Insurance, taxes, PMI)
_____	Maximum Principal and Interest Payment
_____	**MAXIMUM LOAN AMOUNT** (using calculator or interest factor tables)

INCOME QUALIFYING — CONVENTIONAL LOANS
FIXED-RATE, MORE THAN 90% LTV

Monthly Gross Income: **Long-Term Monthly Debt:**

Base salary	_____	Car payment	_____
Overtime	_____	Child support	_____
Bonuses	_____	Credit cards	_____
Commissions	_____	Other loans	_____
Other	_____	Other debts	_____
Total	_____	**Total**	_____

(Consider 5% payments on all revolving charges)

Housing Expense-to-Income Ratio:

_____	Stable Monthly Income
x .28	Income Ratio
_____	Maximum Mortgage Payment (PITI)

Total Debt Service Ratio:

_____	Stable Monthly Income
x .33	Income Ratio
_____	Maximum Monthly Obligations

_____	Maximum Monthly Obligations
_____	Monthly Obligations
_____	Maximum Mortgage Payment (PITI)

MAXIMUM MORTGAGE PAYMENT (PITI)_____

_____	Maximum PITI
	(less 10% of mortgage payment)
− _____	(Insurance, taxes, PMI)
_____	Maximum Principal and Interest
	Payment

_____	**MAXIMUM LOAN AMOUNT** (using calculator or interest factor tables)

INCOME QUALIFYING — CONVENTIONAL LOANS
ADJUSTABLE-RATE, 90% OR LESS LTV

Monthly Gross Income: **Long-Term Monthly Debt:**

Base salary   _____   Car payment   _____
Overtime   _____   Child support   _____
Bonuses   _____   Credit cards   _____
Commissions   _____   Other loans   _____
Other   _____   Other debts   _____
Total   _____   **Total**   _____

(Consider 5% payments on all revolving charges)

Housing Expense-to-Income Ratio:

_____   Stable Monthly Income
_____x .28_____   Income Ratio
_____   Maximum Mortgage Payment (PITI)

Total Debt Service Ratio:

_____   Stable Monthly Income
_____x .36_____   Income Ratio
_____   Maximum Monthly Obligations

_____   Maximum Monthly Obligations
_____ — _____   Monthly Obligations
_____   Maximum Mortgage Payment (PITI)

MAXIMUM MORTGAGE PAYMENT (PITI)_____

_____   Maximum PITI
                       (less 10% of mortgage payment)
_____ — _____   (Insurance, taxes, PMI)
_____   Maximum Principal and Interest
                       Payment

_____   **MAXIMUM LOAN AMOUNT** (using
                       calculator or interest factor tables)

INCOME QUALIFYING — FHA-INSURED LOANS
Income Ratio Method

Monthly Gross Income:

Base salary	_____
Overtime	_____
Bonuses	_____
Commissions	_____
Other	_____
Total	_____

Long-Term Monthly Debt:

Car payment	_____	_____
Child support	_____	_____
Credit cards	_____	_____
Other loans	_____	_____
Other debts	_____	_____
Total	_____	_____

(Consider 5% payments on all revolving charges)

Housing Expense-to-Income Ratio: 29%

_____	Stable Monthly Income
_____ x .29 _____	Income Ratio
_____	Maximum Mortgage Payment (PITI)

Total Debt Service Ratio: 41%

_____	Stable Monthly Income
_____ x .41 _____	Income Ratio
_____	Maximum Monthly Obligations

_____	Maximum Monthly Obligations
_____ − _____	Monthly Obligations
_____	Maximum Mortgage Payment (PITI)

MAXIMUM MORTGAGE PAYMENT (PITI)_____

_____	Maximum PITI
	(less 10% of mortgage payment)
_____ − _____	(Insurance, taxes, MIP)
_____	Maximum Principal and Interest Payment

_____	**MAXIMUM LOAN AMOUNT** (not to exceed regional mortgage amount limitations)

284

INCOME QUALIFYING — VA GUARANTEED LOANS
Residual Income Method

Monthly Gross Income:

Base salary	_____
Overtime	_____
Bonuses	_____
Commissions	_____
Other	_____
Total	_____

Long-Term Monthly Debt:

Car payment	_____
Child support	_____
Credit cards	_____
Other loans	_____
Other debts	_____
Total	_____

(consider 5% payments
on all revolving charges)

Less All Taxes:

Federal Income tax	_____
Social Security (7.65%)	_____
State Income tax	_____
Other Tax	_____
Total	_____

Net Income _____

less:

long-term debts	_____
required reserves	_____
Total	_____

RESIDUAL INCOMES BY REGION FOR LOAN AMOUNTS OF $69,999 AND BELOW					RESIDUAL INCOMES BY REGION FOR LOAN AMOUNTS OF $70,000 AND ABOVE				
Family Size*	NORTH-EAST	MID-WEST	SOUTH	WEST	Family Size*	NORTH-EAST	MID-WEST	SOUTH	WEST
1	$348	$340	$340	$379	1	$401	$393	$393	$437
2	583	570	570	635	2	673	658	658	733
3	702	687	687	765	3	810	792	792	882
4	791	773	773	861	4	913	893	893	995
5	821	803	803	894	5	946	925	925	1031

*For families with more than five members, add $70 for each additional member up to a family of seven.   *For families with more than five members, add $75 for each additional member up to a family of seven.

MAXIMUM HOUSING EXPENSE_____

Total Housing Expense	_____
less 20% (taxes,	— _____
insurance, maintenance,	
utilities)	_____

Maximum Principal and Interest Payment_____

_____ **MAXIMUM LOAN AMOUNT** (not to exceed lender limitations)

Income Ratio Method

Total Debt Service Ratio: 41%

_____	Stable Monthly Income
___x .41___	Income Ratio
_____	Maximum Monthly Obligations
_____	Maximum Monthly Obligations
— _____	Monthly Obligations
_____	Maximum Mortgage Payment (PITI)

MAXIMUM MORTGAGE PAYMENT (PITI)_____

_____	Maximum PITI
	(less 10% of mortgage payment)
— _____	(Insurance, taxes, PMI)
_____	Maximum Principal and Interest Payment
_____	**MAXIMUM LOAN AMOUNT** (not to exceed lender limitations)

CHAPTER SUMMARY

1. The loan underwriting process evaluates both the borrower and the property. The lender will ask:

   - Does the borrower's overall financial situation indicate that he/she will make the payments?, and
   - Is there enough value in the property to secure the debt if the borrower defaults?

2. The lender will answer these questions based on the guidelines of the various agencies involved, specifically FNMA, FHLMC, the FHA, and the VA. Conventional loans that follow FNMA and FHLMC guidelines are called conforming loans.

3. The process of answering the questions listed above is called qualifying the buyer. The lender considers the buyer's current income and monthly debts, overall net worth, and credit history to evaluate the borrower's ability and inclination to repay the loan.

4. Although the specific standards are different for conventional (FNMA/FHLMC), FHA and VA loans, the underwriting procedure is virtually the same. The lender first determines the amount of the borrower's income. Many rules apply as to what constitutes "stable monthly income," including quality, quantity, and durability. Once the lender determines the borrower's income, it applies the appropriate monthly income-to-debt ratios for both housing expense and total monthly obligations, and/or evaluation of the borrower's cash flow or residual income after paying all monthly debts.

5. The lender then checks the borrower's net worth (to determine financial responsibility and ability to meet financial emergencies) and credit history (to determine willingness to pay financial obligations).

6. Conventional and FHA standards emphasize income-to-debt ratios. (FHA standards are more lenient than FNMA's and FHLMC's). VA standards emphasize residual income requirements but also include an income-to-total debt ratio (VA standards are the most lenient of all.)

Chapter 14
QUALIFYING THE PROPERTY

Qualifying a property involves an analysis of its many features to determine whether it has sufficient value to serve as collateral for a real estate loan and whether its value can be expected to remain stable in the months and years to come.

Lenders do not make loans in anticipation of foreclosure; they make loans in anticipation of being repaid (with interest) in a timely manner. Virtually every underwriting decision is based on this premise. However, regardless of the quality of the borrower, the property will serve as security for the debt, and the lender will make certain before making the loan that there is enough value in the property to protect its investment.

LENDER'S PERCEPTION OF VALUE

When an appraiser is retained by a lender to estimate the market value of a residence, he or she is being asked to make a thorough analysis of the property and its surroundings and to issue an objective estimate of its market value. As such, the appraiser's conclusions may not coincide with the purchase price set by the buyer and seller. It is not unusual for the deposit receipt to reflect emotional or subjective considerations that are valuable to the buyer and seller, but are not pertinent to the actual market value of the property. It is the true market value that the lender seeks, because if a foreclosure is ever necessary, the lender will want to know that the property can be resold at a price that will permit recovery of most, if not all, of the investment.

LOAN-TO-VALUE RATIOS

Until recently, market trends have been towards an increasing number of high loan-to-value (LTV) loans. Loan-to-value refers to the maximum loan a lender is willing to make in relation to the appraised value of the property; for instance, if a lender's maximum loan-to-value ratio is 80% and a property appraises for $100,000, the maximum loan is $80,000.

Loan Based on Sales Price or Value

Loan is based on sales price or appraised value, whichever is lower

It is universal lender policy for maximum loan amounts to be based on the appraised value or the selling price, whichever is less.

Example:

$150,000   sales price
$180,000   appraised value

$150,000   sales price
× .80   80% loan-to-value ratio
$120,000   maximum loan

In the example, the maximum loan is predicated on the lower of the two figures, the sales price. If the lender were willing to base the loan amount on the higher of the two figures, the appraised value, an 80% loan-to-value ratio would result in a loan that is nearly 100% of the sales price, which is unacceptable to conventional lenders. Lenders make loans in anticipation of repayment, not foreclosure, and history has shown that borrowers who make normal downpayments are better risks than those who do not.

ESTIMATING MARKET VALUE

It is not necessary for real estate agents to be able to appraise real estate, at least not with the sophistication of a professional appraiser. It is helpful, however, to know something about the mechanics of the appraisal process and the reasoning that underlies many of the appraiser's conclusions. If an agent understands how lenders and their appraisers perceive value, it makes it much easier to write and arrange financing for sales that will hold together.

There are three ways to appraise residential real estate:

1) the market data method,
2) the replacement cost method, and
3) the income method.

Three methods of appraisal:
1. market data
2. replacement cost
3. income

MARKET DATA METHOD

Of the three appraisal methods, the market data method is the one preferred by appraisers. Sometimes called the market comparison method, this technique involves a comparison of the property being appraised against similar properties in the same neighborhood that either are for sale or have sold recently. Appraisers know that competitive forces influence prices and that no informed buyer who is acting free of pressure will pay more for a particular property than he or she would have to pay for an equally desirable substitute property. Nor will an informed property owner sell for less than is necessary, and, if he or she is objective, the owner will base the pricing decision on the prices recently paid in the area for similar properties.

SALES PRICE vs. LIST PRICE

Prices paid for properties are better indications of values in the area than are list prices (asking prices) because they represent actual agreements between buyers and sellers in a competitive marketplace. Asking prices are helpful to an appraiser to the extent that they represent the ceiling of values in the area.

> **Example:** If the asking price for a property being appraised is $174,500 and there are several comparable properties for sale in the area with list prices of $160,000 and below, the appraiser knows that, in the absence of some extraordinary circumstance, the ceiling of value for the subject property is $160,000 or less. Prices asked and prices paid are more often than not entirely different.

IDENTIFYING LEGITIMATE COMPARABLES

Identifying comparables:
1. date of sale
2. location of sale
3. physical characteristics
4. terms of sale
5. arm's length transaction

When appraising by the market data method, one must be certain that the sales used as a basis for comparison are in fact capable of comparison in the areas of greatest consequence. When evaluating a sale to see if it qualifies as a legitimate comparable, the appraiser is concerned with five issues:

1. **Date of comparable sale.** The sale should be recent, within the past six months if possible. Recent sales more accurately indicate what is happening in today's marketplace.

   If the market has been inactive and there are not enough valid comparable sales from the past six months (three comparables are necessary), the appraiser can go back farther, but he or she would have to make adjustments for the time factor, allowing for inflationary or deflationary trends or any other forces that have affected prices in the area during that period.

Example: A comparable residential property sold one year ago for $127,000. In general, the values of local properties have risen by 13% over the last year. The subject property, then, should be worth 13% more than the comparable from a year ago.

$127,000	value one year ago
× 1.13	inflation factor
$143,510	approximate present value

It stands to reason that the more adjustments an appraiser has to make, the more imperfect and questionable the conclusions will be. Adjustments in this context mean allowances for more or less value based on differences between a comparable and the subject property. Adjustments are made for differences in the locations and physical characteristics of the properties as well as differences in time of sales.

2. **Location of comparable sale.** Whenever possible, comparables should be selected from the neighborhood of the subject property. In the absence of any legitimate comparables in the neighborhood, the appraiser can select comparable properties from elsewhere, but the properties selected should at least come from comparable neighborhoods. If a comparable that is selected from an inferior neighborhood is structurally identical to the subject property, it is probably less valuable; conversely, a structurally identical comparable in a superior neighborhood is probably more valuable than the subject property. It is generally conceded that location contributes more to the value of real estate than any other characteristic.

3. **Physical characteristics.** To qualify as a comparable, a property should have physical characteristics that are

similar to those of the subject property.

4. **Terms of sale.** With the increase in seller participation in financing today, the terms of sale have become much more of a factor when estimating value. Buyers have demonstrated a readiness that borders on eagerness to pay top prices—in many cases inflated prices—to sellers willing to sell their properties on attractive terms, which often include extended repayment periods and low interest rates. These inflated prices distort values, and an appraiser has to take into account the influence terms of sale may have had on the price paid for a comparable property. Where a seller made property available on highly favorable terms, there is an excellent chance the sales price did not represent the true market value of the comparable.

Arm's length transaction:
• both parties informed of property's attributes
• both are acting free of undue pressure
• property is offered for sale on open market

5. **Must be arm's length transaction.** Finally, before a comparable sale can be relied upon as an indication of what the subject property is worth, it must be an arm's length transaction. This means the buyer and seller are both informed of the property's attributes and deficiencies and are acting free of unusual pressure, and the property is offered for sale and tested on the open market.

REPLACEMENT COST METHOD

The replacement cost method for appraising real estate is based on the presumption that the value of a property is limited by the cost of replacing it. Residential appraisers keep abreast of construction costs in the area and refer to them when using the cost method. There are three steps in the cost method:

Step 1: Estimate the cost of replacing the house.
Step 2: Estimate and deduct any accrued depreciation.

Step 3: Add the value of the lot to the depreciated value of the house.

SQUARE FOOT REPLACEMENT COST METHOD

By analyzing the average cost per square foot of construction for recently built comparable homes, the appraiser can determine what the square foot cost of replacing the house under appraisement would be. The number of square feet in a home is identified by measuring the dimensions of each floor of the structure, including the outer wall surfaces.

Replacement cost method:
1. estimate cost of replacing house
2. deduct depreciation
3. add value of land

Example:

	Cost To Build*	Square Feet	Cost Per Square Foot	
Comparable #1				$46.90
	$68,000	1,450	1,450	68,000.00
Comparable #2				$48.40
	$72,600	1,500	1,500	72,600.00
Comparable #3				$50.31
	$65,400	1,300	1,300	65,400.00

*Construction costs per square foot include cost of materials, labor, builder administrative costs, and builder profit.

Square-foot replacement uses average cost to construct comparables

Presuming that the three comparables are all equally similar to the subject property with respect to style and quality of construction, the appraiser could form a reliable estimate of the average per square foot cost of construction by adding the three costs per square foot together and dividing by three. (If they are not all equally similar to the subject property, greater weight would be given to the one that is most similar.)

Example:

Comparable #1	$ 78.90/sq.ft.
Comparable #2	68.40/sq.ft.
Comparable #3	73.31/sq.ft.
	$220.61

$$\underline{\$73.54} \text{ average cost per square foot}$$
$$3\overline{)220.61}$$

Next, the appraiser would multiply the average cost per square foot by the number of square feet in the subject property. For sake of example, presume the subject property has 1,600 square feet.

$$\begin{array}{r} 1600 \\ \times\ 73.54 \\ \hline \$117,664 \end{array}$$ estimated cost to replace subject property

DEPRECIATION

If the home being appraised is a used home, the presumption is that it is not as valuable as a comparable new home, that it has depreciated in value. Estimating depreciation is the most difficult part of the replacement cost appraisal process. Depreciation is a loss in value due to any cause. Value can be lost due to physical wear and tear (**deferred maintenance**); functional inadequacies, often caused by age or poor design (**functional obsolescence**); and factors outside the property, such as a deteriorating neighborhood or poor access to important regions, such as downtown shopping and employment centers (**economic obsolescence**).

Depreciation: loss in value due to any source
• deferred maintenance
• functional obsolescense
• economic obsolescence

Example:

$117,664	estimated cost to replace
− 4,100	deferred maintenance (roof in need of repair; garage door should be replaced)
− 5,500	functional obsolescence (living room too small; family room too far from kitchen)
− 4,000	economic obsolescence (obnoxious odors from nearby industrial plant)
$104,064	depreciated value of improvements

The last step in the replacement cost process is to add the value of the land to the depreciated value of the improvements.

Example:

$104,064	depreciated value of improvements
35,000	land value
$139,064	depreciated value of the property

The value of the land is determined by the market data method. Prices recently paid for lots similar to the subject are compared and relied upon as indications of what the subject lot is worth.

INCOME METHOD

Residences are not generally thought of as income producing properties, so traditional income analysis and appraisal techniques do not apply. If a residential appraiser uses an income method at all, he or she will use the **gross income multiplier method**, also called the **gross rent multiplier**

Gross rent multiplier:
rental income equals
percentage of price paid
for rental property

method. As a rule, it is applicable only when appraising residential rental properties.

The assumption underlying the gross rent multiplier approach to value is that rental income represents a percentage of the price paid for a rental property.

Example:

Sales Price: $90,000
Monthly Rent: $900
Conclusion: Monthly rent is equal to
                  1% of the sales price
                  or the sales price is 100
                  times the monthly rent.

Monthly rents may run about one percent of selling prices in one market, and more or less in another. A market exists where specific rental properties compete with each other for tenants. For competitive reasons, rental prices for similar properties tend to be much alike within the same market. As a result, if one rental property has a monthly income that is one percent of its sales price, comparable properties will have similar income-to-price ratios.

A monthly gross income multiplier is established by dividing the sales price by the monthly rental income. An annual multiplier is achieved by dividing the sales price by the annual rental income.

Example:

Sales Price	**Monthly Rent**	**Monthly Multiplier**
$90,000 ÷	$900 =	100

Sales Price	**Annual Rent**	**Annual Multiplier**
$90,000 ÷	$10,800 =	8.33

After locating at least four comparable residential rental properties, the appraiser can determine their monthly or annual multipliers (either is acceptable—appraiser's preference) by dividing the rents into their respective selling prices. We will use the monthly multipliers.

Example:

Comp. No.	Sales Price	Monthly Rent	Monthly Multiplier
1	$117,500	$800	146.88
2	$125,000	$825	151.52
3	$132,600	$895	148.16
4	$137,800	$950	145.05

The appraiser uses the multiplier from the property that is most similar to the subject property. The appraiser may raise or lower the amount of the monthly multiplier to account for any significant differences between the properties.

Example:

The subject property is most similar to comparable number three above, which has a monthly multiplier of 148.16. However, the subject property is slightly older. It is the same age as comparable number one, which has a monthly multiplier of 146.88. So the appraiser may determine the monthly multiplier for the subject property to be slightly less than 148.16 but more than 146.88.

Next the appraiser multiplies the rent that the subject property is generating by the determined monthly multiplier for a rough estimate of its income-producing value.

Principal weakness: does not take vacancies or operating expenses into account

The principal weakness to the gross multiplier method is that it is based on gross income figures and does not take into account vacancies or operating expenses. If two rental

[Handwritten margin notes at top: "Inc less Expenses = 600k / 1200,000 vacancies / Oper Expenses = ___ / Net Inc ÷ Cap Rate = 4.6 million / 13%"]

[Handwritten margin notes at left: "Important for Investors", "Cap Rate = What you want for ROI (eg .11%) + S/L Depr on Property eg Bldg will last 50 yrs / 100% ÷ 50yr = Depr is 2% yr / (eg) 2% / 13%"]

homes have the same rental income, the gross multiplier method would indicate they are worth the same amount; but if one is older and has higher maintenance costs, the net return to the owner would be less, and so would its value.

If possible, the appraiser should use the subject property's **economic rent** (the rent the property could command in today's marketplace if it were available for lease) as opposed to the **contract rent** (the rent it is actually receiving). If the owner leased the property two years ago for $650 a month and the lease contract has another year to go, use of the $650 figure (if it is unrealistically low in today's market) would distort the estimate of value.

WHY SHOULD AN AGENT UNDERSTAND THE APPRAISAL PROCESS?

Below is a replica of a residential appraisal report form, the type used by FNMA, FHLMC, FHA and VA. A review of the report should give you a reasonable understanding of what the appraiser must do before he or she can issue a responsible estimate of value—an appraisal.

Agents should understand the appraisal process because it will help eliminate or at least minimize the most prevalent of all real estate selling problems, the low appraisal. The low appraisal has plagued the real estate industry since the beginning. No one gets through an entire career without facing the appraisal problem at least a few times; some agents never seem to escape it. A low appraisal is an estimate of value that is below (sometimes way below) the actual selling price. A sale is written, and one to three weeks later the appraiser gives the agent the bad news. You will recall that the loan to finance a transaction is based upon the sales price or appraised value, whichever is lower.

300

Property Description & Analysis **UNIFORM RESIDENTIAL APPRAISAL REPORT** **File No.**

SUBJECT		
Property Address	Census Tract	LENDER DISCRETIONARY USE
City County State	Zip Code	Sale Price $
Legal Description		Date
Owner/Occupant	Map Reference	Mortgage Amount $
Sale Price $ Date of Sale	PROPERTY RIGHTS APPRAISED	Mortgage Type
Loan charges/concessions to be paid by seller $	☐ Fee Simple	Discount Points and Other Concessions
R.E. Taxes $ Tax Year HOA $/Mo.	☐ Leasehold	Paid by Seller $
Lender/Client	☐ Condominium (HUD/VA)	
	☐ De Minimis PUD	Source

NEIGHBORHOOD

LOCATION	☐ Urban	☐ Suburban	☐ Rural	NEIGHBORHOOD ANALYSIS	Good	Avg.	Fair	Poor
BUILT UP	☐ Over 75%	☐ 25-75%	☐ Under 25%	Employment Stability	☐	☐	☐	☐
GROWTH RATE	☐ Rapid	☐ Stable	☐ Slow	Convenience to Employment	☐	☐	☐	☐
PROPERTY VALUES	☐ Increasing	☐ Stable	☐ Declining	Convenience to Shopping	☐	☐	☐	☐
DEMAND/SUPPLY	☐ Shortage	☐ In Balance	☐ Over Supply	Convenience to Schools	☐	☐	☐	☐
MARKETING TIME	☐ Under 3 Mos.	☐ 3-6 Mos.	☐ Over 6 Mos.	Adequacy of Public Transportation	☐	☐	☐	☐

PRESENT LAND USE %	LAND USE CHANGE	PREDOMINANT	SINGLE FAMILY HOUSING			
Single Family ___	Not Likely ☐	OCCUPANCY	PRICE AGE	Recreation Facilities	☐☐☐☐
2-4 Family ___	Likely ☐	Owner ☐	$ (000) (yrs)	Adequacy of Utilities	☐☐☐☐
Multi-family ___	In process ☐	Tenant ☐		Property Compatibility	☐☐☐☐
Commercial ___	To: ___	Vacant (0-5%) ☐	Low	Protection from Detrimental Cond.	☐☐☐☐
Industrial ___		Vacant (over 5%) ☐	High	Police & Fire Protection	☐☐☐☐
Vacant ___			Predominant	General Appearance of Properties	☐☐☐☐
				Appeal to Market	☐☐☐☐

Note: Race or the racial composition of the neighborhood are not considered reliable appraisal factors.
COMMENTS: _____

SITE

Dimensions		Topography
Site Area		Size
Zoning Classification	Corner Lot	Shape
HIGHEST & BEST USE: Present Use	Zoning Compliance	Drainage
	Other Use	

UTILITIES	Public	Other	SITE IMPROVEMENTS	Type	Public	Private	View
Electricity	☐		Street		☐	☐	Landscaping
Gas	☐		Curb/Gutter		☐	☐	Driveway
Water	☐		Sidewalk		☐	☐	Apparent Easements
Sanitary Sewer	☐		Street Lights		☐	☐	FEMA Flood Hazard Yes* ___ No ___
Storm Sewer	☐		Alley		☐	☐	FEMA* Map/Zone

COMMENTS (Apparent adverse easements, encroachments, special assessments, slide areas, etc.): _____

IMPROVEMENTS

GENERAL DESCRIPTION	EXTERIOR DESCRIPTION	FOUNDATION	BASEMENT	INSULATION
Units	Foundation	Slab	Area Sq. Ft.	Roof ☐
Stories	Exterior Walls	Crawl Space	% Finished	Ceiling ☐
Type (Det./Att.)	Roof Surface	Basement	Ceiling	Walls ☐
Design (Style)	Gutters & Dwnspts.	Sump Pump	Walls	Floor ☐
Existing	Window Type	Dampness	Floor	None ☐
Proposed	Storm Sash	Settlement	Outside Entry	Adequacy ☐
Under Construction	Screens	Infestation		Energy Efficient Items:
Age (Yrs.)	Manufactured House			
Effective Age (Yrs.)				

ROOM LIST

ROOMS	Foyer	Living	Dining	Kitchen	Den	Family Rm.	Rec. Rm.	Bedrooms	# Baths	Laundry	Other	Area Sq. Ft.
Basement												
Level 1												
Level 2												

Finished area above grade contains: Rooms; Bedroom(s); Bath(s); Square Feet of Gross Living Area

INTERIOR

SURFACES	Materials/Condition	HEATING	KITCHEN EQUIP.	ATTIC	IMPROVEMENT ANALYSIS	Good	Avg.	Fair	Poor
Floors		Type	Refrigerator ☐	None ☐	Quality of Construction	☐	☐	☐	☐
Walls		Fuel	Range/Oven ☐	Stairs ☐	Condition of Improvements	☐	☐	☐	☐
Trim/Finish		Condition	Disposal ☐	Drop Stair ☐	Room Sizes/Layout	☐	☐	☐	☐
Bath Floor		Adequacy	Dishwasher ☐	Scuttle ☐	Closets and Storage	☐	☐	☐	☐
Bath Wainscot		COOLING	Fan/Hood ☐	Floor ☐	Energy Efficiency	☐	☐	☐	☐
Doors		Central	Compactor ☐	Heated ☐	Plumbing-Adequacy & Condition	☐	☐	☐	☐
		Other	Washer/Dryer ☐	Finished ☐	Electrical-Adequacy & Condition	☐	☐	☐	☐
		Condition	Microwave ☐		Kitchen Cabinets-Adequacy & Cond.	☐	☐	☐	☐
Fireplace(s)		Adequacy	Intercom ☐		Compatibility to Neighborhood	☐	☐	☐	☐

AUTOS

CAR STORAGE:	Garage ☐	Attached ☐	Adequate ☐	House Entry ☐	Appeal & Marketability	☐	☐	☐	☐
No. Cars ___	Carport ☐	Detached ☐	Inadequate ☐	Outside Entry ☐	Estimated Remaining Economic Life				Yrs.
Condition ___	None ☐	Built-In ☐	Electric Door ☐	Basement Entry ☐	Estimated Remaining Physical Life				Yrs.

Additional features: _____

COMMENTS

Depreciation (Physical, functional and external inadequacies, repairs needed, modernization, etc.): _____

General market conditions and prevalence and impact in subject/market area regarding loan discounts, interest buydowns and concessions: _____

Freddie Mac Form 70 10/86 12Ch. AJ   Forms and Worms Inc.,® 315 Whitney Ave., New Haven, CT 06511 1(800) 243-4545   Item #111710   Fannie Mae Form 1004 10/86

Valuation Section | **UNIFORM RESIDENTIAL APPRAISAL REPORT** | **File No.**

Purpose of Appraisal is to estimate Market Value as defined in the Certification & Statement of Limiting Conditions.

COST APPROACH

BUILDING SKETCH (SHOW GROSS LIVING AREA ABOVE GRADE)
If for Freddie Mac or Fannie Mae, show only square foot calculations and cost approach comments in this space.

ESTIMATED REPRODUCTION COST-NEW-OF IMPROVEMENTS:

Dwelling _____ Sq. Ft. @ $_____ = $_____
_____ Sq. Ft. @ $_____ = $_____
Extras _____ = _____
_____ = _____
Special Energy Efficient Items _____ = _____
Porches, Patios, etc. _____ = _____
Garage/Carport _____ Sq. Ft. @ $_____ = _____
Total Estimated Cost New .... = $_____

	Physical	Functional	External
Less
Depreciation _____ | | | = $_____
Depreciated Value of Improvements .... = $_____
Site Imp. "as is" (driveway, landscaping, etc.) = $_____
ESTIMATED SITE VALUE .... = $_____
(If leasehold, show only leasehold value.)
INDICATED VALUE BY COST APPROACH .... = $_____

(Not Required by Freddie Mac and Fannie Mae)
Does property conform to applicable HUD/VA property standards? ☐ Yes ☐ No
If No, explain: _____

Construction Warranty ☐ Yes ☐ No
Name of Warranty Program _____
Warranty Coverage Expires _____

The undersigned has recited three recent sales of properties most similar and proximate to subject and has considered these in the market analysis. The description includes a dollar adjustment, reflecting market reaction to those items of significant variation between the subject and comparable properties. If a significant item in the comparable property is superior to, or more favorable than, the subject property, a minus (–) adjustment is made, thus reducing the indicated value of subject; if a significant item in the comparable is inferior to, or less favorable than, the subject property, a plus (+) adjustment is made, thus increasing the indicated value of the subject.

SALES COMPARISON ANALYSIS

ITEM	SUBJECT	COMPARABLE NO. 1		COMPARABLE NO. 2		COMPARABLE NO. 3	
Address							
Proximity to Subject							
Sales Price	$		$		$		$
Price/Gross Liv. Area	$	$		$		$	
Data Source							
VALUE ADJUSTMENTS	DESCRIPTION	DESCRIPTION	+ (–) $ Adjustment	DESCRIPTION	+ (–) $ Adjustment	DESCRIPTION	+ (–) $ Adjustment
Sales or Financing Concessions							
Date of Sale/Time							
Location							
Site/View							
Design and Appeal							
Quality of Construction							
Age							
Condition							
Above Grade Room Count	Total : Bdrms : Baths	Total : Bdrms : Baths		Total : Bdrms : Baths		Total : Bdrms : Baths	
Gross Living Area	Sq. Ft.	Sq. Ft.		Sq. Ft.		Sq. Ft.	
Basement & Finished Rooms Below Grade							
Functional Utility							
Heating/Cooling							
Garage/Carport							
Porches, Patio, Pools, etc.							
Special Energy Efficient Items							
Fireplace(s)							
Other (e.g. kitchen equip., remodeling)							
Net Adj. (total)		☐ + ☐ –	$	☐ + ☐ –	$	☐ + ☐ –	$
Indicated Value of Subject			$		$		$

Comments on Sales Comparison: _____

INDICATED VALUE BY SALES COMPARISON APPROACH .... $_____
INDICATED VALUE BY INCOME APPROACH (If Applicable) Estimated Market Rent $_____ /Mo. x Gross Rent Multiplier _____ = $_____
This appraisal is made ☐ "as is" ☐ subject to the repairs, alterations, inspections or conditions listed below ☐ completion per plans and specifications.
Comments and Conditions of Appraisal: _____

Final Reconciliation: _____

RECONCILIATION

This appraisal is based upon the above requirements, the certification, contingent and limiting conditions, and Market Value definition that are stated in
☐ FmHA, HUD &/or VA instructions.
☐ Freddie Mac Form 439 (Rev. 7/86)/Fannie Mae Form 1004B (Rev. 7/86) filed with client _____ 19____ ☐ attached.
I (WE) ESTIMATE THE MARKET VALUE, AS DEFINED, OF THE SUBJECT PROPERTY AS OF _____ 19____ to be $_____
I (We) certify: that to the best of my (our) knowledge and belief the facts and data used herein are true and correct; that I (we) personally inspected the subject property, both inside and out, and have made an exterior inspection of all comparable sales cited in this report; and that I (we) have no undisclosed interest, present or prospective therein.

Appraiser(s) SIGNATURE _____
NAME _____
Review Appraiser SIGNATURE _____ (if applicable) NAME _____
☐ Did ☐ Did Not Inspect Property

Freddie Mac Form 70 10/86 **12Ch.** | Forms and Worms Inc.,® 315 Whitney Ave., New Haven, CT 06511 1(800) 243-4545 | Fannie Mae Form 1004 10/86

Example:

1. Buyer is prepared to make a 20% downpayment and secure an 80% loan.
2. Sales price is $125,000.
3. Appraisal is issued at $117,000.
4. Maximum loan is 80% of $117,000.

$117,000
× .80
$93,600 maximum loan amount

In the example, the sales price is $125,000, but the maximum loan is restricted to $93,600 because of the low appraisal. The buyer was expecting to make a $25,000 downpayment ($125,000 sales price × 80% = $100,000 loan), but would now have to make a $31,400 downpayment ($125,000 − $93,600 loan = $31,400) if the appraisal is not increased or the sales price reduced.

RESPONSES TO A LOW APPRAISAL

When an appraisal comes in below the sales price, there are five possible responses:

1. Reduce the sales price to the appraised value.
2. Keep the price as is and have the buyer make up the difference in cash.
3. Strike a compromise price somewhere between the appraised value and the initial selling price.
4. Ask for a reconsideration of the appraised value in the hope it will be increased to a level more acceptable to buyer and seller.
5. Terminate the sale.

Once a seller has become accustomed to a certain selling figure, he or she gives it up very reluctantly. If the seller is agreeable to a price reduction, the first response is the simplest and quickest solution, but do not be surprised if your seller resists a price reduction.

Responses two and three are the least likely of the solutions because buyers are understandably reluctant to pay more for a property than a professional appraiser says it is worth. Where a transaction is contingent on financing, the buyer does not have to complete the sale if the appraisal comes in low. Transactions are infrequently salvaged by buyers agreeing to pay over value.

Response four—a request for reconsideration of value—is a viable response if done properly. The correct way to request reconsideration of value will be explained subsequently.

Finally, where there is a significant gap between the sales price and the appraised value, response number five—a termination of the sale—is often the result.

HOW TO SOLVE PROBLEMS CAUSED BY LOW APPRAISALS

Of course, the best way to eliminate the problems created by low appraisals is to avoid them in the first place by pricing properties realistically. A seller should not be given an unrealistic estimate of his or her property's worth; even if a buyer can be persuaded to pay the inflated price, the appraisal will come back low and the real problems of trying to keep the sale together will set in.

If you cannot price the property correctly when you list it, at least attempt to do so when the sale is written. No case can be made for overstating values when properties are listed and sold, because sooner or later every sale that is dependent on financing must yield to the conclusions of a professional appraiser.

Request for Reconsideration of Value

Regardless of how objective an appraiser might try to be, subjective considerations and conclusions are a part of every appraisal. In the end the appraiser's findings can only be termed an opinion of value. If you are affected by a low appraisal and sincerely believe the appraiser has made a mistake, there is a chance you can appeal his or her decision and, with the proper documentation, get the appraisal increased, possibly to the figure originally requested.

Earlier you were given an opportunity to review a uniform residential appraisal report form. The section of the report that makes direct comparisons between the subject and comparable properties is the "market analysis section" of the report.

The undersigned has recited three recent sales of properties most similar and proximate to subject and has considered these in the market analysis. The description includes a dollar adjustment, reflecting market reaction to those items of significant variation between the subject and comparable properties. If a significant item in the comparable property is superior to, or more favorable than, the subject property, a minus (−) adjustment is made, thus reducing the indicated value of subject. If a significant item in the comparable is inferior to, or less favorable than, the subject property, a plus (+) adjustment is made, thus increasing the indicated value of the subject.

ITEM	SUBJECT	COMPARABLE NO. 1		COMPARABLE NO. 2		COMPARABLE NO. 3	
Address							
Proximity to Subject							
Sales Price	$		$		$		$
Price/Gross Liv. Area	$	$		$		$	
Data Source							
VALUE ADJUSTMENTS	DESCRIPTION	DESCRIPTION	+ (−) $ Adjustment	DESCRIPTION	+ (−) $ Adjustment	DESCRIPTION	+ (−) $ Adjustment
Sales or Financing Concessions							
Date of Sale/Time							
Location							
Site/View							
Design and Appeal							
Quality of Construction							
Age							
Condition							
Above Grade Room Count	Total / Bdrms / Baths	Total / Bdrms / Baths		Total / Bdrms / Baths		Total / Bdrms / Baths	
Gross Living Area	Sq. Ft.	Sq. Ft.		Sq. Ft.		Sq. Ft.	
Basement & Finished Rooms Below Grade							
Functional Utility							
Heating/Cooling							
Garage/Carport							
Porches, Patio, Pools, etc.							
Special Energy Efficient Items							
Fireplace(s)							
Other (e.g. kitchen equip., remodeling)							
Net Adj. (total)		+	− $	+	− $	+	− $
Indicated Value of Subject			$		$		$
Comments on Sales Comparison:							

INDICATED VALUE BY SALES COMPARISON APPROACH .... $

The market analysis is the heart of the appraisal, as it shows what informed buyers have been willing to pay for similar properties in the recent past, and the lender can only presume that the value indicated by these comparable sales is what informed buyers will be willing to pay for the property if it is foreclosed and resold. Stated another way, lenders rely heavily on the values suggested by comparable sales.

What this means is, if you disagree with an appraisal and plan to ask the lender to reconsider the appraisal amount, you will have to support your request by submitting at least three comparable sales that indicate a higher value estimate is in order. If you are to persuade the lender to accept your comparables over the appraiser's, they must be at least as similar to the subject property as the comparables contained in the initial appraisal report.

Format for Reconsideration Request

Lenders are familiar with and understand the market data analysis format used in the residential appraisal report. Thus it makes sense to arrange your reconsideration request in much the same way. Write a cover letter making your request and attach your market data information in roughly the following form. Market data information can be obtained from a variety of sources, including real estate office files, multiple listing services, and appraisers' records. Acquaint yourself with the most thorough and accessible record systems in your area. If you are doing your job, you will be referring to them often.

Sometimes appraisers get sloppy, and when they do, their findings can be successfully challenged. If your request for reconsideration of value contains well-researched, properly documented information and is presented in a professional manner, your chances of success skyrocket. Make your request carelessly and the reverse is true.

REQUEST FOR RECONSIDERATION OF VALUE

Dear Mr. Jewel:

Attached is a market data analysis that supports this request for reconsideration of your value estimate for 412 Acme Drive, dated April 17, 199x.

I believe the market data presented indicate that an estimate of value in the amount of $138,000 is justified.

Your earliest consideration of this request will be appreciated.

Sincerely,

Thomas M. Crane

MARKET DATA ANALYSIS
412 Acme Drive

Item	Subject Prop.	Comparable 1	Comparable 2	Comparable 3
Address	412 Acme Drive	131 Skip Road	221 Sutter St.	168 Bow Road
Sales price	$135,000	$141,000	$134,500	$129,500
Data source	sales contract	pres. owner	MLS	selling broker
Date of sale	9/1/9x	6/29/9x	7/14/9x	5/17/9x
Location	high qual. suburb	same	same	same
Site/view	inside lot	corner lot	corner lot	inside lot
Design/appeal	rambler/exc.	same	same	same
Constr. quality	good	good	good	good
Age	7 yrs.	6 yrs.	8 yrs.	8 yrs.
Condition	good	good	good	good
No. of rooms	8	7	7	6
No. of bedrooms	4	4	3	3
No. of baths	2½	2½	2	2
Liv. area (sq. ft.)	2,700	3,300	2,350	2,150
Garage/carport	2-car attached gar.	same	same	same
Patios, pools, etc.	15' x 21' patio	15' x 26' patio	18' x 16' patio	15' x 17' patio
Additional data	2 fireplaces range, oven D/W, disposal central air	2 fireplaces range, oven D/W central air	1 fireplace range, oven D/W central air	1 fireplace range, oven D/W
Comments	Subject has superior energy efficiency to comps 2 and 3 and is at least equal in this respect to comp 1. Principal difference between comps 1 and 2 is square footage.			

307

KEY CONSIDERATIONS TO A RESIDENTIAL APPRAISER

There are many things to consider during the residential appraisal process; some of them are very important, others are not. The principal method for appraising residential real estate is the market data method. Since this amounts to a series of comparisons between the subject property and similar properties that have sold recently, it stands to reason that the most critical elements of comparison are the ones that will have the greatest impact on value. If you know what is most likely to contribute to or detract from value, which is what will most influence a lender's thinking, then low appraisals that threaten your transactions will be fewer and farther between. And when you are confronted with the problem of a low appraisal, you will be better equipped to resolve it.

SUMMARY OF IMPORTANT PROPERTY FEATURES

Important features:
- date of sale
- location
- site/view
- design and appeal
- construction quality
- age/condition
- basement
- functional utility
- air conditioning
- energy efficiency
- number of bedrooms and bathrooms
- size of house

Date of Sale

Presuming the subject property has just sold or is presently for sale, the best comparables are those which have sold within the past six months.

Location

It is preferred that the subject property and the comparables be situated in the same neighborhood. When there are no acceptable comparables from the subject's neighborhood, homes from comparable neighborhoods can be used. When this happens there is not only a comparison between the properties, but their respective neighborhoods as well. Neighborhood considerations include:

Percentage of homeownership. Is there a high degree of owner-occupancy or do rental properties predominate? Owner-occupied neighborhoods are generally better maintained and less susceptible to deterioration.

308

Vacant homes and lots. Is there an unusual number of vacancies in the neighborhood? Vacant homes or lots suggest a low level of interest in the area. If less than 25% of the lots are developed or occupied for residential use, the area is not considered desirable for residential lending purposes.

Rental levels. Where there is a prevalence of rental properties, how do the rents compare to other rental-dominated neighborhoods?

Construction activity. Significant construction activity in a neighborhood signals strong current interest in the area and this has a positive effect on values.

Conformity. Values are protected if there is a reasonable degree of social and economic homogeneity (conformity) in the neighborhood. This includes styles, ages, prices, sizes and quality of structures. Strictly enforced zoning ordinances and private restrictions do much to promote conformity.

Changing land use. Is the neighborhood in the midst of a transition from residential to some other use? If so, the properties within are probably losing their value as residences, even though the change promises higher values overall because of the potential for more productive use of the land in the future.

Sizes and shapes of lots. How do the sizes and shapes of the lots in the subject property's neighborhood compare to the sizes and shapes of lots in comparable neighborhoods? Rectangular lots are more useful than irregularly shaped lots. Street frontage and area of land are the most influential factors.

Contour of the land. Mildly rolling topography is preferred to flat, monotonous or excessively hilly terrain.

Street patterns. Do the neighborhood's streets have good access to main traffic arteries? Wide, gently curving streets are more appealing than narrow or straight streets. Streets should be hard-surfaced, unless the community standard does not require hard-surfaced streets. If a property does not front on a publicly dedicated and maintained street, the lender will require a legally enforceable road maintenance agreement signed by the owners of the properties on the street.

Availability of utilities. Is the neighborhood adequately serviced by necessary utilities such as electricity, water, gas, sewers and telephones?

Nuisances. Are there any nuisances present in or near the neighborhood that might be detrimental to its value? Nuisances include odors, industrial noises or pollutants, and exposure to unusual winds, smog or fog.

Prestige. Is there a prestige factor that makes one neighborhood more valuable than another?

Proximity to city. How far is the neighborhood from important points, such as downtown, industrial (employment) regions, and major shopping centers?

School district. What schools serve the neighborhood? Are they highly regarded? Are they within walking distance? The quality of a school or school district can make a major difference with respect to value.

Public services. Is the neighborhood properly serviced by public transportation, police and fire units?

Government influences. Does zoning in and around the neighborhood promote residential use and insulate the property owner from nuisances like unpleasant sights, sounds and odors from nearby industrial lands? Are property taxes and special assessments consistent and equitable? How do they compare with the tax levels of other neighborhoods nearby?

No two neighborhoods can ever be exactly alike, and it is the differences between them which must be analyzed to determine what, if any, effect they have on value. Keep in mind, a high-quality property by itself cannot overcome the adverse influences on value caused by a low-quality neighborhood. On the other hand, the value of a relatively weak property can be enhanced and sustained if it is situated in a stable and desirable neighborhood.

Site/View

Is the property a corner lot or an inside lot? Nowadays corner lots do not have the extra value they were once accorded. Views can add considerably to value.

Design and Appeal

Ranch style (rambler), colonial, split-level, etc. Comparisons between one- and two-story homes generally are not valid. A one-story house can be compared to a split-level with certain adjustments. Is the property's appeal good, average, or poor?

Construction Quality

Is the quality of the materials and craftsmanship good, average or poor?

Age/Condition

When the subject property and comparables are in similar condition, a difference in age up to five years is generally inconsequential. Older properties are eligible for maximum residential loans if the bath(s), kitchen, plumbing and electrical facilities are up to code and of a quality acceptable to typical purchasers and renters in the area.

Basement/Basement Finished Rooms

A functional basement, especially a finished basement, will contribute to value, but not usually by enough to recover the cost of the finish work.

Functional Utility

Is the floor plan and building orientation functional?

Air Conditioning

The presence or absence of an air conditioning system is more critical in hot regions than in regions with milder climates.

Energy-efficient Items

With spiraling energy costs, an energy-efficient home is more valuable than a comparable one which is not. Examples of energy-efficient items include double- or triple-paned windows, clock-controlled thermostats, insulation-wrapped water heaters, insulated ducts and pipes in unheated areas, adequate insulation for floors, walls and attic, and weather stripping for doors and windows.

Number of Rooms

This includes the total number of rooms in the house, excluding bathrooms and, usually, basement rooms.

Number of Bedrooms

Differences in the number of bedrooms have a major impact on value; for instance, with all else being equal, a two-bedroom comparable is worth noticeably less than a three-bedroom subject.

Number of Bathrooms

A full bath is a lavatory (wash bowl), toilet and bathtub, with or without a shower; a ¾ bath is a lavatory, toilet and shower (no tub); a ½ bath is a lavatory and toilet only. A difference in the number of bathrooms can have a notable effect on value.

Size of House (square footage)

This includes the improved living area, excluding garage and basement. There is no minimum number of square feet required, but the home must contain sufficient square footage to be generally acceptable to typical purchasers or renters in the area.

RURAL AND SUBURBAN HOMES

Properties in outlying areas are eligible for maximum residential financing provided:

1. the value of the land does not exceed 30% of the total property value;
2. there are adequate sewer, water and other utilities available and in service on the premises;
3. the property is readily accessible by a federal, state or county highway or an all-weather secondary road;
4. the present or anticipated use of adjacent real estate does not unfavorably affect the value of the property as a residence.

WORK ORDERS

Frequently, certain parts of the subject property are in need of repair. When this happens, the lender may require that the repairs be made as a condition of granting the loan. Sometimes the required repairs are minor; in other cases they are substantial. When a property is in such poor condition as to make it a marginal risk, the lender will either reject the property as security for the loan or require so many repairs that the cost to the owner becomes prohibitive.

Buyer does work.

When repairs have been required by the lender, someone will have to do the work. It has become a regular practice in the business to arrange to have the buyer do some or all of the repairs for credit. The credit is added to the borrower's list of assets available for closing the transaction.

> **Example:** The lender requires the entire exterior of the house be painted. Estimates from professional painters range between $1,000 and $1,200. The seller agrees to credit the buyer with $1,100 for painting the house.

The advantages to this arrangement are obvious. The seller gets the work done as required by the lender and the buyer earns $1,100 that can be used to satisfy his or her

313

U.S. Department of Housing and Urban Development   FORM 477B
INSPECTION REPORT
REPAIR RECOMMENDATIONS AND ESTIMATES

1. Property Address:	2. HUD Case Number
Condo 0-Lot SFH 2-3-4 Plex	
3. Name of Mortgagee:	4. Name of Servicer:
5. Area Management Broker:	6. HUD Office:

EXTERIOR INSPECTION	YES	NO	RECOMMENDATION/ESTIMATES
7. Is the lawn cut? Has snow removal been performed?			
8. Is the yard free of debris?			
9. Are the doors and windows secure?			
10. Are the windows boarded?			
11. Are there storm windows and/or doors?			
12. If there is a garage, is it secure?			
13. Is a lock box being used to allow access?			Type: Key/Combo Missing: Key/L.B./Cover
14. Is the condition of the exterior paint and siding okay?			
15. Does the roof look okay? Are there gutters, spouts, splashblocks?			Snow Covered?
16. Is the site grading and drainage okay?			
17. Is the condition of masonry, fireplace, chimneys okay?			If no, explain:
18. Any problems/hazards in yard or with exterior?			
19. Is the general exterior appearance good?			
Additional Remarks:			

INTERIOR INSPECTION			
20. Is all personal property removed from interior?			
21. Is the heating system in good working condition? and ON?			
22. Is the domestic plumbing and fixtures in good condition?			
23. Is the electricity ON?			
24. Is the water turned ON?			
25. What is condition of interior paint and decorating?			
26. What is condition of floors, carpets, sheet goods?			
27. What is condition of cabinets, doors, millwork, trim?			
28. Any evidence of roof leaks or damage caused by leakage?			
29. Any evidence of flooding/water damage?			
30. Any major structural or foundation damage?			
31. Any pest control needed?			
32. Any vandalism?			
33. Are emergency or preventive maintenance needed?			
34. Additional remarks			

EXISTING APPLIANCES	#1	#2	#3	#4	EXISTING ITEMS	#1	#2	#3	#4
Range					Heating stove				
Refrigerator					Light fixtures				
Stove top					Washer				
Wall oven					Dryer				
Microwave					Type furnace: Boiler? Leaks? Y/N				
Compactor					Hot water heater? Y/N Leaks? Y/N				
Disposal					Crawl space? WET/DRY				
Range hood					Working smoke detectors? Y/N				

Certification: FORM 477B ANC

By signing below the undersigned certifies that the information reported on this form is based on an acutal site inspection of the property and is complete and accurate. Warning Section 1001, Title 18, U.S.C., provides, "Whoever, in any matter within the jurisdiction of any department... knowingly and will fully falsifies, conceals, or covers up... or makes false, fictitious or fraudulent statements or representations... shall be fined not more than $10,000 or imprisoned not more than five years, or both."

Signature and title: Date:

downpayment and settlement costs. Sometimes the work/credit arrangement is called sweat equity. There are five prerequisites to a sweat equity plan:

1. The work (repairs) for which credit is given must have been called for in the appraisal.
2. The work must be completed prior to closing the transaction.
3. The labor performed must be completed in a workmanlike manner.
4. The amount of credit must not exceed what it would normally cost if the work were given to an outside contractor.
5. The completion and quality of the work must be certified by the appraiser.

Requirements for work repairs:
- work must be required
- work must be completed before closing
- work must be performed adequately
- amount of credit must not exceed normal cost
- work must be inspected by appraiser

The previous page shows a partial list of repair requirements used by an FHA area office. While it is not identical to preprinted repair lists used by every FHA area office, it gives you an idea of the kinds of repairs typically called for by appraisers. If the necessary work is not covered by the preprinted list, the appraiser can add additional requirements at the bottom of the list under "other."

CHAPTER SUMMARY

1. Lenders demand professional appraisals because they want an objective estimate of the true market value of the property offered as collateral for the loan. Loan-to-value ratios are based upon the sales price or appraised value, whichever is lower.

2. Residential real estate is appraised three ways:

   - the market data method,
   - the replacement cost method, and
   - the gross income method.

3. The market data method is an appraisal based on the analysis of other recently sold properties and a comparison between their values and the value of the subject property. The comparables are chosen on the basis of date of sale, location, physical similarity, and terms of the sale (it must be an arm's length transaction). The market data method is usually chosen to appraise residential properties because competitive forces influence value, and no informed buyer will pay more for a property than he or she would have to pay for an equally desirable substitute property.

4. The cost method is based on the theory that the value of a property is limited by the cost of replacing it. The three steps of the cost method are:

   - estimate the cost of replacing the home,
   - estimate and deduct depreciation, and
   - add the value of the lot.

   The cost to replace the home is usually estimated by using the square-foot method.
   Depreciation may be deferred maintenance, functional obsolescence, or economic obsolescence.

5. The income method is based upon the gross rent and a gross rent multiplier derived from analysis of other recently sold comparable rental properties. Once the gross rent multiplier is found, the annual rent the property is generating is multiplied by the multiplier to arrive at a rough estimate of value.

The principal weakness to this method is that the multiplier does not take vacancies or operating expenses into account.

6. A real estate agent should understand the appraisal process so that he or she can effectively respond to and solve problems created by a low appraisal. The agent may want to submit a request for reconsideration of value.

7. A reconsideration of value is essentially the market data portion of an appraisal. Comparable properties (they must be at least as comparable as the properties used in the original appraisal) are listed to indicate the market value of the subject property.

AITD
ALL INCLUSIVE DEED of TRUST
WRAP
WRAP AROUND MORTGAGE

Chapter 15
SELLER FINANCING IN CALIFORNIA

In tight money markets, sometimes the only way a seller can make a deal is to finance part of the purchase price him or herself. Mortgage money from traditional lenders may be too costly in terms of interest rates or it may be simply unavailable. Buyers may be unable to come up with the cash necessary for the downpayment required by a conventional mortgage, or they may wish to take advantage of the low interest rate on the seller's existing mortgage. In any case, sellers can often enhance the salability of their properties by offering financing in the form of a land contract or a purchase money mortgage. A purchase money mortgage is one given by a buyer to a seller to finance the purchase; the seller is the mortgagee or beneficiary.

Seller financing attractive when:
1. interest too high on institutional loans
2. buyer unable to qualify
3. buyer has insufficient cash for conventional mortgage downpayment
4. seller's loan has a low interest rate

PURCHASE MONEY MORTGAGE/TRUST DEED

Institutions such as banks and savings and loans are not the only ones who make loans secured by mortgages or deeds of trust. An individual seller can just as easily be a mortgagee or beneficiary. The central advantage of this arrangement is that sellers are not bound by institutional policies regarding loan ratios, interest rates or qualifying standards. To make the sale, a seller may finance the entire purchase price for the buyer (relying on a mortgage as security), charge below market interest, and offer financing to a buyer who is considered a credit risk by institutional lenders. In all of these instances the seller is taking a risk, but the risk may be justified

Purchase money mortgage/trust deed:
- between buyer and seller for part of purchase price
- may provide tax advantage to seller
- property may be unencumbered or (most likely) encumbered by existing mortgage

if it allows the sale to proceed or enables the seller to get a higher price for his or her home.

As with any other form of seller financing, the seller must not need an immediate cashout from the sale. If the seller does not need immediate cash, purchase money financing can be advantageous. Since receipt of the profit from the sale is spread over several years, the seller may benefit from a lower rate of income taxation. Taking the full profit at the time of sale could push the seller into a higher tax bracket, but when the profit is paid on an installment basis, only the amount actually received in a given year is considered taxable income for that year.

UNENCUMBERED PROPERTY

The simplest form of purchase money financing is where the seller has clear title to the property, free of any mortgages or other liens. The buyer and seller simply negotiate the amount and terms of their financing arrangement and draw up the appropriate documents. Purchase money financing may take any of the many forms discussed in earlier chapters, such as variable interest rates, graduated payments, or partial amortization with balloon payment. Virtually the only limit is the imagination of the parties.

Example: Grandma Perkins decided to move to her sister's farm in the country and wants to sell her townhouse. The mortgage on the townhouse has long since been paid. The Jenkins, a young couple from Grandma's church, are interested in buying the townhouse, but could not qualify for conventional financing. However, Grandma believes they are honest and reliable people who can be trusted to pay off a loan, so she offers them the following deal: sales price of $90,000, with $8,000 down and the balance in the form of a purchase money loan, secured by a deed of trust with

Grandma as the beneficiary. Interest will accrue at the rate of 8% for the first year, and increase ½ of 1% per year until it reaches 11%, where it will stay for the balance of the 30-year loan term. Payments are to be interest only for the first six years, and the principal then fully amortized over the balance of the term.

ENCUMBERED PROPERTY

Since most California residential property is encumbered by existing mortgages or deeds of trust, seller financing often involves assumption or refinancing of existing debt. There are several ways to deal with an existing mortgage. Perhaps the simplest is to let the buyer assume liability for the existing note.

Assumption
FHA and VA mortgages (and some conventional mortgages) may be assumed. This means they do not contain an enforceable alienation or due-on-sale clause. The buyer can simply agree to take over payment of the seller's debt and the terms of the note remain unchanged. The property still serves as the basic security for the loan, but the buyer becomes primarily liable for repayment of the debt. If there is a foreclosure and the proceeds are insufficient to satisfy the debt, the lender may sue the buyer for the deficiency (if the property is not covered by California's anti-deficiency rule).

Assumption and Release
An assumption can take two forms. In the first case, it is an agreement strictly between the buyer and the seller. The buyer assumes liability for the loan, but the seller is not completely released from responsibility; he or she remains **secondarily liable**. If the lender cannot recover the loan amount from the buyer or through foreclosure, it may still sue the seller for the deficiency.

In order for the seller to be relieved of this responsibility, he or she must obtain a **release** from the lender. In this instance, the lender agrees to accept the buyer as the new mortgagor and to release the seller from all obligations on the mortgage. The lender will normally charge a loan assumption fee on assumable loans (such as FHA or VA loans) or renegotiate the interest rate if the mortgage is not assumable (that is, if it contains an alienation clause). To determine whether or not a loan is assumable, always consult the lender and/or an attorney who is familiar with real estate finance.

> **Example:** Ned Taylor sells a rental house to Sam Jones, who assumes Ned's existing $90,000 mortgage. Ned does not get a release from the lender. A year later, with $88,000 still owing on the mortgage, Sam Jones encounters financial difficulties and decides to bail out. He leaves California (and his obligations) behind, but does not leave a forwarding address. The mortgage payments are not made, so the lender forecloses, obtaining only $70,000 at the foreclosure sale due to the dilapidated condition in which Sam's tenants left the property. By the time of the sale, the total amount owed, including delinquent interest and the costs of foreclosure and sale, reaches $93,500, leaving a deficiency of $23,500 ($93,500 debt − $70,000 sale proceeds = $23,500 deficiency). The lender cannot locate Sam to attempt to collect the deficiency, so it sues Ned. Ned may be held responsible for the deficiency because he was never released from liability on the mortgage when it was assumed by Sam.

If no alienation clause:
1. assumption without release of seller (seller remains secondarily liable)
2. assumption with release of seller (requires approval and release from lender)

If there is an alienation clause, lender may:
1. consent to sale and assumption of loan with existing terms
2. consent to sale and assumption with interest rate adjustment
3. refuse to consent and call note

Alienation Clause

If the seller has a conventional mortgage, the mortgage instrument may contain an alienation clause, which is designed to restrict the seller's right to transfer the property. The clause may be triggered by the transfer of title or by the transfer of a significant interest in the property (e.g., a long-term lease). The alienation clause may give the lender the right to declare the entire loan balance immediately due and payable (a **due-on-sale** clause), the right to raise the interest rate on the loan or the right to do either at its option.

PURCHASE MONEY SECOND MORTGAGE

Even in cases where there is an assumable loan, or where the buyer can obtain financing from an institutional lender, it may be beneficial for the seller to provide additional financing in the form of a second mortgage or second deed of trust. If the buyer does not have sufficient cash to cover the difference between the sales price and the institutional financing, a purchase money second can become the key to closing the sale.

Purchase money second mortgage and assumption:
- second mortgage to seller for part of downpayment
- mortgage to seller is junior in lien priority to existing mortgage

> **Example:** George Hatfield owns property with an existing $45,000 mortgage. The mortgage is assumable, and has 120 payments of $582.30 remaining. Ray McCarthy is interested in buying the property, but does not have the $55,000 cash needed to meet the sales price of $100,000. Ray offers to buy the house with a $20,000 downpayment if George will take back a second deed of trust for the remaining $35,000. George agrees and the sale is finalized.

Exercise No. 1

Use the facts from the preceding example and the tables in the back of the book. Assume that the $35,000 second loan bears interest at 11%, and is fully amortized over a 15-year term.

1. What is the monthly payment of the second loan?

2. What is the interest rate on the existing first mortgage?

Seller-sponsored second mortgages are subject to the same lien priority rules as institutional mortgages. In the event of default and foreclosure, the first mortgage is paid in full from the proceeds of sale before any proceeds are allocated to the second mortgage. Sellers who take back second mortgages should keep this in mind when negotiating the amount of seller financing. This is especially true if there is a possibility of declining property values, or if the financing is set up to result in negative amortization over the early years of the loan.

SELLER-SPONSORED WRAPAROUND FINANCING

Wraparound: wraps around, or includes, existing financing

The wraparound mortgage or all-inclusive trust deed is a device sometimes used in place of an assumption. By using a wraparound installment mortgage sales contract, the seller can pass on the benefit of an existing loan at lower than market interest rates, even if the buyer is unwilling to directly assume the loan. While the wrap is sometimes used to get around the provisions of an alienation clause (which limits the assumability of the loan), if the lender becomes aware of the subterfuge the transaction can be foreclosed under the terms of the alienation clause.

Example: Mary Cudahy wants to sell her house for $91,000. There is an existing $32,000, 8% deed of trust on the property. Jeff Cochran offers to buy with $20,000 down and a seller-financed second deed of trust for the balance of $71,000. Under the terms of the agreement, a portion of Jeff's monthly payments will be used to make the payment on Mary's loan, which remains a lien on the property.

The attractiveness of the wraparound is that it enables the buyer to obtain financing at below market interest rates while still providing a market rate of return for the seller. An example will illustrate this apparent contradiction.

Wraparound advantages:
• buyer may pay below market interest rate, or
• seller may receive above market interest rate, or
• in some cases, both of the above

Example: Seller Johnson has a $51,000, 10% trust deed against his property. He sells to Abernathy for $69,000, with $8,000 down and the $61,000 balance secured by a wraparound deed of trust at 12% interest based on 30-year amortization with a balloon payment for the entire balance in 15 years. Seller Johnson will receive 12% interest on the $61,000 wraparound, but has actually extended only $10,000 in credit.

$69,000	sales price
− 8,000	downpayment
− 51,000	underlying trust deed
$10,000	credit extended—net owed to seller

To determine the seller's yield in the first year:

1. Calculate the interest the seller will receive in the first year on the wraparound trust deed.

$$\begin{array}{r} \$61,000 \\ \times\ .12 \\ \hline \$7,320 \end{array}$$

Calculating the seller's yield on wraparound:

2. Calculate the interest the seller will pay the same year on the underlying trust deed.

$$\begin{array}{r} \$51,000 \\ \times\ .10 \\ \hline \$5,100 \end{array}$$

Interest seller will receive
− Interest seller will pay
Net interest to seller

325

Credit extended by seller | Yield to seller / Net interest to seller

3. Determine the net interest to the seller.

$7,320
−5,100
$2,220

4. Divide the net interest to the seller by the amount of credit actually extended.

$$\frac{22\%}{10,000\overline{)2,220}}$$

Stated more simply, the seller is paying out $5,100 a year in interest on the original deed of trust and is receiving $7,320 in interest on the wrap from the buyer. This leaves the seller with a net gain of $2,220. The amount of credit actually extended by the seller under the wrap is $10,000, so the seller is receiving $2,220 in interest payments on $10,000 of credit. The yield on the credit extended is thus 22%. If the market interest rates are at 12.5%, the seller is receiving 9.5% over the market rate while the buyer is paying .5% below the market rate. Even if the rate charged by the seller on the wrap is not below the market rate, the arrangement may still be attractive to the buyer because of the greater flexibility of seller financing.

The example shows the excellent return that is available to the seller when the amount of credit actually extended by the seller is relatively small. The more credit extended by the seller, the lower the return.

Exercise No. 2

Compute the seller's yield during the first year in the following three situations.

1. Underlying mortgage of $39,700 at 9½%; wraparound trust deed of $67,000 at 14%. What is the seller's yield?

326

2. **Underlying mortgage of $62,000 at 9¾%; wraparound contract of $74,000 at 13½%. What is the seller's yield?**

3. **Underlying mortgage of $52,000 at 10¾%; wraparound mortgage of $71,000 at 14¼%. What is the seller's yield?**

WRAPAROUND vs. ASSUMPTION PLUS SELLER SECOND

In an assumption, the buyer receives the benefit of an existing low interest rate loan. If the transaction is structured with a wraparound loan at market rates, the seller receives the benefit of the existing low interest rate loan and is able to receive a very attractive rate of return on the portion of the financing that is actually extended by the seller.

> **Example:** A sale is made for a price of $100,000, with the buyer making a $20,000 downpayment. The seller's existing loan with a balance of $60,000 carries an interest rate of 9%. Prevailing market interest rates at the time of sale are approximately 12%.

Wraparound vs. assumption and seller second:

If low rate on existing mortgage:
1. wraparound at market rate gives seller high yield and benefit of low rate on existing mortgage
2. assumption and second mortgage at market rate gives buyer low overall interest rate and benefit of low rate on existing mortgage

	WRAPAROUND	**ASSUME + 2nd**
Sales price:	$100,000	$100,000
Downpayment:	20,000	20,000
Balance financed:	80,000 @ 12% wrap	60,000 @ 9% assumed 20,000 @ 12% 2nd
Credit extended by seller:	20,000	20,000
Approximate yield to seller on credit extended:	21%	12%
Approximate overall interest to buyer on $80,000 financed:	12%	9¾%

As you can see from the above example, if a wraparound loan is made at market rates, the seller enjoys a high yield on the portion of credit extended by the seller. If the transaction is structured with an assumption and a second mortgage to the seller at market rates, the buyer enjoys financing at a very low overall rate.

Wraparound can benefit both buyer and seller:
1. seller receives above market rate yield
2. buyer pays below market rate interest

A wraparound transaction can also be structured so that the seller receives above market rates on the credit actually extended and, at the same time, the buyer pays below market rates on the total amount financed. It can appear as if both of them are getting a good deal. If in the example just given, the wraparound loan were made at an interest rate of 10½%, the buyer would be paying an overall rate 1½% less than the prevailing market rates of 12%. At the same time, the seller would be receiving a rate of approximately 15% on the $20,000 of credit extended by the seller.

Exercise No. 3

A house is sold on the following terms: $15,000 down; $50,000 deed of trust to seller at 12%, fully amortized over

20 years. The seller is retaining an existing 10% mortgage with a balance of $25,000 and 240 remaining payments.

1. What is the monthly payment on the existing mortgage?

2. What is the monthly payment on the deed of trust?

3. What amount is the seller actually financing (the net amount owed to seller)?

4. What is the seller's yield on the amount in question three?

RESALE OF PURCHASE MONEY SECURITIES

If a seller wants the option of cashing out at some time in the future, he or she can do so without giving up the ability to offer purchase money financing. Since 1980, FNMA has been willing to buy purchase money securities on the secondary market. The catch is that the securities must conform to FNMA underwriting standards, which defeats some of the advantages of seller financing such as freedom from loan-to-value ratios and other institutional limitations. If the seller desires to resell his or her loan immediately or in the future, the seller should use standard FNMA forms for writing the financing agreement with the buyer. This will ensure that the loan meets FNMA standards. The only other requirement

FNMA purchase of seller-financed purchase money loans:
1. loan terms, documents and qualifying ratios must meet FNMA standards
2. loan serviced by FNMA approved lender

is that the loan be serviced by a FNMA approved lender. The seller then has the option at any time of ordering the lender to pass the loan through to FNMA, thereby cashing out the seller. By choosing the proper time to resell (when market interest rates are low), the seller can pass the loan through with a minimum discount.

LAND CONTRACT

Land contract:
1. alternative to mortgage or deed of trust financing
2. seller retains legal title until buyer pays off contract

In some areas of California, a popular form of purchase money financing is the land contract. This type of financing has many of the same advantages as purchase money mortgages and trust deeds, such as freedom from institutional loan qualifying standards, deferral of income taxation and flexibility of terms. Its main disadvantage when compared to purchase money mortgages is that land contracts cannot be resold to FNMA, although a few private secondary market investors may be willing to buy contracts.

The land contract or installment sales contract was outlined in Chapter 5. The distinguishing feature of this financing instrument is that the seller retains legal title to the subject property until the buyer has made all of the payments on the contract. In its simplest form, the land contract is made by a seller who owns his or her property free and clear. Such a seller need only negotiate the term and interest rate of the contract, along with the amount of downpayment, if any.

Example: ten-year, fully amortized contract at 12%.

> ### Real Estate Contract
>
> Buyer agrees to pay $15,000 as downpayment, including deposit. The balance shall be paid as follows: $85,000 in the form of a real estate contract, payable at $1,219.50 or more per month, including principal and interest at the rate of 12% per year, for 120 months until the balance is paid in full.

If encumbered by existing financing:
1. wraparound contract subject to existing mortgage
2. contract and assumption of existing mortgage
3. contract, assumption of existing mortgage, and institutional second mortgage for part of downpayment

Example: five-year, partially amortized contract at 14%.

> ### Real Estate Contract
>
> Buyer agrees to pay $15,000 as downpayment, including deposit. The balance shall be paid as follows: $85,000 in the form of a real estate contract, payable at $1,007.14 or more per month, including principal and interest at the rate of 14% per year, computed on the basis of a 30-year amortization, for 60 months, at which time the balance shall be due and payable in full.

Notice that in a partially amortized contract, a portion of the principal balance remains unpaid at the conclusion of the contract term. The buyer will have to pay this balance ("balloon" payment) in cash at that time, or else refinance the property.

Exercise No. 4

Fred Ferret is selling a house for $71,000, by means of a land contract calling for a $10,000 downpayment with the balance to be paid as follows: equal monthly payments over a term of seven years, at 10½% interest computed on the basis of a 30-year amortization, the unpaid balance due at the end of the seven-year period. Fill in the contract form with the appropriate information. (To compute the monthly payment and the amount of the balloon payment, refer to the loan amortization and loan progress tables in the appendix.)

REAL ESTATE CONTRACT

Buyer agrees to pay _____ as downpayment, including deposit. The balance shall be paid as follows: _____ in the form of a real estate contract, payable at _____ or more per month, including principal and interest at the rate of _____ per year, computed on the basis of a _____ year amortization, for _____ months, at which time the balance of _____ shall be due and payable in full.

_____ (Buyer)

_____ (Seller)

CONTRACT SUBJECT TO EXISTING MORTGAGE

It is rare to find a seller whose property is not encumbered by some form of mortgage lien. When this is the case, the existing mortgage(s) must be taken into account. The simplest way to do this is to make the contract subject to the existing mortgage. The contract is written for the full purchase price, but the buyer's property rights under the contract are subject to the rights of the seller's mortgagee. The seller remains liable to make the payments on the loan and the property may be foreclosed if the seller defaults.

The obvious problem with this arrangement from the buyer's point of view is how to make sure the seller does not default on the loan payments. If this should occur, the buyer may lose everything; the seller will no longer have title to convey after a foreclosure (remember that the buyer doesn't get a deed until the contract is paid in full) and the buyer will be forced to resort to a lawsuit to try to recover his or her payments on the contract. The solution is to include in the contract a provision requiring the seller to make timely payments on his or her loan and allowing the buyer to make such payments directly to the lender if the seller fails to do so.

> Seller shall maintain the existing mortgage in good standing; in the event that seller fails to make any payment when due, or in any other way causes or allows the loan to go into default, buyer shall be entitled to cure such default, and deduct all costs from the amounts next falling due to seller on this contract.

In order for a provision like the one above to be effective in preventing foreclosure, there must be some way for the buyer to receive notice when the seller falls into arrears. This may be the true crux of the problem, since the only sure way to obtain such notice is to request it from the seller's lender. This is a routine procedure, unless the seller's mortgage contains an enforceable alienation (due-on-sale) clause. There is always the possibility that when the lender learns of the proposed sale, it will elect to enforce the alienation provision in the existing mortgage, thus frustrating the sale.

Contract Escrow

To prevent default on underlying mortgage:
1. provision in contract giving buyer right to cure default, or
2. buyer makes payments to an escrow

One approach that is sometimes used to ensure the seller makes the payments on the existing mortgage is to set up an escrow account or servicing agreement for the contract payments. This is fairly simple to do, especially since a deed is usually placed in escrow pending completion of the contract anyway. In a contract escrow, the buyer makes payments into the escrow account, and the escrowee pays the seller's loan payments out of the account. The balance in the account (after the loan payments are made) is disbursed to the seller. In this fashion, the buyer is protected from the consequences of a default by the seller.

Sample Escrow Instructions

1. Seller shall place a deed to the property in escrow, to be conveyed to buyer upon full payment of the contract debt.
2. Buyer shall make all payments into an escrow account to be maintained by the escrow agent.
3. Upon receipt of each monthly payment, the escrow agent shall immediately make all payments due on seller's mortgage.
4. The escrow agent shall maintain a balance in the account equal to two monthly mortgage payments; all funds in excess of this minimum balance shall be disbursed to seller, after compliance with provision three of these instructions.

Estoppel Letter

It is always good practice, in any transaction where an existing mortgage is to be left in place, to obtain the lender's written consent to the proposed transaction. This is not necessary where there is no alienation clause in the seller's promissory note or mortgage, as with all FHA and VA loans. Where alienation clauses do exist, most lenders will insist on renegotiation of the loan to reflect current interest rates, or demand that the loan be paid off entirely. But occasionally a lender will consent to a sale without any change in the existing mortgage. The lender's consent is given in the form of a letter, called an estoppel letter, acknowledging the transfer and waiving the lender's right to accelerate the loan on account of the transfer. By writing the letter, the lender is estopped (legally prevented) from later trying to accelerate the loan on the basis of the sale.

An estoppel letter is often requested even in transactions where the underlying financing does not contain an alienation clause. The holder of the underlying mortgage or contract is asked to state in the estoppel letter the amount of the outstanding principal balance and to acknowledge that the loan is not in default. The buyer then has written confirmation from the lienholder as to the amount of the obligation the buyer is planning to assume or take subject to and is also assured that the seller is current on the payments and other obligations.

Estoppel letter from holder of existing mortgage or contract:
1. consent to sale if underlying mortgage has due-on-sale clause
2. statement of outstanding balance
3. statement that loan not in default

Exercise No. 5

Kate Voss has a home encumbered by a $50,000 note and deed of trust. She makes an agreement to sell the home to Sally Strump on the following terms: $80,000 sales price, $15,000 down, the balance to be paid over ten years in equal monthly installments with interest at the rate of 13%, subject to the existing $50,000 deed of trust. Kate's deed of trust gives her lender the option of accelerating the note if the property is sold.

1. **What will be Sally's monthly payment on the contract?**

2. **Cite two potential problems with this deal.**

3. State two ways that Sally could avoid the risk of Kate defaulting on the note and deed of trust.

CONTRACT WITH ASSUMPTION OF EXISTING MORTGAGE

Contract and assumption of existing mortgage:
- buyer assumes existing mortgage
- gives seller downpayment and contract for remainder

In the previous section, we saw how a seller could enter into a land contract while still maintaining his or her existing mortgage. If the seller does not wish to remain liable for the mortgage payments, but the buyer cannot (or will not) refinance the debt, the buyer may be able to assume (take over) the seller's mortgage and pay the balance of the purchase price under a contract. In this arrangement, the buyer becomes personally liable for payment of the mortgage debt; the buyer makes one payment to the mortgagee and another payment to the seller.

Example: Jim Dalton wishes to sell his home for $70,000. The property is encumbered by an assumable 9½% mortgage with a balance of $34,000 and monthly payments of $336.35 (204 payments remain to be made). Andy Entwhistle agrees to buy the property at the proposed price, with $10,000 down, assumption of the mortgage and the balance to be paid over ten years on a contract at 12¾%.

$70,000 purchase price
− 10,000 downpayment
− 34,000 assumed loan
$26,000 balance due on contract

$26,000   contract balance
×.0147840   10 yr/12¾% amortization factor
$384.38   monthly contract payment

Thus, Andy will pay:

1) $10,000 downpayment to seller
2) $336.35/mo. for 204 months to seller's mortgagee
3) $384.38/mo. for 120 months to seller

The advantage of an assumption for the buyer is the ability to get financing at lower than market interest rates. Of course, if the seller's loan bore a higher interest rate than the buyer could obtain elsewhere, there would be no point in assuming the loan. The advantage for the seller is that his or her property is more attractive when it can be financed at the lower rate, and he or she is also relieved of responsibility for making the monthly payments to the lender.

Exercise No. 6

A property is sold on the following terms: $120,000 sales price; $24,000 down; assumption of $70,000 mortgage balance; $26,000 land contract at 11%, fully amortized over 15 years. The existing mortgage is for a fully amortized 30-year loan in the original amount of $75,000 at 10% interest.

1. What is the monthly payment on the mortgage?

2. What is the monthly payment on the contract?

3. Using the loan progress tables, calculate the approximate number of payments remaining on the mortgage.

CONTRACT PLUS ASSUMPTION PLUS INSTITUTIONAL SECOND

Contract, assumption of existing mortgage, and second mortgage for part of downpayment: arranging a second mortgage from an institutional lender may be difficult

In some transactions, the seller will be willing to let the buyer assume the existing mortgage and also be willing to finance part of the price on a land contract, but he or she will desire at least a partial cashout of his or her equity, perhaps to use as a downpayment on another purchase. This is no problem if the buyer can provide a sufficient downpayment to cover the seller's cash requirements. But even if the buyer cannot come up with the cash from his or her own assets, there is still an alternative: an institutional second mortgage.

Example: Arthur Dodge has listed his house with a sales price of $160,000. He has an assumable first mortgage in the amount of $95,000, and is willing to finance a portion of the balance on a land contract, but he needs at least $50,000 in cash from the sale. Olga Turner would like to buy Art's house, but has only $20,000 towards a downpayment. Olga asks Art whether he would agree to a second mortgage from an institutional lender, which would take priority over the land contract. Art says yes, and the deal is closed on the following terms:

$20,000 cash from Olga
+ 30,000 cash from 2nd mortgage
$50,000 cash to seller

$50,000   cash to seller
 95,000   assumed 1st mortgage
+ 15,000   land contract
$160,000   total purchase price

Olga applies to Sam's Mortgage Company, which loans her $30,000 secured by a second mortgage on the property. The original (assumed) mortgage remains first in priority, and both mortgages have priority over the land contract.

Note that the buyer may have difficulty obtaining an institutional second because most lenders would hesitate to loan money on property where the title remains with the seller (as with a land contract).

Lien priority.

The significance of lien priority becomes apparent only when the borrower defaults. If the property must be sold through foreclosure to satisfy a debt, then each lender is paid from the proceeds of the sale according to its priority. If there is only enough money to pay the first lender, then the other (secondary) lenders are out of luck because their security has been exhausted.

> **Example:** Using the facts from the previous example, assume that Olga defaults and the property is sold under foreclosure, the proceeds of the sale (after taxes, costs, etc.) amounting to $120,000. The first mortgage is paid first, in the amount of $95,000, leaving $25,000 in proceeds. The remaining $25,000 is paid to the second mortgagee, which takes a $5,000 loss because its loan was for $30,000. Art gets nothing at all, because he is last in priority and there are no more proceeds.

Deeds and security.

In the preceding example, Olga did not receive a deed to the property because part of the purchase price was secured by a land contract; Art still holds the deed as security for the repayment of the contract debt. If Olga did not have legal title to the property, how could she get a second mortgage? There are two possible answers. The most likely is that Art, the legal title holder, consented to the mortgage. Art could agree to let the property stand as security for the loan without assuming personal responsibility for its repayment, meaning that the second mortgagee could recover the property if Olga defaulted, but could not sue Art for any deficiency.

The other alternative would have been for Olga to mortgage her equitable interest in the property, that is, her right to acquire title by making timely payments on the land contract. Such an equitable interest may be used as security, but it is not preferred by most lenders. In foreclosure of such an interest, the lender would merely acquire Olga's contract rights, not the property itself. In order to obtain title, the lender would still have to pay off the contract. Under this second arrangement, the so-called "second" mortgage is really third in priority, since it can never result in a sale of the property until after the contract has been paid off.

> **Example:** Using the same circumstances as in the foregoing example, assume that Art did not consent to a second mortgage, but that Olga was still able to borrow $30,000 with her equitable interest (contract rights) as security. If Olga defaults on the loan, Sam's Mortgage Company can take over her rights under the contract. Sam's can acquire title by paying off the contract, then attempt to sell the property in order to recover its loan. Note that the property is still encumbered by the original $95,000 mortgage.

Exercise No. 7

Tillie Taylor has agreed to buy a house from Boris Ivanoff, on the following terms:

$95,000   sales price

40,000   assumed 1st mortgage (192 payments of $412.16 remain)
20,000   new 2nd mortgage (15 yrs at 10½%)
30,000   land contract (10 yrs at 10%)
 5,000   cash

1. What is the monthly payment on the second mortgage?

2. Assuming that the contract payments are partially amortized on the basis of a 30-year schedule, what will be the balloon payment after 10 years?

3. How much will Boris receive at closing?

OTHER FORMS OF CREATIVE FINANCING

As mentioned at the beginning of this chapter, imagination is the only limit to the types of seller financing that are possible. In the final section of this chapter, we will review some of the less conventional arrangements that are being used today.

Other creative financing arrangements:
- lease/option
- lease and option
- lease/purchase
- exchange
- participation plans

LEASE/OPTIONS

Lease/option:
• lease with option to buy
• specified period of time
• non-refundable consideration for the option

The lease/option plan is comprised of two elements: a lease and an option to purchase the leased property within a specific time period (usually within the term of the lease). Obviously the lease/option is not the equivalent of a sale, but there is at least a strong possibility that a sale will eventually take place under the terms of the lease/option.

An option is an agreement to keep open, for a predetermined period of time, an offer to purchase or sell property. The prospective purchaser is referred to as the optionee; the property owner is the optionor. For the most part, the option contract is designed to assure the optionee the right to purchase the property at an agreed price and within a specified period of time. Usually, the optionee is keenly interested in the property, but will not exercise the right to complete the purchase unless certain problems are resolved or questions are answered beforehand. Some of the instances in which an option might be used are:

Reasons for lease/option:
1. speculation
2. investment
3. comparison
4. profit
5. delay for buyer to be financially ready for transaction
6. qualifying to buyer
7. rent credit applied to downpayment, loan, or price

1. **Speculation:** the prospective purchaser believes that the property will increase in value. For example, it is soon to be rezoned. However, the purchaser wants to wait until the change in zoning actually occurs before purchasing the property.
2. **Investment:** the prospective purchaser thinks the property will be a good investment but wants to wait until he or she can find other investors willing to contribute capital and share the risk before actually purchasing the property.
3. **Comparison:** the prospective purchaser thinks the property is a good buy but wants to investigate other properties before coming to a final decision.
4. **Profit:** the purchaser plans on selling the option (if the option is assignable) for a profit.
5. **Time to acquire cash to close:** the prospective purchaser needs additional time to save up the downpayment, to sell other property to obtain the

342

downpayment, or otherwise obtain the cash needed to close the transaction.

6. **Qualifying:** the buyer is unable to qualify for a loan at present, but has reason to believe that circumstances will change shortly and that he or she will be able to qualify for a large enough loan within the next year. For example, perhaps the buyer is expecting a raise, will soon pay off another debt and thereby reduce his or her monthly obligations, will be able to save or otherwise obtain a larger downpayment, or perhaps simply hopes that the property will increase in value enough over the next year so that he or she can obtain a larger loan than is now possible and be able to pay the seller the purchase price.

7. **Rent credit:** the buyer and seller may agree to credit part or all of the lease payments to the downpayment, loan amount, or sales price (which would reduce both the downpayment and the necessary loan amount), making it easier for the buyer to make the purchase in another six months or year.

Consideration for an Option

To be enforceable, an option must be supported by consideration. The consideration is something of value given by the optionee to the optionor in return for a commitment to sell the property to the optionee at some time in the future. The consideration is usually a sum of money, but it can be anything of value. It is sometimes called the **option money**.

In most cases, the consideration must pass to the optionor for the option contract to be binding. In other words, if the purchaser simply promised to pay the property owner $5,000 in return for the owner's promise to sell him the property but had not actually delivered the option money to the owner, the option contract would not be enforceable.

Once paid, the option money is not refundable, regardless of whether the optionee proceeds with the purchase. In many instances, purchasers and sellers agree that the option money will be credited to the purchase price, much like a good faith deposit in an ordinary purchase and sale agreement.

Example:

$73,000	purchase price
− 5,000	option money
$68,000	balance due if sale is consummated

This is not always the case, however, so such an arrangement should be clearly spelled out in the option contract. In fact, if the buyer and seller have not clearly agreed in the written option contract to credit the option money against the purchase price, the presumption is that the balance due would be the entire price recited in the option.

Example:

$73,000	purchase price
5,000	option money
$73,000	balance due

Other Option Essentials

An option is required to include all of the terms of the underlying contract of sale. This means that a binding contract is formed at the moment the optionee decides to exercise his or her option to purchase. Required information includes, but is not necessarily limited to, the following:

1. names and addresses of optionors and optionees;
2. date of the option;
3. nature and amount of consideration;
4. words indicating an option is being given;
5. date option expires; and
6. purchase price and essential terms.

How Does a Lease/option Work?

The seller/lessor leases the property to the buyer/tenant for a specific term (six months, one year, etc.) with the provision that part of the rental payments may be applied to the purchase price if the tenant decides to buy before the lease expires.

> **Example:** Mavis Ritland is selling her house for $75,000. Huey Lawrence is interested in the property, but will not be able to qualify for a loan until he receives a raise which he expects in two months. Huey and Mavis agree that Huey will rent the property for six months at $500.00/month, with half the rental payments being applicable to the sales price if Huey buys within six months. Huey also gets an option, which means that Mavis agrees not to sell to anyone else within the six-month lease period. If Huey decides to buy after six months, he will pay $73,500, the amount still due after deducting half the rental payments. However, failure to exercise the option will not entitle Huey to a refund of the portion that would have been applied to the purchase price had the property been purchased.

The essential terms of a lease/option, in addition to the option requirements recited previously, include:

1. rental amount;
2. rent credit, if any;
3. reference to a security deposit, if any;
4. a statement that a default by the optionee/lessee in connection with the lease agreement will result in a forfeiture of option rights; and
5. type of acceptable financing.

Advantages and Disadvantages of the Lease/option

The main advantage of the lease/option is keeping a sale

Lease/option advantages:
1. keeps sale alive when parties unwilling or unable to close
2. seller receives some rental income
3. through rent credit, buyer may reduce price, loan amount, and/or downpayment

Lease/option disadvantages:
1. seller cannot accept other offers
2. seller cannot occupy property
3. small initial cash investment by buyer
4. long occupation by buyer before sale

alive until the parties are in a position to close. Although this could be done with a simple option agreement, the lease/option also allows the "buyer" to reduce the selling price over a period of time, making it easier to come up with a downpayment or to qualify for a loan when the option is exercised. Also, the "seller" is receiving some income from the property which can be used to make payments on a new house until the old house is sold, or to cover payments on existing financing on the old house.

The primary disadvantage of the lease/option is that the "seller" cannot sell the property to anyone other than the tenant during the term of the option. Thus the lease/option is used only when it seems unlikely that other offers will be forthcoming in the near future. In addition, the "seller" cannot occupy the property during the term of the lease, so this plan normally involves sellers who have already purchased a new home or who have been holding the subject property for income production rather than as a personal residence.

Ways to Structure a Lease/option

The crediting of rental payments may be done in a variety of ways, depending on the needs of the buyer. Rental payments may be credited towards the amount needed for a downpayment if the buyer is short on cash, or they may be used to reduce the amount of financing required if the buyer cannot qualify for a large enough loan. If desired, part of the credit may be applied to the purchase price, reducing both the downpayment and the loan balance.

Example: Here are three different ways of structuring the following transaction: $80,000 sales price, with 20% down, balance at 13% interest for 30 years; one-year lease/option at $750/month with one half of rent applicable to purchase.

346

	Credit Applied To Downpayment	Credit Applied To Loan Balance	Credit Applied To Purchase Price
sales price	$80,000	$80,000	$80,000
credit	$ 4,500	$ 4,500	$ 4,500
downpayment	$11,500	$16,000	$15,100
balance financed	$64,000	$59,500	$60,400
monthly payment	$707.97	$658.19	$668.14

None, part, or all of rent may be credited to:
1. downpayment
2. loan
3. price (reduces both downpayment and loan)

Exercise No. 8

Buyer and Seller agree on a one-year lease/option with half of the $600/month rental payments being applicable to the required 20% downpayment on purchase at $72,000. Buyer exercises the option at the end of the lease term.

1. How much credit has the buyer established?

2. If the credit is applied to the required downpayment, how much will the buyer still owe on the downpayment?

LEASE CONTRACT SEPARATE FROM OPTION CONTRACT

A problem with the lease/option agreement is that too often the optionee/lessee does not exercise the right to purchase. The result is wasted effort, with no sale and no commission.

Separate lease and option
1. triple net lease
2. large option consideration

Why the lease/option has such a high mortality rate is arguable, but there are at least two characteristics inherent in every lease/option agreement that promise trouble:

- the prospective buyer's minimal cash investment— sometimes as little as a first and last lease payment; and
- the prospective buyer's extended occupancy of the property before a commitment is made.

Every property, especially a resale property, is flawed to some extent, and frequently optionees who have not yet committed themselves to a purchase will point to every minor imperfection when the time for a decision arrives. They will either refuse to exercise their right to buy or they will try to use the problems with the property, however inconsequential they might be, to negotiate further concessions on the part of the owner.

A more forceful, and consistently more successful, method of structuring lease/option arrangements is to treat the lease and the option as two separate contracts. Generally, the transaction would be formed as follows:

1. The lease agreement would be written on a triple-net basis (in addition to rent, buyer is responsible for payment of property taxes, insurance and utilities). If possible, rental payments would be set at above market rates. The above normal rental commits the buyer to the property and acts as an incentive to exercise the option to buy at the earliest possible date.
2. Secure the option with substantial cash consideration. Since it is not refundable, the consideration immediately passes to the seller. Because of the substantial nature of the option money, it is usually applied to the purchase price when the option to buy is exercised.

The agent's commission can be paid from the option money immediately, thereby emphasizing to the prospective buyer that a lease/option is a viable form of seller financing.

Experience has taught us that once a purchaser is financially committed to a property, he or she is not likely to walk away from it. Minor imperfections seem less important to someone who has already made a substantial investment in a property.

Of course, the amount of consideration to be paid by the optionee is negotiable. The general rule is simple: the more option money paid, the more secure the transaction. To make the effort worthwhile for an agent, the option money should, at a minimum, equal the amount of the commission.

LEASE/PURCHASE OR LEASE/SALE

A lease/purchase or lease/sale is quite similar to a lease/option. The primary difference is that, along with a lease, the buyer and seller sign a purchase and sale agreement instead of an option. The purchase contract is normally written with a substantial nonrefundable deposit and with a closing date set six months or a year in the future.

Most agents believe that a lease/purchase arrangement is more likely to result in a successful sale than a lease/option. The fact that the buyer is willing to sign a purchase agreement is an indication that he or she has already decided to buy the property and will do so, instead of delaying that decision for another six months or year, as would be the case with an option.

Although the buyer's willingness to sign a written contract to buy the property may certainly be an indication of the buyer's intent, the differences between a lease/purchase and a lease/option may be more psychological than financial. The practical consequences of a lease/purchase are pretty much the same as a lease/option. Lease/purchase agreements are usually written so that the seller is entitled to the deposit if the buyer does not close the transaction as agreed in the purchase and sale agreement. This means that the buyer forfeits the deposit if he or she fails to go through with the purchase, which is little different from paying the option money. As with a lease/option, probably the most reliable indicator of a successful lease/purchase is the amount of money put up by the buyer.

However, even though the economic realities of lease/purchase and lease/option transactions may be essentially the same, many sellers prefer a lease/purchase (lease/sale). Therefore, structuring a transaction as a "sale" with a closing one year later instead of as a one-year option may be acceptable to some sellers who would be reluctant to agree to an option.

EQUITY EXCHANGES

Equity exchange:
- only for income or investment property
- tax on gain is deferred to extent of like-kind property received in exchange
- anything received other than like-kind property is boot and is taxable

When a buyer cannot come up with sufficient cash for a sale, the difference can be made up with other assets, such as land, another house, cars, boats, or any other property in which the buyer has an equity interest and that the seller would be willing to accept as part of the downpayment. If the transaction involves an exchange of real estate that is used in a trade or business or is held for the production of income or for investment, some or all of the capital gain can be deferred in a "tax-free" exchange. The tax-free exchange is not available for residential property or for property held for sale by a dealer. If the transaction does qualify for tax-free exchange treatment, any gain that is purely a result of the exchange is deferred. However, any property or money that does not qualify (i.e., is not like-kind property held for income, business or investment) is treated as "boot" and is taxable.

Example: Ben Hummel owns a rental house which he would like to sell. He lists the house for $174,000, including an assumable mortgage of $127,000. Cathy Collier is interested in the property, but has only $15,000 cash for a downpayment. Bill Broker suggests an exchange of Cathy's triplex, valued at $115,000 with an assumable mortgage of $80,000, for Ben's house, with Cathy to assume Ben's loan. Ben will receive $35,000 in the form of Cathy's equity in the triplex, and $12,000 cash. He will also assume Cathy's loan, which will result in "mortgage relief" of $47,000. (He owed $127,000 on the loan which is to be assumed by Cathy and will owe only $80,000 on the loan which he is to assume—a difference of $47,000.)

In the above example, Cathy would pay no income tax on the sale of her triplex. She received only qualifying property in return for her property. Ben will owe taxes on the $12,000 in cash received and also on the $47,000 of mortgage relief. Both are treated as taxable boot.

PARTICIPATION PLANS

In a participation or shared equity plan, the buyer enters into a form of partnership with an investor who provides cash for the sale. The investor may be the seller, a bank or any private investor. Instead of charging interest, the investor in a participation plan receives a percentage of the equity (the difference between the property's value and the indebtedness secured by the property). Different investors will have varying requirements as to the percentage of equity to be shared, and as to the method of repayment of the investment. These issues are a matter of institutional policy or negotiation between buyer and investor. The important points to consider when arranging a participation loan are listed below.

1. **How will the loan be applied?** An investor may simply put up cash for the downpayment, or the primary lender may reduce the interest rate in exchange for a share of the equity. In the first case, the participation loan is essentially a form of secondary financing, with "interest" paid in the form of a share of the equity instead of a

Participation plans: lender or investor receives percentage of equity in property instead of or in addition to interest

351

percentage of the loan amount.

Example:

$100,000   sales price
  20,000   participation loan
  80,000   conventional loan

In the second instance, the participation loan is a variation of the permanent buydown, except that the buyer must repay the buydown when the equity is divided.

Example: $100,000 sales price; the lender quotes 15% interest rate for $80,000, 30-year conventional loan. The lender agrees to 13% interest rate in exchange for a share of the equity. The buyer makes a $20,000 downpayment.

2. **How will the equity be calculated?** Equity is the difference between the value of the property and the outstanding indebtedness secured by the property. For the purposes of a participation loan, the buyer and investor must agree at the outset as to the method of valuing the property. Any method acceptable to both parties may be used. The value of the property at the time of purchase may be periodically adjusted according to an agreed upon index, or the parties may choose a particular appraiser whose opinion of value they will accept.

   The parties should also determine whether the participation loan is to be considered part of the indebtedness on the property. A critical factor here is whether the participation loan is secured by a lien against the property. If it is, then it reduces the equity.

Example:

$110,000 value of property
− 72,000 balance on participation loan
$38,000 equity to be shared

3. **What percentage of the equity will the investor receive?** This amount is negotiable, but should be large enough to provide at least a market rate of return to the investor. Factors of influence in this regard are:

- the amount of the participation loan in proportion to the value of the property;
- the projected rate of increase in the value of the property;
- the rate at which any conventional financing will be paid off, that is, the rate of equity growth if the value of the property remains constant; and
- the term of the participation loan.

Considerations in participation plans:
1. how the loan or contribution is to be applied
2. how to calculate the equity
3. what percentage of the equity goes to the investor
4. when the investor must be paid
5. how to treat buyer's contributions that improve property value
6. who pays tax and insurance

4. **When will the investor be repaid?** The investor may cash out his or her share of equity at a pre-agreed time (e.g., after five years), or else at the time the property is sold. Notice that if the investor is cashed out before the property is sold, the buyer will most likely have to refinance at that time. If the investor is to be repaid when the property is sold, provision should be made for establishing an acceptable resale price for the property.

5. **How will improvements be handled?** The agreement should specify whether the investor will share in any changes in equity resulting from improvements made on the property. If the buyer invests $5,000 of her own funds in an addition which adds $7,000 to the value of the property, does the investor get a share of the $2,000 equity created by the addition? Conversely, if a $5,000 remodeling project only adds $3,000 to the overall value of the

property, does the investor share in the $2,000 reduction of equity? Questions such as these should be addressed in the original loan agreement.

6. **Who will be responsible for payment of taxes and insurance?** Usually the buyer will pay the property taxes and homeowner's insurance premiums, but this point may be negotiable in the case of some private investors.

You will note from the foregoing discussion that participation plans can be fairly complex in comparison to other creative financing methods. Agreements such as these should be clearly spelled out, with provisions for all possible contingencies. The services of a trained real estate attorney should always be obtained when preparing an agreement of this sort.

BROKER'S RESPONSIBILITIES

Complexity of many creative financing plans imposes obligation on brokers and salespersons to:
- inform clients and customers
- properly represent clients
- make proper disclosures

Several creative financing arrangements have been explained in this chapter, but this is by no means an exhaustive survey of the possibilities for imaginative buyers and sellers. The old saying "where there's a will, there's a way" is the focal point of creative finance. The advantages of open-minded negotiation among buyer, seller, lender and agent cannot be overemphasized. However, when using an arrangement that has not been tried and proven by others in the past, the greatest care should be taken to protect the rights of all parties through detailed specification of all terms of the agreement, preferably with the advice and assistance of legal counsel.

As you have seen, the variety of creative financing plans is almost without limit. The variety of plans and the associated wide variety of rights and obligations of all parties—the buyer, the seller, the lender (if any), and the real estate agent—require that professional real estate agents involved in negotiating creative transactions be particularly well informed and take particular care to properly represent their clients and to make proper disclosures. In many cases, it will be advisable to seek the counsel of real estate attorneys and/or certified public accountants.

The area of law which governs such creative financing transactions is as yet unsettled, but a recent California case should serve as notice to real estate agents working this field. In that case, *Pierce v. Home*, the real estate broker arranged two mortgage loans for the purchaser, who was an elderly widow. When she ultimately was unable to make the payments and lost the property through foreclosure, she sued the broker. The California Court of Appeals held that real estate agents holding themselves out as having professional knowledge in the area of real estate finance have an obligation to give expert advice to their clients regarding the economic consequences of a transaction. In this particular case, the widow, after making both mortgage payments, had scarcely enough money to pay for the necessities of life. The court held that the broker should have inquired into the buyer's ability to repay the loans and possibly advised her of a more prudent way to obtain the money.

CHAPTER SUMMARY

1. Seller financing provides an almost limitless variety of creative alternatives to institutional financing and is particularly attractive in tight money markets when loans from institutional lenders often have prohibitive interest rates. Seller financing is also useful when a borrower could not qualify for an institutional loan, for example, because her employment history was too brief. However, for seller financing to be a feasible alternative, the seller must not need an immediate cashout from the sale.

2. When sellers finance the sales of their homes, they use the same instruments used by other lenders: promissory notes, and mortgages or deeds of trust.

3. The simplest form of seller financing is where the seller has free title to the property (there are no outstanding mortgages or other liens). In this instance, the parties can negotiate the terms of their agreement and close the transaction.

4. However, most seller-financed sales are of encumbered property. The buyer must, therefore, take subject to or assume an existing mortgage, trust deed, or contract. There are various ways to structure such a transaction, including:

   - assumption plus purchase money second mortgage (buyer assumes first mortgage and seller finances remainder of purchase price less downpayment);
   - seller-sponsored wraparound financing (wraparound financing enables the seller to receive an above-market rate of interest yield and the buyer to pay below market interest rates);
   - land contract subject to existing mortgage (contract is for the full purchase price, but buyer's rights are subject to the rights of the seller's mortgagee);
   - contract with assumption of existing mortgage (buyer assumes first mortgage, land contract is for balance of purchase price less downpayment); and
   - contract plus assumption plus institutional second (buyer assumes first mortgage, buyer obtains second mortgage for a portion of price to cashout seller, and contract is written up for the balance of the purchase price).

5. Other creative seller financing plans include:

   - lease/option,
   - lease contract separate from option contract,

- lease/purchase or lease/sale,
- equity exchange, and
- participation plan.

Chapter 16
CALIFORNIA ESCROW PROCEDURES

The last step in the loan process is closing. This is where the loan proceeds are distributed to the seller and the deed to the property is given to the buyer. The steps in the closing process are usually carried out by an escrow agent. The escrow agent makes sure all the necessary documents are prepared and properly signed, calculates the various charges to be assessed against each party, makes sure all the required funds are deposited, and gives each party a settlement statement. Once everything is in order, the loan funds are disbursed, the deed and other documents recorded, the sales transaction has been completed.

DEFINITION OF ESCROW

The State of California defines escrow as "any transaction wherein one person, for the purpose of effecting the sale, transfer, encumbering, or leasing of real property to another person, delivers any written instrument, money, evidence of title to real or personal property, or other thing of value to a third person to be held by such third person until the happening of a specified event or the performance of a prescribed condition, when it is then delivered by such third person to a grantee, grantor, promisee, promisor, obligee, obligor, bailee, bailor, or any agent or employee of any of the latter."

There are two essential requirements for the creation of a valid escrow.

Requirements for valid
escrow:
- legally binding
contract
- conditional delivery
and relinquishment of
control

- First, there must be a legally binding and enforceable contract between the parties. This contract may take the form of a purchase and sale agreement, escrow instructions signed by the buyer and seller, or a combination of the two.
- The second requirement of a valid escrow is "conditional delivery with relinquishment of control." The parties must deposit funds or documents with a third party along with instructions to disburse the funds or deliver the documents only upon the happening of a specified event. If the parties retain any control over the deposited items, there is no valid escrow.

PARTIES

ESCROWEES

Escrowee: neutral third
party, most likely a title
company or an escrow
company

An escrowee is the neutral third party who holds the items deposited by the parties and disburses them after the conditions of the escrow are satisfied. The escrowee also performs additional services such as preparing documents, calculating settlement costs and recording. Factors which may influence the choice of an escrowee include cost of service, professional reputation, and requirements of the third-party lender. (The acceptance of "kickbacks" or similar compensation for referring customers to an escrow business is grounds for suspension or revocation of a real estate license under the California Real Estate Law.)

Title companies are the most common escrowees in northern California. In the southern part of the state, independent escrow companies also close a large number of transactions. Many institutional lenders (banks, savings and loan associations, and insurance companies) have their own escrow departments which are used as closing agents for the transactions they finance. Under certain limited circumstances, attorneys and real estate brokers may also act as escrowees.

Escrow companies must be licensed by the State Department of Corporations under the Escrow Law; only corporations may be licensed as escrow companies, individuals are not eligible. Exempted from this licensing requirement are banks, S&Ls, insurance companies, attorneys, and real estate brokers, all of whom are regulated by other agencies.

Real estate brokers are exempt from the Escrow Law "while performing acts in the course of or incidental to a real estate transaction in which the broker is an agent or a party to the transaction and in which the broker is performing an act for which a real estate license is required." This exemption permits brokers to provide certain services to their clients without becoming subject to regulation from another agency. The exemption does not permit brokers to operate as escrow agents in transactions where they have no bona fide interest other than that of providing escrow services.

Real estate brokers: exempt from license law while in regular course of business

OTHERS INVOLVED IN THE ESCROW PROCESS

The typical escrow involves many people. In addition to the parties (buyer, seller, lender, escrow agent) and the real estate broker, important functions are performed by title companies, notaries public, local county recording officials, and structural pest inspectors.

A notary public is an individual with the power to administer oaths and grant official approval of documents. In real estate transactions, notaries are most commonly employed to witness and verify the signature and acknowledgement of documents which are to be recorded. Acknowledgement, accompanied by notarization, is a prerequisite for the recording of any document affecting title to real estate. The notarization process serves as a protection against forgeries.

Recording documents is one of the key functions of an escrow. The recording system is designed to protect interests in real estate by establishing the relative priority of various

Other parties involved in escrow:
- *title companies*
- *notaries public*
- *recording officials*
- *inspectors*

interested parties. Any document relating to real estate owner-ship (deed, deed of trust, lien, real estate contract, etc.) can and should be recorded.

Each county in the state has its own set of records cover-ing the real estate located in the county. The records are kept at the office of the County Auditor or Recorder. At the close of escrow, each party is charged for the recording of those documents which benefit that party. For example, sellers pay for recording lien releases; buyers pay for recording deeds. Recording charges are imposed on a 'per page' basis, usual-ly a few dollars for the first page of a document and a lesser amount for each additional page. These charges help pay for indexing the documents and maintaining the actual records.

One of the most common contingencies in a sale of real estate is a structural pest inspection. These inspections are required by many buyers, lenders, and insuring agencies to determine whether the security property is in good repair and free from damaging infestation. For a fee, a licensed inspec-tor will prepare a written report of the property's condition, noting any repairs that need to be made. The responsibility for the inspection fee and the cost of needed repairs may be negotiated between the buyer and seller, but is charged to the seller in most areas.

THE ESCROW PROCESS

Although real estate agents are rarely called upon to act as escrow agents, they must be aware of the steps in the escrow process. Agents must be able to advise their clients effectively and can expedite closings by anticipating the needs of the escrowee. Much of the information needed in escrow should be provided by the real estate agent.

The following discussion covers the steps involved in a typical real estate escrow for a single-family residential sale. However, escrow procedures vary significantly from one area of the state to another. Who will perform the escrow, the type of escrow instructions to be used, the timing of the escrow, and the allocation of closing costs all vary depending on local custom.

All escrows involve certain essential steps:

- gathering information necessary to prepare escrow instructions;
- obtaining a preliminary title report from the title company;
- satisfying existing loans secured by the property;
- preparing documents such as escrow instructions, loan documents, deeds, etc.;
- depositing funds by the buyer (and seller if necessary);
- prorating expenses and allocating closing costs;
- preparing a Uniform Settlement Statement;
- issuing title insurance policies for buyer and lender;
- recording necessary documents; and
- disbursing funds and delivering documents.

Essential steps of escrow:
- gather information
- get preliminary title report
- satisfy existing loans
- prepare documents
- deposit funds
- prorate expenses
- prepare Uniform Settlement Statement
- issue title insurance policies
- record documents
- disburse funds and deliver documents

ESCROW INSTRUCTIONS

The escrow instructions are prepared from information obtained from the parties, and the terms of the deposit receipt itself are made a part of the instructions. Joint escrow instructions (a single set of instructions for both buyer and seller) are preferred in southern California, and are normally executed shortly after the deposit receipt is signed. Separate escrow instructions for the buyer and seller are more common in northern California. The buyer's instructions are often signed at the same time the buyer makes his or her deposit of funds into the escrow.

Whether joint or separate, escrow instructions are usually preprinted forms provided by the escrow agent or the lender. Generally speaking, separate escrow instructions tend to be simpler than joint instructions. The advantage of joint instructions is that they eliminate the possibility of conflicts between the instructions received from the buyer and the

Escrow instructions:
- N. California: separate
- S. California: joint

seller. On the other hand, separate instructions allow one party to keep certain information (for example, the amount of the commission) confidential from the other party.

Local custom governs when the instructions are prepared. In northern California, escrow instructions are typically prepared at a much later stage in the transaction than is the case in southern California. In southern counties, where escrows are often handled by escrow companies, the parties typically meet with the escrow agent right after the purchase and sale agreement is executed and the instructions are prepared shortly thereafter.

In northern California, escrow instructions are often prepared only when the transaction is almost ready to close. Real estate agents play a much greater role in the escrow process in northern California, gathering much of the information needed by the escrowee (usually a title company). The escrowee has little if any direct contact with the parties, so it is up to the agent to insure that all the necessary information is forwarded in a timely manner to the escrowee.

ESCROW PROGRESS CHART

It is good idea for agents to use an escrow progress chart (see example below) to keep track of the status of the escrow. By glancing at the chart, the agent can quickly tell the current status of escrow and be reminded of items that still need to be done to close the transaction. One of the agents associated with the transaction is usually responsible for gathering the documents and information required by the escrowee. However, each agent should stay apprised of the process as the escrow progresses.

The first step in the escrow procedure is to open the escrow. This is done by providing the escrowee with the information needed to prepare preliminary escrow instructions. Once the instructions are signed and returned, the escrowee will order a preliminary title report showing the condition of title to the property. This information will be forwarded to

ESCROW PROGRESS CHART

	Sch. Date	Actual Date	Escrow Operations
1			Notice of Sale to multiple listing service
2			Buyer's deposit increased to $
3			Escrow opened with
4			Preliminary title searched
5			Clouds on title eliminated
6			Credit report ordered from
7			Credit report received
8			Report of residential record ordered
9			Report of residential record received
10			Pest control inspection ordered
11			Pest control report received; work —
12			Pest control report accepted by seller
13			Pest control work ordered
14			Pest control work completed
15			Other inspections ordered
16			Report received; work —
17			Report accepted by
18			Special contingencies eliminated
19			Payoff or beneficiary statement ordered
20			Payoff or beneficiary statement received
21			Payoff or beneficiary statement ordered
22			Payoff or beneficiary statement received
23			1st loan commitment ordered from
24			Received: @ % Fee Pts.
25			2nd loan commitment ordered from
26			Received: @ % Fee Pts.
27			Loan application submitted to
28			Loan application approved
29			Loan/assumption papers received by escrow
30			Hazard insurance placed with
31			Escrow closing instructions requested
32			Client called for closing appointment
33			Closing papers signed
34			Closing papers to escrow holder
35			Funds ordered
36			Deed recorded

After Close of Escrow

Received	Delivered	
		Final adjusted closing statement
		Check of seller's proceeds
		Check of buyer's refund
		Commission check
		Seller's "Loss Payee" insurance policy
		Recorded deed
		Title insurance policy

Notations

_____

_____

_____

the buyer's lender, along with a copy of the escrow instructions. Note that the escrow instructions must correspond to the lender's loan terms. Any discrepancy in the loan amount or terms (such as interest rate, repayment period, or discount points) will require signing amended escrow instructions, since the lender will not disburse any loan funds into the escrow until the instructions correspond to the terms of the loan.

Early in the escrow process, the escrowee will also contact the seller's lender to obtain a payoff figure for the seller's loan. This is accomplished by sending a "demand for payoff" or "request for beneficiary's statement" to the lender, who then returns copies of the completed form to the escrowee and the title company. Structural pest inspections are also ordered as soon as possible to avoid delays in closing which may be caused by the need for repairs to the property.

When the buyer's loan is approved, the lender will forward the loan documents (note, deed of trust, and Truth-in-Lending statement) to the escrowee. At this point, the buyer is in a position to complete his or her part of the transaction by depositing the necessary funds into escrow and signing the loan documents, which are then forwarded to the lender.

The seller will be ready to close when the escrowee receives the payoff figures from the seller's lender and the pest control inspection detailing any repairs to be performed. This information will allow a reasonably accurate determination of the seller's proceeds from the sale. The pest control inspection, along with notices of completion of any required repairs, may also be forwarded to the buyer's lender if necessary.

Hazard insurance is another item common to most escrows. A new hazard insurance policy for the buyer, or an assignment of the seller's existing policy, must be forwarded to the new lender prior to disbursal of the loan funds. Before escrow can close, any other contingencies of the sale, such as sale of the buyer's existing home, must be satisfied or waived.

When all contingencies have been satisfied, the lender will disburse the loan funds to the title company. The escrowee will have also sent the seller's grant deed to the title company for recording upon receipt of the loan funds. The title company will record the deed, deed of trust, reconveyance deed and other documents, and then provide the escrowee with the information (final payoff of the seller's loan, title and recording fees, etc.) necessary to prepare the final closing statements. The escrowee prepares the statements and makes the necessary disbursements of funds to the seller, broker and other entities. At this time, the title insurance policy is issued, and the buyer will also receive copies of the completed loan documents, insurance policies and inspection reports.

CLOSING COSTS AND SETTLEMENT STATEMENTS

A settlement statement is a listing of all the amounts payable by or to one of the parties in the transaction. Settlement statements are prepared for both buyer and seller, or a single statement may list charges and credits for both parties. In sales of residential property financed by institutional lenders, a Uniform Settlement Statement form such as the one shown below must be prepared.

Debit: charge payable by party

Items on the settlement statement are listed as either **debits** or **credits**. A debit is a charge payable by a particular party; for example, the purchase price is a debit to the buyer, the sales commission a debit to the seller. Credits are items payable to a party; the buyer would be credited for his or her new loan, the seller for the purchase price. Think of the settlement statement as a check register for a bank account: debits are like checks written against the account, credits are the equivalent of deposits into the account. When the transaction closes, the balances in the buyer's and seller's accounts should equal zero.

Credit: charge payable to party

Although it is virtually impossible to calculate the exact closing costs for a transaction until the time of closing, a reasonably accurate estimate can be prepared in advance.

A. Settlement Statement

U.S. Department of Housing
and Urban Development

OMB No. 2502-0265 (Exp. 12-31-86)

B. Type of Loan

		6 File Number	7 Loan Number	8 Mortgage Insurance Case Number
1. ☐ FHA 2. ☐ FmHa 3. ☐ Conv. Unins.				
4. ☐ VA 5. ☐ Conv. Ins.				

C. Note: This form is furnished to give you a statement of actual settlement costs. Amounts paid to and by the settlement agent are shown. Items marked "(p.o.c.)" were paid outside the closing; they are shown here for informational purposes and are not included in the totals.

D. Name and Address of Borrower	E Name and Address of Seller	F Name and Address of Lender

G. Property Location	H Settlement Agent	
	Place of Settlement	I. Settlement Date

J. Summary of Borrower's Transaction		K. Summary of Seller's Transaction	
100. Gross Amount Due From Borrower		**400. Gross Amount Due to Seller**	
101. Contract sales price		401. Contract sales price	
102. Personal property		402. Personal property	
103. Settlement charges to borrower (line 1400)		403.	
104.		404.	
105.		405.	
Adjustments for items paid by seller in advance		*Adjustments for items paid by seller in advance*	
106. City/town taxes to		406. City/town taxes to	
107. County taxes to		407. County taxes to	
108. Assessments to		408. Assessments to	
109.		409.	
110.		410.	
111.		411.	
112.		412.	
120. Gross Amount Due From Borrower		**420. Gross Amount Due to Seller**	
200. Amounts Paid By Or In Behalf Of Borrower		**500. Reductions In Amount Due To Seller**	
201. Deposit or earnest money		501. Excess deposit (see instructions)	
202. Principal amount of new loan(s)		502. Settlement charges to seller (line 1400)	
203. Existing loan(s) taken subject to		503. Existing loan(s) taken subject to	
204.		504. Payoff of first mortgage loan	
205.		505. Payoff of second mortgage loan	
206.		506.	
207.		507.	
208.		508.	
209.		509.	
Adjustments for items unpaid by seller		*Adjustment for items unpaid by seller*	
210. City/town taxes to		510. City/town taxes to	
211. County taxes to		511. County taxes to	
212. Assessments to		512. Assessments to	
213.		513.	
214.		514.	
215.		515.	
216.		516.	
217.		517.	
218.		518.	
219.		519.	
220. Total Paid By/For Borrower		**520. Total Reduction Amount Due Seller**	
300. Cash At Settlement From/To Borrower		**600. Cash At Settlement To/From Seller**	
301. Gross Amount due from borrower (line 120)		601. Gross amount due to seller (line 420)	
302. Less amounts paid by/for borrower (line 220)	( )	602. Less reductions in amt. due seller (line 520)	( )
303. Cash ☐ From ☐ To Borrower		603. Cash ☐ To ☐ From Seller	

SUBSTITUTE FORM 1099 SELLER STATEMENT

The information contained in Blocks E, G, H and I and on Line 401 (or, if Line 401 is asterisked, Lines 403 and 404) is important tax information and is being furnished to the Internal Revenue Service. If you are required to file a return, a negligence penalty or other sanction will be imposed on you if this item is required to be reported and the Internal Revenue Service determines that it has not been reported.

L. Settlement Charges

		Paid From Borrower's Funds at Settlement	Paid From Seller's Funds at Settlement
700. Total Sales/Broker's Commission based on price $ @ % =			
Division of Commission (line 700) as follows:			
701. $ to			
702. $ to			
703. Commission paid at Settlement			
704.			
800. Items Payable In Connection With Loan			
801. Loan Origination Fee %			
802. Loan Discount %			
803. Appraisal Fee to			
804. Credit Report to			
805. Lender's Inspection Fee			
806. Mortgage Insurance Application Fee to			
807. Assumption Fee			
808.			
809.			
810.			
811.			
900. Items Required By Lender To Be Paid In Advance			
901. Interest from to @$ /day			
902. Mortgage Insurance Premium for months to			
903. Hazard Insurance Premium for years to			
904. years to			
905.			
1000. Reserves Deposited With Lender			
1001. Hazard insurance months @$ per month			
1002. Mortgage insurance months @$ per month			
1003. City property taxes months @$ per month			
1004. County property taxes months @$ per month			
1005. Annual assessments months @$ per month			
1006. months @$ per month			
1007. months @$ per month			
1008. months @$ per month			
1100. Title Charges			
1101. Settlement or closing fee to			
1102. Abstract or title search to			
1103. Title examination to			
1104. Title insurance binder to			
1105. Document preparation to			
1106. Notary fees to			
1107. Attorney's fees to			
(includes above items numbers:)			
1108. Title insurance to			
(includes above items numbers:)			
1109. Lender's coverage $			
1110. Owner's coverage $			
1111.			
1112.			
1113.			
1200. Government Recording and Transfer Charges			
1201. Recording fees: Deed $; Mortgage $; Reseases $			
1202. City/county tax/stamps: Deed$; Mortgage $			
1203. State tax/stamps: Deed $; Mortgage $			
1204.			
1205.			
1300. Additional Settlement Charges			
1301. Survey to			
1302. Pest inspection to			
1303.			
1304.			
1305.			
1400. Total Settlement Charges (enter on lines 103, Section J and 502, Section K)			

SELLER INSTRUCTIONS

If this real estate was your principal residence, file Form 2119, Sale or Exchange of Principal Residence, for any gain, with your tax return; for other transactions, complete the applicable parts of form 4797, form 6252 and/or Schedule D (Form 1040).

The Undersigned Acknowledges Receipt of This Settlement Statement and Agrees to the Correctness Thereof.

_____   _____
Buyer   Seller

Agents are often called upon to make such an estimate of the buyer's cash requirements and the seller's net proceeds from the sale. Worksheets such as the form shown below are commonly used for this purpose.

	BUYER'S STATEMENT		SELLER'S STATEMENT	
SETTLEMENT STATEMENT	Debit	Credit	Debit	Credit
Sales Price	52,000.00			52,000.00
Deposit		1,500.00		
Commission — 7%			3,640.00	
Mortgage Balance			35,822.24	
Prepaid Interest	261.00		156.70	
New Loan		45,000.00		
Taxes — Prorated		327.10	327.10	
Loan Origination Fee - 1%	450.00			
Fire Insurance	192.00			
Title Insurance — standard			238.10	
Title Insurance - extended	135.00			
Tax Reserve — 2 months	183.00			
Appraisal Fee	75.00			
Credit Report	50.00			
Survey Fee	255.00			
Discount Points			2,850.00	
Documentary Stamps			57.20	
Balance Due From Buyer		6,773.90		
Balance Due To Seller			8,908.66	
TOTALS	$53,601.00	$53,601.00	$52,000.00	$52,000.00

Settlement statements are written interpretations of the financial elements of the contract.

BUYER'S COSTS

Obviously, the main cost for the buyer will be the **purchase price**, listed as a debit on the buyer's statement. In most transactions, the purchase price is offset by some form of financing, either an institutional loan or seller financing. New loans or assumptions of existing loans are listed as credits for the buyer. The difference between the sales price and the financing is the downpayment. Some worksheet forms utilize the figure for the downpayment in calculating the buyer's costs, rather than listing the purchase price and loan amounts separately. Either method will yield the same result.

After the purchase price, the largest debit to the buyer at closing is typically the **loan fee**. This is a percentage of the loan amount (usually 1-2%) charged by the lender to cover the administrative costs of making the loan. To calculate the loan origination fee, simply multiply the loan amount by the percentage of the fee.

The lender may also charge **discount points** on the loan. Points are a percentage of the loan amount charged in order to increase the lender's yield on the loan. The seller often pays some or all of the loan discount, but (except in VA loans) the buyer may be responsible for the points. If the buyer pays the points, they should be shown as a debit on the buyer's statement.

Several other loan costs are customarily charged to the buyer in a real estate sale. These include the **appraisal fee, credit report fee**, amounts for impound or reserve accounts for **taxes** and **insurance**, lender's **title insurance premium**, and **prepaid interest**.

Impound or reserve accounts are trust accounts maintained by the lender to pay property taxes and hazard insurance premiums. The borrower pays a portion (1/12 of the annual amount) of these expenses each month along with the principal and interest payment; when the taxes or insurance premium become payable, the lender pays them out of the reserve account. When the loan is originated, the lender asks the borrower to deposit an initial amount into the reserve account. This is usually in the range of six months' to one year's worth of the taxes and insurance premium. The borrower's monthly deposits will then maintain a positive balance in the account as the items are paid.

Prepaid or interim interest is the amount of interest due on the new loan during the first (partial) month of the loan term. Interest on real estate loans is normally paid in arrears, that is, the interest for a given month is paid at the end of the month. However, when a new loan is made, the interest

Buyer's costs:
- purchase price
- loan fee
- discount points
- appraisal fee
- credit report fee
- taxes
- insurance
- title insurance
- pre-paid interest
- attorney's fees
- notary fees
- escrow fees
- recording fees

371

	BUYER'S STATEMENT		SELLER'S STATEMENT	
	DEBIT	**CREDIT**	**DEBIT**	**CREDIT**
Purchase Price	X			X
Deposit		X		
Documentary Transfer Tax			X	
Sales Commission			X	
Pay-Off Existing Loan			X	
Assume Existing Loan		X	X	
New Loan		X		
Purchase Money Loan		X	X	
Title Search	X			
Standard Title Insurance	VARIES ACCORDING TO LOCAL CUSTOM			
Title Insurance - extended coverage	X			
Loan Discount (Points)	BY AGREEMENT, EXCEPT VA (DEBIT SELLER)			
Loan Fee	X			
Property Taxes				
Arrears		X	X	
Current/Not Due		X	X	
Prepaid	X			X
Insurance				
Assume Policy	X			X
New Policy	X			
Interest				
Pay-off Existing Loan			X	
Assume Existing Loan		X	X	
New Loan	X			
Impound Accounts				
Pay-off Existing Loan				X
Assumption	X			X
New Loan	X			
Credit Report	X			
Survey, Inspection	BY AGREEMENT			
Appraisal	X			
Escrow Fee	BY AGREEMENT, EXCEPT VA (DEBIT SELLER)			
Sale of Chattels	X			X
Misc. Recording Fees	X		X	
Balance Due From Buyer		X		
Balance Due Seller			X	
TOTALS	**X**	**X**	**X**	**X**

is paid in advance for the month of closing. For example, if closing occurs on June 15, interest for the period June 15 through June 30 is paid at closing. The first regular payment on the loan is then due on August 1 and covers the interest due for the month of July (payment in arrears). To calculate the amount of interim interest that will be due, multiply the daily interest rate times the number of days between the closing date and the end of the month times the amount of the loan.

Other items which are typically charged to the buyer in a real estate sale include: **attorney fees, notary fees**, a share of the **escrow fee** and **recording fees**. Depending on the agreement of the parties or local custom, the buyer may also be charged for all or a portion of the owner's **title insurance policy**. (This expense is paid by the seller in most southern California counties; in most northern counties it is either paid by the buyer or the cost is split between buyer and seller. Note, however, that the parties are free to ignore local custom and allocate this expense by agreement in the deposit receipt or escrow instructions if they so desire.) If a **pest control inspection** and/or **repairs** are one of the contingencies to the sale, the buyer may also be responsible for all or part of this expense, depending on the allocation agreed to by the parties. Finally, the buyer will be charged for any special costs incurred by the buyer, such as the cost of a **home warranty contract**.

Depending on the status of the **property taxes**, the buyer may be due a credit or may owe an amount to the seller. If the property taxes have been paid for a period after the closing date, the buyer will have to reimburse the seller for taxes applicable to the time after the closing date. On the other hand, if taxes are in arrears, the seller will owe the buyer for the amount of arrears.

In calculating the amount of tax payable by or to the seller or buyer, it is necessary to know the daily rate of the tax and the number of days for which each party is responsible. The expense can then be prorated (divided and allocated) between the parties. The process of proration is also used to allocate such items as interest on assumed loans, premiums on assumed insurance policies, and rents for income property.

Example: Assume that the annual property taxes are $3,600 and have been paid through the end of June for the current year. If the sale is to close on April 17, the taxes would be prorated as follows.

Step 1: calculate the daily rate of the expense by dividing the annual rate by 360 (for monthly expenses, divide by 30)

$3600 ÷ 360 = $10 daily rate of tax

> NOTE: Although it is more accurate to use the actual number of days in the year or month, it is easier and sufficiently accurate for the purposes of estimation to assume that each month contains 30 days, for a 360-day year.

Step 2: calculate the number of days for which each party is responsible for the expense.

In this case, the taxes are paid in advance, so the buyer must reimburse the seller for the taxes paid from April 17 through June 30. (The buyer is responsible for taxes that apply to the date of closing.)

14 days in April (30 − 16 = 14)
30 days in May
30 days in June
74 days total

Step 3: multiply the daily rate times the number of days.

$10 × 74 = $740 prorated amount of taxes

The buyer will owe the seller approximately $740 for property taxes at closing. This amount will be listed as a debit for the buyer and a credit for the seller.

BUYER'S CREDITS

To determine the amount that the buyer will owe at closing, certain credits must be deducted from the buyer's closing costs. For example, the buyer is credited for the amount of the good faith (earnest money) **deposit** and for any deposit given to the lender to cover the initial loan costs such as the **appraisal** and **credit report**. The buyer may also be due a credit for **prorated taxes** or **rents**. The cash needed by the buyer for closing can then be calculated as follows:

Buyer's credits:
- earnest money deposit
- deposit for credit report or appraisal
- prorated taxes or rents

> total of closing costs payable by buyer
> − total of credits due to buyer
> + downpayment
> cash required to close

SELLER'S COSTS

The seller's primary cost at closing is normally the **payoff of any existing loans**. The seller may also be charged a **prepayment penalty** in connection with the payoff, and will be responsible for the interest due for the month of closing. The interest due may be calculated using the proration formula: daily rate times number of days equals prorated expense.

The seller is usually responsible for paying the **sales commission** and **attorney fees, escrow fee, notary**

Seller's costs:
- payoff any loans
- prepayment penalty (if any)
- sales commission
- attorney's fees
- escrow fee
- rotary fee
- recording fees
- title insurance
- inspection/repairs
- prorated taxes
- documentary transfer taxes

fees and **recording fees**. Depending on custom or agreement, the seller may also be responsible for the owner's **title insurance premium**, the **structural pest control inspection** and/or **repairs**, the buyer's **loan discount** and such miscellaneous items as a **home warranty contract**. If the property taxes are in arrears, the seller will also owe for the **prorated taxes** due up to the date of closing.

Documentary transfer taxes are normally paid by the seller. This is a tax that applies to the transfer of real estate. It is charged at the rate of 55 cents for each $500 of the purchase price.

Example: sales price: $100,000

$$\frac{\$100,000}{\div\ 500}$$
$$200$$

$$\frac{200}{\times\ .55}$$
$$\$110 \quad \text{transfer tax}$$

NOTE: The documentary transfer tax does not apply to the amount of any assumed loans or loans the buyer takes subject to. If the buyer in the example above had assumed the seller's existing $70,000 loan, the tax would be due on only the $30,000 difference between the sales price and the assumed loan.

SELLER'S CREDITS

Seller's credits:
- prorated taxes, insurance, rents
- impound accounts

In addition to the purchase price, the seller may be due credits for such items as **prorated taxes** and **insurance premiums**, and the balances in any **impound accounts** in connection with existing loans. If the property is income property, there may be a credit (or a debit) for **prorated rents**. The seller's net proceeds from the sale can then be calculated as follows:

    purchase price
    − existing loans (to be paid/assumed/taken subject to)
    − seller financing (if any)
    − seller's closing costs
    + seller's credits
    ─────────────
    net cash to seller

Seller Financing

When the seller takes back a note from the buyer as part of the purchase price, or when the buyer assumes or takes subject to the seller's existing loan(s), the financing amounts are listed as credits to the buyer and debits to the seller. In the case of an assumption, the buyer is debited and the seller credited for any reserve account balances in connection with the assumed loan. If there is an assumption fee charged by the lender, it may be debited to either party, or shared, depending upon their agreement in the deposit receipt or escrow instructions.

Income Property

When income property is sold, it is necessary to prorate the rents from the property. If rents are paid in advance, the buyer will be due a credit, and the seller a debit, for the amount of rents applicable to the time after closing. If rents are in arrears, the reverse is true: the seller is due a credit and the buyer is debited for the arrears applicable to the time the seller owned the property.

RESPA

The Real Estate Settlement Procedures Act, commonly known as RESPA, applies to most sales of one- to four-unit residential property (including condominiums, coops and mobile homes) involving institutional financing where the purchase loan is secured by a first mortgage on the property. The Act does not apply to loans used to finance the purchase of 25 acres or more, loans for the purchase of vacant land, or transactions where the buyer assumes or takes subject to an existing first lien loan.

In transactions subject to RESPA, the lender must give the borrower a good faith estimate of the closing costs at the time of the loan application (see form below). The lender is also required to give the borrower a booklet published by the Department of Housing and Urban Development which describes closing costs, settlement procedures and the bor-rower's rights. The entity handling the closing must prepare the settlement statement on a HUD form called a Uniform Settlement Statement, and the buyer must be allowed to in-spect the statement on the day before closing if requested. (There is an exception to the inspection requirement when the buyer or his or her agent does not attend the settlement or when the escrowee does not require a meeting of the par-ties. Thus the inspection provision does not apply to most escrows in California. In these circumstances, the escrowee is required to mail the statement to the borrower as soon as possible after closing.)

RESPA also prohibits kickbacks and unearned fees in con-nection with covered transactions, and provides for criminal penalties and triple damages in the event of a violation. This provision does not apply to referral fees paid between real estate brokers, but will apply to any other fees received by a broker other than the commission.

Other important RESPA provisions concern providers of services. If the lender requires the use of a particular closing agent, it must disclose any business relationship between the lender and the agent, and give an estimate of the agent's

Good Faith Estimate
of Real Estate Settlement Costs

Borrower(s) _____

Property Address_____

THIS FORM IS AN ESTIMATE OF ANTICIPATED COSTS YOU WILL BE REQUIRED TO PAY IN CASH AT TIME OF SETTLEMENT. IT MAY NOT INCLUDE ADDITIONAL UNANTICIPATED COSTS WHICH YOU MAY BE REQUIRED TO PAY AT SETTLEMENT.

101	CONTRACT SALES PRICE	$ _____
202	Principal Amount of New Loan	− $ _____
	DOWNPAYMENT	$ _____

ESTIMATED LOAN COSTS

801	Loan Origination Fee_____%	$ _____
802	Loan Discount to Borrower	_____
803	Appraisal Fee	_____
804	Credit Report	_____
809	Tax Service Fee	_____
902	Mortgage Insurance Premium	_____
1101	Settlement or Closing Fee (Escrow)	_____
1108	Title Insurance	_____
1201	**Recording Fees:** Deed	_____
	Deed of Trust/Mortgage	_____
	Releases	_____
1301	Survey	_____
1302	Pest Inspection	_____

TOTAL . . . . . $_____

ESTIMATED RESERVES AND ADJUSTMENTS

901	Interest for 30 days @ $_____/day*	$ _____
903	Hazard Insurance Premium for _____ years to _____	
1001	Hazard Insurance _____ months @ $_____ per month	_____
1002	Mortgage Insurance	
	_____ months @ $_____ per month	_____
1004	County Property Taxes (Reserves)	
	_____ months @ $_____ per month	_____
107	County Property Taxes (Pro-Rates)	
	_____ to _____	_____
	_____ to _____	_____

TOTAL . . . . . $_____

ESTIMATED DUE AT CLOSING . . . . $_____

Less: 201 Deposit or Earnest Money _____

ESTIMATED AMOUNT REQUIRED TO CLOSE . . . . $_____

*This interest calculation represents the greatest amount of interest you could be required to pay at settlement unless you have applied for an FHA or VA loan. The actual amount could be more if the FHA/VA interest rate increases between the time you apply and the time of closing. The actual amount will also vary depending on the day of the month your loan is closed.

I acknowledge receipt of the "Settlement Costs Booklet".

Borrower_____Date_____

Borrower_____Date_____

Prepared by_____Date_____

ESTIMATED PAYMENT SCHEDULE

Principal and Interest	$_____
Reserve for Taxes	_____
Reserve for Insurance	_____
Reserve for PMI	_____
Total Estimated Payment	$_____

charges for the service. Also, the sale may not be conditioned on the use of a particular title insurer or escrow company chosen by the seller.

CHAPTER SUMMARY

1. In California, real estate closings are usually handled by an escrow agent (which may be an independent escrow company or a title insurance company).

2. To be valid escrow, there must be:
   - a legally binding contract, and
   - a conditional delivery and relinquishment of control.

3. The escrow agent prepares necessary documents, allocates charges and credits between the parties, prepares a closing statement, records documents and disburses funds according to escrow instructions signed by the parties. Escrow instructions may be either separate or joint.

4. Costs and credits for the buyer and seller are shown as debits and credits on the closing statement. The responsibility for some costs varies depending upon local custom in different parts of California.

5. RESPA applies to most purchase money loans made by institutional lenders for residential property. If the transaction is covered by RESPA, the lender must give the buyer a good faith estimate of closing costs, an informational pamphlet on closing costs, and prepare the closing statement on the HUD Uniform Settlement Statement form. Kickbacks and other unearned fees are prohibited.

Chapter 17
REAL ESTATE FINANCE MATHEMATICS

Math is a fundamental tool used in the financing process. As you explain the various finance programs, qualify a buyer for a loan, describe discounts and buydowns, and determine closing costs, you will be using mathematical formulas. While the prospect of mathematical computations arouses fear in the hearts of many of us, the math principles you will need to know are actually very simple. The following is a brief description of those formulas.

APPROACH TO SOLVING MATH PROBLEMS

Solving math problems is simplified by using a step-by-step approach. The most important step is to thoroughly understand the problem. You must know what answer you want before you can successfully work any math problem. Once you have determined what it is you are to find (for example, interest rate, loan to value ratio or amount of profit) you will know what formula to use.

Then choose the correct mathematical formula. For example, the profit and loss formula is *value after = percent × value before (VA = % × VB).* The formulas you will most likely be using will be explained in this chapter.

The next step is to substitute the numbers you know into the formula. In many problems you will be able to substitute the numbers into the formula without any additional steps. However, in many other problems it will be necessary to take one or more preliminary steps, for instance, converting fractions to decimals.

Once you have substituted the numbers into the formula you will have to do some computations to find the unknown. Most of the formulas have the same basic form (A = B × C). You will need two of the numbers (or the information that enables you to find two of the numbers) and then you will either have to divide or multiply them to find the third number, the answer you are seeking.

Whether you will need to multiply or divide is determined by which quantity (number) in the formula you are trying to discover. For example, the formula A = B × C may be converted into three different formulas. All three formulas are equivalent but are put into different forms depending upon the quantity (number) to be discovered. If the quantity A is unknown, then the following formula is used:

$$A = B \times C$$

The number B is multiplied by C; the product of B times C is A.

If the quantity B is unknown, the following formula is used:

$$B = A \div C$$

The number A is divided by C; the quotient of A divided by C is B.

If the quantity C is unknown, the following formula is used:

$$C = A \div B$$

The number A is divided by B; the quotient of A divided by B is C. Notice that in all these instances, the unknown quantity is always by itself on one side of the "equals" sign.

CONVERTING FRACTIONS TO DECIMALS

There will be many times when you will want to convert a fraction into a decimal. Most people find it much easier to work with decimals than fractions. Also, hand calculators can multiply and divide by decimals. To convert a fraction into a decimal, you simply divide the top number of the fraction (called the numerator) by the bottom number of the fraction (called the denominator).

Example: To change ¾ into a decimal, you must divide 3 (the top number) by 4 (the bottom number):

Converting fractions to decimals: divide numerator by denominator

$$
\begin{array}{r} .75 \\ 4\overline{)3.00} \end{array}
$$ ¾ becomes .75.

To change 1/5 into a decimal, divide 1 by 5:

$$
\begin{array}{r} .20 \\ 5\overline{)1.00} \end{array}
$$ 1/5 becomes .20.

If you are using a hand calculator, it will automatically give you the right answer with the decimals in the correct place.

To add or subtract by decimals, line the decimals up by decimal point and add or subtract.

Example:

$$
\begin{array}{r}
23.77 \\
746.1 \\
1.567 \\
82.6 \\
+\,1134.098 \\
\hline
1988.135
\end{array}
$$

To multiply by decimals, do the multiplication. The answer should have as many decimal places as the total number of decimal places in the multiplying numbers. Just add up the decimal places in the numbers you are multiplying and put the decimal point the same number of places to the left.

Example:

$$
\begin{array}{r}
23.7 \\
\times\ 57.999 \\
\hline
1374.5763
\end{array}
$$

To divide by decimals, move the decimal point in the outside number all the way to the right and then move the decimal point in the inside number the same number of places to the right.

Example: 44.6 divided by 5.889

$$
5889\overline{)44600}^{\ 7.57}
$$

Just as with addition and multiplication, the above steps are unnecessary if you use a hand calculator. If the numbers are punched in correctly, the calculator will automatically give you an answer with the decimal in the right place.

PERCENTAGE PROBLEMS

You will often be working with percentages in real estate finance problems. For example, loan-to-value ratios and interest rates are stated as percentages. It is necessary to convert the percentages into decimals and vice versa, so that the arithmetic in a percentage problem can be done in decimals.

To convert a percentage to a decimal, remove the percentage sign and move the decimal point two places to the left. This may require adding zeros.

Example:

80% becomes .80
9% becomes .09
75.5% becomes .755
8¾% becomes .0875

To convert percentage to decimal: remove the percentage sign and move decimal point two places to the left.

To convert a decimal to a percentage, do just the opposite. Move the decimal two places to the right and add a percentage sign.

Example:

.88 becomes 88%
.015 becomes 1.5%
.09 becomes 9%

Whenever something is expressed as a percent of something, it means multiply. The word "of" means to multiply.

LTV

Example: If a lender requires a loan-to-value ratio of 75% and a house is worth $89,000, what will be the maximum loan amount? (What is 75% of $89,000?)

.75 × $89,000 = $66,750 maximum loan amount

Percentage problems are usually similar to the above example. You have to find a part of something, or a percentage of the total.

A general formula is:

A percentage of the total equals the part, or part = percent × total

$$P = \% \times T$$

Example: Smith spends 24% of her monthly salary on her house payment. Her monthly salary is $2,750. What is the amount of her house payment?

1. Find amount of house payment.
2. Write down formula: $P = \% \times T.$
3. Substitute numbers into formula:
   $P = 24\% \times \$2,750$

Before you can perform the necessary calculations, you must convert the 24% into a decimal. Move the decimal two places to the left: .24.

$$P = .24 \times \$2,750$$

4. Calculate: multiply the percentage by the total. $.24 \times \$2,750 = \$660$
   Smith's house payment is $660.

INTEREST PROBLEMS

Interest can be viewed as the "rent" paid by a borrower to a lender for the use of money (the loan amount, or principal). Interest is the cost of borrowing money. There are two types of interest, "simple" or "compound." Simple interest is interest paid only on the principal owed; compound interest is interest paid on accrued interest as well as on the principal owed.

Simple interest problems are worked in basically the same manner as percentage problems except that the simple interest formula has four components rather than three: interest, principal, rate and time.

$$\text{Interest} = \text{Principal} \times \text{Rate} \times \text{Time}$$
$$I = P \times R \times T$$

- Interest: the cost of borrowing expressed in dollars; money paid for the use of money.
- Principal: the amount of the loan in dollars on which the interest is paid.
- Rate: the cost of borrowing expressed as a percentage of the principal paid in interest for one year.
- Time: the length of time of the loan, usually expressed in years.

One must know the number values of three of the four components in order to compute the fourth (unknown) component.

a. Interest unknown.
   Interest = Principal × Rate × Time

   Example: find the interest on $3500 for six years at 11%.

   1. $I = PRT$
   2. $I = \$3500 \times .11 \times 6$
   3. $I = \$385 \times 6$
   4. $I = \$2310$

b. Principal unknown.
   Principal = Interest divided by Rate × Time

   $$P = I \div (R \times T)$$

Example: How much money must be loaned to receive $2310 interest at 11% if the money is loaned for six years?

1. $P = I \div RT$

2. $P = \$2310 \div (.11 \times 6)$

3. $P = \$2310 \div .66$

4. $P = \$3500$

  c. Rate unknown.
Rate = Interest divided by Principal × Time

$$R = I \div (P \times T)$$

Example: In six years $3500 earns $2310 interest. What is the rate of interest?

1. $R = I \div (P \times T)$

2. $R = \$2310 \div (\$3500 \times 6)$

3. $R = \$2310 \div \$21,000$

4. $R = .11 \text{ or } 11\%$

  d. Time unknown.
Time = Interest divided by Rate × Principal

$$T = I \div (R \times P)$$

Example: How long will it take $3500 to return $2310 at an annual rate of 11%?

1. $T = I \div (R \times P)$

2. $T = \$2310 \div (\$3500 \times .11)$

3. $T = \$2310 \div \$385$

4. $T = 6\ years$

COMPOUND INTEREST

Compound interest is more common in advanced real estate subjects, such as appraisal and annuities. Compound interest tables are readily available but the principle is discussed here to further your understanding.

As previously stated, compound interest is interest on the total of the principal plus its accrued interest. For each time period (called the "conversion period"), interest is added to the principal to make a new principal amount. Therefore, each succeeding time period has an increased principal amount on which to compute interest. Conversion periods may be monthly, quarterly, semi-annual or annual.

The compound interest rate is usually stated as an annual rate and must be changed to the appropriate "interest rate per conversion period" or "periodic interest rate." To do this, you must divide the annual interest rate by the number of conversion periods per year. This periodic interest rate is called "i." The formula used for compound interest problems is interest = principal × periodic interest rate, or

$$I = P \times i$$

Compound interest formula:
interest = principal × periodic interest rate

Example: A $5000 investment at 9% interest compounded annually for three years earns how much interest at maturity?

$$I = P \times i$$

$$I = \$5,000 \times (.09 \text{ divided by } 1)$$

First year's I = $5,000 × .09 or $450.
Add to $5,000.

Second year's I = $5,450 × .09 or $490.50.
Add to $5,450.

Third year's I = $5,940.50 × .09 or $534.65.
Add to $5,940.50

At maturity, the borrower will owe $6,475.15. The $5,000 loan has earned interest of $1,475.15 in three years.

Example: How much interest will a $1,000 investment earn over two years at 12% interest compounded semi-annually?

Since the conversion period is semi-annual, the interest is computed every six months. Thus, the periodic interest rate (i) is 12% divided by two conversion periods: $i = 6\%$.

$$I = P \times i$$

1. *Original principal amount*.............$1,000.00
2. *Interest for 1st period ($1,000 × .06)*........60.00
3. *Balance beginning 2nd period*...........1,060.00
4. *Interest for 2nd period ($1,060 × .06)*.......63.60
5. *Balance beginning 3rd period*............1,123.60
6. *Interest for 3rd period ($1,123.60 × .06)*.....67.42
7. *Balance beginning 4th period*............1,191.02
8. *Interest for 4th period ($1,191.02 × .06)*.....71.46
9. *Compound principal balance*............1,262.48

I for 2 years = $1,262.48 − $1,000 or $262.48

390

The same problem using annual simple interest results in $22.48 less interest for the lender: *$1,000 × .12 × 2 = $240 simple interest.*

Obviously, no one in actual practice is going to go through the tedious process outlined above to calculate compound interest, especially if it is compounded daily over a 30-year period! Instead, standardized compound interest tables or calculators can be used to find the answer quickly.

EFFECTIVE RATE OF INTEREST

The "nominal" or "named" interest rate is the rate of interest stated in the loan documents. The effective interest rate is the rate the borrower is actually paying. In other words, the loan papers may say one thing when the end result is another, depending upon how many times a year the actual earnings rate is compounded. The effective rate of interest equals the annual rate which will produce the same interest in a year as the nominal rate converted a certain number of times. For example, 6% converted semi-annually produces $6.09 per $100; therefore, 6% is the nominal rate and 6.09% is the effective rate. A rate of 6% converted semi-annually yields the same interest as a rate of 6.09% on an annual basis.

DISCOUNTS

As discussed in the chapter on alternative methods of financing, often the loan proceeds disbursed by the lender are less than the face value of the note. This occurs when the borrower (or a third party) pays discount points. The lender deducts the amount of the points from the loan amount up front as compensation for making the loan on the agreed terms. The borrower thus receives less than must be repaid under the contract. When a discount is paid, the interest costs to the borrower (and the yield to the lender) are higher than the contract interest rate.

When more accurate yield and interest tables are un-available, it is possible to approximate the effective interest cost to the borrower and the yield rate to the lender when discounted loans are involved. The formula for doing so is as follows:

$$i = [r + (d/n)] \div (P - d)$$

- i: approximate effective interest rate (expressed as a decimal)
- r: contract interest rate (expressed as a decimal)
- d: discount rate, or points deducted (expressed as a decimal)
- P: principal of loan (expressed as the whole number 1 for all dollar amounts)
- n: term (years, periods, or fraction thereof)

Example: What is the estimated effective interest rate on a $60,000 mortgage loan, with a 20-year term, contract rate of interest being 10% per an-num, discounted 3%, so that only $58,200 is disbursed to the borrower?

$$i = \frac{.10 + (.03/20)}{1 - .03} = \frac{.10 + .0015}{.97} = \frac{.10150}{.97} = .10463 \text{ or } 10.46\%$$

The effective interest rate (or yield) on the loan is 10.46%.

PROFIT AND LOSS PROBLEMS

Every time a homeowner sells a house, a profit or loss is made. If the house is sold for more than was initially paid for it, the owner makes a profit. If it is sold for less, the owner suffers a loss. Many times you will want to be able to calculate the amount of that profit or loss. Profit and loss problems are solved with a formula that is a variation of the percent formula: value after = percentage × value before.

$$VA = \% \times VB$$

Profit and loss formula: value after = percentage × value before

The value after is the value of the property after the profit or loss is taken. The value before is the value of the property before the profit or loss is taken. The percent is 100% plus the percent of profit or minus the percent of loss. The idea is to express the value of the property after a profit or loss as a percentage of the property's value before the profit or loss. If there is no profit or loss, the value after is exactly 100% of the value before, because the value has not changed. If there is a profit, the value after will be greater than 100% of the value before, since the value has increased. If there is a loss, the value after is less than 100% of the value before, since the value has decreased.

Example: Green bought a house ten years ago for $50,000 and sold it last month for 45% more than she paid for it. What was the selling price of the house?

$VA = \% \times VB$
$VA = 145\% \times VB$ *(to get the percent, you must add the percent of profit to or subtract the percent of loss from 100%.)*
$VA = 1.45 \times \$50,000$
$VA = \$72,500$ *was the selling price*

Example: Now we will use the profit and loss formula to calculate another one of the components.

Green sold his house last week for $117,000. He paid $121,000 for it five years ago. What was the percent of loss?

$$VA = \% \times VB$$
$$\$117{,}000 = \% \times \$121{,}000$$
$$\% = \frac{\$117{,}000}{\$121{,}000}$$ *(Since the percent is the unknown, you must divide the value after by the value before.)*

$$\% = 97\%$$
Now subtract 97% from 100% to find the percent of loss.
$$\% = 100\% - 97\% = 3\% \text{ loss}$$

Example: Your customer just sold a house for 17% more than was paid for it. The seller's portion of the closing costs came to $4,677. The seller received $72,500 in cash at closing. What did the seller originally pay for the house?

$$VA = \% \times VB$$
$$\$72{,}500 + 4{,}677 = 117\% \times VB$$
$$VB = \frac{\$72{,}500 + 4{,}677}{117\%}$$ *(Since the value after is unknown, you must divide the value before [the total of the closing costs and the escrow proceeds] by the percent of profit.)*

$$VB = \frac{\$77{,}177}{1.17}$$
$$VB = \$65{,}963.25 \text{ was the original price}$$

394

PRORATIONS

There are some expenses connected with owning real estate that are often paid for either in advance or in arrears. For example, fire insurance premiums are normally paid for in advance. Landlords usually collect rents in advance, too. On the other hand, mortgage interest accrues in arrears.

When expenses are paid in advance and the owner then sells the property, part of these expenses have already been used up by the seller and are rightfully the seller's expense. Often, however, a portion of the expenses of ownership still remain unused and when title to the property transfers to the buyer, the benefit of these advances will accrue to the buyer. It is only fair that the buyer, therefore, reimburse the seller for the unused portions of these expenses of homeowner-ship. For example, suppose the seller of a home paid a $1400 annual property taxes for the coming year one month before the property was sold. The seller has only benefited from one month of the tax year, but the buyer will benefit from the next 11 months of the prepaid taxes. Unless the buyer reimburses the seller for 11 months worth of the taxes, the seller will be stuck with paying the taxes for someone else's property.

These adjustments, or reimbursements, are made by the process of proration. This simply means apportioning the expenses (or benefits) fairly to each party.

For example, a seller sells the property six months after paying the annual property taxes for the ensuing year. One half of the tax payment will thus accrue to the benefit of the buyer. In this case, the buyer should pay half of the tax amount to the seller. (This example is over-simplified because in practice, prorations are figured down to the day, with the so-called banker's rule of 30 days to a month and 360 days to a year usually applying.)

Prorations are usually calculated at real estate closings, where the costs of such items as taxes and insurance are allocated between the buyer and the seller. The formula for proration is: share = daily rate × number of days.

$$S = R \times D$$

To work a proration problem:

1. Find the annual or monthly amount of the expense.
2. Then find the daily rate of the expense (per diem). Under the "banker's rule" the daily rate equals 1/30 of the monthly rate or 1/360 of the annual rate.
3. Next determine the number of days for which the person is responsible for the expense.
4. Finally, substitute the daily rate and number of days into the formula and calculate.

> **Example:** Seller paid the month's homeowner's insurance premium of $28 on the first of the month. The transaction closes on the 18th of the month. How much of the insurance premium does the buyer owe to the seller?

$$S = R \times D$$

The premium is $28 per month. To find the daily rate of the expense, divide $28 by 30.

$$30 \overline{)\ 28} \quad \frac{.93}{}$$ The rate is $.93 per day.

Next find out how many days the buyer is responsible for. (The buyer pays for the day of closing.) There are 13 days left in the month that the buyer is responsible for.

$$S = R \times D$$
$$S = .93 \times 13$$
$$S = \$12.09 \text{ is the amount owed to the seller.}$$

Example: A sale closes on September 14. The annual property taxes of $1,750 have not been paid. How much will the seller owe the buyer at closing?

The property tax year runs from July 1 through June 30. The seller owes for the period from July 1 up to September 14.

The annual amount is $1,750 which must be divided by 360 days to get the daily rate.

$$360 \overline{)1{,}750} \quad \$4.86 \text{ per day}$$

Next, you must figure the number of days.

$$
\begin{array}{r}
July \text{ - } 30 \\
August \text{ - } 30 \\
September \text{ - } \underline{13} \\
73 \quad days
\end{array}
$$

$S = R \times D$
$S = 4.86 \times 73$
$S = \$354.78$ *owed to the buyer at closing.*

MATHEMATICAL TABLES AND THEIR USE

The scope of this course does not permit a full discussion of the use of the various tables relating to real estate finance. Generally speaking, the following tables are most commonly used.

AMORTIZATION TABLES

These are commonly available in booklet form from various title companies, escrow companies, and banks. They indicate the monthly payment needed for the periodic repayment of both the principal amount of the loan and the interest due. One form of amortization table has a list of possible loan terms (expressed in years) along one axis. The other axis is the interest rate. There is a separate table for each loan amount. At the intersection of any two axes in the table is the monthly payment in dollars and cents. (See next page for an example of a loan amortization table.)

An alternate type of table for figuring loan payments is the Interest Rate Factors Table. An example of this table is found is Appendix 1. It would be helpful to take a moment to examine this table and follow the instructions set out at the beginning of the table. This table gives you interest rate factors, which, multiplied by the loan amount, give you the amount of the monthly loan payment.

PRORATION TABLE

This is simply a table that gives the number of days between various dates. It is used to prorate such items as interest, insurance premiums, or rents. Below is an example of a proration table.

REMAINING BALANCE TABLES OF LOAN PROGRESS CHARTS

Remaining balance tables show the remaining balance of a loan expressed as a percentage of the original loan amount, using the data: original loan amount, interest rate, age of loan and original term of loan. A loan progress chart also allows you to find the remaining loan balance by giving you the

LOAN AMORTIZATION

MONTHLY PAYMENT FOR A $1,000 LOAN

YEARS	7%	7½%	8%	8½%	8¾%	9%	9¼%	9½%	9¾%	10%	10¼%	10½%
1.0	86.53	86.76	86.99	87.22	87.34	87.45	87.57	87.68	87.80	87.92	88.03	88.15
1.5	58.69	58.91	59.14	59.37	59.48	59.60	59.71	59.83	59.94	60.06	60.17	60.29
2.0	44.77	45.00	45.23	45.46	45.57	45.68	45.80	45.91	46.03	46.14	46.26	46.38
2.5	36.43	36.66	36.89	37.12	37.23	37.35	37.46	37.58	37.70	37.81	37.93	38.04
3.0	30.88	31.11	31.34	31.57	31.68	31.80	31.92	32.03	32.15	32.27	32.38	32.50
3.5	26.91	27.15	27.38	27.61	27.73	27.84	27.96	28.08	28.20	28.32	28.44	28.55
4.0	23.95	24.18	24.41	24.65	24.77	24.89	25.00	25.12	25.24	25.36	25.48	25.60
4.5	21.64	21.88	22.11	22.35	22.47	22.59	22.71	22.83	22.95	23.07	23.19	23.32
5.0	19.80	20.04	20.28	20.52	20.64	20.76	20.88	21.00	21.12	21.25	21.37	21.49
5.5	18.30	18.54	18.78	19.02	19.14	19.27	19.39	19.51	19.64	19.76	19.88	20.01
6.0	17.05	17.29	17.53	17.78	17.90	18.03	18.15	18.27	18.40	18.53	18.65	18.78
6.5	15.99	16.24	16.48	16.73	16.86	16.98	17.11	17.23	17.36	17.49	17.61	17.74
7.0	15.09	15.34	15.59	15.84	15.96	16.09	16.22	16.34	16.47	16.60	16.73	16.86
7.5	14.31	14.56	14.81	15.06	15.19	15.32	15.45	15.58	15.71	15.84	15.97	16.10
8.0	13.63	13.88	14.14	14.39	14.52	14.65	14.78	14.91	15.04	15.17	15.31	15.44
8.5	13.04	13.29	13.54	13.80	13.93	14.06	14.19	14.33	14.46	14.59	14.73	14.86
9.0	12.51	12.76	13.02	13.28	13.41	13.54	13.68	13.81	13.94	14.08	14.21	14.35
9.5	12.03	12.29	12.55	12.81	12.95	13.08	13.22	13.35	13.49	13.62	13.76	13.90
10.0	11.61	11.87	12.13	12.40	12.53	12.67	12.80	12.94	13.08	13.22	13.35	13.49
10.5	11.23	11.49	11.76	12.02	12.16	12.30	12.43	12.57	12.71	12.85	12.99	13.13
11.0	10.88	11.15	11.42	11.69	11.82	11.96	12.10	12.24	12.38	12.52	12.66	12.80
11.5	10.57	10.84	11.11	11.38	11.52	11.66	11.80	11.94	12.08	12.22	12.37	12.51
12.0	10.28	10.55	10.82	11.10	11.24	11.38	11.52	11.66	11.81	11.95	12.10	12.24
12.5	10.02	10.29	10.57	10.85	10.99	11.13	11.27	11.41	11.56	11.70	11.85	12.00
13.0	9.78	10.05	10.33	10.61	10.75	10.90	11.04	11.19	11.33	11.48	11.63	11.78
13.5	9.56	9.83	10.11	10.40	10.54	10.68	10.83	10.98	11.12	11.27	11.42	11.57
14.0	9.35	9.63	9.91	10.20	10.34	10.49	10.64	10.78	10.93	11.08	11.23	11.38
14.5	9.16	9.44	9.73	10.02	10.16	10.31	10.46	10.61	10.76	10.91	11.06	11.21
15.0	8.99	9.27	9.56	9.85	9.99	10.14	10.29	10.44	10.59	10.75	10.90	11.05
15.5	8.82	9.11	9.40	9.69	9.84	9.99	10.14	10.29	10.44	10.60	10.75	10.91
16.0	8.67	8.96	9.25	9.54	9.69	9.85	10.00	10.15	10.30	10.46	10.62	10.77
16.5	8.53	8.82	9.11	9.41	9.56	9.71	9.87	10.02	10.17	10.33	10.49	10.65
17.0	8.40	8.69	8.98	9.28	9.43	9.59	9.74	9.90	10.05	10.21	10.37	10.53
17.5	8.27	8.56	8.86	9.16	9.32	9.47	9.63	9.78	9.94	10.10	10.26	10.42
18.0	8.16	8.45	8.75	9.05	9.21	9.36	9.52	9.68	9.84	10.00	10.16	10.32
18.5	8.05	8.34	8.64	8.95	9.11	9.26	9.42	9.58	9.74	9.90	10.06	10.23
19.0	7.94	8.24	8.55	8.85	9.01	9.17	9.33	9.49	9.65	9.81	9.98	10.14
19.5	7.84	8.15	8.45	8.76	8.92	9.08	9.24	9.40	9.56	9.73	9.89	10.06
20.0	7.75	8.06	8.36	8.68	8.84	9.00	9.16	9.32	9.49	9.65	9.82	9.98
20.5	7.67	7.97	8.28	8.60	8.76	8.92	9.08	9.25	9.41	9.58	9.74	9.91
21.0	7.58	7.89	8.20	8.52	8.68	8.85	9.01	9.17	9.34	9.51	9.68	9.85
21.5	7.51	7.82	8.13	8.45	8.61	8.78	8.94	9.11	9.27	9.44	9.61	9.78
22.0	7.43	7.75	8.06	8.38	8.55	8.71	8.88	9.04	9.21	9.38	9.55	9.73
22.5	7.36	7.68	8.00	8.32	8.48	8.65	8.82	8.99	9.15	9.33	9.50	9.67
23.0	7.30	7.61	7.93	8.26	8.43	8.59	8.76	8.93	9.10	9.27	9.44	9.62
23.5	7.24	7.55	7.88	8.20	8.37	8.54	8.71	8.88	9.05	9.22	9.40	9.57
24.0	7.18	7.50	7.82	8.15	8.32	8.49	8.66	8.83	9.00	9.17	9.35	9.52
24.5	7.12	7.44	7.77	8.10	8.27	8.44	8.61	8.78	8.95	9.13	9.31	9.48
25.0	7.07	7.39	7.72	8.05	8.22	8.39	8.56	8.74	8.91	9.09	9.26	9.44
25.5	7.02	7.34	7.67	8.01	8.18	8.35	8.52	8.70	8.87	9.05	9.23	9.40
26.0	6.97	7.29	7.63	7.96	8.13	8.31	8.48	8.66	8.83	9.01	9.19	9.37
26.5	6.92	7.25	7.58	7.92	8.09	8.27	8.44	8.62	8.80	8.97	9.15	9.33
27.0	6.88	7.21	7.54	7.88	8.06	8.23	8.41	8.58	8.76	8.94	9.12	9.30
27.5	6.84	7.17	7.50	7.85	8.02	8.20	8.37	8.55	8.73	8.91	9.09	9.27
28.0	6.80	7.13	7.47	7.81	7.99	8.16	8.34	8.52	8.70	8.88	9.06	9.25
28.5	6.76	7.09	7.43	7.78	7.95	8.13	8.31	8.49	8.67	8.85	9.03	9.22
29.0	6.72	7.06	7.40	7.75	7.92	8.10	8.28	8.46	8.64	8.82	9.01	9.19
29.5	6.69	7.02	7.37	7.72	7.89	8.07	8.25	8.43	8.62	8.80	8.98	9.17
29.8	6.67	7.00	7.35	7.70	7.88	8.06	8.24	8.42	8.60	8.79	8.97	9.16
30.0	6.65	6.99	7.34	7.69	7.87	8.05	8.23	8.41	8.59	8.78	8.96	9.15
35.0	6.39	6.74	7.10	7.47	7.65	7.84	8.03	8.22	8.41	8.60	8.79	8.98
40.0	6.21	6.58	6.95	7.33	7.52	7.71	7.91	8.10	8.30	8.49	8.69	8.89

Counting Days of the Year*
Numbering from January 1

Day of the month	Jan.	Feb.	March	April	May	June	July	Aug.	Sept.	Oct.	Nov.	Dec.
1	1	32	60	91	121	152	182	213	244	274	305	335
2	2	33	61	92	122	153	183	214	245	275	306	336
3	3	34	62	93	123	154	184	215	246	276	307	337
4	4	35	63	94	124	155	185	216	247	277	308	338
5	5	36	64	95	125	156	186	217	248	278	309	339
6	6	37	65	96	126	157	187	218	249	279	310	340
7	7	38	66	97	127	158	188	219	250	280	311	341
8	8	39	67	98	128	159	189	220	251	281	312	342
9	9	40	68	99	129	160	190	221	252	282	313	343
10	10	41	69	100	130	161	191	222	253	283	314	344
11	11	42	70	101	131	162	192	223	254	284	315	345
12	12	43	71	102	132	163	193	224	255	285	316	346
13	13	44	72	103	133	164	194	225	256	286	317	347
14	14	45	73	104	134	165	195	226	257	287	318	348
15	15	46	74	105	135	166	196	227	258	288	319	349
16	16	47	75	106	136	167	197	228	259	289	320	350
17	17	48	76	107	137	168	198	229	260	290	321	351
18	18	49	77	108	138	169	199	230	261	291	322	352
19	19	50	78	109	139	170	200	231	262	292	323	353
20	20	51	79	110	140	171	201	232	263	293	324	354
21	21	52	80	111	141	172	202	233	264	294	325	355
22	22	53	81	112	142	173	203	234	265	295	326	356
23	23	54	82	113	143	174	204	235	266	296	327	357
24	24	55	83	114	144	175	205	236	267	297	328	358
25	25	56	84	115	145	176	206	237	268	298	329	359
26	26	57	85	116	146	177	207	238	269	299	330	360
27	27	58	86	117	147	178	208	239	270	300	331	361
28	28	59	87	118	148	179	209	240	271	301	332	362
29	29	—	88	119	149	180	210	241	272	302	333	363
30	30	—	89	120	150	181	211	242	273	303	334	364
31	31	—	90	—	151	—	212	243	—	304	—	365

* In a leap year, add one to each number after 59 (February 28)

amount still owing for every $1000 borrowed. There is a loan progress chart presented in Appendix 2.

MORTGAGE YIELD TABLES

These are used to determine the yield on a mortgage at a specified discount. A point discount table (which does the same thing) is presented in Appendix 3 .

BALLOON PAYMENT TABLES

These are used to determine the unpaid balance due and payable on a loan before it has been amortized. Loans, especially second trust deed loans, often have terms of four or five years but are amortized over 12 or 15 years. This will leave a large lump sum payment of principal owing at the end of the loan term.

CONSTANT ANNUAL PERCENTAGE TABLES

An annual constant is the sum of 12 monthly payments expressed as a percent of a principal loan amount. When multiplied by the loan amount, the annual loan payment may be determined. The remaining term of a loan, remaining loan balance, and interest rate of a loan may also be determined by use of a constant annual percent table.

CHAPTER SUMMARY

In order to be able to answer questions from buyers and sellers and to provide professional service to their clients, real estate agents need to be able to solve math problems which frequently arise in connection with real estate sales and financing. Of particular importance are the ability to answer questions regarding interest, appreciation in value and prorations of closing costs.

Appendix 1
Interest Rate Factors

find monthly Payment

Example: $50,000 loan @ 12¼% for 30 years

Problem: find monthly payment

YEARS	12%	12¼%
1	888487	889657
1½	609820	610982
2	470734	471903
2½	387481	388661
3	332143	333338
3½	292756	293968
4	263338	264567
4½	240565	241812
5	222444	223709
6	195501	196804
7	176527	177867
8	162528	163905
9	151842	153255
10	143470	144919
12	131341	132859
15	120016	121629
20	110108	111856
21	108869	110641
22	107793	109586
23	106856	108670
24	106038	107871
25	105322	107174
26	104695	106564
27	104144	106030
28	103661	105562
29	103235	105150
30	102861	104789

Step 1: Find the **column** that corresponds to the interest rate of the proposed loan.

Step 2: Find the **row** that corresponds to the term of the proposed loan. For example, calculations for a loan of 30 years would use the last (bottom) row of the charts.

Step 3: Take the number found at the intersection of the appropriate column and row, and **add a decimal point and a zero at the front** of the number. In our example, the chart shows a figure of 104789, which should be converted to **.0104789**.

Step 4: **Multiply** the proposed **loan amount** by the answer from step 3 to get the monthly loan payment. In our example, multiply $50,000 times .0104789.

$$\begin{array}{r} \textbf{\$50,000} \\ \times\textbf{.0104789} \\ \hline \textbf{\$523.95} \end{array}$$

Thus, the monthly payment on a $50,000 30-year loan at 12¼% is $523.95 per month.

YEARS	8%	8¼%	8½%	8¾%	9%	9¼%	9½%	9¾%	10%	10¼%	10½%	YEARS
1	869884	871041	872198	873356	874515	875675	876835	877996	879158	880322	881486	1
1½	591403	592544	593687	594831	595977	597123	598271	599420	600570	601722	602875	1½
2	452273	453414	454557	455701	456847	457995	459144	460296	461449	462603	463760	2
2½	368883	370030	371178	372329	373482	374637	375793	376952	378114	379277	380443	2½
3	313364	314518	315675	316835	317997	319162	320329	321499	322671	323846	325024	3
3½	273770	274934	276102	277272	278445	279621	280800	281982	283168	284356	285547	3½
4	244129	245304	246483	247665	248850	250039	251231	252426	253625	254828	256033	4
4½	221124	222311	223501	224696	225894	227096	228301	229510	230724	231941	233161	4½
5	202764	203963	205165	206372	207584	208779	210018	211242	212470	213702	214939	5
6	175332	176556	177784	179017	180255	181499	182746	184000	185258	186521	187789	6
7	155862	157111	158365	159625	160891	162162	163439	164722	166011	167306	168606	7
8	141367	142641	143921	145208	146502	147802	149108	150422	151741	153067	154400	8
9	130187	131487	132794	134108	135429	136758	138093	139436	140786	142144	143508	9
10	121328	122653	123986	125327	126676	128033	129397	130770	132150	133539	134934	10
12	108245	109621	111006	112400	113803	115216	116637	118068	119507	120956	122414	12
15	095565	097014	098474	099945	101427	102919	104422	105936	107460	108995	110539	15
20	083644	085207	086782	088371	089973	091587	093213	948516	096502	098164	099837	20
21	082043	083627	085224	086835	088458	090094	091743	093404	095078	096763	098459	21
22	080618	082222	083841	085472	087117	088775	090446	092129	093824	095531	097250	22
23	079345	080970	082609	084261	085927	087606	089297	091001	092718	094446	096186	23
24	078205	079850	081508	083181	084866	086566	088277	090002	091738	093487	095248	24
25	077182	078845	080523	082214	083920	085638	087369	089113	090870	092638	094418	25
26	076260	077942	079638	081348	083072	084810	086559	088322	090097	091884	093682	26
27	075428	077128	078842	080570	082313	084068	085836	087616	089409	091214	093030	27
28	074676	076393	078125	079871	081630	083403	085188	086986	088796	090617	092450	28
29	073995	075729	077477	079240	081016	082805	084607	086421	088247	090085	091934	29
30	073376	075127	076891	078670	080462	082268	084085	085915	087757	089610	091473	30

YEARS	10¾%	11%	11¼%	11½%	11¾%	12%	12¼%	12½%	12¾%	13%	13¼%
1	882650	883816	884983	886150	887318	888487	889657	890828	892001	893173	894347
1½	604029	605185	606342	607500	608659	609820	610982	612145	613311	614476	615643
2	464918	466078	467239	468403	469568	470734	471903	473073	474245	475419	476594
2½	381610	382780	383952	385126	386302	387481	388661	389844	391029	392216	393405
3	326045	327387	328572	329760	330950	332143	333338	334536	335737	336940	338145
3½	286741	287938	289138	290341	291547	292756	293968	295182	296401	297621	298845
4	257242	258455	259670	260890	262112	263338	264567	265799	267036	268275	269518
4½	234386	235614	236846	238082	239322	240565	241812	243063	244319	245577	246839
5	216179	217424	218673	219926	221183	222444	223709	224979	226254	227531	228813
6	189062	190340	191623	192911	194204	195501	196804	198111	199425	200742	202063
7	169912	171224	172541	173864	175193	176527	177867	179212	180564	181920	183282
8	155739	157084	158435	159793	161157	162528	163905	165288	166678	168073	169475
9	144880	146258	147644	149036	150436	151842	153255	154675	156103	157536	158977
10	136338	137750	139168	140595	142029	143470	144919	146376	147840	149311	150789
12	123880	125355	126839	128331	129832	131341	132859	134385	135912	137463	139014
15	112094	113659	115234	116818	118413	120016	121629	123252	124884	126525	128174
20	101522	103218	104925	106642	108370	110108	111856	113614	115382	117158	118944
21	100167	101887	103617	105357	107108	108869	110641	112421	114213	116012	117820
22	098980	100722	102474	104237	106010	107793	109586	111389	113202	115023	116853
23	097382	099700	101474	103258	105052	106856	108670	110493	112327	114168	116018
24	097019	098802	100596	102400	104214	106038	107871	109714	111567	113427	115296
25	096209	098011	099823	101646	103479	105322	107174	109035	110906	112784	114671
26	095492	097312	099143	100984	102835	104695	106564	108442	110330	112225	114128
27	094857	096695	098542	100400	102268	104144	106030	107924	109828	111738	113656
28	094293	096147	098012	099885	101769	103661	105562	107471	109389	111314	113246
29	093793	095662	097542	099431	101329	103235	105150	107074	109005	110944	112889
30	093348	095232	097126	099029	100940	102861	104789	106725	108670	110620	112578

YEARS	13½%	13¾%	14%	14¼%	14½%	14¾%	15%	15¼%	15½%	15¾%	16%	YEARS
1	895521	896696	897872	899048	900226	901404	902584	903764	904945	906126	907309	1
1½	616812	617981	619152	620324	621498	622672	623848	625026	626204	627384	628565	1½
2	477771	478949	480129	481311	482495	483680	484867	486056	487246	488438	489632	2
2½	394596	395789	396984	398181	399381	400582	407186	402992	404199	405209	406621	2½
3	339353	340564	341777	342992	344210	345431	346654	347879	349107	350338	351571	3
3½	300071	301301	302533	303768	305006	306247	307491	308738	309988	311240	312496	3½
4	270764	272013	273265	274521	275780	277042	278308	279577	280849	282125	283403	4
4½	248105	249374	250647	251924	253205	254489	255777	257068	258363	259662	260964	4½
5	230099	231389	232683	233981	235283	236590	237900	239214	240532	241855	243181	5
5½	215476	216787	218102	219422	220746	222074	223407	224744	226086	227432	228782	5½
6	203390	204722	206058	207399	208745	210095	211451	212811	214175	215545	216919	6
6½	193254	194606	195964	197326	198694	200066	201444	202827	204215	205607	207005	6½
7	184649	186022	187401	188784	190174	191568	192968	194373	195784	197200	198621	7
8	170882	172296	173716	175141	176573	178011	179455	180904	182360	183821	185288	8
9	160424	161877	163338	164804	166278	167758	169244	170737	172236	173741	175253	9
10	152275	153767	155267	156774	158287	159808	161335	162870	164411	165959	167514	10
12	140572	142139	143713	145295	146885	148483	150088	151701	153321	154948	156583	12
15	129832	131499	133175	134858	136551	138251	139959	141675	143400	145131	146871	15
20	120738	122541	124353	126172	128000	129836	131679	133530	135389	137254	139126	20
21	119637	121463	123297	125139	126989	128847	130712	132585	134464	136351	138244	21
22	118692	120538	122393	124256	126127	128005	129890	131783	133682	135587	137500	22
23	117877	119743	121618	123500	125390	127287	129190	131101	133018	134942	136871	23
24	117173	119058	120951	122851	124758	126673	128593	130521	132454	134394	136340	24
25	116565	118467	120377	122293	124217	126147	128084	130026	131975	133929	135889	25
26	116038	117956	119881	121813	123752	125697	127648	129604	131567	133535	135508	26
27	115582	117514	119454	121400	123352	125310	127274	129244	131219	133199	135184	27
28	115185	117132	119084	121043	123008	124978	126954	128936	130922	132913	134909	28
29	114841	116800	118764	120735	122712	124693	126680	128672	130669	132670	134675	29
29½	114686	116651	118621	120597	122579	124566	126558	128555	130556	132562	134572	29½
30	114542	116512	118488	120469	122456	124448	126445	128446	130452	132462	134476	30

YEARS	18¾%	18½%	18¼%	18%	17¾%	17½%	17¼%	17%	16¾%	16½%	16¼%	YEARS
1	920374	919182	917991	916800	915611	914423	913235	912048	910862	909677	908493	1
1½	641639	640444	639251	638058	636867	635677	634489	633301	632115	639031	629747	1½
2	502873	501661	500450	499242	498034	496829	495625	494423	493223	492024	490827	2
2½	420091	418856	417623	416392	415164	413937	412713	411490	410270	409052	407835	2½
3	365298	364038	362780	361524	360272	359021	357773	356528	355285	354044	352806	3
3½	326496	325209	323924	322643	321365	320089	318816	317546	316279	315015	313754	3½
4	297684	296370	295058	293750	292446	291144	289846	288551	287259	285971	284685	4
4½	275530	274188	272849	271514	270183	268855	267531	266210	264894	263580	262270	4½
5	258032	256663	255297	253935	252577	251223	249872	248526	247184	245846	244511	5
5½	243918	242521	241128	239739	238354	236974	235598	234226	232859	231495	230136	5½
6	232339	230914	229494	228078	226667	225261	223859	222462	221069	219681	218298	6
6½	222705	221254	219807	218365	216928	215496	214068	212646	211228	209816	208408	6½
7	214598	213120	211647	210179	208716	207258	205806	204359	202916	201479	200048	7
8	201804	200275	198751	197233	195720	194213	192711	191215	189725	188240	186761	8
9	192287	190709	189136	187569	186009	184454	182905	181362	179826	178295	176771	9
10	185042	183417	181798	180186	178579	176979	175386	173798	172217	170643	169075	10
12	175021	173312	171609	169912	168223	166539	164863	163193	161530	159874	158225	12
15	166467	164653	162845	161043	159247	157458	155676	153901	152133	150371	148617	15
20	160127	158190	156258	154332	152410	150495	148585	146681	144782	142891	141005	20
21	159455	157501	155551	153606	151666	149732	147802	145879	143961	142049	140143	21
22	158902	156932	154966	153004	151048	149096	147149	145208	143272	141342	139418	22
23	158446	156461	154481	152505	150533	148566	146604	144647	142695	140748	138807	23
24	158069	156072	154078	152089	150104	148123	146147	144176	142209	140247	138291	24
25	157757	155749	153744	151743	149746	147753	145765	143780	141800	139825	137855	25
26	157499	155481	153467	151456	149448	147444	145444	143448	141456	139469	134786	26
27	157286	155259	153236	151216	149198	147185	145175	143167	141166	139167	137173	27
28	157109	155075	153044	151015	148990	146968	144949	142933	140921	138913	136909	28
29	156963	154922	152884	150848	148816	146786	144759	142735	140715	138698	136684	29
29½	156899	154856	152814	150776	148739	146706	144675	142648	140624	138603	136585	29½
30	156841	154795	152751	150709	148670	146633	144599	142568	140540	138515	136494	30

YEARS	19%	19½%	20%	20½%	21%	YEARS
1	921566	923954	926346	928740	931138	1
1½	642835	645231	647633	650039	652450	1½
2	504087	506519	508959	511404	513857	2
2½	421328	423808	426296	428793	431298	2½
3	366561	369094	371636	374189	376751	3
3½	327785	330374	332973	335584	338206	3½
4	299002	301647	304304	306974	309657	4
4½	276875	279577	282293	285024	287768	4½
5	259406	262165	264939	267729	270534	5
5½	245320	248135	250968	253817	256682	5½
6	233768	236639	239529	242436	245360	6
6½	224161	227088	230034	232998	235981	6½
7	216081	219062	222062	225083	228123	7
8	203339	206425	209533	212661	215811	8
9	193871	197057	200266	203496	206749	9
10	186673	189953	193256	196583	199932	10
12	176737	180187	183661	187159	190681	12
15	168288	171948	175630	179335	183062	15
20	162069	165967	169883	173816	177765	20
21	161415	165347	169295	173260	177239	21
22	160877	164839	168816	172808	176814	22
23	160434	164423	168426	172442	176470	23
24	160069	164081	168106	172144	176192	24
25	159769	163801	167846	171901	175967	25
26	159520	163571	167632	171704	175784	26
27	159315	163382	167458	171543	175637	27
28	159146	163226	167315	171412	175517	28
29	159006	163098	167198	171306	175419	29
29½	158945	163043	167148	171260	175378	29½
30	158890	162993	167102	171219	175314	30

Appendix 2
Loan Progress Charts

balance owed after X years

Example: $50,000 loan @ 12¼% for 30 years

Problem: find balance after three years

Step 1

Choose the **chart** that corresponds to the interest rate of the loan in question.

Step 2

Choose the **column** that corresponds to the original term of the loan. For example, 30-year loans are found in the farthest right hand column of the chart.

12¼%

ORIGINAL LOAN TERM

		22	23	24	25	26	27	28	29	30		
AGE	1	990	992	993	994	994	995	996	996	997	1	DOLLARS STILL
OF	2	980	982	984	986	988	989	991	992	993	2	OWED FOR EVERY
LOAN	3	968	972	975	978	981	983	985	987	988	3	$1000 BORROWED
	4	954	959	964	969	972	976	979	981	983	4	
	5	938	946	952	958	963	968	971	975	978	5	

Step 3

Choose the **row** that corresponds to the age of the loan. For example, a three-year-old loan would utilize row three of the chart.

Step 4

Multiply the number at the intersection by the number of **$1,000 increments** in the original loan.

$988
× 50 ($50,000)
$49,400 present balance

If the original loan amount had been **$50,600**, you would multiply 988 times 50.6.

409

8%

ORIGINAL LOAN TERM

AGE OF LOAN	5	8	10	12	15	16	17	18	19	20	21	22	23	24	25	26	27	28	29	30
1	831	907	932	948	964	968	971	974	977	979	981	983	984	986	987	988	989	990	991	992
2	647	806	858	892	925	933	940	946	951	956	960	964	967	970	973	975	977	979	981	983
3	448	697	778	831	883	895	906	916	924	931	938	943	949	953	957	961	964	968	970	973
4	233	579	692	766	837	854	869	883	894	904	913	921	929	935	941	946	951	955	959	962
5		451	598	694	788	810	830	847	862	875	887	897	907	915	923	930	936	941	946	951
6		313	497	617	734	762	787	808	827	844	858	872	883	894	903	912	919	926	933	938
7		162	387	534	676	710	740	766	789	810	828	844	858	871	882	892	902	910	918	925
8			268	443	613	654	690	721	749	773	794	813	830	846	859	872	883	893	902	910
9			139	345	545	593	635	672	704	733	758	780	800	818	834	849	862	874	885	894
10				239	471	527	576	619	656	689	719	745	768	789	808	824	840	853	866	877
11				124	391	456	512	561	604	642	676	706	733	757	779	798	815	831	846	859
12					305	379	443	499	548	592	630	664	695	722	747	769	789	807	824	839
13					211	295	368	431	487	537	580	619	654	685	713	738	761	781	800	817
14					110	204	287	358	421	477	526	570	609	645	676	704	730	753	774	793
15						106	199	279	350	412	468	517	561	601	636	668	697	723	746	768
16							103	193	273	343	405	460	509	553	593	628	661	690	716	740
17								100	189	267	336	398	452	502	546	586	622	654	684	710
18									98	185	262	330	391	446	495	539	579	615	648	678
19										96	181	257	325	386	440	489	533	574	610	643
20											94	178	253	320	381	435	484	528	568	605
21												93	175	249	316	376	430	479	523	564
22													91	173	246	312	372	426	475	519
23														90	171	243	309	368	422	471
24															89	168	241	306	365	418
25																88	167	238	303	362
26																	87	165	236	300
27																		86	163	234
28																			85	162
29																				84

8½%

ORIGINAL LOAN TERM

AGE OF LOAN	5	8	10	12	15	16	17	18	19	20	21	22	23	24	25	26	27	28	29	30
1	832	909	934	950	966	969	973	975	978	980	982	984	985	987	988	989	990	991	992	992
2	650	810	861	895	928	936	943	949	954	958	962	966	969	972	975	977	979	981	983	984
3	451	701	783	836	887	899	910	919	928	935	941	947	952	956	960	964	967	970	973	975
4	235	584	697	771	843	860	875	888	899	909	918	926	933	939	945	950	954	958	962	966
5		456	604	701	794	817	836	853	868	881	893	903	912	921	928	934	940	946	951	955
6		317	503	624	742	770	794	816	834	851	865	878	890	900	909	918	925	932	938	943
7		165	393	541	684	719	749	775	798	818	836	851	865	878	889	899	908	917	924	931
8			273	450	622	663	699	730	758	782	803	822	839	854	867	880	890	900	909	917
9			142	352	554	603	645	682	714	743	768	790	810	828	844	858	871	882	893	902
10				244	480	537	586	629	667	700	729	755	778	799	818	834	849	863	875	886
11				127	399	465	522	572	615	653	687	717	744	768	789	809	826	842	856	868
12					312	387	452	509	559	603	642	676	707	734	759	781	801	818	835	849
13					217	302	377	441	498	548	592	631	666	697	725	750	773	793	812	828
14					113	210	294	367	432	488	538	582	622	657	689	717	743	766	787	806
15						109	204	287	359	423	479	529	574	614	649	681	710	736	760	781
16							106	199	280	352	415	472	522	566	606	642	675	704	730	754
17								104	195	275	346	409	465	515	559	600	636	668	698	725
18									101	191	270	340	403	458	508	553	594	630	663	693
19										99	187	266	335	397	453	503	548	588	625	658
20											98	184	262	331	392	448	498	543	583	620
21												96	182	258	327	338	443	493	538	579
22													95	179	255	323	384	439	489	534
23														93	177	252	320	381	436	485
24															92	175	250	317	378	432
25																91	173	247	314	375
26																	90	172	245	312
27																		89	170	243
28																			89	169
29																				88

9%

ORIGINAL LOAN TERM

AGE OF LOAN	5	8	10	12	15	16	17	18	19	20	21	22	23	24	25	26	27	28	29	30
1	834	911	935	951	967	971	974	977	979	981	983	985	986	988	989	990	991	992	992	993
2	653	813	865	898	931	939	945	951	956	961	965	968	971	974	977	979	981	983	984	986
3	454	706	787	840	891	903	914	923	931	938	945	950	955	959	963	967	970	973	975	978
4	237	589	703	777	848	865	880	893	904	914	923	930	937	943	949	954	958	962	965	969
5		461	610	707	801	823	842	859	874	887	898	909	918	926	933	939	945	950	955	959
6		321	509	631	749	777	802	823	841	858	872	885	896	906	915	923	931	937	943	948
7		167	398	548	692	727	757	783	806	826	843	859	873	885	896	906	915	923	930	936
8			277	457	630	672	708	739	767	791	812	831	847	862	875	887	898	907	916	924
9			145	358	563	612	654	691	724	752	777	799	819	837	852	866	879	890	900	910
10				249	489	546	596	639	677	710	740	765	789	809	827	844	858	872	884	894
11				130	408	474	532	582	626	664	698	728	755	779	800	819	836	851	865	878
12					319	396	462	519	570	614	653	688	718	746	770	792	812	829	845	859
13					222	310	385	451	509	559	604	643	678	710	737	762	785	805	823	839
14					116	215	301	376	442	499	550	595	634	670	702	730	755	778	799	817
15						113	210	294	368	433	491	541	586	627	662	695	723	749	772	793
16							110	205	288	361	426	483	534	579	620	656	688	717	743	767
17								107	201	283	355	420	477	527	573	613	650	682	712	738
18									105	197	278	350	414	471	522	567	608	644	677	707
19										103	194	274	345	409	466	516	562	603	640	673
20											101	191	270	341	404	461	512	557	598	635
21												100	188	267	337	400	457	507	553	594
22													98	186	264	334	396	453	503	549
23														97	184	261	331	393	449	500
24															96	182	259	328	390	446
25																95	180	257	325	388
26																	94	179	255	323
27																		93	177	253
28																			93	176
29																				92

9½%

ORIGINAL LOAN TERM

AGE OF LOAN	5	8	10	12	15	16	17	18	19	20	21	22	23	24	25	26	27	28	29	30
1	836	912	937	953	968	972	975	978	980	982	984	986	987	989	990	991	992	992	993	994
2	656	816	868	901	934	941	948	954	959	963	967	970	973	976	978	981	982	984	986	987
3	457	710	792	845	895	907	918	927	935	942	948	953	958	962	966	969	972	975	977	980
4	239	593	708	782	853	870	885	898	909	918	927	934	941	947	952	957	961	965	968	971
5		465	616	714	807	829	849	865	880	893	904	914	923	930	937	943	949	954	958	962
6		325	515	638	756	784	809	830	848	864	879	891	902	912	921	929	936	942	947	953
7		170	404	555	700	735	765	791	813	833	851	866	880	892	903	912	921	929	935	942
8			282	464	639	681	717	748	775	799	820	839	855	870	883	894	905	914	922	930
9			148	364	571	621	664	701	733	762	787	809	828	845	861	875	887	898	908	917
10				254	497	555	606	649	687	720	750	775	798	819	837	853	867	880	892	902
11				133	416	483	542	592	636	675	709	739	766	789	810	829	846	861	874	886
12					326	404	471	530	581	625	664	699	730	757	781	803	822	839	855	869
13					227	317	394	461	519	570	615	655	690	721	749	774	796	816	834	850
14					119	221	309	385	452	510	561	607	647	682	714	742	767	790	810	828
15						116	216	302	378	444	502	553	599	639	675	707	736	762	785	805
16							113	211	296	371	437	495	546	592	633	669	701	730	756	780
17								110	207	291	365	431	489	540	586	627	663	696	725	752
18									108	203	286	360	425	483	535	580	622	658	691	721
19										106	200	282	355	420	478	530	576	617	654	687
20											105	197	279	351	416	474	525	571	613	650
21												103	194	276	348	412	470	521	567	609
22													102	192	273	344	409	466	518	564
23														101	190	270	342	406	463	514
24															100	188	268	339	403	460
25																99	187	266	337	400
26																	98	185	264	335
27																		97	184	262
28																			96	183
29																				96

413

10%

ORIGINAL LOAN TERM

AGE OF LOAN	5	8	10	12	15	16	17	18	19	20	21	22	23	24	25	26	27	28	29	30
1	838	914	939	955	970	973	976	979	981	983	985	987	988	989	991	992	992	993	994	994
2	658	819	871	904	936	944	950	956	961	965	969	972	975	978	980	982	984	986	987	988
3	460	714	796	849	899	911	922	930	938	945	951	956	961	965	969	972	975	977	979	982
4	242	598	713	788	858	875	890	902	913	923	931	938	945	951	956	960	964	968	971	974
5		470	622	720	813	835	855	871	885	898	909	919	927	935	942	948	953	958	962	966
6		329	521	645	763	791	816	837	855	871	885	897	908	918	926	934	940	946	952	957
7		173	410	562	708	743	773	799	821	841	858	873	886	898	909	918	927	934	941	946
8			286	471	647	689	725	757	784	807	828	847	863	877	890	901	911	920	928	935
9			150	370	580	630	673	710	743	771	796	817	837	854	869	882	894	905	914	923
10				259	506	565	615	659	697	730	759	785	808	828	846	861	876	888	899	909
11				136	424	492	551	602	647	685	719	749	776	799	820	838	855	870	883	894
12					333	412	481	540	591	636	675	710	741	768	792	813	832	849	864	878
13					233	324	403	471	530	581	627	666	702	733	760	785	807	826	844	859
14					122	227	316	394	462	521	573	618	659	694	726	754	779	801	821	839
15						119	221	310	387	454	513	565	611	652	688	720	748	774	796	817
16							116	217	304	380	447	506	559	605	645	682	714	743	769	792
17								114	213	299	375	442	500	553	599	640	677	709	738	765
18									112	209	295	370	436	495	547	594	635	672	705	734
19										110	206	291	366	432	491	543	589	631	668	701
20											108	203	287	362	428	486	539	585	627	664
21												107	201	284	358	424	483	535	582	623
22													105	199	282	355	421	479	532	578
23														104	197	279	353	418	476	529
24															103	195	277	350	415	474
25																102	194	275	348	413
26																	102	192	273	346
27																		101	191	272
28																			100	190
29																				100

10¼%

ORIGINAL LOAN TERM

AGE OF LOAN	5	8	10	12	15	16	17	18	19	20	21	22	23	24	25	26	27	28	29	30
1	839	915	939	955	970	974	977	980	982	984	986	987	989	990	991	992	993	993	994	995
2	660	821	872	906	937	945	952	957	962	966	970	973	976	979	981	983	985	986	988	989
3	462	716	798	851	901	913	923	932	940	947	952	958	962	966	970	973	976	978	980	982
4	243	601	716	790	861	878	892	904	915	925	933	940	947	952	957	962	966	969	972	975
5		473	625	723	816	838	857	874	888	901	912	921	930	937	944	950	955	959	964	967
6		331	524	648	767	795	819	840	858	874	888	900	911	920	929	936	943	949	954	959
7		174	412	566	712	747	777	802	825	844	861	876	890	901	912	921	929	936	943	949
8			289	475	651	693	730	761	788	812	832	850	867	881	893	904	914	923	931	938
9			152	373	584	634	678	715	747	775	800	822	841	858	873	886	898	908	918	926
10				261	510	569	620	664	702	735	764	790	812	832	850	866	880	892	903	913
11				137	428	497	556	607	652	691	725	754	781	804	825	843	859	874	887	898
12					337	417	485	545	596	641	681	715	746	773	797	818	837	854	869	882
13					236	328	407	475	535	587	632	672	707	738	766	790	812	831	849	864
14					124	229	320	399	467	526	578	624	664	700	732	760	785	807	827	844
15						121	224	314	391	459	519	571	617	658	694	726	754	779	802	822
16							118	220	308	385	453	512	565	611	652	688	720	749	775	798
17								115	216	303	380	447	506	559	605	646	683	716	745	771
18									113	212	299	375	442	501	554	600	642	679	711	741
19										112	209	295	371	437	497	549	596	638	675	708
20											110	207	292	367	433	493	545	592	634	671
21												109	204	289	364	430	489	542	589	630
22													107	202	286	361	427	486	538	585
23														106	200	284	358	424	483	536
24															105	199	282	356	422	480
25																104	197	280	354	419
26																	104	196	278	352
27																		103	195	277
28																			102	194
29																				102

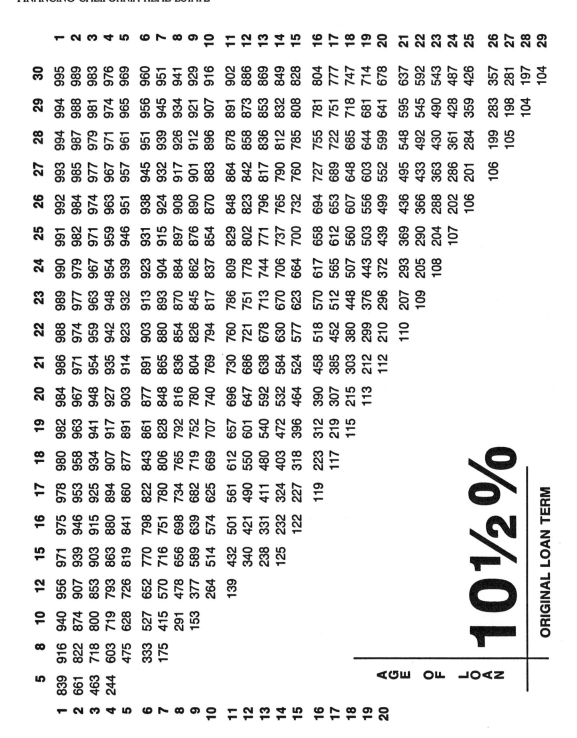

10½%

ORIGINAL LOAN TERM

AGE OF LOAN	5	8	10	12	15	16	17	18	19	20	21	22	23	24	25	26	27	28	29	30
1	839	916	940	956	971	975	978	980	982	984	986	988	989	990	991	992	993	994	994	995
2	661	822	874	907	939	946	953	958	963	967	971	974	977	979	982	984	985	987	988	989
3	463	718	800	853	903	915	925	934	941	948	954	959	963	967	971	974	977	979	981	983
4	244	603	719	793	863	880	894	907	917	927	935	942	948	954	959	963	967	971	974	976
5		475	628	726	819	841	860	877	891	903	914	923	932	939	946	951	957	961	965	969
6		333	527	652	770	798	822	843	861	877	891	903	913	923	931	938	945	951	956	960
7		175	415	570	716	751	780	806	828	848	865	880	893	904	915	924	932	939	945	951
8			291	478	656	698	734	765	792	816	836	854	870	884	897	908	917	926	934	941
9			153	377	589	639	682	719	752	780	804	826	845	862	876	890	901	912	921	929
10				264	514	574	625	669	707	740	769	794	817	837	854	870	883	896	907	916
11				139	432	501	561	612	657	696	730	760	786	809	829	848	864	878	891	902
12					340	421	490	550	601	647	686	721	751	778	802	823	842	858	873	886
13					238	331	411	480	540	592	638	678	713	744	771	796	817	836	853	869
14					125	232	324	403	472	532	584	630	670	706	737	765	790	812	832	849
15						122	227	318	396	464	524	577	623	664	700	732	760	785	808	828
16							119	223	312	390	458	518	570	617	658	694	727	755	781	804
17								117	219	307	385	452	512	565	612	653	689	722	751	777
18									115	215	303	380	448	507	560	607	648	685	718	747
19										113	212	299	376	443	503	556	603	644	681	714
20											112	210	296	372	439	499	552	599	641	678
21												110	207	293	369	436	495	548	595	637
22													109	205	290	366	433	492	545	592
23														108	204	288	363	430	490	543
24															107	202	286	361	428	487
25																106	201	284	359	426
26																	106	199	283	357
27																		105	198	281
28																			104	197
29																				104

10¾%

ORIGINAL LOAN TERM

AGE OF LOAN	5	8	10	12	15	16	17	18	19	20	21	22	23	24	25	26	27	28	29	30
1	840	917	941	957	972	975	978	981	983	985	987	988	989	991	992	993	993	994	995	995
2	663	824	875	909	940	947	954	959	964	968	972	975	978	980	982	984	986	987	989	990
3	465	720	802	855	905	917	927	935	943	950	955	960	965	969	972	975	978	980	982	984
4	245	605	721	795	866	882	897	909	920	929	937	944	950	956	960	965	969	972	975	978
5		477	631	729	822	844	863	879	893	906	916	926	934	941	948	953	958	963	967	970
6		335	530	655	774	802	826	846	864	880	894	906	916	925	933	941	947	953	958	962
7		176	418	573	720	754	784	810	832	851	868	883	896	907	918	926	934	941	948	953
8			293	482	660	702	738	769	796	820	840	858	874	888	900	911	920	929	936	943
9			154	380	593	643	687	724	756	784	809	830	849	866	880	893	905	915	924	932
10				266	519	578	629	673	711	745	774	799	821	841	858	874	887	899	910	919
11				140	436	506	566	617	662	701	735	764	791	814	834	852	868	882	894	906
12					344	425	495	555	607	652	691	726	756	783	807	828	846	863	877	890
13					241	335	416	485	545	598	643	683	718	749	777	801	822	841	858	873
14					127	235	328	408	477	537	590	636	676	712	743	771	795	817	837	854
15						124	230	321	401	470	530	583	629	670	706	738	766	791	813	833
16							121	226	316	395	463	524	576	623	664	700	733	761	787	809
17								119	222	311	389	458	518	571	618	659	696	728	757	783
18									117	218	307	385	453	513	566	613	655	692	724	754
19										115	215	303	381	449	509	562	609	651	688	721
20											113	213	300	377	445	505	558	605	647	685
21												112	211	297	374	442	502	555	602	644
22													111	209	295	371	439	499	552	599
23														110	207	293	369	436	496	549
24															109	205	291	367	434	494
25																108	204	289	365	432
26																	107	203	288	363
27																		107	202	286
28																			106	201
29																				106

11%

ORIGINAL LOAN TERM (per $1000 of original loan — remaining balance)

AGE OF LOAN	5	8	10	12	15	16	17	18	19	20	21	22	23	24	25	26	27	28	29	30
1	841	917	942	957	972	976	979	981	983	985	987	989	990	991	992	993	994	994	995	995
2	664	825	877	910	941	949	955	960	965	969	973	976	979	981	983	985	987	988	989	990
3	466	722	805	857	907	918	928	937	945	951	957	962	966	970	973	976	979	981	983	985
4	246	608	724	798	868	885	899	911	922	931	939	946	952	957	962	966	970	973	976	979
5		480	634	732	825	847	866	882	896	908	919	928	936	943	950	955	960	964	968	972
6		337	533	659	777	805	829	850	867	883	896	908	919	928	936	943	949	955	960	964
7		178	421	577	724	758	788	813	836	855	872	886	899	910	920	929	937	944	950	955
8			296	485	664	706	742	773	800	823	844	862	877	891	903	914	923	931	939	945
9			156	383	597	648	691	728	760	788	813	834	853	869	884	897	908	918	927	935
10				269	523	583	634	678	716	749	778	803	826	845	862	877	891	903	913	923
11				142	440	510	570	622	667	706	740	769	795	818	838	856	872	886	898	909
12					347	429	499	560	612	657	697	731	762	788	812	832	851	867	881	894
13					244	339	420	490	550	603	649	689	724	755	782	806	827	846	863	877
14					129	238	332	412	482	542	595	641	682	717	749	776	801	822	842	859
15						125	233	325	405	475	535	588	635	676	712	743	771	796	818	838
16							123	229	320	399	469	529	582	629	670	706	739	767	792	815
17								121	225	315	394	463	524	577	624	665	702	734	763	789
18									119	221	311	390	459	519	572	619	661	698	731	760
19										117	219	308	386	454	515	568	616	657	694	727
20											115	216	305	382	451	511	565	612	654	691
21												114	214	302	379	448	508	562	609	651
22													113	212	299	377	445	505	559	606
23														112	210	297	374	442	503	556
24															111	209	295	372	440	500
25																110	207	294	370	438
26																	109	206	292	368
27																		109	205	291
28																			108	204
29																				108

11 1/4%

ORIGINAL LOAN TERM

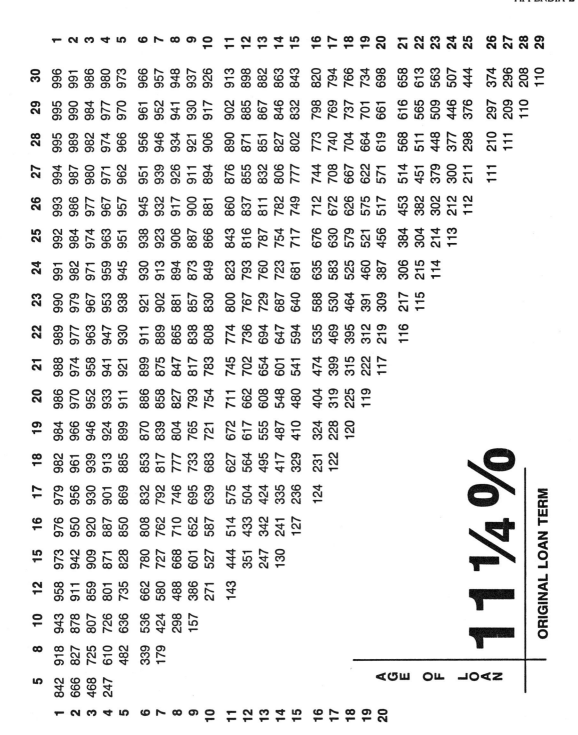

AGE OF LOAN	5	8	10	12	15	16	17	18	19	20	21	22	23	24	25	26	27	28	29	30
1	842	918	943	958	973	976	979	982	984	986	988	989	990	991	992	993	994	995	995	996
2	666	827	878	911	942	950	956	961	966	970	974	977	979	982	984	986	987	989	990	991
3	468	725	807	859	909	920	930	939	946	952	958	963	967	971	974	977	980	982	984	986
4	247	610	726	801	871	887	901	913	924	933	941	947	953	959	963	967	971	974	977	980
5		482	636	735	828	850	869	885	899	911	921	930	938	945	951	957	962	966	970	973
6		339	536	662	780	808	832	853	870	886	899	911	921	930	938	945	951	956	961	966
7		179	424	580	727	762	792	817	839	858	875	889	902	913	923	932	939	946	952	957
8			298	488	668	710	746	777	804	827	847	865	881	894	906	917	926	934	941	948
9			157	386	601	652	695	733	765	793	817	838	857	873	887	900	911	921	930	937
10				271	527	587	639	683	721	754	783	808	830	849	866	881	894	906	917	926
11				143	444	514	575	627	672	711	745	774	800	823	843	860	876	890	902	913
12					351	433	504	564	617	662	702	736	767	793	816	837	855	871	885	898
13					247	342	424	495	555	608	654	694	729	760	787	811	832	851	867	882
14					130	241	335	417	487	548	601	647	687	723	754	782	806	827	846	863
15						127	236	329	410	480	541	594	640	681	717	749	777	802	832	843
16							124	231	324	404	474	535	588	635	676	712	744	773	798	820
17								122	228	319	399	469	530	583	630	672	708	740	769	794
18									120	225	315	395	464	525	579	626	667	704	737	766
19										119	222	312	391	460	521	575	622	664	701	734
20											117	219	309	387	456	517	571	619	661	698
21												116	217	306	384	453	514	568	616	658
22													115	215	304	382	451	511	565	613
23														114	214	302	379	448	509	563
24															113	212	300	377	446	507
25																112	211	298	376	444
26																	111	210	297	374
27																		111	209	296
28																			110	208
29																				110

11½%

ORIGINAL LOAN TERM

AGE OF LOAN

AGE	5	8	10	12	15	16	17	18	19	20	21	22	23	24	25	26	27	28	29	30
1	843	919	943	959	973	977	980	982	984	986	988	989	991	992	993	993	994	995	995	996
2	667	828	880	913	944	951	957	962	967	971	974	977	980	982	984	986	988	989	990	991
3	470	727	809	861	910	922	932	940	947	954	959	964	968	972	975	978	980	983	985	986
4	248	612	729	803	873	889	903	915	926	935	942	949	955	960	965	969	972	975	978	981
5		485	639	738	831	853	871	887	901	913	923	932	940	947	953	958	963	967	971	974
6		341	539	665	784	812	835	856	873	889	902	913	924	932	940	947	953	958	963	967
7		180	426	584	731	766	795	821	843	861	878	892	905	916	925	934	941	948	954	959
8			300	492	672	714	750	781	808	831	851	869	884	897	909	919	929	937	944	950
9			159	389	606	656	700	737	769	797	821	842	860	877	891	903	914	924	932	940
10				274	531	592	643	687	725	759	787	812	834	853	870	885	898	909	920	929
11				145	448	519	580	632	677	716	749	779	805	827	847	864	880	893	905	916
12					354	437	508	569	622	667	707	741	772	798	821	841	859	875	889	902
13					249	346	429	499	560	613	659	699	734	765	792	816	837	855	871	886
14					132	244	339	421	492	553	606	653	693	728	759	787	811	832	851	868
15						129	239	333	414	485	546	600	646	687	723	755	782	807	829	848
16							126	234	328	409	479	540	594	641	682	718	750	778	805	825
17								124	231	323	404	474	535	589	636	678	714	746	775	800
18									122	228	319	400	470	531	585	632	674	710	743	772
19										120	225	316	396	466	527	581	628	670	707	740
20											119	223	313	393	462	523	577	625	667	704
21												118	220	311	390	459	520	575	622	664
22													117	219	308	387	457	518	572	620
23														116	217	306	385	454	515	570
24															115	216	304	383	452	513
25																114	214	303	381	450
26																	113	213	302	380
27																		113	212	300
28																			112	211
29																				112

11 3/4%

AGE OF LOAN (rows) × **ORIGINAL LOAN TERM** (columns)

AGE	5	8	10	12	15	16	17	18	19	20	21	22	23	24	25	26	27	28	29	30
1	844	920	944	960	974	977	980	983	985	987	988	990	991	992	993	994	994	995	996	996
2	668	830	881	914	945	952	958	963	968	972	975	978	981	983	985	987	988	990	991	992
3	471	729	811	863	912	924	933	942	949	955	961	965	969	973	976	979	981	983	985	987
4	249	615	731	806	875	891	905	917	927	936	944	951	957	962	966	970	973	977	979	982
5		487	642	741	834	855	874	890	903	915	925	934	942	949	955	960	965	969	972	975
6		343	542	669	787	815	839	859	876	891	905	916	926	935	942	949	955	960	965	969
7		182	429	587	735	769	799	824	846	865	881	895	908	919	928	936	944	950	956	961
8			302	495	676	718	754	785	812	835	855	872	887	900	912	922	931	939	946	952
9			160	392	610	661	704	741	773	801	825	846	864	880	894	906	917	927	935	942
10				276	535	596	648	692	730	763	792	817	838	857	874	889	901	913	923	931
11				146	452	523	584	636	681	720	754	784	809	832	851	868	884	897	909	919
12					358	442	513	574	627	672	712	746	776	803	826	846	864	879	893	905
13					252	350	433	504	566	619	665	705	740	770	797	821	841	859	875	890
14					133	246	343	425	497	558	611	658	698	734	765	792	816	837	856	872
15						130	242	337	419	490	552	605	652	693	729	760	788	812	834	852
16							128	237	332	413	484	546	600	647	688	724	756	784	809	830
17								126	234	327	409	479	541	595	642	684	720	752	780	805
18									124	231	324	404	475	537	591	638	680	717	749	777
19										122	228	320	401	471	533	587	635	676	713	746
20											121	226	317	398	468	530	584	631	674	711
21												119	224	315	395	465	527	581	629	671
22													118	222	313	392	462	524	578	626
23														117	220	311	390	460	522	576
24															117	219	309	388	458	520
25																116	218	308	387	456
26																	115	217	306	385
27																		115	216	305
28																			114	215
29																				114

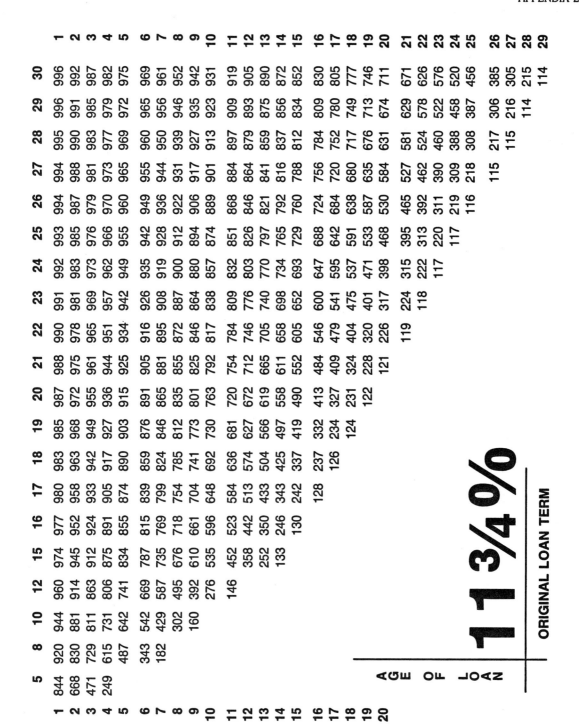

12%

ORIGINAL LOAN TERM

AGE OF LOAN	5	8	10	12	15	16	17	18	19	20	21	22	23	24	25	26	27	28	29	30
1	845	921	945	960	975	978	981	983	985	987	989	990	991	992	993	994	995	995	996	996
2	670	831	883	915	946	953	959	964	969	973	976	979	982	984	986	987	989	990	991	992
3	473	731	813	865	914	925	935	943	950	956	962	966	970	974	977	980	982	984	986	988
4	250	617	734	808	877	894	907	919	929	938	946	952	958	963	967	971	975	978	980	982
5		489	645	744	837	858	877	892	906	917	928	936	944	951	957	962	966	970	974	977
6		345	545	672	790	818	842	862	879	894	907	918	928	937	944	951	957	962	966	970
7		183	432	590	738	773	802	828	849	868	884	898	910	921	930	939	946	952	958	963
8			305	499	680	722	758	789	815	838	858	875	890	903	915	925	934	941	948	954
9			161	395	614	665	708	745	777	805	829	850	868	884	897	909	920	929	938	945
10				279	540	600	652	696	735	767	796	821	842	861	878	892	905	916	926	934
11				148	456	528	589	641	686	725	759	788	814	836	855	872	887	900	912	922
12					361	446	518	579	632	677	717	751	781	807	830	850	868	883	897	909
13					255	353	437	509	571	624	670	710	745	775	802	825	846	864	880	894
14					135	249	347	430	501	563	617	663	704	739	770	797	821	842	860	876
15						132	245	341	424	495	557	611	657	698	734	765	793	817	838	857
16							130	240	336	418	489	551	605	652	694	730	761	789	814	835
17								127	237	332	413	485	547	601	648	689	726	758	786	811
18									126	234	328	409	480	542	597	644	686	723	755	783
19										124	231	325	406	477	539	593	641	683	720	752
20											123	229	322	403	473	536	590	638	680	717
21												121	227	319	400	471	533	587	635	677
22													120	225	317	398	468	530	585	633
23														119	224	315	395	466	528	583
24															119	222	314	394	464	526
25																118	221	312	392	462
26																	117	220	311	391
27																		117	219	310
28																			116	219
29																				116

12¼%

ORIGINAL LOAN TERM

AGE OF LOAN	5	8	10	12	15	16	17	18	19	20	21	22	23	24	25	26	27	28	29	30
1	846	922	946	961	975	979	981	984	986	988	989	990	992	993	994	994	995	996	996	997
2	671	833	884	917	947	954	960	965	970	974	977	980	982	984	986	988	989	991	992	993
3	474	733	815	867	915	927	936	945	952	958	963	968	972	975	978	981	983	985	987	988
4	251	620	736	811	880	896	909	921	931	940	947	954	959	964	969	972	976	979	981	983
5		492	648	747	839	861	879	895	908	920	930	938	946	952	958	963	968	971	975	978
6		347	548	675	794	821	845	865	882	897	910	921	930	939	946	953	958	963	968	971
7		184	437	594	742	777	806	831	852	871	887	901	913	924	933	941	948	954	960	964
8			307	502	684	726	762	793	819	842	862	879	893	906	918	928	936	944	950	956
9			163	399	618	669	713	750	782	809	833	853	871	887	901	912	923	932	940	947
10				282	544	605	657	701	739	772	800	825	846	865	881	895	908	919	928	937
11				149	460	532	593	646	691	730	763	793	818	840	859	876	891	904	915	925
12					365	450	522	584	637	682	722	756	786	812	835	854	872	887	900	912
13					258	357	441	514	576	629	675	715	750	780	807	830	850	868	884	897
14					138	252	350	434	506	568	622	669	709	744	775	802	826	846	865	880
15						134	247	345	428	500	562	616	663	704	740	771	798	822	843	862
16							131	243	340	423	495	557	611	658	699	735	767	795	819	840
17								129	240	336	418	490	552	606	654	695	732	763	791	816
18									127	237	332	414	486	548	603	650	692	728	761	789
19										126	234	329	411	482	545	599	647	689	726	758
20											124	232	326	408	479	541	596	644	686	723
21												123	230	324	405	476	539	593	642	684
22													122	229	322	403	474	536	591	639
23														121	227	320	401	472	534	589
24															120	226	318	399	470	532
25																120	225	317	397	468
26																	119	224	315	396
27																		119	223	314
28																			118	222
29																				118

12 1/2 %

AGE OF LOAN	\ ORIGINAL LOAN TERM → 5	8	10	12	15	16	17	18	19	20	21	22	23	24	25	26	27	28	29	30
1	846	922	946	962	976	979	982	984	986	988	990	991	992	993	994	995	995	996	996	997
2	673	834	886	918	948	955	961	966	971	974	978	980	983	985	987	988	990	991	992	993
3	476	735	817	869	917	928	938	946	953	959	964	969	973	976	979	981	984	986	987	989
4	253	622	739	813	882	898	911	923	933	942	949	955	961	966	970	974	977	980	982	984
5		494	651	750	842	863	882	897	910	922	932	940	948	954	960	965	969	973	976	979
6		349	551	678	797	824	848	868	885	899	912	923	933	941	948	954	960	965	969	973
7		186	438	597	746	780	809	834	856	874	890	904	916	926	935	943	950	956	961	966
8			309	506	688	730	766	797	823	845	865	882	896	909	920	930	939	946	952	958
9			164	402	622	673	717	754	786	813	837	857	875	890	904	915	926	935	942	949
10				284	548	609	661	705	743	776	804	829	850	869	885	899	911	922	931	939
11				151	464	536	598	651	696	735	768	797	822	844	869	880	894	907	918	928
12					368	454	527	589	642	687	727	761	791	816	839	858	876	891	904	915
13					261	361	446	518	580	634	680	720	755	785	811	834	854	872	887	901
14					138	255	354	439	511	573	627	674	714	750	780	807	830	851	869	884
15						135	250	349	433	505	567	622	668	709	745	776	803	827	848	866
16							133	246	344	427	500	562	617	664	705	741	772	800	824	845
17								131	243	340	423	495	558	612	660	701	737	769	797	821
18									129	240	336	419	491	554	608	656	698	734	766	794
19										128	238	333	416	488	550	605	653	695	731	764
20											126	235	330	413	485	547	602	650	692	729
21												125	234	328	410	482	545	600	648	690
22													124	232	326	408	480	542	597	646
23														123	230	324	406	478	540	596
24															122	229	323	404	476	539
25																122	228	321	403	474
26																	121	227	320	402
27																		121	226	319
28																			120	226
29																				120

12 3/4%

ORIGINAL LOAN TERM / AGE OF LOAN

Age of Loan	5	8	10	12	15	16	17	18	19	20	21	22	23	24	25	26	27	28	29	30
1	847	923	947	962	976	980	982	985	987	988	990	991	992	993	994	995	995	996	996	997
2	678	836	887	919	949	956	962	967	972	975	978	981	983	986	987	989	990	991	993	993
3	477	737	819	871	919	930	939	947	954	960	965	970	974	977	980	982	984	986	988	989
4	254	624	741	815	884	900	913	925	935	943	950	957	962	967	971	975	978	980	983	985
5		496	653	753	845	866	884	899	913	924	934	942	949	956	961	966	970	974	977	980
6		351	554	682	800	827	851	870	887	902	915	925	935	943	950	956	962	966	970	974
7		187	440	601	749	784	813	838	859	877	893	906	918	928	937	945	952	958	963	967
8			312	509	692	734	770	800	826	849	868	885	899	912	923	932	941	948	954	960
9			166	405	626	677	721	758	790	817	840	861	878	893	907	918	928	937	945	951
10				287	552	613	665	710	748	780	809	833	854	872	888	902	914	925	934	942
11				152	468	541	603	655	700	739	773	801	826	848	867	883	898	910	921	931
12					372	458	531	593	647	692	732	766	795	821	843	863	879	894	907	918
13					263	364	450	523	585	639	685	725	760	790	816	839	859	876	891	904
14					140	258	358	443	516	579	633	679	720	755	785	812	835	855	873	888
15						137	253	352	437	510	573	627	674	715	750	781	808	832	852	870
16							135	249	348	432	505	568	622	669	710	746	778	805	829	850
17								133	246	344	428	500	563	618	665	707	743	774	802	826
18									131	243	340	424	496	559	614	662	704	740	772	800
19										129	241	337	421	493	556	611	659	701	737	769
20											128	239	335	418	490	553	608	656	698	735
21												127	237	332	415	488	551	606	654	696
22													126	235	330	413	485	549	604	652
23														125	234	329	411	483	547	602
24															124	233	327	410	482	545
25																124	232	326	408	480
26																	123	231	325	407
27																		123	230	324
28																			122	229
29																				122

425

13%

Remaining loan balance per $1,000 — AGE OF LOAN vs. ORIGINAL LOAN TERM

Age of Loan	5	8	10	12	15	16	17	18	19	20	21	22	23	24	25	26	27	28	29	30
1	848	924	948	963	977	980	983	985	987	989	990	991	993	994	994	995	996	996	997	997
2	675	837	888	921	950	957	963	968	972	976	979	982	984	986	988	989	991	992	993	994
3	479	739	821	873	920	931	941	949	956	961	966	971	974	978	981	983	985	987	989	990
4	255	626	744	818	886	902	915	927	936	945	952	958	964	968	972	976	979	981	984	986
5		499	656	756	847	869	887	902	915	926	936	944	951	957	963	967	971	975	978	981
6		354	557	685	803	830	854	873	890	905	917	928	937	945	952	958	963	968	972	975
7		188	443	604	753	787	816	841	862	880	896	909	921	931	940	947	954	960	965	969
8			314	512	695	738	774	804	830	852	871	888	902	915	926	935	943	950	956	962
9			167	408	630	682	725	762	794	821	844	864	881	896	910	921	931	939	947	954
10				289	556	618	670	714	752	785	813	837	858	876	891	905	917	927	936	944
11				154	472	545	607	660	705	744	777	806	831	852	871	887	901	913	924	934
12					376	462	536	598	651	697	736	770	800	825	847	866	883	898	910	922
13					266	368	454	528	590	644	690	730	765	795	820	843	863	880	895	908
14					142	261	362	447	521	584	638	684	725	760	790	816	839	859	877	892
15						139	256	356	442	515	578	632	679	720	755	786	813	836	857	874
16							136	253	352	437	510	573	628	675	716	752	783	810	833	854
17								134	249	348	432	506	569	623	671	712	748	780	807	831
18									133	246	344	429	502	565	620	668	709	746	777	805
19										131	244	341	426	499	562	617	665	707	743	775
20											130	242	339	423	496	559	614	662	704	741
21												129	240	337	420	493	557	612	660	702
22													128	239	335	418	491	555	610	658
23														127	237	333	417	489	553	606
24															126	236	332	415	488	551
25																126	235	330	414	486
26																	125	234	329	412
27																		125	233	328
28																			124	233
29																				124

AGE OF LOAN · ORIGINAL LOAN TERM

13½%

ORIGINAL LOAN TERM

AGE OF LOAN

Age of Loan	5	8	10	12	15	16	17	18	19	20	21	22	23	24	25	26	27	28	29	30
1	850	925	949	964	978	981	984	986	988	989	991	992	993	994	995	995	996	997	997	997
2	678	840	891	923	953	959	965	970	974	977	980	983	985	987	989	990	992	993	994	994
3	482	743	825	876	924	934	944	951	958	964	969	973	976	979	982	982	986	988	990	991
4	257	631	749	823	890	906	919	930	940	948	955	961	966	970	974	978	981	983	985	987
5		504	662	761	853	874	891	906	919	930	939	947	954	960	965	970	974	977	980	983
6		358	562	691	809	836	859	879	895	909	921	932	941	949	955	961	966	970	974	978
7		191	449	611	760	794	823	847	868	886	901	914	925	935	944	951	957	963	968	972
8			319	519	703	745	781	811	837	859	878	894	908	920	930	939	947	954	960	965
9			170	414	638	690	733	770	801	828	851	871	888	902	915	926	936	944	951	957
10				294	564	626	679	723	761	793	821	844	865	883	898	911	923	932	941	949
11				157	480	554	616	669	714	753	786	814	839	860	878	894	907	919	930	939
12					383	470	544	607	661	707	746	779	808	834	855	874	890	904	917	927
13					272	375	463	537	600	654	700	740	774	804	829	851	871	887	902	914
14					145	267	369	456	530	594	648	695	735	769	799	825	848	868	885	899
15						142	262	364	451	525	588	643	690	730	765	796	822	845	865	882
16							140	259	360	446	520	584	638	686	727	762	793	819	843	863
17								138	255	356	442	516	580	635	682	723	759	790	817	840
18									136	253	353	438	512	576	631	679	720	756	788	815
19										135	250	350	435	509	573	628	676	718	754	786
20											134	248	347	433	507	571	626	674	716	752
21												133	247	345	431	504	568	624	672	714
22													132	245	343	429	502	566	622	670
23														131	244	342	427	501	565	620
24															130	243	341	425	499	563
25																130	242	339	424	498
26																	129	241	338	423
27																		129	240	338
28																			128	240
29																				128

427

14%

ORIGINAL LOAN TERM

AGE OF LOAN	5	8	10	12	15	16	17	18	19	20	21	22	23	24	25	26	27	28	29	30
1	851	927	951	965	979	982	985	987	989	990	992	993	994	995	995	996	996	997	997	998
2	681	843	894	926	955	961	967	971	975	979	982	984	986	988	990	991	992	993	994	995
3	485	747	829	880	927	937	946	954	960	966	971	975	978	981	984	986	988	989	991	992
4	259	636	754	827	895	910	923	934	943	951	958	963	968	973	976	979	982	985	987	988
5		508	667	767	858	878	896	911	923	934	943	951	957	963	968	972	976	979	982	984
6		362	568	697	815	842	865	884	900	914	926	936	945	952	959	964	969	973	977	980
7		193	454	618	767	801	829	853	874	891	906	919	930	939	948	955	961	966	970	974
8			323	526	711	753	788	818	844	865	884	900	913	925	935	944	951	958	963	968
9			173	420	646	698	741	778	809	835	858	877	894	908	921	931	940	948	955	961
10				299	572	635	687	731	769	801	828	852	872	889	904	917	928	937	946	953
11				160	487	562	625	678	723	761	794	822	846	867	885	900	913	925	935	943
12					390	479	553	617	670	716	755	788	817	842	863	881	897	911	922	933
13					277	383	471	546	609	664	710	749	783	812	838	859	878	894	908	920
14					148	272	377	465	540	603	658	705	745	779	809	834	856	875	892	906
15						146	268	372	460	534	598	653	700	740	775	805	831	854	873	890
16							143	265	367	455	530	594	649	696	737	772	802	829	851	871
17								141	262	364	451	526	590	645	693	734	769	800	826	849
18									140	259	361	448	523	587	642	690	731	767	798	824
19										138	257	358	445	520	584	640	688	729	765	796
20											137	255	356	443	517	582	637	686	727	763
21												136	253	354	441	515	580	635	684	725
22													135	252	352	439	513	578	634	682
23														135	251	351	437	512	576	632
24															134	250	350	436	510	575
25																134	249	348	435	509
26																	133	248	347	434
27																		133	247	347
28																			132	247
29																				132

15%

ORIGINAL LOAN TERM

AGE OF LOAN	5	8	10	12	15	16	17	18	19	20	21	22	23	24	25	26	27	28	29	30
1	855	930	953	968	981	984	986	988	990	991	993	994	995	995	996	997	997	997	998	998
2	686	849	899	930	958	965	970	975	978	981	984	986	988	990	991	993	994	995	995	996
3	491	754	836	887	933	943	951	959	965	970	974	978	981	984	986	988	990	991	992	993
4	264	645	763	836	902	917	930	940	949	956	963	968	973	977	980	983	985	987	989	991
5		518	678	778	868	888	905	919	931	941	949	957	963	968	973	977	980	983	985	987
6		370	580	710	827	853	875	894	910	923	934	943	952	958	964	969	974	977	981	983
7		199	465	631	780	813	842	865	885	902	916	928	938	947	955	961	967	971	975	979
8			333	539	725	767	802	832	856	877	895	910	923	934	943	951	958	964	969	973
9			179	433	662	713	757	793	823	849	871	889	905	919	930	940	949	956	962	967
10				310	588	651	704	748	785	816	843	865	885	901	915	927	937	946	954	960
11				166	503	579	642	695	740	778	810	838	861	881	898	912	924	935	944	952
12					404	495	571	635	688	734	772	805	833	857	877	894	909	922	933	942
13					289	397	488	564	628	682	728	767	801	829	853	874	892	907	920	931
14					155	284	392	482	558	623	677	724	763	797	826	850	872	890	905	918
15						153	280	387	477	554	618	673	720	760	794	823	848	869	888	903
16							150	277	383	473	549	614	669	717	757	791	821	846	867	886
17								149	274	380	470	546	611	666	714	754	789	819	844	866
18									147	272	377	467	543	608	664	711	752	787	817	842
19										146	270	375	464	541	606	661	709	750	785	815
20											145	268	373	462	538	604	660	707	749	784
21												144	266	371	460	537	602	658	706	747
22													143	265	369	459	535	600	656	705
23														142	264	368	457	534	599	655
24															142	263	367	456	532	598
25																141	262	366	455	532
26																	141	262	365	454
27																		141	261	365
28																			140	261
29																				140

lender yield after points

Appendix 3
Points Discount Tables

Example: $50,000 loan @ 12¼% for 30 years

Problem: find lender's yield if two points are charged

Step 1
Choose the **chart** that corresponds to the stated interest rate.

Step 2
Choose the **column** that corresponds to the term of the loan. For a 30-year loan, use the third column from the right.

INTEREST RATE	NET %				LOAN TERM IN YEARS				
		5	10	15	20	25	30	35	40
	95	14.54	13.55	13.23	13.08	13.00	12.96	12.93	12.92
	96	14.07	13.28	13.03	12.91	12.85	12.81	12.79	12.78
12¼%	97	13.60	13.02	12.83	12.74	12.69	12.67	12.65	12.64
	98	13.15	12.76	12.63	12.57	12.54	12.53	12.52	12.51
	99	12.69	12.50	12.44	12.41	12.40	12.39	12.38	12.38

Step 3
Choose the **row** that corresponds to the discount. For a two-point discount, the net % of the loan (the amount the borrower actually receives) is 98 (100% − 2% = 98%).

Step 4
Locate the number at the intersection of the appropriate column and row. This is the lender's yield. For a 30-year, 12¼% loan with two points charged, the yield is **12.53%**.

If the discount had been **four** points, the net % would be **96** (100 − 4 = 96) and the lender's yield would be **12.81%**.

INTEREST RATE	NET %	LOAN TERM IN YEARS							
		5	10	15	20	25	30	35	40
8%	95	10.20	9.19	8.86	8.70	8.61	8.55	8.51	8.48
	96	9.74	8.95	8.68	8.55	8.48	8.44	8.40	8.38
	97	9.30	8.70	8.51	8.41	8.36	8.32	8.30	8.29
	98	8.86	8.47	8.34	8.27	8.24	8.21	8.20	8.19
	99	8.43	8.23	8.17	8.14	8.12	8.11	8.10	8.09
8¼%	95	10.45	9.45	9.12	8.96	8.86	8.81	8.77	8.74
	96	10.00	9.20	8.94	8.81	8.74	8.69	8.66	8.64
	97	9.55	8.96	8.76	8.67	8.61	8.58	8.56	8.54
	98	9.11	8.72	8.59	8.53	8.49	8.47	8.45	8.44
	99	8.68	8.48	8.42	8.39	8.37	8.36	8.35	8.35
8½	95	10.71	9.70	9.37	9.21	9.12	9.07	9.03	9.00
	96	10.25	9.46	9.19	9.07	8.99	8.95	8.92	8.90
	97	9.80	9.21	9.02	8.92	8.87	8.83	8.81	8.80
	98	9.36	8.97	8.84	8.78	8.74	8.72	8.71	8.70
	99	8.39	8.73	8.67	8.64	8.62	8.61	8.60	8.60
8¾%	95	10.96	9.96	9.63	9.47	9.38	9.32	9.29	9.26
	96	10.51	9.71	9.45	9.32	9.25	9.21	9.18	9.16
	97	10.06	9.46	9.27	9.18	9.12	9.09	9.07	9.05
	98	9.62	9.22	9.09	9.03	9.00	8.97	8.96	8.95
	99	9.18	8.98	8.92	8.89	8.87	8.86	8.85	8.85
9%	95	11.12	10.11	9.78	9.63	9.54	9.48	9.44	9.42
	96	10.66	9.86	9.60	9.48	9.40	9.36	9.33	9.31
	97	10.21	9.62	9.42	9.33	9.27	9.24	9.22	9.21
	98	9.77	9.37	9.25	9.18	9.15	9.13	9.11	9.10
	99	9.33	9.14	9.07	9.04	9.02	9.01	9.01	9.00
9¼%	95	11.47	10.47	10.14	9.99	9.90	9.84	9.81	9.78
	96	11.01	10.22	9.96	9.83	9.76	9.72	9.69	9.67
	97	10.56	9.97	9.78	9.68	9.63	9.60	9.58	9.56
	98	10.12	9.73	9.60	9.54	9.50	9.48	9.47	9.46
	99	9.68	9.49	9.42	9.39	9.38	9.36	9.36	9.35

INTEREST RATE	NET %	LOAN TERM IN YEARS							
		5	10	15	20	25	30	35	40
9½%	95	11.73	10.73	10.40	10.24	10.16	10.10	10.07	10.05
	96	11.27	10.47	10.21	10.09	10.02	9.98	9.95	9.93
	97	10.82	10.22	10.03	9.94	9.89	9.85	9.83	9.82
	98	10.37	9.98	9.85	9.79	9.76	9.73	9.72	9.71
	99	9.93	9.74	9.67	9.64	9.63	9.62	9.61	9.61
9¾%	95	11.98	10.98	10.66	10.50	10.41	10.36	10.33	10.31
	96	11.52	10.73	10.47	10.35	10.28	10.23	10.21	10.19
	97	11.07	10.48	10.29	10.19	10.14	10.11	10.09	10.08
	98	10.62	10.23	10.10	10.04	10.01	9.99	9.97	9.97
	99	10.18	9.99	9.93	9.90	9.88	9.87	9.86	9.86
10%	95	12.24	11.34	10.91	10.76	10.67	10.62	10.59	10.57
	96	11.78	10.98	10.72	10.60	10.53	10.49	10.47	10.45
	97	11.32	10.73	10.54	10.45	10.40	10.37	10.35	10.33
	98	10.88	10.48	10.36	10.30	10.26	10.24	10.23	10.22
	99	10.43	10.24	10.18	10.15	10.13	10.12	10.11	10.11
10¼%	95	12.49	11.50	11.17	11.02	10.93	10.88	10.85	10.83
	96	12.03	11.24	10.98	10.86	10.79	10.75	10.72	10.71
	97	11.58	10.99	10.79	10.70	10.65	10.62	10.60	10.59
	98	11.13	10.74	10.61	10.55	10.52	10.50	10.48	10.47
	99	10.69	10.49	10.43	10.40	10.38	10.37	10.37	10.36
10½%	95	12.75	11.75	11.43	11.27	11.19	11.14	11.11	11.09
	96	12.29	11.49	11.24	11.11	11.05	11.01	10.98	10.97
	97	11.83	11.24	11.05	10.96	10.91	10.88	10.86	10.85
	98	11.38	10.99	10.86	10.80	10.77	10.75	10.74	10.73
	99	10.94	10.74	10.68	10.65	10.63	10.62	10.62	10.61
10¾%	95	13.01	12.01	11.68	11.53	11.45	11.40	11.37	11.35
	96	12.54	11.75	11.49	11.37	11.30	11.26	11.24	11.22
	97	12.08	11.49	11.30	11.21	11.16	11.13	11.11	11.10
	98	11.63	11.24	11.11	11.06	11.02	11.00	10.99	10.98
	99	11.19	10.99	10.93	10.90	10.89	10.88	10.87	10.87
11%	95	13.26	12.26	11.94	11.79	11.71	11.66	11.63	11.61
	96	12.80	12.00	11.75	11.63	11.56	11.52	11.50	11.48
	97	12.34	11.75	11.56	11.47	11.42	11.39	11.37	11.36
	98	11.88	11.49	11.37	11.31	11.28	11.26	11.24	11.24
	99	11.44	11.25	11.18	11.15	11.14	11.13	11.12	11.12

INTEREST RATE	NET %	LOAN TERM IN YEARS							
		5	10	15	20	25	30	35	40
11¼%	95	13.52	12.52	12.20	12.05	11.97	11.92	11.89	11.87
	96	13.05	12.26	12.00	11.88	11.82	11.78	11.76	11.74
	97	12.59	12.00	11.81	11.72	11.67	11.64	11.63	11.62
	98	12.14	11.75	11.62	11.56	11.53	11.51	11.50	11.49
	99	11.69	11.50	11.43	11.40	11.39	11.38	11.37	11.37
11½%	95	13.77	12.78	12.46	12.31	12.23	12.18	12.15	12.13
	96	13.30	12.51	12.26	12.14	12.08	12.04	12.02	12.00
	97	12.84	12.25	12.06	11.98	11.93	11.90	11.88	11.87
	98	12.39	12.00	11.87	11.81	11.78	11.76	11.75	11.75
	99	11.94	11.75	11.69	11.66	11.64	11.63	11.63	11.62
11¾%	95	14.03	13.03	12.71	12.57	12.49	12.44	12.41	12.39
	96	13.56	12.77	12.51	12.40	12.33	12.30	12.27	12.26
	97	13.10	12.51	12.32	12.23	12.18	12.16	12.14	12.13
	98	12.64	12.25	12.13	12.07	12.04	12.02	12.01	12.00
	99	12.19	12.00	11.94	11.91	11.89	11.88	11.88	11.87
12%	95	14.28	13.29	12.97	12.82	12.74	12.70	12.67	12.66
	96	13.81	13.02	12.77	12.65	12.59	12.55	12.53	12.52
	97	13.35	12.76	12.57	12.49	12.44	12.41	12.40	12.39
	98	12.89	12.50	12.38	12.32	12.29	12.27	12.26	12.25
	99	12.44	12.25	12.19	12.16	12.14	12.13	12.13	12.13
12¼%	95	14.54	13.55	13.23	13.08	13.00	12.96	12.93	12.92
	96	14.07	13.28	13.03	12.91	12.85	12.81	12.79	12.78
	97	13.60	13.02	12.83	12.74	12.69	12.67	12.65	12.64
	98	13.15	12.76	12.63	12.57	12.54	12.53	12.52	12.51
	99	12.69	12.50	12.44	12.41	12.40	12.39	12.38	12.38
12½%	95	14.79	13.80	13.49	13.34	13.26	13.22	13.19	13.18
	96	14.32	13.53	13.28	13.17	13.11	13.07	13.05	13.04
	97	13.86	13.27	13.08	13.00	12.95	12.92	12.91	12.90
	98	13.40	13.01	12.88	12.83	12.80	12.78	12.77	12.76
	99	12.95	12.75	12.69	12.66	12.65	12.64	12.63	12.63
12¾%	95	15.05	14.06	13.74	13.60	13.52	13.48	13.46	13.44
	96	14.58	13.79	13.54	13.42	13.36	13.33	13.31	13.30
	97	14.11	13.52	13.34	13.25	13.21	13.18	13.17	13.16
	98	13.65	13.26	13.14	13.08	13.05	13.03	13.02	13.02
	99	13.20	13.00	12.94	12.91	12.90	12.89	12.89	12.88

INTEREST RATE	NET %	LOAN TERM IN YEARS							
		5	10	15	20	25	30	35	40
13%	95	15.31	14.32	14.00	13.86	13.78	13.74	13.72	13.70
	96	14.83	14.04	13.79	13.68	13.62	13.59	13.57	13.56
	97	14.36	13.78	13.59	13.51	13.46	13.44	13.42	13.41
	98	13.90	13.51	13.39	13.33	13.30	13.29	13.28	13.27
	99	13.45	13.26	13.19	13.17	13.15	13.14	13.14	13.14
13¼%	95	15.56	14.57	14.26	14.12	14.04	14.00	13.98	13.97
	96	15.09	14.30	14.05	13.94	13.88	13.85	13.83	13.82
	97	14.62	14.03	13.85	13.76	13.72	13.69	13.68	13.67
	98	14.15	13.77	13.64	13.59	13.56	13.54	13.53	13.53
	99	13.70	13.51	13.45	13.42	13.40	13.39	13.39	13.39
13½	95	15.82	14.83	14.52	14.38	14.30	14.26	14.24	14.23
	96	15.34	14.55	14.31	14.19	14.14	14.10	14.09	14.08
	97	14.87	14.28	14.10	14.02	13.97	13.95	13.94	13.93
	98	14.41	14.02	13.90	13.84	13.81	13.80	13.79	13.78
	99	13.95	13.76	13.70	13.67	13.65	13.65	13.64	13.64
13¾%	95	16.07	15.09	14.77	14.63	14.56	14.52	14.50	14.49
	96	15.59	14.81	14.56	14.45	14.39	14.36	14.35	14.34
	97	15.12	14.54	14.35	14.27	14.23	14.21	14.19	14.18
	98	14.66	14.27	14.15	14.09	14.07	14.05	14.04	14.04
	99	14.20	14.01	13.95	13.92	13.91	13.90	13.89	13.89
14%	95	16.33	15.34	15.03	14.89	14.82	14.78	14.76	14.75
	96	15.85	15.07	14.82	14.71	14.65	14.62	14.60	14.60
	97	15.38	14.79	14.61	14.53	14.48	14.46	14.45	14.44
	98	14.91	14.52	14.40	14.35	14.32	14.30	14.30	14.29
	99	14.45	14.26	14.20	14.17	14.16	14.15	14.15	14.14
14¼%	95	16.58	15.60	15.29	15.15	15.08	15.05	15.02	15.01
	96	16.10	15.32	15.08	14.97	14.91	14.88	14.86	14.85
	97	15.63	15.05	14.86	14.78	14.74	14.72	14.71	14.70
	98	15.16	14.78	14.66	14.60	14.57	14.56	14.55	14.55
	99	14.70	14.51	14.45	14.42	14.41	14.40	14.40	14.40
14½%	95	16.84	15.86	15.55	15.41	15.34	15.31	15.29	15.28
	96	16.36	15.58	15.33	15.22	15.17	15.14	15.12	15.11
	97	15.88	15.30	15.12	15.04	15.00	14.97	14.96	14.96
	98	15.42	15.03	14.91	14.86	14.83	14.81	14.81	14.80
	99	14.95	14.76	14.70	14.68	14.66	14.66	14.65	14.65

INTEREST RATE	NET %	LOAN TERM IN YEARS							
		5	**10**	**15**	**20**	**25**	**30**	**35**	**40**
14¾%	95	17.10	16.11	15.81	15.67	15.60	15.57	15.55	15.54
	96	16.61	15.83	15.59	15.48	15.43	15.40	15.38	15.37
	97	16.14	15.55	15.37	15.29	15.25	15.23	15.22	15.21
	98	15.67	15.28	15.16	15.11	15.08	15.07	15.06	15.06
	99	15.21	15.01	14.95	14.93	14.91	14.91	14.90	14.90
15%	95	17.35	16.37	16.07	15.93	15.86	15.83	15.81	15.80
	96	16.87	16.09	15.84	15.74	15.68	15.66	15.64	15.63
	97	16.39	15.81	15.63	15.55	15.51	15.49	15.48	15.47
	98	15.92	15.54	15.42	15.36	15.34	15.32	15.31	15.31
	99	15.46	15.27	15.21	15.18	15.17	15.16	15.16	15.15
15¼%	95	17.61	16.63	16.32	16.19	16.12	16.09	16.07	16.06
	96	17.12	16.34	16.10	16.00	15.94	15.92	15.90	15.89
	97	16.64	16.06	15.88	15.80	15.77	15.74	15.73	15.73
	98	16.17	15.79	15.67	15.62	15.59	15.58	15.57	15.57
	99	15.71	15.52	15.46	15.43	15.42	15.41	15.41	15.41
15½%	95	17.86	16.88	16.58	16.45	16.39	16.35	16.33	16.33
	96	17.38	16.60	16.36	16.25	16.20	16.17	16.16	16.15
	97	16.90	16.32	16.14	16.06	16.02	16.00	15.99	15.99
	98	16.42	16.04	15.92	15.87	15.84	15.83	15.82	15.82
	99	15.96	15.77	15.71	15.68	15.67	15.66	15.66	15.66
15¾%	95	18.12	17.14	16.84	16.71	16.65	16.61	16.60	16.59
	96	17.63	16.85	16.61	16.51	16.46	16.43	16.42	16.41
	97	17.15	16.57	16.39	16.32	16.28	16.26	16.25	16.24
	98	16.68	16.29	16.18	16.12	16.10	16.09	16.08	16.08
	99	16.21	16.20	15.96	15.94	15.92	15.92	15.91	15.91
16%	95	18.38	17.40	17.10	16.97	16.91	16.88	16.86	16.85
	96	17.89	17.11	16.87	16.77	16.72	16.69	16.68	16.67
	97	17.40	16.83	16.65	16.57	16.53	16.51	16.51	16.50
	98	16.93	16.55	16.43	16.38	16.35	16.34	16.33	16.33
	99	16.46	16.27	16.21	16.19	16.17	16.17	16.17	16.16
16¼%	95	18.63	17.66	17.36	17.23	17.17	17.14	17.12	17.11
	96	18.14	17.37	17.13	17.03	16.98	16.95	16.94	16.93
	97	17.66	17.08	16.90	16.83	16.79	16.77	16.76	16.76
	98	17.18	16.80	16.68	16.63	16.61	16.59	16.59	16.58
	99	16.71	16.52	16.46	16.44	16.43	16.42	16.42	16.42

INTEREST RATE	NET %	LOAN TERM IN YEARS							
		5	10	15	20	25	30	35	40
16½%	95	18.89	17.91	17.62	17.49	17.43	17.40	17.38	17.38
	96	18.40	17.62	17.38	17.28	17.24	17.21	17.20	17.19
	97	17.91	17.33	17.16	17.08	17.05	17.03	17.02	17.01
	98	17.43	17.05	16.93	16.89	16.86	16.85	16.84	16.84
	99	16.96	16.77	16.72	16.69	16.68	16.67	16.67	16.67
16¾%	95	19.14	18.17	17.87	17.75	17.69	17.66	17.65	17.64
	96	18.65	17.88	17.64	17.54	17.49	17.47	17.46	17.45
	97	18.16	17.59	17.41	17.34	17.30	17.29	17.28	17.27
	98	17.69	17.30	17.19	17.14	17.12	17.10	17.10	17.09
	99	17.21	17.03	16.97	16.94	16.93	16.93	16.92	16.92
17%	95	19.40	18.43	18.13	18.01	17.95	17.92	17.91	17.90
	96	18.90	18.13	17.90	17.80	17.75	17.73	17.72	17.71
	97	18.42	17.84	17.67	17.59	17.56	17.54	17.53	17.53
	98	17.94	17.56	17.44	17.39	17.37	17.36	17.35	17.35
	99	17.47	17.28	17.22	17.19	17.18	17.18	17.17	17.17
17¼%	95	19.66	18.68	18.39	18.27	18.21	18.18	18.17	18.16
	96	19.16	18.39	18.16	18.06	18.01	17.99	17.98	17.97
	97	18.67	18.10	17.92	17.85	17.82	17.80	17.79	17.79
	98	18.19	17.81	17.70	17.65	17.62	17.61	17.61	17.60
	99	17.72	17.53	17.47	17.45	17.44	17.43	17.43	17.43
17½%	95	19.91	18.94	18.65	18.53	18.47	18.45	18.43	18.43
	96	19.41	18.64	18.41	18.32	18.27	18.25	18.24	18.23
	97	18.92	18.35	18.18	18.11	18.07	18.06	18.05	18.04
	98	18.44	18.06	17.95	17.90	17.88	17.87	17.86	17.86
	99	17.97	17.78	17.72	17.70	17.69	17.68	17.68	17.68
17¾%	95	20.17	19.20	18.91	18.79	18.73	18.71	18.70	18.69
	96	19.67	18.90	18.67	18.57	18.53	18.51	18.50	18.49
	97	19.18	18.61	18.43	18.36	18.33	18.31	18.31	18.30
	98	18.70	18.32	18.20	18.15	18.13	18.12	18.12	18.11
	99	18.22	18.03	17.97	17.95	17.94	17.93	17.93	17.93
18%	95	20.42	19.46	19.17	19.05	19.00	18.97	18.96	18.95
	96	19.92	19.16	18.96	18.83	18.79	18.77	18.76	18.75
	97	19.43	18.86	18.69	18.62	18.59	18.57	18.56	18.56
	98	18.95	18.57	18.46	18.41	18.39	18.38	18.37	18.37
	99	18.47	18.28	18.23	18.20	18.19	18.19	18.18	18.18

Appendix 4
Using The Texas Instruments BA II

INTRODUCTION

The Texas Instruments Business Analyst II is designed to perform a wide variety of algebraic, statistical and financial calculations. Many of these functions are beyond the knowledge needed by residential real estate sales agents. This supplement will cover only those functions that pertain to the financial aspects of residential transactions covered in the book. Explanations of particular calculations (such as calculating the monthly payment for a mortgage) will be covered in the same order in this supplement as the corresponding material and calculations first appear in the text.

While explaining the key sequences used to work various types of calculations, the keys will be designated in two ways:

1) the digit keys (1, 2, 3, 4, 5, 6, 7, 8, 9, 0) will be indicated by the corresponding arabic numeral;

2) the function keys will be indicated by a symbol placed within brackets.

EXAMPLE:

The problem, "What is seven plus four?" will be shown as:

7 [+] 4 [=] 11.00

CALCULATOR OVERVIEW

BASIC CALCULATIONS

[+] The add key tells the calculator to add the next number you enter to the number displayed.

EXAMPLE:

5 [+] 1 [=]   6.00

[−] The subtract key tells the calculator to subtract the next number you enter from the number displayed.

EXAMPLE:

5 [−] 1 [=]   4.00

[×] The multiply key tells the calculator to multiply the displayed number by the next number you enter.

EXAMPLE:

4 [×] 2 [=]   8.00

[÷] The divide key tells the calculator to divide the displayed number by the next number you enter.

EXAMPLE:

6 [÷] 2 [=]   3.00

[=] The equals key completes any of the basic calculations.

THE [2nd] KEY

[2nd]   Pressing this key allows you to use the operations printed ABOVE the keys. For example, [2nd] [FIX] gives you the MODE function; [2nd] [STO] gives you the CORR function; etc.

MEMORY OPERATIONS

[ON/C][STO]   Clears display and memory

[STO]   Stores the displayed value in memory

[RCL]   Recalls the value in memory to the display

[SUM]   Adds the displayed value to the value previously stored in memory

[EXC]   Exchanges the displayed value with the value previously stored in memory

SPECIAL FUNCTION KEYS

[K]   This key stores the displayed number AND an operation (+, −, ×, ÷, %) for performing repetitive calculations.

[+/−]   This key changes the sign of the displayed number.

[X = Y]   This key exchanges the displayed number ("X") with the number in the "Y" register.

MODE FUNCTIONS KEYS

[2nd] [FIX]   This sequence gives you the MODE function. It changes the calculator function to the next mode in sequence: profit margin, financial or statistical. Here, we will always be using the financial mode. Press [2nd] [FIX] and repeat until "FIN" appears at the left side of the display.

[2nd] [DUE]   This sequence gives you the CMR function. It clears all the data sorted in the mode registers.

FINANCIAL MODE KEYS

[N]   This key places the displayed number into the "N" register, which represents the number of payments or compounding periods. For example, a 30-year loan with monthly payments would have a total of 360 payments (30 x 12 = 360), so the number 360 would be placed in the "N" register.

[%i]   This key places the displayed number into the "%i" register, which represents the interest rate per compounding period. For example, a loan with monthly payments and an interest rate of 10% per year would have .83 interest per month (10 ÷ 12 = .83), so .83 would be placed in the "%i" register.

NOTE: The time period of the data stored in the "N" register MUST correspond to the time period of the data stored in the "%i" register. For example, if the payment periods are monthly, then the interest rate must also be a monthly rate.

[PMT]   This key places the displayed number into the "PMT" register, which represents the periodic payment amount.

[PV]   This key places the displayed number into the "PV" register, which represents the present value of something in today's dollars (in our case, usually a loan amount).

[FV]   This key places the displayed number into the "FV" register, which represents the future value of something at some specified time in the future.

REAL ESTATE FINANCIAL CALCULATIONS

CALCULATING THE MONTHLY PAYMENT

Procedure: You can solve for the loan amount, interest rate, number of payments or amount of payment by entering three of the values and then pressing the "2nd" key and the key for the value being sought. To solve for the monthly payments, calculate and enter the number of monthly payments, calculate and enter the monthly percentage rate, enter the loan amount, and then press the "2nd" key and the "PMT" key to find the amount of the payments. Remember to convert years to months and annual interest to monthly interest when solving for a monthly payment.

Example: What would be the monthly payment of principal and interest for a loan with a principal amount of $92,000, an annual interest rate of 10.5%, and a term of 30 years?

NUMBER OF PAYMENTS: Monthly for 30 years
INTEREST RATE: 10.5% per year
LOAN AMOUNT: $92,000
MONTHLY PAYMENT: ?

STEP 1: Calculate and enter the number of payments.

STEP 2: Calculate and enter the monthly interest rate.

STEP 3: Enter loan amount.

STEP 4: Compute monthly payment.

STEP	KEY SEQUENCE	DISPLAY
1	30 [×] 12 [=] [N]	360.00
2	10.5 [÷] 12 [=] [%i]	0.88
3	92000 [PV]	92000.00
4	[2nd] [PMT]	841.56

Answer: The monthly payment is $841.56.

CALCULATING TEMPORARY BUYDOWNS

Procedure: For an estimate of the cost of a buydown, compute the monthly payment at the note rate. Then find the amount of the subsidized payment. If the buydown is a graduated payment buydown, such as a "3-2-1 Buydown," the amount of the subsidized payment will be different for each year of the buydown period. Then calculate the difference between the actual payments (at the bought down rate) and the note rate payments for the entire buydown period.

Example: The lender offers an $80,000 loan for 30 years at an annual interest rate of 12%. The builder offers to buy down the interest rate by 3% the first year, 2% the second year, and 1% the third year. What would be the cost of the buydown?

NUMBER OF PAYMENTS: monthly for 30 years
NOTE INTEREST RATE: 12% per year
PAYMENT RATE IN THE FIRST YEAR: 9%
PAYMENT RATE IN THE SECOND YEAR: 10%
PAYMENT RATE IN THE THIRD YEAR: 11%
LOAN AMOUNT: $80,000
COST OF BUYDOWN: ?

STEP 1: Calculate and enter the number of payments.

STEP 2: Calculate and enter the periodic note rate.

STEP 3: Enter the loan amount.

STEP 4: Compute the payment at the note rate; store this value in memory.

STEP 5: Substitute the buydown rate for year 1.

STEP 6: Compute the payment amount for year 1.

STEP 7: Subtract the first year payment from the note rate payment and multiply by 12 for the total subsidy in year 1; WRITE DOWN THE RESULT.

STEP 8: Enter the buydown rate for year 2.

STEP 9: Compute the payment amount for year 2.

STEP 10: Subtract the second year payment from the note rate payment and multiply by 12 for the total subsidy in year 2; WRITE DOWN THE RESULT.

STEP 11: Enter the buydown rate for year 3.

STEP 12: Compute the payment amount for year 2.

STEP 13: Subtract the third year payment from the note rate payment and multiply by 12 for the total subsidy in year 3; WRITE DOWN THE RESULT.

STEP 14: Add the values from steps 7, 10 and 13 to find the total buydown amount.

STEP	KEY SEQUENCE	DISPLAY
1	30 [×] 12 [=] [N]	360.00
2	12 [÷] 12 [=] [%i]	1.00
3	80000 [PV]	80000.00
4	[2nd] [PMT] [STO]	822.89
5	9 [÷] 12 [=] [%i]	0.75
6	[2nd] [PMT]	643.70
7	[−] [RCL] [=] [+/−] [×] 12 [=]	2150.30
8	10 [÷] 12 [=] [%i]	0.83
9	[2nd] [PMT]	702.06
10	[−] [RCL] [=] [+/−] [×] 12 [=]	1449.99
11	11 [÷] 12 [=] [%i]	0.92
12	[2nd] [PMT]	761.86
13	[−] [RCL] [=] [+/−] [×] 12 [=]	732.38
14	2150.30 [+] 1449.99 [+] 732.38 [=]	4332.67

Answer: The cost of the 3-2-1 buydown would be $4,332.67.

CALCULATING PAYMENTS FOR ADJUSTABLE-RATE MORTGAGES

Procedure: First find the monthly payment for the first year. Next compute the loan balance after the first year, and then compute the payment needed to pay off this balance over the remainder of the loan term at the new interest rate. Repeat the process to find the payment for the third year and any succeeding year(s).

Example: The lender offers an adjustable-rate loan for $90,000 with a term of 30 years. The initial interest rate is 7.5%, with annual adjustments not to exceed 2% per year and a lifetime cap of 5% above or below the initial rate. If the rate increases to 9.5% the second year, what will the payments be for the second year? If the interest rate is decreased to 8.5% for the third year, what will the payments be for the third year?

NUMBER OF PAYMENTS: monthly for 30 years
FIRST YEAR INTEREST RATE: 7.5%
SECOND YEAR INTEREST RATE: 9.5%
THIRD YEAR INTEREST RATE: 8.5%
LOAN AMOUNT: $90,000
MONTHLY PAYMENT IN YEAR 2: ?
MONTHLY PAYMENT IN YEAR 3: ?

STEP   1:   Calculate and enter the number of payments.

STEP   2:   Calculate and enter the periodic interest rate for the first year.

STEP   3:   Enter the loan amount.

STEP   4:   Compute the first year payment.

447

STEP 5: Compute the loan balance after one year and enter this value as the new loan amount for determining the second year payment.

STEP 6: Calculate and enter the number of payments remaining after one year.

STEP 7: Calculate and enter the second year periodic interest rate.

STEP 8: Compute the second year payment.

STEP 9: Compute the loan balance at the end of the second year and enter this value as the new loan amount for determining the third year payment.

STEP 10: Calculate and enter the number of payments remaining after the second year.

STEP 11: Calculate and enter the third year periodic interest rate.

STEP 12: Compute the third year payment.

STEP	KEY SEQUENCE	DISPLAY
1	30 [×] 12 [=] [N]	360.00
2	7.5 [÷] 12 [=] [%i]	0.63
3	90000 [PV]	90000.00
4	[2nd] [PMT]	629.29
5	12 [2nd] [K] [x=y] [PV]	89170.35
6	[2nd] [N]	348.00
7	9.5 [÷] 12 [=] [%i]	0.79
8	[2nd] [PMT]	754.44
9	12 [2nd] [K] [x=y] [PV]	88562.16
10	[2nd] [N]	336.00
11	8.5 [÷] 12 [=] [%i]	0.71
12	[2nd] [PMT]	691.89

Answer: The second year payment would be $754.44 and the third year payment would be $691.89.

CALCULATING PAYMENTS ON A GEM LOAN

Procedure: Enter the three known values and compute the monthly payment. Then compute each of the following years' payments in order.

Example: A lender offers a GEM loan of $85,000 with a fixed interest rate of 10.5% and a term of 30 years. Monthly payments are to increase 3% per year. What would the buyer's monthly payments be for each of the first five years of the loan?

NUMBER OF PAYMENTS: monthly for 30 years
INTEREST RATE: 10.5% per year
LOAN AMOUNT: $85,000
MONTHLY PAYMENT FOR YEAR 1, 2, 3, 4, 5: ?

STEP 1: Calculate and enter the number of payments.

STEP 2: Calculate and enter the monthly interest rate.

STEP 3: Enter the loan amount.

STEP 4: Compute the first year payment amount.

STEP 5: Calculate the second year payment amount using the [K] key to store the "add 3%" operation for calculating payments for successive years.

STEPS 6-8: Calculate the payments for years 3-5.

STEP	KEY SEQUENCE	DISPLAY
1	30 [×] 12 [=] [N]	360.00
2	10.5 [÷] 12 [=] [%i]	0.88
3	85000 [PV]	85000.00
4	[2nd] [PMT]	777.53
5	[+] 3 [%] [K] [=]	800.85
6	[=]	824.88
7	[=]	849.63
8	[=]	875.12

Answer: The monthly payments for years 1-5 are $777.53, $800.85, $824.88, $849.63, and $875.12.

CALCULATING THE LOAN BALANCE (BALLOON PAYMENT) AT THE END OF A SPECIFIED TERM

Procedure: First calculate the monthly payment by entering the known values and pressing [2nd] [PMT]. You must then REENTER the payment amount to the nearest penny because the actual payments will not reflect the fractions of a penny in the calculator's "PMT" register. Now you can calculate the loan balance.

Example: The seller has agreed to take back a second note and trust deed in the amount of $25,000 with an annual interest rate of 10%. Monthly payments are to be made based upon a 30-year amortization schedule with the outstanding balance due in five years. What will the balloon payment be in five years?

NUMBER OF PAYMENTS: monthly for 30 years
INTEREST RATE: 10% per year
LOAN AMOUNT: $25,000
MONTHLY PAYMENT: ?
LOAN BALANCE (BALLOON PAYMENT) AFTER
5 YEARS: ?

STEP 1: Enter the number of payments.

STEP 2: Enter the periodic interest rate.

STEP 3: Enter the loan amount.

STEP 4: Calculate the payment.

STEP 5: Reenter the payment amount to the
nearest penny.

STEP 6: Recalculate the number of payments
at the revised payment amount.

STEP 7: Calculate the loan balance after 5
years.

STEP	KEY SEQUENCE	DISPLAY
1	30 [×] 12 [=] [N]	360.00
2	10 [÷] 12 [=] [%i]	0.83
3	25000 [PV]	25000.00
4	[2nd] [PMT]	219.39
5	219.39 [PMT]	219.39
6	[2nd] [N]	360.03
7	5 [×] 12 [=] [2nd] [K] [x=y]	24143.80

Answer: The remaining principal balance at the
end of five years would be $24,143.80. The balloon
payment would be the remaining principal balance
plus the last monthly payment of $219.39, for a
total of $24,363.19.

CALCULATING THE NUMBER OF PAYMENTS REMAINING ON A LOAN

Procedure: Enter the three known values and then press [2nd] [N] to calculate the number of payments remaining.

Example: The seller has an existing loan with monthly principal and interest payments of $797.11. The annual interest rate is 10.75%. The current outstanding principal balance is $78,000. How many monthly payments remain on the loan?

INTEREST RATE: 10.75% per year
MONTHLY PAYMENT: $797.11
CURRENT LOAN BALANCE: $78,000
NUMBER OF PAYMENTS REMAINING: ?

STEP	KEY SEQUENCE	DISPLAY
1	10.75 [÷] 12 [=] [%i]	0.90
2	797.11 [PMT]	797.11
3	78000 [PV]	78000.00
4	[2nd] [N]	234.61

Answer: There are 234.61 payments remaining on the loan.

CALCULATING THE LOAN AMOUNT THE BUYER CAN AFFORD

Procedure: Calculate the amount the buyer can afford for principal and interest per month. Use this value with the other two known values to compute the loan amount at a particular interest rate.

Example:

Based on the conventional loan housing expense-to-income ratios, the buyer can afford a monthly housing expense of $967. If approximately 10% of the monthly housing expense would be needed for taxes and insurance, what would be the maximum loan the buyer could afford for a 30-year, fixed-rate loan at an annual interest rate of 11%?

STEP 1: Calculate and enter the number of payments.

STEP 2: Calculate and enter the periodic interest rate.

STEP 3: Calculate and enter the amount for monthly principal and interest payment.

STEP 4: Calculate the loan amount.

STEP	KEY SEQUENCE	DISPLAY
1	30 [×] 12 [=] [N]	360.00
2	11 [÷] 12 [=] [%i]	0.92
3	967 [−] 10 [%] [=] [PMT]	870.30
4	[2nd] [PV]	91387.02

Answer: The maximum loan amount would be approximately $91,387.

Answer Key

Chapter 8 Exercises—Answer key

Exercise No. 1
1.   Both interest rates and loan fees are generally higher fo

2.   NO. The buyer must make the downpayment on his ow dary financing or gift money.

3.   YES. FNMA guidelines allow a 95% loan to a first-time buyer if the borrower has good credit and sufficient financial assets to carry the mortgage payment. The borrower must normally have on deposit sufficient assets to cover three months of mortgage payments.

Exercise No. 2
1. $85,000 × .75 = $63,750 first loan amount
$85,000 × .15 = $12,750 second loan amount

2. $63,750 × .015 = $956.25 loan fee
$85,000 × .10 = $8,500 one time PMI
$956.25 + 8,500 = $9,456.25 total costs

3.   12.75 × $972 = $12,393 balloon payment

Chapter 9 Exercises—Answer Key

Exercise No. 1
1. $137,000 × .08 = $10,960 8% discount

Exercise No. 2
1. $110,000 × .90 = $99,000 loan amount
$99,000 × .06 = $5,940 buydown (6 points = 1%)

2. $99,000   loan amount
× .0116512   13¾%, 30-year factor
$1,153.47   monthly payment

Exercise No. 3
1. $92,000 × .0087757 = $807.36 1st year payment (10%)
$994 × 92 = $91,448 loan balance after first year
$91,448 × .0103235 = $944.06 payment @ 12%, 29 years
$807.36 × 1.075 = $867.91 maximum payment in year 2

2. $91,448 × .12 (12%) = $10,973.76 interest due in year 2
$867.91 × 12 = $10,414.92 total payments in year 2
$10,973.76 − 10,414.92 = $558.84 interest shortfall in year 2
$558.84 ÷ 12 = $46.57 monthly interest shortfall

No. 4

$82,000 × .0087757 = $719.61 monthly payment @ 10%

$719.61 × 1.03 = $741.20 2nd year payment
$741.20 × 1.03 = $763.44 3rd year payment
$763.44 × 1.03 = $786.34 4th year payment

Chapter 10 Exercises—Answer Key

Exercise No. 1

1.
$73,700	loan amount
× .0114542	13½%, 30-year factor
$844.17	monthly payment

2.
$73,700	loan amount
× .038	financed MIP factor
$2,800.60	MIP

$73,700 + 2,800.60 = $76,500.60
$76,500.60 rounded down to next $1 increment = $76,500

$76,500	loan amount
× .0114542	13½%, 30-year factor
$876.25	monthly payment

Exercise No. 2

1. $25,000 × .97 = $24,250
    $122,000 − $25,000 = $97,000
    $97,000 × .95 = $92,150
    $24,250 + $92,150 = $116,400 (loan amount)

2. $2,000 estimated closing costs

3. $122,000 + $2,000 = $124,000
    $25,000 × .97 = $24,250
    $124,000 − $25,000 = $99,000
    $99,000 × .95 = $94,050
    $24,250 + $94,050 = $118,300 (loan amount)

Exercise No. 3

1.
$70,250	sales price
+ 1,500	allowable closing costs
$71,750	

$25,000 \times .97 = \$24,250$
$\$71,750 - \$25,000 = \$46,750$
$\$46,750 \times .95 = \$44,412.50$
$\$24,250 + \$44,412.50 = \$68,662.50$
$\$68,662.50 \times 1.038 = \$71,271.68$
$71,272 maximum loan, including financed MIP

2. $71,173   loan amount
     × .0116512   13¾%, 30-year factor
     ─────────
        $829.25   monthly payment

Chapter 11 Exercises—Answer Key

Exercise No. 1
1.   Yes. $46,000

2. $28,000 (.40 × 70,000)

Exercise No. 2
1. $36,000   maximum bank of remaining entitlement
        − 17,500   entitlement used on existing loan
        ─────────
        $18,500   maximum remaining entitlement

        $18,500
           × 4
        ─────────
        $74,000   maximum zero down loan

2. $80,000
           × .25
        ─────────
        $20,000   lender requirement for guaranty/cash down
        − 18,500   maximum guaranty for Jeffrey
        ─────────
        $1,500   required cash downpayment

Chapter 13 Exercises—Answer Key

Exercise No. 1
1. $13   hourly wage
           × 40
        ─────────
            $520   weekly wage
           × 52
        ─────────
        $27,040   annual income

457

$27,040 ÷ 12 = $2,253.33 husband's monthly income
$385 × 52 = $20,020 wife's annual income
$20,020 ÷ 12 = $1,668.33 wife's monthly income
$2,253.33 + 1,668.33 = $3,921.66 total stable monthly income
$3,921.66 × .28 = $1,098.07 maximum housing expense

2. $3,921.66 × .36 = $1,411.80 maximum total debt service

3. YES. Husband had special training in Air Force; wife is vocational nurse, which implies special training.

Exercise No. 2

1. $700 × 52 = $36,400 annual income
$36,400 ÷ 12 = $3,033.33 monthly income
$878 ÷ $3,033 = .29 (29%)

2. $878   mortgage payment
      + 212   auto payment

     $1,090   total debt service

$1,090 ÷ 3,033 = .36 (36%)

3. YES. Equity in home ($14,000) plus money in bank ($3,800) total $17,800; he needs $18,400 to close. Also might not be approved for loan (.29 housing expense to income ratio).

4. YES. Savings balance significantly higher than average balance.
Savings account opened recently. Where did additional savings come from? Was it borrowed?

Exercise No. 3

POSITIVE: wife with same employer for last eight years; wife shows advancement with firm
NEGATIVE: possible alimony and/or child support from recent divorce; husband changed employers within last two years; three slow ratings on credit report—all of them open accounts; recent loan from ABC Finance may represent funds borrowed to pay closing costs or downpayment

Exercise No. 4

1. $1,800   husband's gross income
    + 785   wife's gross income

   $2,585   total monthly gross income

2. $2,585   gross income
   × .29   FHA ratio

    $750   maximum housing expense

3. $2,585   gross income
            × .41   FHA ratio
          ─────────
            $1,060   maximum housing expense plus fixed payments

Exercise No. 5

1. $3,401   4. $3,401
                                                    − 1,106
2. $1,031   2,295
            + 75   − 953
          ─────────   ─────────
            $1,106 $1,342

3.   510
              136
              210
               52
            + 45
          ─────────
              953

CASE STUDY

1.   Conventional, 90% LTV, fixed-rate: $681
      Conventional, 90% LTV, adjustable-rate: $681
      Conventional, 95% LTV, fixed-rate: $580
      FHA: $945.75
      VA: $851

2.   Conventional, 90% LTV, fixed-rate: $72,952
      Conventional, 90% LTV, adjustable-rate: $88,566
      Conventional, 95% LTV, fixed-rate: $59,716
      FHA: $90,000 (limited by regional maximum loan amount)
      VA: $96,972 (must qualify under both methods)

3.   VA: allows largest mortgage amount at low interest rates.
      Also, no downpayment required (see Chapter 10).

INCOME QUALIFYING — CONVENTIONAL LOANS
FIXED-RATE, 90% OR LESS LTV

Monthly Gross Income:

Base salary	3525	
Overtime	-0-	
Bonuses	-0-	
Commissions	250	
Other	-0-	
Total	3775	

Long-Term Monthly Debt:

Car payment	380	
Child support	-0-	
Credit cards	30	
Other loans	192	
Other debts	-0-	
Total	602	

(Consider 5% payments on all revolving charges)

Housing Expense-to-Income Ratio:

3775	Stable Monthly Income
x .28	Income Ratio
1057	Maximum Mortgage Payment (PITI)

Total Debt Service Ratio:

3775	Stable Monthly Income
x .36	Income Ratio
1359	Maximum Monthly Obligations

1359	Maximum Monthly Obligations
- 602	Monthly Obligations
757	Maximum Mortgage Payment (PITI)

MAXIMUM MORTGAGE PAYMENT (PITI)_____757_____

757	Maximum PITI
- 76	(less 10% of mortgage payment) (Insurance, taxes, PMI)
681	Maximum Principal and Interest Payment

72,952	**MAXIMUM LOAN AMOUNT** (using calculator or interest factor tables)

INCOME QUALIFYING — CONVENTIONAL LOANS
FIXED-RATE, MORE THAN 90% LTV

Monthly Gross Income:

		Long-Term Monthly Debt:	
Base salary	3525	Car payment	380
Overtime	−0−	Child support	−0−
Bonuses	−0−	Credit cards	30
Commissions	250	Other loans	192
Other		Other debts	−0−
Total	3775	**Total**	602

(Consider 5% payments on all revolving charges)

Housing Expense-to-Income Ratio

3775	Stable Monthly Income
x .28	Income Ratio
1,057	Maximum Mortgage Payment (PITI)

Total Debt Service Ratio

3775	Stable Monthly Income
x .33	Income Ratio
1246	Maximum Monthly Obligations

1246	Maximum Monthly Obligations
− 602	Monthly Obligations
644	Maximum Mortgage Payment (PITI)

MAXIMUM MORTGAGE PAYMENT (PITI) _____644_____

644	Maximum PITI
− 64	(less 10% of mortgage payment) (Insurance, taxes, PMI)
580	Maximum Principal and Interest Payment

59,716	**MAXIMUM LOAN AMOUNT** (using calculator or interest factor tables)

INCOME QUALIFYING – CONVENTIONAL LOANS
ADJUSTABLE-RATE, 90% OR LESS LTV

Monthly Gross Income:

		Long-Term Monthly Debt:	
Base salary	3525	Car payment	380
Overtime	–0–	Child support	–0–
Bonuses	–0–	Credit cards	30
Commissions	250	Other loans	192
Other	–0–	Other debts	–0–
Total	3775	**Total**	602

(Consider 5% payments on all revolving charges)

Housing Expense-to-Income Ratio

3775	Stable Monthly Income
x .28	Income Ratio
1057	Maximum Mortgage Payment (PITI)

Total Debt Service Ratio

3775	Stable Monthly Income
x .36	Income Ratio
1359	Maximum Monthly Obligations

1359	Maximum Monthly Obligations
– 602	Monthly Obligations
757	Maximum Mortgage Payment (PITI)

MAXIMUM MORTGAGE PAYMENT (PITI) _____ 757 _____

757	Maximum PITI
	(less 10% of mortgage payment)
– 76	(Insurance, taxes, PMI)
681	Maximum Principal and Interest Payment

88,566	**MAXIMUM LOAN AMOUNT** (using calculator or interest factor tables)

INCOME QUALIFYING — FHA-INSURED LOANS
Income Ratio Method

Monthly Gross Income:		Long-Term Monthly Debt:	
Base salary	3,525	Car payment	380
Overtime	–0–	Child support	–0–
Bonuses	–0–	Credit cards	30
Commissions	250	Other loans	192
Other	–0–	Other debts	–0–
Total	3,775	Total	602

(Consider 5% payments on all revolving charges)

Housing Expense-to-Income Ratio: 29%

3,775	Stable Monthly Income
x .29	Income Ratio
1,094.75	Maximum Mortgage Payment (PITI)

Total Debt Service Ratio: 41%

3,775	Stable Monthly Income
x .41	Income Ratio
1,547.75	Maximum Monthly Obligations

1,547.75	Maximum Monthly Obligations
– 602	Monthly Obligations
945.75	Maximum Mortgage Payment (PITI)

MAXIMUM MORTGAGE PAYMENT (PITI) 945.75

945.75	Maximum PITI
	(less 10% of mortgage payment)
– 94.58	(Insurance, taxes, MIP)
851.17	Maximum Principal and Interest Payment

91,182/90,000	**MAXIMUM LOAN AMOUNT** (not to exceed regional mortgage amount limitations)

INCOME QUALIFYING – VA GUARANTEED LOANS
Residual Income Method

Monthly Gross Income:

Base salary	3,525
Overtime	–0–
Bonuses	–0–
Commissions	250
Other	–0–
Total	3,775

Long-Term Monthly Debt:

Car payment	380
Child support	–0–
Credit cards	30
Other loans	192
Other debts	–0–
Total	602

(consider 5% payments
on all revolving charges)

Less All Taxes:

Federal Income tax	462
Social Security (7.65%)	289
State Income tax	
Other Tax	
Total	751

Net Income 3,024

less:

long-term debts	602
required reserves	893
Total	1,529

	RESIDUAL INCOMES BY REGION FOR LOAN AMOUNTS OF $69,999 AND BELOW					RESIDUAL INCOMES BY REGION FOR LOAN AMOUNTS OF $70,000 AND ABOVE			
Family Size*	NORTH-EAST	MID-WEST	SOUTH	WEST	Family Size*	NORTH-EAST	MID-WEST	SOUTH	WEST
1	$348	$340	$340	$379	1	$401	$393	$393	$437
2	583	570	570	635	2	673	658	658	733
3	702	687	687	765	3	810	792	792	882
4	791	773	773	861	4	913	893	893	995
5	821	803	803	894	5	946	925	925	1031

*For families with more than five members, add $70 for each additional member up to a family of seven.

*For families with more than five members, add $75 for each additional member up to a family of seven.

MAXIMUM HOUSING EXPENSE 1,529

Total Housing Expense	1,529
less 20% (taxes, insurance, maintenance, utilities)	– 306
	1,223

Maximum Principal and Interest Payment 1,223

139,362   **MAXIMUM LOAN AMOUNT** (not to exceed lender limitations)

Income Ratio Method

Total Debt Service Ratio: 41%

3,775	Stable Monthly Income
x .41	Income Ratio
1,548	Maximum Monthly Obligations

1,548	Maximum Monthly Obligations
– 602	Monthly Obligations
946	Maximum Mortgage Payment (PITI)

MAXIMUM MORTGAGE PAYMENT (PITI) 946

946	Maximum PITI
	(less 10% of mortgage payment)
– 95	(Insurance, taxes, PMI)
851	Maximum Principal and Interest Payment

96,972   **MAXIMUM LOAN AMOUNT** (not to exceed lender limitations)

Chapter 15

Exercise No. 1

1.
$35,000 loan amount
× .0113659 11%, 15-year factor
───────
$397.81 monthly payment

2. $582.30 ÷ $45,000 = .01294 factor
A ten-year loan with a factor of .01294 corresponds roughly to 9½% interest.

Exercise No. 2

1. $67,000 × .14 = $9,380 interest on wraparound
$39,700 × .095 = $3,771.50 interest on underlying
$67,000 − 39,700 = $27,300 credit extended
$9,380 − 3,771.50 = $5,608.50 net interest to seller
$5,608.50 ÷ 27,300 = .205 or 20½% yield

2. $74,000 × .135 = $9,990 interest on wraparound
$62,000 × .0975 = $6,045 interest on underlying
$74,000 − 62,000 = $12,000 credit extended
$9,990 − 6,045 = $3,945 net interest to seller
$3,945 ÷ 12,000 = .329 or 32.9% yield

3. $71,000 × .1425 = $10,117.50 interest on wraparound
$52,000 × .1075 = $5,590 interest on underlying
$71,000 − 52,000 = $19,000 credit extended
$10,117.50 − 5,590 = $4,527.50 net interest to seller
$4,527.50 ÷ 19,000 = .238 or 23.8% yield

Exercise No. 3

1.
$25,000 loan balance
× .0096502 10%, 20-year factor
───────
$241.26 monthly payment

2.
$50,000 loan amount
× .0110108 12%, 20-year factor
───────
$550.54 monthly payment

3. $50,000 − 25,000 = $25,000 credit extended

4. $50,000 × .12 = $6,000 interest on wraparound
$25,000 × .10 = $2,500 interest on underlying
$6,000 − 2,500 = $3,500 net interest to seller
$3,500 ÷ 25,000 = .14 or 14% yield

Exercise No. 4

$10,000 down, $61,000 balance
$61,000 × .0091473 = $557.99 monthly payment
10½% interest, 30-year amortization, 84 months
$951 × 61 = $58,011 balance after seven years

Exercise No. 5

1. $80,000 − 15,000 = $65,000 contract balance

   $65,000
   × .0149311   13%, 10-year factor
   _____
   $970.52   monthly payment

2. Possible enforcement of due-on-sale clause; no guaranty that Kate will pay on underlying note.

3. Contract escrow; right to pay delinquencies on underlying note and deduct from amount due on contract.

Exercise No. 6

1. $75,000   original mortgage loan balance
   × .0087757   10%, 30-year factor
   _____
      $658.18   monthly payment

2. $26,000   contract amount
   × .0113659   11%, 15-year factor
   _____
      $295.51   monthly payment

3. $70,000 ÷ 75,000 = .933, so a $933 balance remains for each $1,000 of the original loan; according to the 10% loan progress chart, this loan would be eight years, two months old, so the remaining term is 21 years, ten months (262 payments).

Exercise No. 7

1. $20,000   mortgage loan amount
   × .0110539   10½%, 15-year factor
   _____
      $221.08   monthly payment

2. $909   balance per $1,000 after 10 years @ 10%
      × 30   number of $1,000 increments
   _____
    $27,270   balloon payment

3. $25,000 (before closing costs)

Exercise No. 8

1. $600 × 12 × ½ = $3,600 credit established

2. $72,000 × .20 = $14,400
       $14,400 − 3,600 = $10,800 due as downpayment

Acceleration—the process of calling an entire loan balance immediately due and payable, usually because of default or sale of the security property
SEE: DUE-ON-SALE CLAUSE

Alienation—the transfer of title to real estate, by any means

All-inclusive Trust Deed—a trust deed that is equivalent to a wraparound mortgage

AML—adjustable mortgage loan, the savings and loan equivalent of an ARM

Amortize—to structure loan payments so that level payments will retire the debt in full at the end of the loan term

ARM—adjustable-rate mortgage; a loan in which the interest rate is tied to an index and periodically changed to reflect market trends as indicated by the index
COMPARE: VRM, AML

Arm's Length Transaction—a sale where neither buyer nor seller are acting under unusual pressure, the property is offered in the marketplace for a reasonable period of time, and both buyer and seller are aware of the property's merits and defects

Assumption—the substitution of buyer for seller as the person responsible for payment of an existing loan

Balloon Payment—the payment due at the end of the term of a partially amortized loan

Bank Insurance Fund (BIF)—a fund under the control of the Deposit Insurance Corporation, which insures deposits in commercial banks and savings banks

Beneficiary—the person entitled to payment on a loan secured by a deed of trust

Buydown Plan—a plan where the seller pays a portion of the buyer's loan payments, either for the life of the loan (permanent buydown) or for a shorter period (temporary buydown)

Cash Flow Analysis—a method of qualifying borrowers by analyzing the amount of income left over after all monthly obligations have been met

Commercial Bank—a financial institution whose main function is to facilitate commercial transactions. Commercial banks hold most of their assets in the form of demand deposits (checking accounts)

Compound Interest—interest calculated as a percentage of both principal and accumulated unpaid interest
COMPARE: SIMPLE INTEREST

Conforming/Non-conforming Loans—conforming loans can be resold in the secondary market because they meet nationally accepted underwriting criteria; non-conforming loans are generally not salable in the secondary market

Contingent Interest—a term used to describe the lender's share of the appreciation paid on a SAM loan

Conventional Loan—a fixed-rate, level payment loan

Convertible ARM—an ARM that gives the borrower the option of converting to a fixed-rate loan within the first few years of the loan term

Credit Report—a listing of a borrower's credit history, including amount of debt and record of repayment

CRV—certificate of reasonable value; an appraisal form used by the VA

Deed of Trust—an instrument whereby title to property is given to a trustee who holds the deed as security for the repayment of a debt by the trustor to the beneficiary COMPARE: MORTGAGE

Deferred Interest—interest that is accumulated over the course of one or more payment periods but not payable until some later time; a common element of adjustable-rate and graduated payment loans

Deficiency Judgment—a court judgment ordering a debtor to pay the difference between the amount of a debt and the proceeds raised by foreclosure and sale of the security property

Demand Deposit—a deposit that may be withdrawn at any time, such as a checking account deposit

Deposit Insurance Fund—The Federal Fund which controls the Bank Insurance Fund (BIF) and the Savings Association Insurance Fund (SAIF), which insure customer deposits in commercial and savings banks and savings and loan associations.

Discount—the charging of points on a loan for the purpose of increasing the yield

Discount Rate—the interest rate charged by the Federal Reserve to member banks who borrow funds on a short-term basis

Disintermediation—the process by which savings institutions lose deposits to higher-paying investments

Due-on-sale Clause—a clause in a mortgage allowing the lender to accelerate the loan if the property is sold; also called an alienation clause

Equitable Interest—the real property interest of the vendee in a land contract; includes the right to possession of the property and the right to acquire title by paying the contract according to its terms

Equity—the difference between the value of a property and the outstanding indebtedness secured by the property

Federal Reserve System—the government body that regulates the activities of commercial banks

FHA—a government agency designed to aid the construction and real estate industries by providing mortgage insurance, among other programs

Federal Housing Finance Board (FHFB)—the new board created by FIRREA to take over the duties of the Federal Home Loan Bank Board.

FHLMC—Federal Home Loan Mortgage Corporation, "Freddie Mac," a government agency that performs a similar function to that of FNMA

Financial Institutions Reform, Recovery, and Enforcement Act (FIRREA)—a law enacted in 1989 in response to a crisis in the Savings and Loan industry. It revised the regulation of thrift organizations and created several new agencies such as the Office of Thrift Supervision and the Resolution Trust Corporation

Financial Statement—a summary of facts showing an individual's financial condition, including an itemized list of assets and liabilities which serves to disclose net worth

Fixed-Rate Mortgage—a mortgage wherein the interest rate remains constant throughout the entire loan term

FNMA—the Federal National Mortgage Association, "Fannie Mae," a private corporation supervised by HUD; FNMA is a major secondary market investor

GNMA—Government National Mortgage Association, "Ginnie Mae," a government agency supervised by HUD; GNMA promotes investment in real estate by guaranteeing payment on FHA, FmHA and VA loans

GPM—graduated payment mortgage; a loan in which the payments are increased periodically during the early years of the loan term

Graduated Payment Term—the number of years during which payments may be adjusted in a GPM

Gross Income—a person's income before deductions for income taxation
COMPARE: NET INCOME

Index—a measure of the cost of money used as the basis of interest rate adjustments in an ARM

Interest—a periodic charge for a loan, usually expressed as a percentage of the outstanding loan amount
COMPARE: PRINCIPAL

Interest Rate Cap—a limit on the amount that interest rates may be increased in an ARM

Interest Shortfall—the failure to collect accumulated interest due to the graduated payment or adjustable-rate feature of a loan

Intermediary—a person or institution who originates and/or services loans on behalf of another

471

Judicial Foreclosure—a court-supervised foreclosure proceeding, provided for by law
COMPARE: NON-JUDICIAL FORECLOSURE

Law of Supply and Demand—a basic law of economics stating that prices rise when supply decreases or demand increases, and that prices fall when supply increases or demand decreases

Lease/Option—a combination of a lease on real property and an option to purchase the real property during the term of the lease

Level Payment Loan—a loan that is repaid in equal periodic payments over its entire term

Loan Fee—a one-time fee charged by the lender for origination of a loan; often a percentage of the loan amount; also called a loan service fee or loan origination fee

Loan-to-value Ratio (LTV)—the percentage of a property's market value that a lender is willing to loan with only the property as security

Local/Primary Market—the market in which real estate loans are originated between borrowers and lenders
COMPARE: NATIONAL/SECONDARY MARKET

Margin—the difference between the index rate and the interest charged on an ARM

Market Value—the highest price a property would bring if sold in an arm's length transaction; also called fair market value

MIP—the mortgage insurance program of the FHA; MIP also refers to the premium charged for Mutual Mortgage Insurance

MMI—Mutual Mortgage Insurance
SEE: MIP

Mortgage—an instrument wherein property is pledged as security for a debt, creating a lien on the security property
COMPARE: DEED OF TRUST

Mortgage-Backed Securities—instruments issued by various agencies such as GNMA and FHLMC to raise investment funds

Mortgage Company—an institution designed to originate and service real estate loans on behalf of large investors

Mortgagee—the one who receives a mortgage, usually the lender
COMPARE: MORTGAGOR

Mortgagor—the person who gives a mortgage; the borrower
COMPARE: MORTGAGEE

Mutual Savings Bank—a type of financial institution designed for small savers; found mainly in the Northeast

National/Secondary Market—the market consisting of agencies, institutions and investors who buy and sell real estate mortgages
COMPARE: LOCAL/PRIMARY MARKET

Negative Amortization—an increase in an outstanding loan balance brought about by deferred interest

Negative Amortization Cap—a limit on the amount of negative amortization allowable in an ARM or GPM

Negotiable Instrument—an instrument, such as a promissory note, that is freely transferable

Net Income—a person's after-tax income, calculated by subtracting federal income tax withholding from gross income
COMPARE: GROSS INCOME

Net Worth—the worth of an individual as determined by subtracting personal liabilities from total assets

Non-Judicial Foreclosure—foreclosure of a trust deed without court proceedings by means of a trustee's sale
COMPARE: JUDICIAL FORECLOSURE

Note Rate—the interest rate specified in a promissory note; also called the coupon rate

Office of Thrift Supervision—a new arm of the Treasury Department created to regulate the thrift industry

Origination—the process of making a new loan

Participation Loan—a loan made in exchange for a share of the borrower's equity in the security property, also called a shared appreciation mortgage (SAM), shared equity loan or shared equity mortgage

Payment Adjustment Period—the minimum interval between successive adjustments of payments on an ARM or GPM

Payment Cap—a limit on the size of payments on ARMs

PMI—private mortgage insurance; insurance against loss from default on high loan-to-value conventional loans

Points—a point is one percent of a loan amount; also called discount points, they are charged by lenders in order to increase the yield on loans with lower than market interest rates
SEE: DISCOUNT

Portfolio—the collection of mortgages and other securities held by a lending institution and not resold on the secondary market

Principal—the amount of a loan balance which represents the original funds advanced
COMPARE: INTEREST

Private Mortgage Insurance—insurance for lenders against loss in connection with real estate loans; usually paid for by borrowers

Promissory Note—written evidence of a debt

Purchase Money Loan—a loan made by a lender or a seller to a buyer, and used to finance a purchase of property

Qualifying—the process of insuring that 1) a borrower is not likely to default, and 2) a property is worth enough to satisfy the debt if the borrower does default

Rate Adjustment Period—the minimum interval between successive adjustments of the interest rate on an ARM

Real Estate Contract—an installment sales contract for the purchase of real estate

Reamortization—recalculation of level payments for a loan, necessitated by either a change in the loan term or an increase in the loan balance due to negative amortization
SEE: AMORTIZE

Recast—to reamortize

Redemption—the process of recovering foreclosed property after a sheriff's sale

Reduction-option Mortgage—a fixed-rate mortgage with an option to reduce the interest rate once in the life of the loan

Reserve Requirement—the percentage of a bank's deposits that may not be loaned out by the bank

Resolution Trust Corporation (RTC)—an agency formed to manage the disposition of bankrupt thrifts

SAM—shared appreciation mortgage; a loan in which the lender charges below market interest in exchange for a share in the borrower's equity

Savings Association Insurance Fund (SAIF)—a fund under the control of the Deposit Insurance Fund (DIF), which insures deposits in savings and loan associations. This fund takes the place of the former Federal Savings and Loan Insurance Corporation (FSLIC)

Savings & Loan Association—a financial institution designed to hold long-term savings deposits and to reinvest those deposits in long-term loans such as real estate loans

Secondary Financing—money borrowed from any source to pay a portion of the required downpayment or settlement costs of a loan

Secondary Liability—liability that arises only in the event that the person primarily liable cannot satisfy the debt

Securities—instruments, such as mortgages and trust deeds, that pledge assets as security for a debt

Servicing—the process of collecting loan payments, keeping records and handling defaults

Shared Equity Loan—see participation loan

Simple Interest—interest calculated as a percentage of the principal only
COMPARE: COMPOUND INTEREST

Spread—the difference between the note rate and the payment rate on a GPARM

Stable Monthly Income—a borrower's base income plus earnings from reliable secondary sources

Step Rate Loan—a loan utilizing a temporary buydown which decreases over the buydown period
SEE: BUYDOWN

Total Debt Service Ratio—the ratio between the total of housing expense plus long term obligations (such as installment debt & alimony) and the borrower's stable monthly income

Underwriting—the process of evaluating a loan application; the underwriter is the one who approves the loan

U.S. Treasury—an executive department of the U.S. Government serving as the nation's fiscal manager

VA Entitlement—the dollar amount of loan guaranty to which an eligible veteran is entitled

VA Guaranty—the dollar amount of a loan that will be paid by the VA in the event of borrower's default

Verification of Deposit—a form sent by a lender to a bank requesting verification of a borrower's deposit(s) at the bank

VRM—variable-rate mortgage; any loan in which the interest rate may change, whether the rate is tied to an index or not; considered obsolete—replaced by ARMs and AMLs

Wraparound Mortgage—a type of mortgage where part of the mortgage payments are used to retire an existing loan; used to avoid enforcement of due-on-sale clauses

Yield—the lender's overall rate of return on a loan, taking into account interest, discounts, fees, etc.

Index